PESOS *and* DOLLARS

CONNECTING THE GREATER WEST SERIES

Sterling Evans, Series Editor

PESOS *and* DOLLARS

ENTREPRENEURS IN THE TEXAS-MEXICO BORDERLANDS, 1880–1940

ALICIA M. DEWEY

FOREWORD BY STERLING EVANS

Texas A&M University Press
College Station

This paper meets the requirements of ANSI/NISO Z39.48–1992
(Permanence of Paper).
Binding materials have been chosen for durability.
♾ ♻

Library of Congress Cataloging-in-Publication Data

Dewey, Alicia M., 1962– author.
  Pesos and dollars : entrepreneurs in the Texas-Mexico borderlands, 1880–1940 /
Alicia M. Dewey ; foreword by Sterling Evans.—First edition.
      pages cm. — (Connecting the greater west series)
  Includes bibliographical references and index.
  ISBN 978-1-62349-175-8 (cloth : alk. paper) — ISBN 978-1-62349-209-0 (e-book)
  1. Texas, South—Commerce—History—19th century. 2. Texas, South—Commerce—
History—20th century. 3. Mexican-American Border Region—Commerce—
History—19th century. 4. Mexican-American Border Region—Commerce—
History—20th century. I. Title. II. Series: Connecting the greater west series.
  HF3161.T4D49 2014
  338.'040972109041—dc23
                                                        2014015201

For my parents,
Dick and Marion Dewey

CONTENTS

Illustrations

Maps

Tables

FOREWORD

I T IS WITH A GREAT DEAL OF PLEASURE that I am introducing here
Alicia Dewey's *Pesos and Dollars: Entrepreneurs in the Texas-Mexico Borderlands, 1880–1940.* It is the second book in the Connecting the Greater
West Series, scholarly works designed to explore the changing and growing ways
that historians and others are coming to view the North American West. That
West is the large region that includes the American West, northern Mexico, western Canada, parts of the Pacific Rim, and the borderlands areas between these
places. The books in the series include works on transnational history, borders
and borderlands, immigration, environment and agriculture, and indigenous
negotiations of bordered regions. *Pesos and Dollars* fits well within this set of
studies as it examines the bordered region between southern Texas and the
Mexican states of Tamaulipas, Nuevo León, and Coahuila. This transnational
area is characterized by farming and ranching and by the growth of cities and
towns on both sides of the Rio Grande, which separates the United States from
Mexico in this part of the continent.

Dewey has written here what is one of the only books that examines the history of the South Texas borderlands from a business history perspective, using a
wide array of records not usually consulted by historians (e.g., banking accounts,
credit records, bankruptcy court documents). The book then tells the story of
the rise and fall of various business ventures to explore the larger story of the
economic development of the US/Mexico borderlands in general. Along the way,

it also details a concurrent story of diversity in the region, that of the development of a highly ethnically diverse entrepreneurial middle class that formed in
South Texas. Immigrants from a wide variety of cultures and heritages, including Latino/Hispanic, Middle Eastern, Jewish, African American, Canadian, and
European—eastern, southern, and northern—all converged in the South Texas
borderlands to help build communities and the economy. This dimension of *Pesos
and Dollars* illustrates how the book includes much more transnational history
than one might think at first glance. As Dewey has written, it was these immigrants' "adaptability at navigating the cultural and social frontiers of borderland
society and also at nurturing relationships in diverse communities" that makes
this such an important study.

Dewey also points out that the book's objective is to show "how people created and navigated changing business opportunities in South Texas between
1880 and 1940." In doing so, *Pesos and Dollars* "explores how and why local
entrepreneurs started new business ventures, utilized the power of credit, employed methods of risk management, and discovered ways to start over again
after failure," all of which were "necessary for success in [the] increasingly capitalistic and entrepreneurially oriented economy" of that region. And that is
exactly what she accomplishes in the book's eight chapters, divided nicely along
the lines explained here, and in a very logical chronological and thematic se-
quence. Dewey concludes in her introduction that, while the book is a study of a
"particular region at a particular time and place," it also "grapples with larger
questions about opportunity in American society . . . how people pursued it, how
it eluded them, and how they found new chances"—especially as South Texas
is indeed part of the American West, a region that has long been historically
imbued with a sense of opportunity—and sometimes failure. And readers will
get to meet some of the economic leaders, as Dewey introduces each chapter with
anecdotes about individual entrepreneurs. She then uses these introductory stories to draw readers into the larger thematic context in the rest of the chapter.
Her own background in law and bankruptcy cases certainly has served her well
with this project, as she portrays an excellent understanding of legal history and
uses it to analyze appropriate court cases and business law, but without falling
into the trap of legalese or jargon.

Dewey's research is solid, based primarily on primary materials (court
records, business indices of the times, newspapers, booster literature, etc.), and
demonstrates a very solid understanding and engagement of secondary works.
The book will be an important work in the field, as currently there are few to

no other books on business history of the Texas-Mexico borderlands or on the development of the middle class there. As such, it will be important to border-lands historians, Texas historians, business historians, agricultural historians (since much of the business discussed here centered on farming and ranching), geographers, and social scientists (historical anthropologists and sociologists). It also taps into the fast-growing literature of a transnational North America, not only by being a study of borderlands but also through effective analysis of immigration from many parts of the Middle East, Europe, Canada, and Mexico to South Texas. Dewey shows how Mexican immigrants to this region more often than not faced hard times, both socially and economically. But, as she writes, "Hundreds of small shopkeepers, grocers, and other businesspeople from Mexico who chose to become American citizens and live permanently in South Texas must have seen the possibility of a better life north of the border than in Mexico despite the segregation and discrimination they often experienced."

All of these varying facets were part of the building of communities in the borderlands. All are needed to understand the history of this transnational zone more thoroughly, especially as the region became a place for chasing dreams for such a wide variety of peoples. Dewey shows us here exactly how that was played out in this enlightening and well-researched study.

—Sterling Evans
Series Editor

PREFACE

SOUTH TEXAS HAS CAPTURED my imagination for as long as I can remember. I grew up in Houston, Texas, where I followed the familiar routines of school, sports, work, and church. But on long weekends and in the summer, I could leave all of those routines behind as we piled into the family station wagon and drove the four hours to Corpus Christi, where my grandmother lived, and on to Padre Island. Those days were filled with adventure, long hours riding the waves, or running with my dog on the beach, sometimes past hundreds of Anglo-American and Mexican American beachgoers sitting on their cars with radios blaring. My brother and I would explore the sand dunes, hoping to find a Karankawa arrowhead or old Spanish gold coins. I also looked forward to our occasional, brief trips to the border. To me, the mysterious King Ranch consisted of those seemingly endless miles of mesquite and cactus we passed along the way. We were always glad to see grapefruit groves, often filled with migrant farmworkers, because it meant we had arrived in the Lower Rio Grande Valley, our destination. One of the main attractions was the market in Matamoros, across the Rio Grande from Brownsville, where we would wander for hours, gazing at the colorful and varied merchandise. I understood little of the society I saw on either side of the border, but the images stayed with me.

I do not have long-standing roots in South Texas. My mother's family was part of the stream of Anglo-American migrants who moved to South Texas between 1880 and 1940. In 1935 a friend urged my grandfather to join him in

Corpus Christi, suggesting that there was a lot of opportunity there for a young doctor to start a new medical practice. So, during the depths of the Great Depression, my grandfather convinced my grandmother to leave Salisbury, North Carolina, where their families had lived for generations, and start a new life on the edge of the Texas-Mexico borderlands, a place the rest of the family still considered "the Wild West." My father's family arrived twenty years later, in the mid-1950s, when his parents were ready to leave Boston's cold winters forever.

When I decided to return to graduate school to study the history of the American West and the US/Mexico borderlands at Southern Methodist University after practicing law for several years, I naturally turned to topics about South Texas. I wondered what would motivate people like my grandfather to leave everything they knew to move to a completely unfamiliar place. It was in a class with Professor John Chávez that I also became intrigued with what had happened to the original Tejano landowners in the twentieth century. Much had been written about their experiences through the end of the nineteenth century, mostly emphasizing land loss, but there was very little after that. I knew some had held on to their land because my grandfather had taken bird-hunting trips with Tejano patients who owned ranches near the border. I was also interested in the connections between South Texas and the Mexican American middle class in the rest of the state. I knew that members of the family of one of my law partners had left Mexico during the Mexican Revolution of 1910 and initially settled in South Texas before making their way up to Dallas, where they had opened a tortilla factory. I learned of others who had had similar experiences. How had these different people fared in South Texas? How had they changed it?

These were some of the questions I had in mind as I searched the bankruptcy case records for South Texas. As a former bankruptcy lawyer, I knew how bankruptcy cases record much of how people make a living as well as the disappointments, losses, and failures they experience. The cases raised even more questions as I discovered Russian Jews, Italians, and Syrians alongside the Anglo-Americans and Mexicans. Why would these immigrants move to South Texas rather than New York, Chicago, or San Francisco? My dissertation was only the beginning of an effort to uncover more about what I call the "business class" in South Texas. It seemed to me that some of the recent literature gave the impression that the ethnic Mexican middle class of the early twentieth century was too small to be of any significance and that most Anglo-Americans who came to the region were relatively wealthy, exploitative capitalists. It also tended to overlook or minimize the presence of foreign immigrants. Older literature, by contrast, had turned the Anglo-American elite developers, lawyers, merchants, and ranchers into heroes and pioneers. It had ignored the contributions of ethnic Mexican business owners as well as small Anglo proprietors, both men and women. I wanted to complicate and humanize our understanding of the businesspeople in the region by looking more closely at who they were, where they came from, how they tried to make a living, and the kinds of challenges and disappointments they faced. I discovered an ethnically and socioeconomically diverse group of people who, in their search for economic opportunities, had embraced risk, employed similar business practices, and collectively participated in the growth of a more commercial, urbanized, and consumer-oriented society in South Texas. I also discovered that many of them, both large and small, had faced failure at some point in their lives.

I wrote the dissertation in Texas, but I have written much of this book on the far western edge of the US/Mexico border, in Southern California. I look out my window at a landscape very different from that of my home state. I can see rugged mountains rising in the distance, often with a hint of snow on the peaks. On many occasions I have wandered along the jagged Pacific coastline, where cold waves crash on rocks and cliffs, so different from the warm, wide beaches and sand dunes of Padre Island. As I have contemplated the similarities and differences between my home state and my current residence, my perspective of the land about which I write, its people and its history, has been considerably broadened. One of my goals in this book has been to provide a better understanding not only of how the history of South Texas cannot be understood apart from that of northern Mexico but also how its history is inextricably intertwined with that of other parts of the US/Mexico border.

I wish to express my sincere gratitude to Sterling Evans, the series editor, and Mary Lenn Dixon, former editor-in-chief at Texas A&M University Press, both of whom have encouraged this project almost since its inception. I also want to thank the reviewers and others who read all or a portion of the manuscript and gave me very insightful comments, especially Sterling Evans, Armando Alonzo, Ed Perkins, and Brian DeLay. Their critiques helped me hone my arguments and enhance my narrative. Thanks to Carol Hoke, my copyeditor, for her assistance with my language and writing style, and to Pat Clabaugh, associate editor at the press, who shepherded me through the publishing process. The members of my dissertation committee, Hal Williams, Ben Johnson, Sherry Smith, and Joe McKnight, provided excellent feedback in the earliest stages of the project. Alexis McCrossen gave me the idea to incorporate a study of failure and bankruptcy into my work. John Mears also provided comments at various stages. I am extremely grateful to David Weber, who assisted with my book proposal and believed in its importance. His memory continues to inspire me. I also want to recognize Art Goddard and John German, my middle and high school history teachers at the Kinkaid School in Houston, Texas, who inspired and encouraged my love of history at a young age.

This book would not have been possible without the assistance of a number of librarians, archivists, and others in the field of historical research. I wish to thank the following people: George Gause and Janette García in Special Collections, University of Texas–Pan American; Barbara Rust and her staff at the National Archives in Fort Worth; the staff at the Dolph Briscoe Center for American History and at the Nettie Lee Benson Latin American Collection, both at the University of Texas at Austin; Joan Gosnell, Russell Martin, and other staff at the DeGolyer Library at Southern Methodist University; Andrea Boardman and Ruth Ann Elmore at the William P. Clements Center for Southwest Studies; Brian Bingham at the South Texas Archives, Jernigan Library, Texas A&M University–Kingsville; Laura Linard, Katherine Fox, and their staff at the Baker Library Historical Collections, Harvard Business School; Peter Blodgett at the Huntington Library; Walter Brem and Theresa Salazar at the Bancroft Library, University of California at Berkeley; Barbara Stokes, Steve Lomas, and Phyllis Kinnison at the Margaret H. McAllen Memorial Archives, Museum of South Texas History.

I appreciate the ongoing camaraderie of fellow graduate students from Southern Methodist University, including Helen McLure, Paul Nelson, Matt Babcock, Tim Bowman, George Diaz, Gabriel Martinez-Serna, Jimmy Bryan, Francis Galán, David Rex Galindo, Carla Mendiola, Houston Mount, and Eduardo Morález, which has enabled us to continue to exchange ideas about our research even after we have taken faculty positions in different states. I also want to recognize my colleagues in the history and political science department at Biola University with whom I have shared the joys and challenges of faculty life over the course of the last seven years, including work on this book: Susan Lim, Judith Rood, Paul Rood, Daniel Christensen, Dave Peters, Evanson Wamagatta, Scott Waller, Darren Guerra, Ruth Mills-Robbins, James Petitfils, George Giacumakis, and Carolyn Kemp. My students at Biola played a role in my writing by constantly challenging me to consider how to make history relevant, accessible, and interesting. Members of the community, by praying for this project and supporting me in other areas of my life, also contributed to the publication of this book. Special thanks to Dr. Jim Rosscup, Lonnie Wick, Barb Wick, Tom Badin, Karla Fosburg, Sue Hunt, John Barnewall, Michelle Lee-Barnewall, and other friends at Kindred Community Church. I am thankful for fellow hikers, especially Gary, Betty, Debby, Penny, Rebecca, Jim VT, Susan, Debra, Anne, Steve, Andy, Estela, Chuck Two Knives, Mitra, Jumping Jim, Doug, and Marc from Modjeska Canyon, who share my love of the western landscape and gave me a reason to leave my computer for a few hours every week to explore the natural beauty of Southern California so that I could return to my manuscript with a fresh perspective.

I want to mention my former law partners, Arnie Cavazos, Chuck Hendricks, and Rod Poirot, because they were the ones who first introduced me to the arena of bankruptcy law and helped me to consider its history and impact beyond the courtroom. I have often recalled our many discussions about bankruptcy policy and business issues while writing this manuscript. This book is, in many ways, a product of the years I spent practicing law with them. I will always appreciate their friendship.

Most important, I am grateful to my family for their loyalty and ongoing support. My parents, Dick and Marion Dewey, have always backed my effort to forge a new direction in life, for which I will be forever thankful. Without their love and commitment, none of this would have been possible. In addition, my father has read chapters and helped with the analysis. His keen insights have made this a better book than it would have been otherwise. My brother, Rich Dewey, and his wife, Debbie, along with my niece Beall and nephews Richard, Campbell, and Chad, have encouraged me frequently throughout this long journey. Finally, although writing a book can be a lonely endeavor, my dog, Cody, made it less so by being my faithful companion during many long hours spent in front of the computer.

A NOTE ON TERMINOLOGY

ERMINOLOGY IN THE BORDER REGION is complex. In South Texas, the term "Anglo-American" or "Anglo" refers to any "white" American who is not Hispanic or an ethnic Mexican. The term masks the diversity of the ethnic groups that existed even within the larger category, including, for example, those from eastern or southern Europe. In order to differentiate between native-born white Americans and foreign immigrants from Western Europe, I use the term "Anglo-American" to refer to the native born and "European" to refer to the foreign born. I also use the terms "Italian," "Syrian," "Jew," or "Greek" in order to identify ethnic groups that were somewhat distinct from the native-born Anglos and the western Europeans. The complexity of the Spanish-speaking population in South Texas makes choosing one term with which to identify them especially difficult. Terms used to identify ethnic Mexicans during the period were fluid and interchangeable. Throughout the book, "ethnic Mexican" is used to identify people whose ethnicity was Mexican, whether they were born in the United States or in Mexico. "Tejano" refers to descendants of the families who had lived in the South Texas border region since the time of Spain and Mexico. "Mexican" refers to Mexican nationals. "Mexican American" includes people of Mexican ethnicity, regardless of birthplace, who were citizens of the United States. "Hispanic" refers to anyone with a Spanish surname; use of this term is particularly necessary when referring to the R. G. Dun records because they provide no way to determine birthplace or citizenship. I use the term "Río Bravo" to describe the river dividing the United States and Mexico when I view it from the perspective of Mexico and "Rio Grande" when discussing it as part of Texas. I use the term "Río Bravo/Rio Grande" when discussing the river as part of the entire region.

PESOS *and* DOLLARS

INTRODUCTION

"THE RIO GRANDE IS NOT THE BORDER," wrote a correspondent for the *Dallas Morning News* in 1928. "It is a mere dividing line for Generals and Sheriffs, sometimes ineffectual for that. . . . It loves to remind folks living along its banks of the uncertainty of national boundaries by writhing its great torso and flopping over behind some man's farm, so that overnight he moves lock, stock, and barrel, horse, chattel and cattle, from the jurisdiction of Texas to Mexico and vice versa. But moist sandbars do not divide populations, neither for barter nor banter, commerce nor culture. The real dividing line shades off into the north like a changing color of the spectrum, and extends even beyond Dallas."[1]

The porous nature of the US/Mexico border served to enhance economic opportunities in South Texas and contributed to the rise of a new class of diverse businesspeople as the region became more integrated into the system of global capitalism. Once the railroads linked the US and Mexican economies together after 1880, tying the once isolated Texas-Mexico borderlands more effectively to markets in both countries and to sources of financing in the United States, South Texas became an attractive destination for many people seeking to start new enterprises. A fresh wave of entrepreneurs from the United States, Europe, the Middle East, and the interior of Mexico converged on the lower Río Bravo/Rio Grande between 1880 and 1940. They regularly crossed the literal, physical border and navigated linguistic and cultural borders on a daily basis as they cultivated customers and interacted with creditors, business partners, and employees. Residents of northern Mexico, for example, routinely rode ferries or walked across bridges to shop in South Texas stores for the latest fashions or to search for appliances and other products that were scarce in Mexico. The temporary closing of the international bridge between Laredo and Nuevo Laredo during the Christmas season in 1929 resulted in at least a 50 percent drop in the business of local stores like La Victoria and La Moderna, owned by Leon Shapu and Isadore Frelich, revealing the extent to which shopkeepers relied on Mexican customers. A number of entrepreneurs in the region operated businesses on both sides of the border. Vicente Cantú, for instance, owned a general store in Hidalgo, Texas, in the 1920s and also operated a movie theater in Reynosa, Mexico, just a few miles away across the Río Bravo/Rio Grande. Although W. L. Bradbury, a local farmer, was seemingly less dependent on Mexico for business, he could not have survived without the assistance of Mexican laborers when he bought 167 acres of land near Mission in 1918 and planted broom corn.[2]

Even as the border brought people together, it also divided the region between two very different legal and political regimes. South Texas was part of a nation that from its inception had sought to create an environment favorable to business enterprise. Americans had always had a particular "love affair" with small businesses, which exemplified liberal democratic values of autonomy and freedom and seemed to provide a path to upward mobility. With varying degrees of success, the United States had pursued policies designed to facilitate those small businesses. This promise of opportunity lured many, including Mexican citizens, to the US side of the Rio Grande, but they discovered, like so many others, that success often eluded them.[3]

This book tells the story of how people created and navigated changing business opportunities in the South Texas borderlands between 1880 and 1940. It explores how and why local entrepreneurs started new business ventures, utilized the power of credit, employed methods of risk management, and discovered ways to start over again after failure, all of which were necessary for success in an increasingly capitalistic and entrepreneurially oriented economy. It argues that a newly formed business environment, forged by the intersection of American industrial capitalism and Porfirian modernization and later influenced by the Mexican Revolution, created favorable conditions for the emergence of a diverse, modern "business class" along the South Texas border between 1880 and 1940. It argues further that members of this class shared similar business goals regardless of background or ethnicity, their collective efforts led to the economic development of the region, and their individual successes and failures depended largely on their access to markets, capital, and credit, their ability to manage debt and risk, and the ups and downs of the business cycle. Race and ethnicity played a role in the degree to which they were successful but did not prevent them from becoming participants in the business class. Together, they remade the relatively isolated ranching society of the borderlands into one that was thoroughly commercialized, urbanized, and integrated into global markets. They also contributed to and participated in the emergence of a diverse, consumer-oriented, urban middle class. Although ethnic Mexicans and their descendants who had lived in the region for generations lost ground both politically and economically in the changing environment, many pursued new entrepreneurial opportunities and became the core of a new Mexican American middle class.

Typical of the migrant entrepreneurs who moved into South Texas in the late nineteenth and early twentieth centuries were Joseph Netzer and Morris Edelstein. Netzer, born in Germany, spent some time fighting Indians on the western plains before he arrived in Laredo in the 1880s. He set up a plumbing and hardware store and quickly became a prominent businessman in the town. His fortunes began to fail in the late 1910s, and he filed a bankruptcy case in 1922. Just a few years later, he had restored his fortunes and was praised for "his good business ability and thrifty habits."[4] Edelstein, a Lithuanian Jew, joined a brother in Eagle Pass in 1906 when he was just sixteen years old. He peddled various wares door to door before he was able to open his own furniture store in Brownsville in 1912. This store expanded into a chain across the Lower Rio Grande Valley in the early 1930s. Edelstein filed for bankruptcy during the depths of the Great Depression in 1932 and sold off many of his assets. By the end of the decade he had rebounded and started opening new stores once again.[5]

Eusebio García's family, by contrast, had long-standing roots in the region. Born in Guerrero, Mexico, he spent some time working for his uncle, a foreman on the King Ranch, before moving to Los Ojuelos Ranch near Laredo, where he and his brother ran a general store. In 1882 he married Josefa Guerra, daughter of Dionisio Guerra, owner of the Los Ojuelos grant. His wife inherited land from the grant, and García purchased more acreage with profits from his store. By the 1920s, he owned more than fifty thousand acres. He bred and sold cattle and leased land for development to oil and gas companies. He, too, faced hardship during the Great Depression and filed for bankruptcy in 1935. Though he died at the age of seventy-eight in December, 1937, too soon to recover his losses, the headline on the front page of the *Laredo Times* proclaimed that he "Was an Outstanding Pioneer Who Aided This Area's Development."[6]

The lives of Joseph Netzer, Morris Edelstein, and Eusebio García illustrate the risks, challenges, successes, and failures that accompanied the pursuit of new business opportunities in the Texas-Mexico borderlands between 1880 and 1940. All three became respected leaders of their communities. Each relied to some extent on borrowed funds to build and expand their businesses. Each faced virtual ruin and the collapse of what they had built. Yet each man was able to overcome his experience of failure and emerge once again as someone whom friends and family considered a "successful pioneer." Countless other lesser-known entrepreneurs had similar experiences, revealing how much the willingness to take risks, the availability of credit, success, and failure were intertwined as people seized new opportunities and navigated economic change.

South Texas provides a unique context in which to study the lives and experiences of individual entrepreneurs because of its location and history. The area was once a part of the northern frontier of New Spain and later Mexico. In the mid-eighteenth century the Spaniards established a number of towns along the lower Río Bravo in the province of Nuevo Santander, which later became the state of Tamaulipas after Mexican independence in 1821. For nearly a century, these towns were the focal points of a ranching society that extended more than one hundred miles north of the river, where settlers grazed thousands of cattle, goats, and sheep. Then, in the mid-nineteenth century, the Mexican north met the American West. Out of the confrontation of these two frontiers emerged a borderland environment that was very different from the rest of the United States and Mexico.[7] After the US conquest of Mexico in 1848, the river became the international boundary line, cutting through the heart of the Hispanic settlements. South Texas legally became part of the western United States, but economic, social, and cultural interaction continued across the river. As the century wore on, Anglo-Americans came in greater and greater numbers, part of a general migration westward from the more densely populated eastern seaboard. They carved out their own space within the region, bringing an entrepreneurial spirit and drive that transformed the local economy into one that was highly competitive and capitalistic.

This study focuses on the portion of South Texas that is closest to the Rio Grande River and extends from Brownsville near the Gulf Coast all the way to Del Rio. This book identifies that area as the "South Texas border region," the "South Texas borderlands," and sometimes simply as "South Texas." It includes the border towns of Brownsville, Rio Grande City, Roma, Laredo, Del Rio, and Eagle Pass as well as the Winter Garden District and the Lower Rio Grande Valley (map 1). It does not encompass the parts of South Texas farther from the river, including San Antonio, Corpus Christi, and the surrounding areas, emphasizing instead the region lying within about one hundred miles of the international border.

Although the study is about the South Texas border region in particular, it endeavors to place it in a transnational context and explore its links with northern Mexico. Borderland historian David Weber's notion of the border region as a "zone of contact and exchange" between peoples of different ethnicities, cultures, and nationalities is central to my understanding of how the South Texas economy developed and how people interacted within it. Additionally, Oscar Martínez's concept of a borderland as a "zone of transition, a place where people and institutions are shaped by natural forces not felt in the heartland" in an area next to an international border has influenced my thinking about the region.[8] Proximity to Mexico shaped life and business in South Texas and gave ethnic Mexicans living there potential advantages that they did not experience in other parts of the United States. They were familiar with the language and customs of Mexican business and often had contacts and customers south of the border. South Texas also attracted foreign immigrants from Greece, Spain, Italy, eastern Europe, and the Middle East and Jews from New York and other cities in the eastern United States. The fluidity of social and economic life along the border allowed greater mobility for members of these groups who might be marginalized elsewhere.[9]

Despite its porousness, the international border was a dividing line that made a difference in the lives of those who resided in South Texas. Divergent legal systems governing aspects of economic life such as property rights, credit, taxes, and insolvency as well as the nature of both federal and state governments in the United States and Mexico created dissimilar business environments north and south of the Río Bravo/Rio Grande. In this regard, South Texas was more similar to New York than to northeastern Mexico. The purpose of this study is to explore what it was like for people to pursue opportunity in the developing periphery of the United States, where influences from and links with Mexico affected the economy and the society.

The period of study, 1880 to 1940, was a time of significant economic change in South Texas and the greater US/Mexico borderlands. These changes were part of larger, global patterns. After the Civil War, the American West, Mexico,

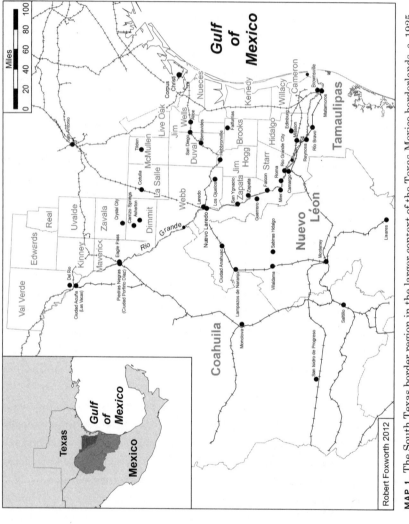

MAP 1. The South Texas border region in the larger context of the Texas-Mexico borderlands, c. 1925. Map by Robert Foxworth.

and Latin America increasingly provided raw materials for the industrializing regions of the United States and western Europe. The expansion of the railway network beyond the Mississippi River and into Mexico facilitated the shipment of mineral resources and agricultural products out of the American West and Mexico into the northeastern and midwestern United States, and US trade with and investment in Mexico increased substantially. The railroads in turn made it possible for thousands of retail merchants to bring newly manufactured consumer goods from Chicago, New York, and Pittsburgh into rural parts of the United States and Mexico. In the 1880s, as railroad lines snaked south into Mexico, new towns such as Nogales, Arizona, sprang up along the border, while the dusty, adobe twin towns of El Paso/Juarez and Laredo/Nuevo Laredo became "international gateways to commerce," later blossoming into major import/export centers between Mexico and the United States.[10]

Convinced that railroads were the key to capitalist modernization, local entrepreneurs offered land and capital for the construction of tracks across South Texas. By 1904, the region was fully connected to the North American and Mexican railway networks. As a result, commercial agriculture, both extensive and intensive, began developing in the lower Rio Grande Valley, outside Laredo, and in the Winter Garden District alongside commercial ranching. Older border towns expanded, and newer towns emerged to serve a growing population. Urbanization enlarged the opportunities for specialized retailers of a growing variety of goods and services.

Economic change disrupted familiar patterns and displaced thousands of people from the land. By the early twentieth century, Anglo ranchers had acquired millions of acres of South Texas ranchland from financially struggling Tejano *rancheros,* forcing them to find ways to make a living as artisans, laborers, clerks, or merchants. Between 1880 and 1910, a period of relative peace and stability in Mexico known as the Porfiriato, policies instituted by Mexican president Porfirio Díaz that were designed to encourage modernization by consolidating land into private hands uprooted millions of peasants from their ancestral villages by disrupting their traditional subsistence patterns of agriculture. The peasants migrated north, seeking work on the railroads and in the fields of the American Southwest. The Mexican Revolution of 1910 forced thousands more to flee, increasing the population of South Texas dramatically and creating a class of migratory laborers who had little choice but to work for low wages.[11]

The arrival of the railroads, the availability of cheap labor, and the commodification of land made possible the rapid growth of a more expansive business class along the South Texas border with Mexico between 1880 and 1940. Despite the importance of the businesspeople to economic development in South Texas during this period, few scholars have written about them. Older works, such as Stambaugh and Stambaugh's *Lower Rio Grande Valley* and Allhands' *Gringo Builders,* emphasized the role of the Anglo-American elite in developing the region and described and chronicled key economic events.[12] These works did not explore the nature and roles of small business owners, women, and ethnic Mexican entrepreneurs, nor did they evaluate the impact of global, national, and regional economic trends on the region.

More recent scholarship about South Texas has concentrated primarily on the Tejano community, Tejano land loss in the nineteenth century, ethnic conflict, and labor relations between Anglo farmers and migratory Mexican laborers. One of the latest works, *River of Hope,* by Omar Valerio-Jiménez, explores the construction of identity as residents adopted various strategies of resistance and accommodation to the different regimes that controlled the region in the eighteenth and nineteenth centuries. One key issue that pervades the more recent literature is the nature of relations between Anglo-Americans and ethnic Mexicans in the region: were they characterized primarily by cooperation and accommodation or by conflict and oppression? In attempting to answer this question, the role of Anglo-American businesspeople in the towns and cities has not been fully explored, and there is very little about ethnic Mexican business owners in the late nineteenth and early twentieth centuries. Furthermore, scholars have not yet examined the multiethnic nature of the business class after the arrival of the railroads. Historians have explored the merchant class in the nineteenth century, particularly on the Mexican side, but there is little work on merchants in the twentieth century.[13] Moreover, few business historians have studied either the American West or the US/Mexico border region, preferring to concentrate primarily on areas east of the Mississippi, and thus no scholarship exists that investigates issues such as credit availability or business failure in the Texas-Mexico borderlands. The only recent business history about South Texas, Adams's *Conflict and Commerce on the Rio Grande,* focuses exclusively on Laredo.[14]

The limited nature of our knowledge about the region's business owners leaves a substantial gap in our understanding of the South Texas borderlands because of the central role they played in both economic and social change in this period. There is a need for a fresh perspective on the business history of the region that places local developments in a larger economic context in order to better understand the environment in which local businesspeople operated, analyzes the nature and identity of these local businesspeople and the enterprises they started, and evaluates how they navigated capitalist changes in the borderlands in both the urban and agricultural spheres. This book emphasizes the importance of US industrialization and Porfirian modernization in the late nineteenth century and the Mexican Revolution and the Great Depression in the twentieth century to the shaping of the evolving business environment of South Texas. In particular, it highlights the significance of town development and the growth of the urban population after 1900, a frequently overlooked trend that created new kinds of business opportunities outside of the rural economy, where ranching and agriculture increasingly became capital intensive. Furthermore, it shows that transnational links as well as national boundaries, which determined the underlying legal structures that affected businesses, influenced economic opportunities.

This book illuminates and explores for the first time the multiethnic composition of the South Texas business class between 1880 and 1940. It examines the kinds of enterprises that these individuals operated and why they chose them. It stresses the importance of individual agency in navigating capitalist change in the borderlands, which is especially significant to the analysis of ethnic Mexican business owners, farmers, and ranchers; they were able to persist and succeed in this period despite ongoing problems of segregation, discrimination, and limited resources, although these obstacles often curbed what they could accomplish. This study also complicates current understandings of ethnic relations by showing that they differed depending on geographic location as well as on considerations of wealth, occupation, and class. Finally, this study evaluates how the uncertainty endemic to the capitalist system (i.e., whether one's venture would succeed or fail) affected South Texas entrepreneurs by examining three crucial aspects of business life: the ability to access credit when one lacked sufficient capital to start or continue a business; the impact of failure on individuals and their businesses; and their ability to start over again by taking advantage of insolvency and bankruptcy statutes. It sheds light on the extent to which wealth, class, and ethnicity influenced these things.

This book contains substantial original information about businesspeople in South Texas based on underutilized sources. My historical approach draws on elements of the methodologies of business history, the new social history, and the new Western history. I am interested in exploring the lives of businesspeople not just as economic actors but also as ordinary people, including the ways in which they adapted to their environment and interacted with others and how class and ethnicity shaped their opportunities and experiences. The two main sources for this history, the federal bankruptcy case files and the R. G. Dun & Co. Reference Books, have never been used by historians of South Texas. These sources, increasingly consulted by business historians in studies of other parts of the United States, are underutilized by western and borderlands historians generally. The federal bankruptcy case files contain a variety of documents, including copies of bankruptcy petitions, schedules of debts and assets, creditor meeting transcripts, proofs of claim filed by creditors, various pleadings filed in the case, and sometimes photographs and drawings. County tax rolls provide information about changing land ownership over several decades. Local newspapers, magazines, personal papers, promotional materials from land-development campaigns, business directories, county histories, oral histories, biographical sketches of prominent businesspeople, and published law cases augment material from the R. G. Dun & Co. Reference Books, the bankruptcy case files, and the county tax rolls. These sources give the social history and tell the stories that allow a glimpse into the more personal side of many of the entrepreneurs' lives.

In order to facilitate my analysis, I created several databases. One database contains the names, as well as statistics such as gender, ethnicity, approximate net worth, and credit rating, of 4,915 individuals and corporations listed in the R. G. Dun & Co. Reference Books from selected towns in the region for the years 1901, 1910, 1918, 1925, 1930, and 1938. These lists are not exhaustive; they include only those businesses that R. G. Dun & Co. discovered and attempted to evaluate, but they nonetheless constitute a good representative sample of the businesses in the South Texas border region. Separate databases cover the bankruptcy cases filed in each of the courts that served the counties of the region (Brownsville, Laredo, Corpus Christi, San Antonio, and Del Rio). They include detailed information about the 1,160 bankruptcy cases filed between 1898 and 1941. Of these, 827 of the individuals who filed for bankruptcy (70 percent of the total) appeared in the census records. Data about the birthplace, ethnicity, parents' and spouse's birthplaces, marriage status, literacy, native language, and citizenship of each bankrupt debtor, if available, were included in the bankruptcy databases.

The R. G. Dun Reference Books, which contain information about business size and type, reveal that most businesspeople in South Texas organized their enterprises as small proprietorships, partnerships, or closely held corporations. Despite the small size of many of their enterprises, each of these individuals was still an "entrepreneur," which means "a person who organizes and manages a business undertaking, assuming the risk for the sake of the profit."[15] Although the word "entrepreneur" carries different connotations, arguably a person operating any kind of business between 1880 and 1940 in South Texas, regardless of size or type, was both assuming risk and practicing innovation, characteristics typically associated with entrepreneurs. People had to be creative risk takers to identify customers and figure out how to run a business during that time of rapid change and political, economic, and social instability. Farmers and ranchers are included in the definition of "entrepreneur" as well and were therefore part of the new business class because they, like other businesspeople of the time, embraced a market-oriented outlook that pervaded everything they did.[16]

The businesspeople along the border between 1880 and 1940 operated a wide variety of enterprises. The R. G. Dun Reference Books, by identifying the nature of local businesses, made it possible to trace changes over time in terms of the kinds of enterprises that people started. Initially, general merchants, artisans, and ranchers predominated, but eventually there was increasing specialization, especially in areas of substantial population growth. Small country stores gave way to an array of boutiques—millinery shops, gents' furnishings, ladies' ready-to-wear, local grocery stores, drug stores, and gift shops. Orange groves and grapefruit orchards replaced general farms. Cotton gins, petroleum refineries, and major warehouses sprang up along railroad tracks. In the 1920s there was an explosion of businesses devoted to the automobile, including gas stations and auto repair shops.

The business class was diverse in terms of gender and ethnicity. All too often, the border region is conceived of as a place sharply divided between male Anglo-American business owners and Mexican laborers. The reality is more complex. Although Anglo-American men predominated, a number of women ran a variety of small shops as well as ranches and farms. In addition to native-born Americans of western European descent, there were Italians, Jews, immigrants from eastern Europe and Russia, Greeks, Lebanese Christians (or Syrians), Spaniards, and ethnic Mexicans. The R. G. Dun Reference Books, the bankruptcy case files, the manuscript census, and the census summaries all reveal this rich diversity.

The study of these entrepreneurs along the border is important not only because it helps us to understand the transformation of the South Texas economy but also because it provides a window into the middle class in the United States as it existed on the border at the time.[17] Some individuals moved to South Texas, as they did to other parts of the American West at the time, because of the mythic promise of unlimited opportunity and the hope that they could improve their status. They believed that there they would find more prospects for new, independent start-up ventures that seemed foreclosed to them in the East, where big business was rapidly taking over most sectors of the economy. A few became wealthy, but most remained in the unstable middle, living as it were, a "dream" on the one hand while "fearful of falling" on the other. The vast majority ran small businesses or farms with few employees and values of $10,000 or less.[18] Among the middle-class migrants were ethnic Mexicans who either came by choice or were forced out of their nation due to revolutionary violence after 1910. Despite rhetoric about the importance of the middle class in Mexico both before and after the revolution, which echoed a transnational discourse about the crucial role members of the middle class played in the development of a stable, democratic society, the reality was often very different, and the elite continued to dominate much of Mexico's society and economy. Those who left for South Texas hoped they would find greater opportunities, more money, and a better lifestyle in the United States.[19]

The idea of the American dream, "the promise that all Americans have a reasonable chance to achieve success as they define it—material or otherwise—through their own efforts, and to attain virtue and fulfillment through success," an important aspect of entrepreneurial and middle-class culture in the United States, was the ideological basis for the pursuit of economic opportunity.[20] This American dream had transnational dimensions for borderland entrepreneurs. Independent business ownership was still a major path to achieving the American dream in this period, and for most of these business owners, their success depended in part on connections they made in Mexico or on laborers who migrated from Mexico. Moreover, US ideals influenced borderland entrepreneurs both north and south of the Río Bravo/Rio Grande. Mexican historian John Hart has argued that during the Porfiriato, Americans sought to export to Mexico "their unique 'American dream,'" which "incorporated social mobility, Protestant values, a capitalist free market, a consumer culture, and a democracy of elected representation."[21]

The ability to start small businesses was especially important for ethnic minorities and women as a means of upward mobility in an age when prejudice and other limitations shut them out of many salaried white-collar jobs.[22] Ethnic Mexicans in particular faced obstacles to accumulating wealth. The R. G. Dun Reference Books reveal that disproportionate numbers of ethnic Mexican-owned businesses had a net worth of less than $500, and very few Hispanic-surnamed individuals ranked among the most affluent. As more and more Anglo-Americans moved into the region, many towns were segregated into "Anglo" and "Mexican" areas, forcing most ethnic Mexican business owners to operate in the *barrios,* where they catered primarily to impoverished migratory farmworkers. Out of this intense crucible of change and difficulty, however, emerged a separate Mexican American middle class that eventually had a national influence through organizations like the League of United Latin American Citizens.[23]

A significant development along the border between 1880 and 1940 that placed independent business ownership within the reach of more people was the increasing availability of credit.[24] Greater availability of credit would ultimately lead not only to the growth of entrepreneurship in South Texas but also to the expansion of a middle class. Without it, the economy of South Texas and the rest of the country would have remained largely in the hands of a small and powerful group of the elite. Access to credit, however, was not guaranteed; it depended on the willingness of those with capital to lend it to others and on the uneven growth of lending facilities in the region. Anglo-American men in particular had an advantage in borrowing money from a variety of sources and hence in establishing a permanent business presence in the area. Credit was not unavailable for ethnic Mexicans, but their ability to access it was more limited, mainly because they tended to have smaller businesses, fewer assets, and fewer connections to those supplying the credit. This book covers new ground about access to credit in South Texas in the early twentieth century, a topic largely overlooked by historians, exploring who was able to borrow money and the sources they used. The credit ratings listed in the R. G. Dun Reference Books give some hint as to the extent to which people could borrow, but the bankruptcy case files were most revealing. Lists of the debts of bankrupts contained in those files show that even individuals with low credit ratings were sometimes able to borrow money from a wide range of creditors.

Uncertainty accompanied the expansion of capitalism in the South Texas borderlands. The concept of "risk" as applied to ordinary businesses had emerged in the nineteenth-century United States with the rapid expansion of the market economy across the continent and the explosion of industry after the Civil War. Once applied only to the perils faced on the high seas, risk became part of everyday life on the land as more and more people became dependent on fluctuating international markets and an expanding web of credit, as historian Jonathan Levy has explained in his recent work on the history of risk, *Freaks of Fortune.*[25] Risk had an upside; chance coupled with hard work could lead to unimagined profits. It also had a downside. The ever-present specter of failure made the achievement of the American dream elusive and uncertain. As a 1916 article in the *Cattleman* put it, many individuals "chased the phantom of sudden riches only to find themselves 'broke' in a cabbage patch with a strong smell of onions in the air."[26] Reliance on credit, which was escalating throughout the period, made borrowers more vulnerable to failure. Circumstances, moreover, often made life difficult. Episodes of violence and military conflict along the border periodically disrupted people's ability to make a living. Two major depressions occurred in the initial decades of the twentieth century, first in the early 1920s and again in the decade of the 1930s. Competition from big business was one of the mounting risks to individual entrepreneurship. Between 1880 and 1940, there was a trend toward consolidation of land into the hands of large ranchers, a shift from small to large farms, the penetration of the mail-order catalog companies into rural parts of South Texas, and the proliferation of chain stores in the towns. It became more and more difficult to operate a small or medium-sized business in this environment. There were also everyday challenges: customers who had trouble paying their bills, disability, illness and death, fires, fraud of a partner, inexperience, and failure to keep good books. This book is the very first to explore the history of failure along the border. The bankruptcy case files, particularly those that include a narrative transcript of the creditors' meeting, provide the best evidence as to the kinds of circumstances that led to business failures.

One of the keys to surviving in the increasingly competitive environment of South Texas was the ability to start over again after failure. The legal system in Texas and in the United States evolved to manage risk in such a way that it cushioned the impact of business failure on entrepreneurs and provided a framework for creditors to receive a fair distribution from insolvent estates so that they could assess the costs of lending. The passage of the Bankruptcy Act of 1898, the first permanent bankruptcy law in the United States, coincided with the development of South Texas. Many of the people who filed under this act along the border succeeded in starting over again. The willingness of friends, family, and creditors to lend a helping hand as well as the cultural belief in second chances went a long way in making a fresh start possible. Relying on case law, statutes, and bankruptcy case files, this study analyzes the extent to which businesspeople in South Texas utilized the federal bankruptcy act and explores other ways in which they attempted to mitigate or avoid failure and how the border may have played a role. Tracing individuals through the census provides evidence as to what happened to people after a bankruptcy filing.

This book is organized thematically in three sections. Part I, "Commercial Society in the Lower Río Bravo/Rio Grande Borderlands" discusses the development of the business environment in South Texas that attracted entrepreneurs. The first chapter, "Borderlands in Transition," gives the historical context of the study. It begins with a brief description of the Spanish ranching era but focuses mainly on the period from 1820 until 1880, when global commerce first began to penetrate the region in a significant way through the port of Matamoros. It addresses some of the early obstacles to economic growth, the rise of frontier merchants who accumulated large fortunes, and Tejano land loss, which paved the way for commercial ranching. Chapter 2, "Forging a Landscape of Opportunity," continues the history of the region's economy between 1880 and 1940, arguing that during this time a more favorable business environment for a wide range of enterprises emerged. It identifies the Porfiriato as a crucial turning point; the construction of railroads, a consequence of efforts to more fully integrate the US and Mexican economies, linked South Texas more effectively and efficiently to markets and sources of credit. It also explores the subsequent impact of the Mexican Revolution and the increasing urbanization of the region in shaping the business environment.

Part II, "Texas Borderland Entrepreneurs," analyzes the individual businesspeople in the area. Chapter 3, "Seizing Opportunity," examines how the Anglo-American migrants of the twentieth century took advantage of growing opportunities in the South Texas border region and started new businesses, ranches, and farms. It argues that in the process they brought US entrepreneurial culture, middle-class values, and consumerism to the border and dominated the border economy. Chapter 4, "Searching for the American Dream," is about European immigrants, Jews, and Syrians who resided on the edges of Anglo-American society but made use of their proximity to the border to enhance their business opportunities. Many were among the most upwardly mobile entrepreneurs in the borderlands. Chapter 5, "Navigating Change," addresses how Tejano and Mexican ranchers, farmers, and business owners dealt with the changes brought about by economic development and urbanization and how they, too, seized new opportunities by transitioning to commercial agriculture or by starting businesses in the towns and cities. It argues that the rise of the Mexican American middle class in the region can be explained by the participation of ethnic Mexican entrepreneurs in the increasingly competitive local economy and their experiences in adapting to the influx of Anglo-Americans.

Part III, "The Elusiveness of Success," explores particular aspects of the difficulty and uncertainties of business life and endeavors to shed light on how and why some people succeeded and persisted while others did not or at least experienced more limited success. Chapters 6, 7, and 8 each address a different facet. Chapter 6, "Accessing Credit," argues that the expansion of credit in the region between 1880 and 1940 created new opportunities for those with limited or no capital by enabling them to start and expand businesses that they would not otherwise be able to. By contributing to the growth of small business, credit expanded the middle class in the region. There were disparities, however, in terms of how much credit individuals could acquire. The chapter investigates some of the effects of those disparities. Chapter 7, "Facing Failure," explores the endemic nature of business failure along the border. It examines how reliance on credit exacerbated the possibility of failure and looks at common paths to failure. It focuses especially upon the impact of the Great Depression of the 1930s, when failure was particularly widespread. Chapter 8, "Starting Over," argues that state-created legal regimes, particularly exemption statutes and federal bankruptcy laws, constituted a crucial safety net that enabled people to avoid substantial downward mobility. It analyzes the extent to which South Texas entrepreneurs utilized these statutes and other means to cope with business loss and failure.

Although this is a study of a particular region during a particular time period, the South Texas border region between 1880 and 1940, it grapples with larger questions about opportunity in American society by exploring how people pursued it, how it eluded them, and how they found second chances. Their experiences underscore the risk and uncertainty that underlies all of our efforts. Wealth gained today can be gone tomorrow. This study is situated in a place that is both part of the West, a region long associated with opportunity in American culture, and part of *México de afuera* and Greater Mexico, which includes those southwestern borderland regions in the United States that have beckoned to numerous generations of Mexicans hoping for a better life.[27]

PART I

COMMERCIAL SOCIETY IN THE LOWER
RÍO BRAVO/RIO GRANDE BORDERLANDS

1

BORDERLANDS IN TRANSITION
(1820–1880)

I N THE DARK OF an early September morning in 1859, about seventy
men crossed the Río Bravo/Rio Grande near Matamoros on horseback. Residents of Brownsville, many asleep in their beds, awoke to cries of "¡Viva
Cheno Cortina!" "¡Mueran los Gringos!" and "¡Viva la República Mexicana!" Juan
Nepomuceno Cortina, son of an elite Tejano family, quickly seized control of the
town and dispatched several small bands of his armed followers to search out
and kill individuals who had reportedly harassed, physically abused, murdered,
or defrauded his fellow countrymen. In Cortina's words, some members of the
new, rising Euro-American elite of the border region had "connived with each
other, and form[ed] . . . a perfidious inquisitorial lodge to persecute and rob us,
without any cause, and for no other crime on our part than that of being of
Mexican origin." They "form[ed], with a multitude of lawyers, a secret conclave,
with all its ramifications, for the sole purpose of despoiling the Mexicans of their
lands and usurp[ing] them afterwards."[1] Many of Cortina's countrymen praised
him as a hero.

Anglo-Americans, however, saw things differently, viewing Cortina and his
followers as thieves who sought to steal and destroy that which they had right-
fully acquired. On October 8, 1859, John Hemphill, chief justice of the Supreme
Court of Texas, sent a dispatch to President James Buchanan, reporting that he
had "just heard of an outrage on our frontier, at Brownsville, of a character so
flagrant and astonishing that I would not believe it possible, if the information

were not on undoubted authority. A party of Mexicans crossed the river from
Matamoras [*sic*], captured the town of Brownsville, liberated the prisoners from
jail, and murdered five of the citizens, retaining possession of the town for an
hour. . . . This frontier is encompassed with difficulties from other quarters, and
the ravages of marauders will not be less terrible than the hostilities of the savage. The same force that entered Brownsville could have captured Brazos St.
Jago, with the custom-house and the immense property and funds belonging to
the government and others. I trust that the troops will be speedily ordered to the
abandoned posts of the Rio Grande, and that outrages will become impossible."[2]

This 1859 conflict was the first of several raids known collectively as the
Cortina Wars, which continued through the 1860s and 1870s. The Cortina Wars
were not only ethnic struggles triggered by the US conquest of Mexico in 1848
but also responses to an economic shift that had begun a few decades earlier, almost immediately after Mexico gained its independence from Spain and opened
an international port at Matamoros. The merchants from Europe and the United
States who flocked to Matamoros in the 1820s, drawn by the lucrative trading
potential in the rich silver-mining districts of northern Mexico, were instrumental in incorporating the delta of the lower Río Bravo/Rio Grande into the global
capitalist economy. As they seized control of the region's trade, they began the
process of "creative destruction" (a term coined by economist Joseph Schumpeter) of the local ranching economy; this process lasted for more than seventy
years.[3] The wealth the merchants accumulated as they forged a new economy
based on trade and commercial capital provided the resource base for the dispossession of the land-rich but cash-poor Tejano landholding *rancheros*. Com-
pounding the problems of the *rancheros* was their loss of herds due to periodic
but intense raiding by Comanches, Lipan Apaches, and their allies in the 1810s,
1820s, and 1830s. The US conquest of Mexico and subsequent annexation of the
Trans-Nueces in 1848 only exacerbated the already existing economic disparities
between the Tejano landowners and the new merchant class.[4]

This competition for land and resources among nomadic Indian tribes, the
descendants of the original Spanish *vecinos,* and a rising European and Anglo-
American merchant class was central to the unfolding story of the lower Río
Bravo/Rio Grande Valley borderlands between 1820 and 1880. By 1880, the merchants and their allies had clearly won, paving the way for the modernization of
the region in subsequent decades. They were also responsible for fostering trade
between the United States and Mexico in silver, cotton, and manufactured goods,
which would lay the foundation for transnational economic integration in the

borderlands in subsequent decades. Not all Tejanos followed Cortina's example; some chose to pursue a path of cooperation and accommodation in attempting to adapt to the tremendous changes that occurred during this period.

ROOTS OF THE TEJANO RANCHING SOCIETY ALONG THE LOWER RÍO BRAVO

The land bordering the lower Río Bravo was one of the last areas the Spaniards settled along the rim of their empire in North America. Like much of the rest of New Spain's northern frontier, the region seemingly had very little to offer—no gold or silver, a relatively inhospitable climate, and an unreliable water supply. Yet despite its apparent lack of resources, the area was strategically important as a buffer zone between the valuable silver mines of Durango, Zacatecas, and San Luis Potosí and lands inhabited by the hostile tribes of the North American grasslands and claimed by rival European empires. The threat of British expansion from Jamaica to the Gulf Coast provided the impetus for colonization in 1749, more than 150 years after the founding of Santa Fe on the upper Río Bravo and only twenty years before the Sacred Expedition into Alta California, Spain's final settlement in North America. A colony along the western Gulf Coast would clearly stake Spain's claim to the territory between the towns of Saltillo and Monterrey on the edge of the mining frontier to the south and San Antonio de Béxar, a trading post, mission, and *presidio* about two hundred miles to the north.

The viceroy of New Spain commissioned José de Escandón, a Spanish-born military officer, to lead the exploration and settlement of the new province, Nuevo Santander, named for Escandón's birthplace of Santander, Spain. Within six years, Nuevo Santander (which comprised the territory that is today the Trans-Nueces, or South Texas, as well as the Mexican state of Tamaulipas) had fifteen missions and twenty-three towns, including six along the banks of the Río Bravo. These six towns, Nuestra Señora de Santa Ana de Camargo (Camargo), Villa de Nuestra Señora de Guadalupe de Reynosa (Reynosa), Villa de San Ignacio de Loyola de Revilla (later Guerrero), Lugar de Mier (Mier), Villa de San Augustín de Laredo (Laredo), and Nuestra Señora de los Doloros, a hacienda consisting of about thirty families, became known as the *villas del norte*. Camargo, Revilla, Mier, and Reynosa all lay on the south bank of the river. Laredo was the only *villa* on the north bank to last into the American period. The *villas* were small, consisting of a few wood and adobe buildings with thatched roofs surrounding a central plaza. The population grew steadily, from approximately 1,479 in 1749 to nearly 14,000 by 1821. The region's demographics resembled those of the rest of the frontier; there were a few full-blooded Spaniards and *criollos,* many *mestizos,* and a sprinkling of *mulatos* and local Coahuiltecan Indians who had intermarried with the *vecinos* or served as laborers.[5]

The distribution of land among the original families was unequal and based on considerations of length of residence and military, civilian, or community service as well as political connections. Only a few received the extremely large grants consisting of more than 100,000 acres of land. One of these was Juan Cortina's great-great-grandfather, Blas María de la Garza Falcón, founder of Camargo, and initial grantee of the Potrero del Espíritu Santo grant, north of the Río Bravo. The majority received small and medium-sized land grants, such as the 177-acre irrigable farm plots, or *caballerías,* and larger sections of pasture land, 4,428 acres, labeled either *sitios de ganado mayor* for raising cattle or *sitios de ganado menor* for raising sheep and goats. In order to maximize access to water sources, *vecinos* in the *villas del norte* received narrow slices of land along the north bank of the river, 9/13 of a mile wide and eleven to sixteen miles long. Called *porciones,* these land grants consisted of 4,200 to 6,200 acres, depending on the quality of the tract. Additional land grants called *mercedes de tierras,* tracts of ten to twenty thousand acres each, lay just beyond the *porciones.* A 1794 report listed seventeen *haciendas* and 437 *ranchos* in all of Nuevo Santander, revealing a society with a majority population of small to middling *rancheros.* The remainder included the large landowners, a few government officials, artisans, traveling merchants, and some landless laborers such as *vaqueros* who lived and worked on the larger *ranchos.*[6]

The *vecinos* along the lower Río Bravo in the eighteenth and early nineteenth centuries resided either in the villages for protection or in dispersed *rancho* community settlements. The *villas del norte* and the surrounding *ranchos* had to function in a somewhat self-sufficient manner because of the lack of consistent access to regular markets. They raised cattle and sheep and grew corn, beans, and squash, but frequent droughts and occasional winter freezes precluded the development of agriculture on a large scale. The basic social unit was the extended family, led by the patriarch. Baptisms, weddings, fiestas, and entertainment usually occurred within the context of the home or village community. Literacy rates were low, and education was almost nonexistent. Despite their relative remoteness, however, the residents of the *villas del norte* did engage in a regional trade network with residents of the silver-mining districts, Monterrey, Saltillo, and San Luis Potosí. Barter and credit were the primary forms of personal exchange because of the scarcity of specie. Traveling merchants, or *comerciantes,* used mule trains to carry domestic textiles, metal items, and some foodstuffs to the *villas del norte* along treacherous inland routes winding through mountains and across deserts and plains. *Carreteros* guided oxcarts that carried bulkier items, especially hides, wool, salt, and tallow, from the *ranchos* back to Saltillo or Monterrey. Laredoans exchanged goods with residents of San Antonio to the north.[7] These trade routes established during the Spanish period created a precedent for future commercial pathways, and the lower Río Bravo/Rio Grande region became an important crossroad of commerce and migration between San Antonio, Monterrey, and the Gulf Coast, a status it continues to hold today.

One of the greatest threats to prosperity in the *villas del norte* and sur-rounding ranchlands were the *indíos bárbaros* who inhabited the southern plains. For much of the eighteenth century, the Lipan Apaches, who lived sea-sonally in *rancherías* in the canyon lands of the upper Nueces River, raided *ranchos* around Laredo for livestock and captives. The Comanches arrived out of the north in the latter half of the eighteenth century and developed a vast commercial network of raiding and trade extending south from the banks of the Arkansas River across most of Texas and into northern Mexico. They frequently attacked *ranchos* north and south of the Río Bravo, stealing captives and cattle as well as horses and mules to exchange for guns. In order to pacify the Coman-ches, Tejanos in Laredo and nearby settlements gave gifts of cloth, tobacco, food, metal utensils, and other items, which depleted their resources substantially and on an ongoing basis. The Spaniards managed to achieve a tenuous peace in the late eighteenth century with both the Apaches and the Comanches, which, by providing a respite from the raids, led to a 210 percent increase in the num-bers of cattle, horses, mules, sheep, and goats (799,874) between 1768 and 1795. The peace agreement proved to be temporary, however, collapsing when Spain's defenses crumbled from Tejas to Alta California during the final two decades of Spanish rule.[8]

The wars for independence that erupted as Mexico sought to throw off Span-ish colonial rule created havoc along the border for a decade and disrupted the livelihoods of *rancheros* along the Río Bravo. After Father Hidalgo's revolt in 1810, different groups vied for control in the growing power vacuum in New Spain, leading to protracted civil wars that lasted eleven years. Although the *villas del norte* experienced little of the violence, other than some sporadic rebel activity, they suffered from extreme supply shortages and inflation. The Coman-ches, allied with the Lipan Apaches, took advantage of the chaos to extend their control over the region, participating in especially destructive raids along the Río Bravo in 1814 and 1815.[9]

THE RISE OF MERCANTILE ENTERPRISE

Shortly after gaining independence from Spain in 1821, the Mexican government instituted more liberal trade policies that not only changed life along the Río Bravo forever but also transformed its entire northern frontier by connecting it more fully to transatlantic and transcontinental trade networks. Although Spain had prohibited its colonies from trading outside of the Spanish empire, smuggling was endemic in the far north. *Comercientes* along the Gulf Coast had carried on a limited trade in contraband with the merchants of New Orleans, for example, for a number of years. Still, the policies had curtailed trade between Hispanic frontier communities and the United States. With the opening of Mexico's borders, Mexican commerce with the United States surged despite rather high tariffs frequently instituted by the Mexican republic. Merchants in the United States pioneered new trade routes overland into Mexico such as the Santa Fe Trail, which opened in 1821. While the Mexican economy stagnated, its northern frontier boomed as market ties shifted toward the United States and away from the expensive and lengthy overland trade on the rugged trails through Chihuahua to Mexico City. Cheap, imported foreign goods flooded into the northern territories and states of Alta California, Nuevo Mexico, and Coahuila y Tejas as they moved into the orbit of the US economy.[10]

In 1823, the Mexican government designated the small Villa del Refugio at the mouth of the Río Bravo, Nuestra Señora del Refugio de los Esteros, as a *puerto del altura* and renamed it Matamoros in honor of a hero of the Mexican wars for independence. Matamoros rapidly became one of the most important Mexican Gulf Coast ports. It lay at the crossroad between the silver districts of northern Mexico, serviced by the inland towns of Saltillo and San Luis Potosí, and the maritime routes from the Gulf of Mexico to New Orleans, New York, London, and other Atlantic world ports. If the Río Bravo could be navigated all the way to Santa Fe, it would potentially link the St. Louis–Santa Fe–Chihuahua trade and the Matamoros-Saltillo trade.[11]

Merchants, adventurers, and financiers from the United States and Europe flocked to Matamoros because of its strategic location. Their primary trading partners were the merchants of New Orleans, who carried the much-coveted European goods that northern Mexicans preferred over those coming from the United States. (Great Britain was the primary competitor of the United States for control over the Mexican trade prior to the US/Mexican War.) Most of the foreigners were young men seeking to gain experience and improve their financial position. They were part of a larger migration of Europeans into Mexico, seeking to fill the void left by the *peninsulares,* who had long controlled the international and wholesale trade of New Spain but were forced out due to intense hostility toward Spaniards in the aftermath of independence. The city's population boomed, growing from 2,320 in 1820 to 7,000 in 1829 and 16,372 in 1837. By 1832, at least three hundred foreign residents resided in Matamoros. It became a culturally diverse, cosmopolitan seaport. Walking through its streets, a person could hear the sounds of Spanish, English, French, Italian, and German being spoken.[12]

One of the most prominent of the new foreign merchants in Matamoros was Connecticut-born Yankee Charles Stillman. He remained in the Río Bravo/Rio Grande delta for more than thirty years and played a pivotal role in its economic transformation. In fact, he was so important that virtually every person who became extremely wealthy in South Texas prior to 1880 had some tie to him. He furthered the careers of a number of people in northern Mexico as well. Historian John Mason Hart called him "the most important American capitalist in Mexico" by the 1850s. He built "a trading and manufacturing nexus in northeastern Mexico which was anchored in Monterrey and the Matamoros-Brownsville area" by investing in mines, textile mills, land, and mercantile operations.[13] His career illuminates the important role of access to credit in the economic development and distribution of wealth in the region.

In 1827, when Charles was just seventeen years old, his father, Francis Stillman, sent him to work in Durango, Mexico, as an apprentice in the growing community of foreign merchants. Charles lived there for several months, acquiring the knowledge and skills necessary to participate in the global wholesale trade. He moved to Matamoros, Mexico, in 1828 to open a branch of his father's New York wholesale dry goods company. He was able to take advantage of his father's connections with suppliers and bankers in New York, and he continued to nurture those connections personally and expand them. Ties to suppliers and financiers in their own countries gave foreign merchants like Stillman a considerable advantage throughout Mexico, where they dominated most of the retail sectors as well as wholesale trade.[14]

Through transnational business partnerships with people like the Spanish immigrant José San Román and Monterrey wholesaler Jeremiah Galván, Stillman participated in the lucrative import/export trade between the rich silver mines of northern Mexico and New York and Europe. Ships filled with European manufactured goods, including linens, furniture, dishes, pots and pans, and hardware, entered the harbor at Brazos de Santiago, north of the river, and unloaded their cargo onto ox wagons and two-wheeled carts drawn by burros for transport to Matamoros. The ships carried loads of silver, the primary and most valuable Mexican export, along with hides, tallow, and wool, away to New York, Boston, New Orleans, and London. Traveling merchants from across northern Mexico journeyed to Matamoros to buy from wholesalers like Stillman. Stillman also hired *carreteros* to haul his goods over rough and often treacherous dirt roads to Monterrey, Saltillo, and San Luis Potosí in order to gain wider access to markets. This was often risky because of the prevalence of Indian and bandit raids on the wagon trains.[15]

Wholesalers were far more willing to give credit to the large merchants like Stillman because it was more cost effective than dealing with small traders. The costs of sending goods by sea from New York or London to Matamoros were high. Storms, pirates, and shipwrecks were always a threat. Stillman had the capital to purchase insurance to help share the risk of transport. He could also afford to purchase in large quantities, making it worthwhile for a supplier to bear the high price of transporting goods by ship. He was deemed a good credit risk because the suppliers knew him and his father. All of these things worked to his advantage, helping his business to grow, which in turn improved his profitability and creditworthiness.[16]

Because of his superior access to sources of capital and suppliers, Stillman became a major determinant of who succeeded and who did not. One of those he helped was young Francisco Yturria, son of Manuel María Yturria, a military man who had served in the Royal Spanish Army and in the Mexican Army. With stores on both sides of the Río Bravo/Rio Grande, Yturria later became a wealthy border merchant as well as a private banker, the only one south of San Antonio between 1858 and 1870. Stillman, Yturria, and their associates essentially monopolized access to credit in the region for several decades. Small traders had few other places to turn for supplies and funding. They carried limited goods and served the local market as long as they could. Their small size exacerbated their vulnerability to failure. Many went out of business.[17]

In contrast to Stillman and his associates, many substantial landowners and businesspeople in northern Mexico had difficulty gaining access to credit. The Republic of Mexico lay in shambles after the long wars for independence from Spain; financial institutions were few, and there was virtually no manufacturing base. The Catholic Church had been an important lender during the colonial period, but its power had waned during the Bourbon Era, and by the Mexican period, it was struggling financially. The first state bank of Mexico, Banco del Avío, located in Mexico City, was politically controversial and economically unstable. It failed in 1842. Thus, the major sources of credit lay overseas, especially in cities like New York and London, too far away and expensive for most Mexican landowners and businesspeople to travel to and cultivate contacts with bankers and wholesalers.[18]

Charles Stillman found ways to profit despite the conflict, unrest, and even anarchy that often prevailed along the border in subsequent decades. While many American merchants based in Matamoros left during the Texas Revolution after David G. Burnet, president of the Republic of Texas, ordered a naval blockade of the port of Brazos de Santiago, temporarily disrupting commerce in Matamoros and infuriating local Mexican and European merchants, Stillman stayed. He and other merchants living in Matamoros profited substantially just a few years later by supplying the US Army during the US/Mexican War.[19]

General Zachary Taylor's quartermaster system relied on steamboats to ferry supplies upriver from Matamoros to the troops. As Stillman delivered his goods for shipment on the steamboats, he saw the potential for future trade along the river after the war. Steamboats plied the waters up to Roma, which sat on high bluffs overlooking the river just over one hundred miles from Brownsville. The army had tried, unsuccessfully, to navigate all the way to Fort Duncan, near the present-day town of Eagle Pass. When the war ended, Stillman purchased the steamboats and invited the two young pilots hired by the army, Richard King and Mifflin Kenedy, to join him in a partnership. That partnership held a virtual monopoly over traffic on the Río Bravo/Rio Grande for the next few decades and provided the initial foundation for the King and Kenedy fortunes. Thus began the use of steamboats for river commerce, which continued for many years thereafter (fig. 1). King, a New York orphan of Irish parentage, and Kenedy, the son of Pennsylvania Quakers, were of relatively humble origins, but with Stillman's help, they soon ranked among the wealthiest men in South Texas.[20]

The Treaty of Guadalupe Hidalgo ended the US/Mexican War in 1848 and divided the society that had grown up along the banks of the lower Río Bravo over the course of the last century. Problematically for Mexico, Matamoros's port of Brazos de Santiago ended up on the US side, giving merchants there an advantage in maintaining the upper hand in the competition for control of the silver trade in northern Mexico. The treaty solved the legal dispute over the Trans-

FIGURE 1. Steamboat on the Rio Grande near Brownsville. Courtesy, Lower Rio Grande Valley Historical Collection, Library Archives and Special Collections, University of Texas–Pan American.

Nueces, definitively making it part of Texas and the United States, and defined the Texas-Mexico border as the deepest channel of the middle of the Río Bravo, giving Texas the longest international border of any state, more than twelve hundred miles. The Americans even changed the name of the river itself—to the Rio Grande. This shifting border would prove difficult to delineate and control. The river facilitated interaction more than conflict and division along its banks.[21]

Merchants in the United States promptly took advantage of the drawing of the international boundary by playing an instrumental role in establishing towns near army outposts along the Rio Grande. Some of the forts had been established during the war, while others were built to comply with Article 11 of the Treaty of Guadalupe Hidalgo, which required the United States to stop the threat of Indians in its territory from raiding into Mexico.[22] These new US border towns provided a market for small traders, known as "camp followers," as well as larger merchants. They became important commercial centers and gradually transformed the surrounding rural areas through their connections with world markets and the capital that flowed out from them into the countryside. Built on a standard Anglo-American grid pattern designed to maximize space for businesses along straight and wide streets, their appearance contrasted with that of the Spanish colonial towns, centered around plazas where people often came together to engage in communal, religious, and civic, as well as commercial activities.[23] The US border towns became intimately intertwined with commercial and social activities in nearby Mexican villages and settlements just across the river, some of which were new and others long established in the region.

Charles Stillman planned the first of these new border towns, Brownsville, right across from Matamoros near Fort Brown, with easy access to the port of Brazos Santiago, thereby ensuring its attractiveness to international merchants. In a move that angered local Tejanos, he designed it on disputed Matamoros *ejido* lands (town commons) out of a portion of the Espíritu Santo grant, acquired by questionable means. Juan Cortina claimed the lands still belonged to his mother, Francisca Cavazos, who had never received payment from the city of Matamoros when they were designated as *ejidos*. Title litigation continued for several decades, long after Stillman's death.[24]

Upriver from Brownsville, the towns of Hidalgo (originally Edinburgh), Rio Grande City, and Roma sprang up in the vicinity of *ranchos* dating to the early Spanish period. John Young, a Scotsman, established the town of Edinburgh across from Reynosa on land he had bought before the war. Henry Clay Davis's mercantile business and ranch formed the nucleus of Rio Grande City. Near Fort Ringgold, it fronted the river, across from the town of Camargo. It also lay on a strategic overland trade route from Corpus Christi to Nuevo León. Davis, a former soldier in Zachary Taylor's army, had acquired land along the river through his marriage to María Hilaria de la Garza. Roma, about twelve miles from Rio Grande City, was the only new town on the left bank established by a Tejano. It symbolized the hope of some Tejanos that life would be better in the United States than in Mexico. José María García Sáens arranged for the platting of a townsite on his land just a week after the signing of the Treaty of Guadalupe Hidalgo. He designed the town to include both Anglo and Hispanic elements. It had a plaza, which was typical of Hispanic settlement, but it was far more rectangular in shape than most plazas in Mexican towns. The purpose was to make it more accessible to commercial activity while at the same time preserving the social aspects of the plaza.[25]

Above Roma, settlement initially remained sparse because of the ongoing threat of Indian raids and the lack of access to the river trade. After 1848, a number of Tejano families moved across the river from Laredo into Mexico and founded the town of Nuevo Laredo. A few farmers began settling the rich land north of Fort McIntosh near Laredo. Eagle Pass began as a small settlement near Fort Duncan in 1849. In 1850, San Antonio merchant James Campbell opened a trading post nearby, attracting travelers on the way to the California goldfields. By 1860, Eagle Pass had about five hundred inhabitants. A small Mexican settlement, Piedras Negras, developed across the river at about the same time and became home to nine merchants and their families. Their origins reveal how even remoter parts of the region attracted a diverse group of immigrants: one merchant came from Ireland, one from Nassau, Bahamas, another from Switzerland, a fourth from Prussia, two from France, one from Great Britain, one from Kentucky, and another from Louisiana. The rest of the population, except for the soldiers at Fort Duncan, consisted of ethnic Mexicans, most of whom worked as artisans, *carreteros,* and day laborers.[26] Del Rio's origins came later, in the late 1860s, when an Anglo rancher, John Taylor, and his Mexican wife, Paula, along with some business associates, built a rudimentary canal system near San Felipe Springs. They formed the San Felipe Agricultural, Manufacturing, and Irrigation Company and prepared to sell farm tracts to prospective buyers. As a town began to take shape, the Mexican government founded Ciudad Acuña across the river as a defensive outpost.[27]

American control of the left bank of the Rio Grande encouraged US investment in the area and offered greater assurance of legal protection of those investments, luring more entrepreneurs to the region. Evidence of this lies in the pages of the credit ledgers of the Mercantile Agency (later known as R. G. Dun & Co.), one of the first credit-reporting firms in the United States, which kept pages of records about merchants along the lower Río Bravo/Rio Grande. Brownsville-Matamoros had the largest number of entries, 358, of any of the border towns in the region. There were ninety-seven entries for Starr County, mostly merchants in Rio Grande City, Roma, Mier, and Camargo, eighty-four entries for Laredo, forty-four for Eagle Pass, and seventeen for all of Hidalgo County. Even though the reports technically covered particular counties in Texas, merchants in Matamoros, Camargo, Mier, and Nuevo Laredo were included.[28]

The R. G. Dun records indicate that creditors viewed the Río Bravo/Rio Grande borderlands as an economic unit, which reflected the reality that, in many ways, life along the river in the decades after 1848 continued much as it had before the war. Although South Texas was legally part of the United States, the process of incorporating it into the national economy, culture, and society of the United States would take time. It was still tied more closely to Mexico. The population was well over 90 percent ethnic Mexican, Spanish continued to be the primary language, and the *peso* was the common medium of exchange. There were still families living on the Mexican side of the river who owned property on the Texas side.[29]

Merchants continued partnerships and businesses that spanned the river. This enabled them to take advantage of changing laws and shifting political winds. They would move the focus of their operations from Texas to Mexico and back again depending on tariff policies, local unrest, wars, and other circumstances that might affect business. During times of peace, having stores in two or more cities gave merchants the advantage of reaching more customers. This practice of doing business on both sides of the border became entrenched during the nineteenth century and continues to the present. For example, J. B. Burchard & Co., a partnership headquartered in Brownsville, consisted of "active business men" who had "an extensive trade in the adjoining states of Mexico."[30] John Decker, reportedly the "richest merchant in Rio Grande City" as of August 1, 1874, had a son-in-law and partner, Emile Laffargue, with a significant business in Camargo across the river.[31] Francisco Rodríguez owned stores in both Laredo and Nuevo Laredo.[32] An "old merchant in good standing" lived in Mexico and ran A. Dudlos & Co., a mercantile house in Eagle Pass.[33]

In addition to conducting cross-border trade within the immediate region, a number of businesspeople either ran businesses or had connections with an emerging class of merchants in Monterrey, Nuevo León. Juan Fernández, a "Mexican trade f[ir]mly of this place (Brownsville)," started a business in Monterrey in 1860. In addition, D. N. Brainerd & Co. had operations in both Brownsville and Monterrey. By 1856, Jacob Schwarz, a German Jewish trader, had closed his business in Brownsville and left for Monterrey. Joseph Moses, who came from New York, owned a store and town lot in Brownsville, a house in Roma, and a mercantile business in Monterrey.[34] Lorenzo and Jesús González had operations in Chihuahua, Monterrey, and Brownsville.[35] Members of the Monterrey merchant elite, with whom the border merchants established trade networks, would later play an important role in the capitalist transformation of northern Mexico. After accumulating their wealth through contraband cross-border trade in the 1850s and 1860s, they moved into banking, legitimate commerce, and real estate in the late 1860s and industry by the end of the nineteenth century.[36]

The prominence of Charles Stillman and his associates in and around Brownsville is readily apparent from the credit records. Stillman was the "largest proprietor," "very reliable," and "regarded as the safest on the Rio Grande."[37] Still, by 1859, reports were urging caution. Although Stillman was "undoubtedly wealthy," he was "mixed up in land speculations & has facilities for transferring his [property]." A suit pending against him in New York had the potential of wiping out his entire fortune.[38] Stillman's partner, Samuel Belden, had a business that had "grown as by magic."[39] Francisco Yturria used connections and expertise developed while working for Stillman to start a tailor shop. Credit reports indicate that he had a small business and could be credited for a small amount in 1854. By December 1873 he reportedly "almost always has money," was "never in debt," and was "a man of considerable means."[40] He was "reliable," "prudent," and "energetic."[41]

While commercial networks in the region continued to function after 1848 as they had previously, the border introduced complexities that affected trade. Both countries relied heavily on tariffs for revenues, but Mexican tariffs were prohibitively high, discouraging imports. The comparably lower US tariffs made importing goods far more profitable on the north bank of the Río Bravo/Rio Grande. The primary markets, however, were south of the river. The appetite in the northern Mexican cities of Saltillo and Monterrey for imported wines, linens, textiles, furniture, hardware, and other manufactured items from Europe and the United States continued to grow, and South Texas remained sparsely populated. As a result, between 1848 and 1857, merchants from the older towns of Mier, Reynosa, Camargo, and Matamoros and new immigrants streamed to the towns on the Texas side of the river, where they bought and warehoused their goods and then smuggled them into northern Mexico. The length of the river and the numerous shallow crossings made smuggling difficult to police. Merchants could readily move goods from warehouses in Rio Grande City, Laredo, or Eagle Pass over to the Mexican side, and customshouses in Matamoros and Nuevo Laredo could be easily circumvented.[42]

Smuggling became a lucrative practice engaged in by both large and small merchants. It was not without risks, however. Samuel Belden, an associate of Charles Stillman, faced "occasional seizures and confiscation by the Mexican authorities." He later suffered heavy losses as a result of getting caught smuggling goods into Mexico, and by June 1853 he was "hopelessly bankrupt."[43] These risks made many wholesalers reluctant to do business with known smugglers. Credit reports warned that José Bestiero of Brownsville paid his bills on time and had a solid business, but "he will smuggle, buy stolen goods or do anything by which he can turn a penny."[44] Jesús Ortíz of San Diego, Duval County, and his partner were "smuggling from Mexico and are liable to be caught at any time."[45]

Frustration over Mexican tariffs contributed to a border disturbance known as the Merchants' War in the early 1850s. The merchants had been used to doing business without regard to international tariffs and fees and resented the change. Financed by Charles Stillman and led by José María de Jesús de Carvajal, a Mexican merchant with substantial ties to the United States, a group of revolutionaries supported by local merchants seized control of several border towns, including Camargo and Reynosa. The Merchants' War ended after Carvajal's unsuccessful attempt to capture Matamoros.[46] Partly as a response to the Merchants' War and partly out of concern for the loss of business in his province, the governor of Tamaulipas, Ramón Guerra, declared *zona libre* in 1857, which allowed US goods to flow across the border free of tariffs in a twelve-mile-wide zone. Although this move helped the Mexican border towns, it did not stop the smuggling. It simply moved many of the smugglers into Mexico, stimulating a new boom in the population of Matamoros and a corresponding decline in business in Brownsville.[47] US ranchers complained that the *zona libre* created a "depot for smuggling," which "induc[ed] smugglers, adventurers, and thieves to flock to the right bank of the Rio Grande, from whence they depredate on our exposed frontier."[48]

The elite merchants in the region held a virtual monopoly over local resources during the period. After a branch of the Commercial and Agricultural Bank of Galveston closed in 1858, Francisco Yturria's private bank was the only one along the border before the arrival of the railroads. More remote towns in the interior had no banks of any kind, and so the only available credit was in the hands of local merchants, who were not always willing to lend, especially to their competitors.[49]

The limited availability of local credit coupled with the reluctance of wholesalers to do much business with a merchant who had a minimal net worth, which was always noted in the credit reports, created a high-risk environment for small traders and made it difficult for them to succeed or expand. The entries for small general store owner S. Raveli emphasized that he was honest and industrious but "has a small store." Juan Rios, Servando Cavazos, and Blas Martínez were all reliable "for a small amount."[50] Failure was common; many left after only a few years, some for California, where prospects were much better in the San Francisco area. A Frenchman named R. Duval, who was known for doing considerable business in 1854, had left for New Orleans by 1856. Another Frenchman, D. Baiz, who was doing a "fair" business in 1854, also closed down and moved to Mobile in 1856. Joseph Wellman, a watchmaker, left in 1856, probably for St. Louis. George Dye was "hopelessly insolvent" on August 16, 1857.[51]

A few managed to succeed and stay. John Cross, originally from South Carolina, moved from Louisiana to the lower Rio Grande Valley shortly after the US/Mexican War to engage in cattle ranching. He found that he could not make a living because of the constant threat of raids, so he moved to Matamoros in 1857, where he started a general store. An entry in the R. G. Dun credit ledgers stated that he "married a colored woman" and that his mulatto son, a good businessman, managed his affairs.[52] Within a couple of decades, Cross had built a substantial business. His retail store on Abasolo Street in Matamoros carried groceries, dry goods, notions, boots, shoes, and men's furnishings. Behind the store, warehouses stored furniture, lumber, and munitions that were shipped by oxcart into the interior of Mexico, to places like Linares, San Fernando, and Victoria. His wholesale house in Brownsville supplied the border towns of Reynosa, Camargo, Santa María, Edinburg, Rio Grande City, and Roma by steamboat. By 1893 he and his son owned more than nine thousand acres of land in Cameron County, where they raised cattle.[53]

The Confederate cotton trade in the 1860s brought increased prosperity to the river towns and cemented commercial partnerships between Texas and Mexican merchants even as it unfolded in the midst of conflict. The Union naval blockade along the Atlantic and Gulf coasts, which closed the ports of Galveston and New Orleans, forced the Confederates to search for alternative routes to ship cotton overseas. Matamoros became a logical destination because it was the only foreign port bordering the Confederacy. Oxcarts carried cotton overland through Corpus Christi, across Richard King's ranch, and then south into Brownsville. Once on the banks of the river, the cotton was loaded onto steamboats traveling downriver to Matamoros and the port of Bagdad, where European ships waited to exchange dry goods, coffee, medicines, and military supplies. After Union troops occupied Brownsville in late 1863, pro-Confederate merchants involved in the cotton trade moved to Matamoros, and the trade continued along a more western route through Laredo and Eagle Pass. The shift in the route proved to be a boon to the towns farther upriver that had not seen the prosperity of Brownsville-Matamoros.[54]

As had occurred so many times before, those who profited in the 1860s did so in the midst of tremendous conflict. Skirmishes between Union and Confederate troops battling each other over the occupation of Brownsville threatened business and deterred some investors. Union soldiers ransacked Stillman's home and Richard King's ranch. Simultaneously, civil war raged south of the border between the Juaristas, the liberal faction led by Benito Juárez, and the Imperialistas, conservative supporters of the French regime under Ferdinand Maximilian, installed by the French when Mexico refused to repay its debt. The two groups vied for control of northern Mexico along with Juan Cortina, who was adept at changing sides depending on the political winds. Matamoros alternately fell under the control of the different warring factions over the course of the decade.[55] The manager of one mercantile house was killed, and his store "lost most of its available capital in the train captured by the Liberals."[56]

The Confederate cotton trade created new fortunes and solidified the place of Stillman, King, and Kenedy at the top of the South Texas economy. Entries in the R. G. Dun ledgers for King, Kenedy, & Co., their steamboat partnership, which had carried thousands of bales of cotton during the war, reveal that the men were considered "large capitalists and reliable" in 1868. According to the R. G. Dun & Co. credit ledgers, by September 1870, their estimated worth was at least $350 million, and their potential to grow virtually unlimited. José San Román, one of Stillman's business associates, was reportedly worth at least half a million in 1878 and was a solid, reliable borrower.[57] Stillman invested some of his profits in National City Bank of New York (today Citibank), helping it to become the largest bank in the country by 1894. After he died in 1875, his son James inherited his enterprises. James served as the president of National City Bank between 1891 and 1909.[58]

Farther upriver, Santiago Vidaurri, the powerful *caudillo* of Nuevo León, and his son-in-law, an Irish immigrant, Patrick Mullins, who Hispanicized his name to Patricio Milmo, amassed enormous wealth and power from the cotton trade. Through P. Milmo and Company, Patricio Milmo launched brokerage houses and forwarding agencies all along the northern bank of the Río Bravo/Rio Grande. Although he lived in Monterrey, Laredo became his base of operations in Texas. On July 1, 1880, he organized and funded the Milmo National Bank, one of the key financial institutions in Laredo for half a century.[59]

A community of German Jewish merchants prospered both during and after the Civil War. For example, J. Alexander, A. J. Bloomberg, and G. M. Raphael started a major dry goods house, Alexander & Co., in 1865, which was housed in three brick buildings along Elizabeth Street in Brownsville and sold American products. They also opened a store in Matamoros that sold European clothing, fabrics, and notions. When Alexander was killed by one of Cortina's associates in 1872, the firm's name was changed to Bloomberg & Raphael. Brothers Adolph and Henry Bollack of Bavaria arrived in Brownsville shortly after the Civil War. Adolph had had a successful wholesale business in New Orleans, which he moved to Brownsville. His brother set up a retail enterprise, the Bollack Store. After Henry Bollack died of yellow fever, his widow, Pauline, with the help of her sons significantly expanded the original retail store, renaming it Bollack's Department Store, which occupied a substantial stone building on Market Plaza for many years.[60]

Many Anglo merchants left after the cessation of the Confederate cotton trade and the implementation of the Reconstruction Act of 1867 in Texas, which plunged the region into turmoil and depression. A study of Roma reveals that local Tejano entrepreneurs purchased most of the buildings around the plaza in the late 1860s, and the number of non-Hispanic-surnamed individuals plummeted from twenty-one in 1860 to five in 1870.[61] Merchants who shifted from cotton to deal in hides and wool, however, found new opportunities with the rise of commercial ranching in the late 1860s and 1870s.

Laredo/Nuevo Laredo benefited from this post–Civil War boom in the cattle trade. It had developed more slowly than Brownsville because it was located above the navigable part of the Rio Grande and subject to ongoing Indian raids. In contrast to Brownsville-Matamoros, which had many entries in the R. G. Dun credit ledgers from the 1850s and 1860s, almost all of the entries for Laredo/Nuevo Laredo began in the 1870s. The Anglo-Americans and Europeans who moved to Laredo quickly established themselves. In 1860, only twenty-one Anglos and eleven Europeans were living in Laredo out of a population of approximately 1,306. Despite their small numbers, they owned about one-quarter of the land and one-third of the wealth in the town.[62] German merchant John Z. Leyendecker, who had arrived in the 1850s, made his fortune trading hides in San Antonio and New York. Raymond Martin from France also immigrated in the 1850s and by 1871 was an established merchant who was as "trusty as any man." An entry about Antonio Bruni, an Italian who had arrived there with very little to his name in the early 1870s, noted, "Think he will make money."[63] Bruni eventually became one of the wealthiest men in Laredo. Charles Callaghan, a Confederate veteran whose sheep ranch eventually expanded to cover more than one hundred thousand acres in Webb County, owned only forty-five sheep in 1870 but was deemed trustworthy. In March 1877, people apparently had great confidence in the thirty-five-year-old owner of Villegas & Bro., whom they believed would "no doubt succeed." Villegas & Bro., located in Nuevo Laredo at the time, became one of largest wholesale grocery houses in Laredo in the early twentieth century.[64]

Anglo-Americans and Europeans did not entirely displace the Tejano elite in the borderlands, and not all Tejanos followed Cortina's example by engaging in efforts to drive out the newcomers. The most successful pursued commercial enterprises and embraced change. As historian Joyce Appleby points out, "capitalism relied on people's acting differently: taking risks, endorsing novelty, and innovating."[65] It was not only the Anglo-Americans and Europeans from countries that had already made the complete transition to capitalism who were acting this way; Tejanos and Mexicans were as well. As these groups cooperated in business endeavors, largely in pursuit of their own interests, they furthered the economic integration of South Texas and northern Mexico and mitigated to some degree the harshness of racial, national, and ethnic conflict.[66]

Creditors proved willing to lend to Tejanos and Mexicans, although apparently to a lesser extent than to Anglos and Europeans. The R. G. Dun credit ledgers contain reports on Hispanic individuals in the 1850s, 1860s, and 1870s, yet they were few in number; only about 38 out of 358 proprietorships and partnerships listed in the Brownsville ledger included people with Hispanic surnames.[67] The credit reports emphasized character, habits, net worth, and business ability in descriptions of Hispanic merchants rather than ethnicity, just as they did for Anglo-Americans and Europeans. Manuel Guerra, who later became the political boss of Starr County, ran a hides, wool, and liquor business in Roma. In 1878, he had also had storehouses across the river in Mier, Mexico. He could be trusted and paid his debts promptly.[68] Juan Fernández, who had businesses in both Brownsville and Monterrey, was "prudent," "reliable," and "regarded as a very honest man."[69] Servando Cavazos had a dry goods store with branches in both Brownsville and Matamoros. He was considered prudent and reliable as a borrower.[70] Augustín Morales of Brownsville was "always ready to meet any bill."[71] Francisco Rodríguez, who had stores in Laredo and in Mexico, was "believed to be prompt in payment." Refugio, Santos, and Cristóbal Benavides of Laredo were all considered reliable and "safe to credit."[72] The inability of some to speak English may have been a problem in dealing with potential creditors, virtually all of whom were in the United States. An entry about Cayetano de la Garza, who raised sheep around Laredo and sold their wool, pointed out that he made money but was unable to speak English.[73]

Character was an important consideration, and although the character of a number of Hispanic merchants was questioned, there is no evidence that they were singled out because of their ethnicity. Francis Pérez of San Diego was very industrious and hard working but "sometimes inclined to gamble and speculate too heavily."[74] Manuel Treviño "seems to have use of a [large credit] and some means. But no one knows where they came from. His style of living and expenses are v. heavy."[75] In addition, W. Cavazos, who owned a saloon and small café, was "a very penurious Mexican" and "not safe" to credit.[76] Similar entries about non-Hispanics included one labeling Adam Joseph "a great cheat." William Scanlon spent his money too freely.[77] Theodore Lambertson, a saloon owner, was an alcoholic and known for living "in adultery with a prostitute."[78]

By 1880 a small but growing class of Hispanic merchants and grocers was serving the developing local market. Brownsville had about twenty-nine Hispanic grocers from both Texas and Mexico as well as a number of Hispanics working as bakers, butchers, dressmakers, and cigar makers. Merchants Juan Buentello, Bruno García, José Mora, José María Chapa, and Amado Vela operated small grocery stores on several of the larger *ranchos* in Hidalgo County. In Rio Grande City, Europeans dominated the larger mercantile enterprises, but a group of small Hispanic grocers, fruit dealers, and coffee house proprietors also made a living there. In Laredo, ethnic Mexican merchants of various sizes blended in with Italians, Frenchmen, Poles, Prussians, Bavarians, Spaniards, and Anglo-Americans, many of whom had grown up in Mexico. The town of Eagle Pass had only seven merchants, but two of them were from Mexico.[79]

The presence of growing numbers of Hispanic merchants in South Texas indicates the movement of some ethnic Mexicans away from sole reliance on the pastoral economy. Some were wealthy members of the elite, while others were people of limited means. In either case, these merchants would generally be better equipped to navigate the economic changes ahead than those who remained involved solely in traditional forms of ranching.

GRADUAL TEJANO LAND LOSS NORTH OF THE LOWER RÍO BRAVO/RIO GRANDE

While a coalition of European, Anglo-American, and elite Hispanic merchants controlled the US border towns, Tejanos continued to dominate much of rural South Texas. The recovery in ranching after the US/Mexican War and the boom that occurred after the Civil War preserved border ranching among all classes of rancheros until the 1880s. Yet as conditions in the border region changed, their hold on the land loosened. A rising class of Anglo-American and European ranchers increasingly gained the upper hand, exploiting the uncertainty, chaos, and general lack of law enforcement that prevailed in the years following the US/Mexican War to amass considerable landholdings and cattle and sheep herds. Fraud and outright theft occurred on occasion. However, most Tejanos lost their property, as historian David Montejano has pointed out, as a result of the "play of the market." Although many participated in the transition to commercial ranching, they generally lacked the resources to pay property taxes and legal fees in difficult times, much less expand and modernize, and therefore few became wealthy. They became susceptible to tax foreclosures as well as offers to buy their land. The process of Tejano land loss was uneven, occurring rapidly in the areas closest to the coast and along the Nueces River and more gradually farther inland.[80]

Tejano vulnerability to land loss began before the US conquest. After 1820, a "wealth gap" developed between Hispanic *rancheros* and the relatively small group of Anglo-Americans and Europeans who dominated import/export trade in the border towns. Highly profitable commercial activity in the Río Bravo/Rio Grande borderlands remained confined largely to the coastal and river trade. Although the *rancheros* benefited from enhanced access to markets for hides, cattle by-products, and wool, they did not share in the wealth accumulated by Stillman and others. The value of hides and wool, despite their bulk, was relatively small compared to the manufactured goods and cotton traded by the merchants.[81] As a result, the liquid resources of the new merchant class began to surpass that of even the largest *rancheros,* whose wealth remained tied up primarily in land. Many merchants would later use these resources to acquire land from the cash-poor Tejanos, especially when ranching became very profitable just after the Civil War.

The census records of 1850 foreshadow the eventual dominance of Euro-Americans and the dispossession of the Tejanos in the area. In 1850, the merchant class in the Rio Grande Valley region, which comprised the counties of Cameron, Webb, and Starr, was made up almost entirely of Anglo-Americans and Europeans. Nearly half of those identified as merchants were from Europe, predominantly France and Germany. Only three were born in Mexico. The Anglo-American merchants were almost all from states along the eastern seaboard, with nearly half coming from New England and the mid-Atlantic states. In contrast to the merchant class in the towns, the rural landowning class consisted almost entirely of ethnic Mexicans. More than 92 percent of those classified as "farmers," who principally raised livestock, had Spanish surnames. All of the unskilled laborers were ethnic Mexicans.[82]

Hispanic *rancheros* in South Texas faced other challenges in the years leading up to the US conquest, which weakened the ability of some to retain their lands. Repeated raids by the Comanches, the Lipan Apaches, and their allies had

devastated areas near the Nueces River and inland from the Gulf Coast, resulting in the losses of thousands of horses and cattle. Comanches used the stolen
livestock to trade to farmers and merchants along the Anglo-American southwestern frontier for guns.[83] Lieutenant John L. Haynes, state representative
from Rio Grande City, described the Anglo perception of the *rancheros'* situation:
"Here for years they led a sort of amphibious life, swimming from one side of
the river to the other as the Indians appeared on one or the other bank. The
rich coast was a wilderness; on our earlier maps it was laid down as a 'desert,'
inhabited only by large droves of wild horses and cattle. You have doubtless seen
these maps. It is no desert, but the 'wild horses and cattle' were there, being the
product of the immense droves and herds once obedient to and constituting the
wealth of their owners."[84] The Texas Revolution had also dealt a severe blow.
Uncertainty over the outcome of the boundary dispute between Mexico and the
Republic of Texas over the Trans-Nueces led many to sell their lands.[85]

Then, the US victory over Mexico in 1848 complicated the century-old ranching society by dividing it in half and creating two different real-property regimes
on the border ranges. Despite the recovery of Tejano ranching in the early 1850s
and the return of herds driven to Mexico during the hostilities, requirements
imposed on Mexican landowners to prove title to their landholdings in the Trans-
Nueces created new obstacles that had to be overcome. The Bourland-Miller
Commission, tasked with determining legal ownership of the Spanish and Mexican land grants in South Texas as required by the Treaty of Guadalupe Hidalgo,
required proof of ownership under the applicable laws of Spain and Mexico. Tejanos transferred portions of their acreage to pay for attorneys to represent them
in the title-confirmation process. Stephen Powers and his apprentice, James B.
Wells, were among those who became substantial landowners by taking land
in place of cash to represent Tejanos in need of legal services. Powers became
so influential that Herbert Davenport, a local attorney, referred to him as the
"Uncrowned King of the Tamaulipas session."[86]

Fear of losing land in the title-confirmation process may have played a role
in Tejanos' decisions to sell to Anglos. Mexican law required continual occupation
and possession of land in order to maintain title to land. Abandonment of one's
land for more than five years exposed an owner to forfeiture, and even though the
commission generally recommended confirmation of the title in cases where an
owner had left due to hostilities but returned once they had ceased, the ultimate
outcome of the decision was somewhat uncertain.[87] It is therefore not surprising
that most of the land the Anglos acquired from Tejanos shortly after the con-

quest was in places formerly subject to frequent Indian raids, such as northern Cameron County and Nueces County, where some owners had failed to return to their lands over the course of many years. The manuscript census reveals that in 1850 all of the resident farmers and ranchers on the land just south of the Nueces River were either European or Anglo-American.[88]

Steamboat captain Richard King apparently exploited this particular weakness when he decided to start his own ranching enterprise. In 1853, he traveled to Camargo to visit the widow of Juan Mendiola, offering to buy 15,500 acres out of the Rincón de Santa Gertrudis for less than two cents an acre. She accepted. Mendiola had never lived on or established a ranching enterprise on the land because of the constant threat of Indian raids. In 1854, King sought out the heir of Don José Pérez Rey and paid $1,800 for 53,000 acres of the de la Garza Santa Gertrudis *rancho,* which Pérez had essentially abandoned after Indians drove him out. These Mexican grants formed the core of Richard King's ranching empire; King amassed more than 600,000 acres in his lifetime, and the King Ranch eventually encompassed more than 1,000,000 acres. He built his home and headquarters on the banks of the Santa Gertrudis Creek and ran his Santa Gertrudis Ranch like a Mexican *patrón.* His workers, called *kiñenos,* were tied for generations to the ranch by a system resembling debt peonage.[89]

Rumors about King's shadowy dealings and questionable methods live on among Anglos and Tejanos alike, but little hard evidence of how he amassed his additional holdings can be found. King reportedly fenced in lands that were not his own and used intimidation tactics to enforce questionable title. He hired his owned armed militia to protect his land and also called on the Texas Rangers for protection. Stories of masked riders arriving unannounced in the middle of the night, forcing *rancheros* from their homes, persist in the oral histories of Tejano ranching families in the area.[90] Juan Cortina's raiders targeted the King Ranch in particular. King claimed to have lost 108,336 cattle between 1866 and 1869.[91]

The *rancheros'* situation was more complex closer to the heart of original Spanish settlement along the Río Bravo/Rio Grande because the land there was less likely to be abandoned. The Bourland-Miller Land Commission actually upheld the vast majority of the claims to Spanish and Mexican land grants in this area.[92] Ranching also recovered after the end of hostilities between the United States and Mexico; the wool, hide, and tallow trade was the main source of revenue. In 1859, Tejanos still owned most of the land sixty miles from the river in Cameron County as well as most of the land in Hidalgo, Starr, Webb, and Zapata counties. The transition from Tejano to Anglo ownership in these areas occurred more gradually and as a result of accommodation. Anglos and Europeans cooperated with the local Tejano elite and adapted to their lifestyle and customs. Most learned Spanish because it continued to be the primary language of commerce for the remainder of the nineteenth century. Many also converted to Catholicism and established bonds with families in the area through *compadrazgo* and marriage. Mifflin Kenedy married Petra Vela, a member of one of the oldest families of the Río Bravo/Rio Grande borderlands, who brought to the marriage land along the river in Hidalgo and Starr counties. Similarly, John McAllen acquired a portion of the Santa Anita land grant by marrying Salomé Ballí. Together, they purchased additional tracts from her family and friends.[93]

North and west of Laredo, outside the boundaries of the original Spanish and Mexican land grants, settlement remained sparse until after the Civil War. Here, Anglos battled the Lipáns, Comanches, and Kickapoos for control. The first settlers along this southwestern ranching frontier were Anglo-Americans from the southern United States, a few Europeans from Germany, France, and Ireland, black laborers and servants, and a sprinkling of *pastores, vaqueros,* and *jornaleros.* The 1860 census listed only twenty-six inhabitants of Zavala County and sixty-one residents of Kinney County, which included the area where the town of Del Rio would later emerge. Eagle Pass was the only town of any size for hundreds of miles. The census taker recorded twenty-seven people in Maverick County living outside of Eagle Pass and Fort Duncan.[94]

High market demand for beef, wool, and hides in the late 1860s and 1870s, stimulated by the depletion of livestock along the Atlantic seaboard during the Civil War and the growth of cities and industry in the northeastern and midwestern United States, lured investors, merchants, and other businesspeople into ranching. The grasslands from Canada to northern Mexico transformed into a vast pasture filled with horse, sheep, and cattle herds. Cheap, unfenced lands, a relatively mild climate, and the availability of inexpensive livestock in northern Mexico made South Texas an attractive location. South Texas ranchers rounded up longhorn cattle to drive to distant railheads for shipment to stockyards in Chicago. Sheep raising on the Rio Grande plain expanded. Ranching rapidly transformed into a thoroughly commercial operation enmeshed in national and international markets, subject to the vagaries of supply and demand. It was a transnational enterprise in the Texas-Mexico borderlands; the ranches of northern Mexico reoriented to US markets and supplied much of the breeder stock to Texas ranchers.[95]

Anglo and European stockmen spread westward into Uvalde, Kinney, Maverick, and Zavala counties, spurred on by the defeat of Comanches in the 1870s. Like Richard King, they relied on ethnic Mexicans—*pastores, vaqueros,* and *jornaleros* migrating out of northern Mexico—to do most of the work. Thus, on the fringe of original Spanish settlement, in areas historically controlled by nomadic Indians, once those Indians had been displaced, Anglos quickly dominated, and a system based on Anglo owners and ethnic Mexican laborers developed rather rapidly. Dimmit County provides an excellent illustration of what was happening in these western regions once dominated by the Apaches, Comanches, and other nomadic tribes. The county did not attract settlement before the Civil War. In 1870, there was a very small settlement of about twenty-six families, consisting primarily of Anglo farmers and stock raisers and ethnic Mexican herders, housekeepers, and unskilled laborers. By 1880, a sizeable community of more than one hundred families was living at Carrizo Springs. Smaller Anglo settlements were found at Rocky Creek, Rocky Springs, and San Pedro Creek, and a small Mexican village was established along Apuración Creek.[96]

Anglos and Europeans were not the only ones to benefit from the boom in commercial ranching. Rising prices of livestock products, coupled with the relative abundance of cheap cattle, sheep, and goats in northern Mexico after 1865, benefited Tejanos as well as Mexican citizens, many of whom moved north out of Mexico to participate in the growing market. The 1880 census for Encinal County, northeast of Webb County, records eighty-six ethnic Mexican stock raisers, sixty-seven from Mexico and nineteen from Texas. Only three non-Hispanic individuals were listed, a merchant from France, one from Hanover, and one stock raiser, A. P. Spohn, from Canada. In 1860, according to the census taker, Encinal had a population of fewer than forty-three people, which included only two livestock raisers, both from Mexico, six *pastores,* and a day laborer. Substantial numbers of Mexicans also moved into Duval County, about a hundred miles north of the border, where they provided a market for Hispanic merchants.[97]

With the boom in cattle ranching, displacement of Tejanos closer to the Rio Grande accelerated as more and more Anglo and European merchants looked for land to buy and existing ranchers added to their holdings. By 1862, approximately 385,652 acres (24 percent of the total) in Cameron County was in the hands of non-Hispanic landowners, and by 1877, that number had climbed to 656,899.98 acres (42 percent of the total).[98] One of those was Sheriff James G. Browne, who began as a small shop owner. The R. G. Dun & Co. Credit Volumes reported that he was "of limited means" and "somewhat embarr[asse]d" in December 1860. By 1890, he owned 143,000 acres.[99]

The cross-border Tejano ranching society survived more intact farther inland. In 1880, Tejanos still owned approximately 4,018,796 acres (79 percent) out of a total of 5,089,452 acres in Cameron, Hidalgo, Starr, and Zapata counties combined. Many maintained residences in the river towns of Camargo, Guerrero, Mier, Reynosa, and Nuevo Laredo and operated ranches that spanned the border. There was a sufficient regional market for most small and medium-sized *rancheros* to survive, and as long as the range remained open, their herds could find available water sources. Although the smaller *rancheros* rarely participated in the large cattle drives because of the expenses involved, they marketed hides, meat, and other products locally and sold cattle and horses to middlemen in San Antonio, Santa Margarita, and owners of large ranches in Nueces County. Increasing competition for land, however, made life more and more difficult for the smaller *rancheros*. The arrival of the railroads, coupled with plunging livestock prices and severe droughts, would accelerate Tejano land loss after 1880 and pave the way for Anglo-American and European dominance over the countryside.[100]

. . .

Despite periods of flourishing trade, the entire lower Río Bravo/Rio Grande borderlands remained relatively isolated and sparsely populated for most of the nineteenth century and offered little outside of the commercial activity in the twin cities of Matamoros and Brownsville to attract new migrants. Many of those who came experienced failure and left for greener pastures. Indian raids, wars, ongoing bandit activity, title problems with local land grants, and the expense of sea transport hampered economic growth. Livestock raising continued to dominate the local economy. Commercial agriculture was virtually nonexistent; corn, used for food and feed, was the only crop widely grown in the area. South Texas remained on the periphery of the United States, Mexico, and the global economy.

Mexican society and culture prevailed both north and south of the Río Bravo/Rio Grande throughout the period. Anglo-Americans and Europeans who settled in the area generally assimilated the Hispanic language, values, and customs. People, animals, and goods moved relatively freely across the river border, largely disregarded by the region's inhabitants, who favored long-standing commercial, social, and familial ties over newly drawn political boundaries. Captain John G. Bourke, stationed in the area during the early 1890s, observed that the "Río Bravo del Norte . . . can in no sense be regarded as fulfilling any of the conditions of a line of delimitation . . . the lower part of the Rio Grande valley, which remains to-day, as it has been for more than forty years, a sealed book, a *terra incognita* to the rest of the United States. Twice the waves of North American aggression [US/Mexican War and Civil War] have swept across this region, bearing down all in their path; but as the tempest abated the Mexican population placidly resumed its control of affairs and returned to its former habits of life as if the North American had never existed."[101]

Yet Bourke's words described only how things seemed on the surface. The arrival of Anglo-American and European merchants in Matamoros in the 1820s and the subsequent incorporation of the Trans-Nueces into the United States as a result of the US/Mexican War in 1848 had fundamentally changed the region. The resources of the merchant elite soon surpassed those of local ethnic Mexicans, enabling the former to control major commercial activity in the area. The US conquest facilitated efforts of some members of the new elite to acquire large tracts of land from *rancheros,* particularly on the Texas side of the border. Perhaps most important, between 1820 and 1880, trade links between northern Mexico and the northeastern United States had been established that would provide the foundation for an economic takeoff in the early twentieth century and draw the region more tightly into the orbit of the US economy.

2

FORGING A LANDSCAPE OF
OPPORTUNITY (1880–1940)

D ARK CLOUDS THREATENED overhead on the afternoon of July 4, 1904, in the lower Rio Grande Valley. By evening, a steady rainfall had turned the dusty roads of Brownsville into a thick, muddy soup, almost impassable by the carriages. Undeterred, crowds of people thronged the streets alongside the newly constructed railroad tracks to welcome the first passenger train into Brownsville. They brought floats decorated red, white, and blue, one with a band on board. When the train pulled up at 7:20 P.M., fireworks shot off in every direction. Uriah Lott, builder of the railroad line, gave a speech that received a standing ovation. The next morning, the *Browns-ville Daily Herald* announced that Brownsville had been "born again."[1] A new era had finally dawned, and the hope for the future was palpable. A Southern Pacific Railroad brochure declared, "Opportunity is written in shining letters all over the place."[2] Railroads meant growth, development, and the end of isolation (fig. 2).

This process of building railroads to the border had begun nearly thirty years earlier, when two lines reached Laredo in late 1881, an event celebrated with a fiesta lasting from Christmas Eve until New Year's Day. With the completion of the Mexican National Railway line from Monterrey to Matamoros and construction of the railroad bridge across the river to Brownsville in 1909, the entire length of the lower Río Bravo/Rio Grande Valley was finally connected to the intercontinental railway network.[3]

46

FIGURE 2. Brownsville depot, c. 1919. Railroads stimulated the development of commercial agriculture and the growth of towns and cities in the South Texas border region. Courtesy, Robert Runyon Photograph Collection, 02798, Dolph Briscoe Center for American History, University of Texas at Austin.

The arrival of the railroads enabled local entrepreneurs to create a new landscape of opportunity for business enterprise in South Texas. Railroads became the vehicles through which people, materials, and manufactured goods flowed in and out of the region. They solidified and expanded trade networks with northern Mexico established in previous decades and bound South Texas more tightly to the eastern United States. Railroad owners, land developers, and ranchers cooperated to create and promote farm communities and towns that facilitated small enterprises, in contrast to the western portions of the US/Mexico border, where large corporations involved in mining, smelting, and cattle ranching tended to dominate. The creation of this new landscape inexorably continued the decline of the Tejano ranching society, leading to unrest and ethnic conflict.[4]

LAYING THE FOUNDATION DURING THE PORFIRIATO (1880–1910)

The integration of the US and Mexican economies during the Porfiriato, a period of relative peace in Mexico under the leadership of President Porfirio Díaz that lasted from about 1876 until 1910, became the catalyst for the transformation of

South Texas. During this time, both the US and Mexican governments promoted a relatively open border to facilitate commerce and investment between the two nations. The Texas-Mexico borderlands were strategically located between the primary centers of finance and industry in the northern United States and the newly emerging financial and industrial center of northern Mexico, Monterrey, Nuevo León, situated about 550 miles north of Mexico City in the center of a rich mining district. The region therefore became a critical crossroad for rail lines connecting Monterrey and Mexico City with major US cities like New York and Chicago. Railroad access turned the South Texas border towns into way stations for the flow of capital, goods, and people in and out of Mexico and made it profitable to convert the surrounding lands to productive agriculture and commercial ranching.[5]

US Interest in Mexico

American financiers and railroad builders became interested in investing in Mexico during a time of phenomenal industrial and urban expansion in the United States after the Civil War. The US economy was growing faster than any in Europe and would soon surpass those of England, France, and Germany.[6] The relentless search for raw materials to supply new industries and the hunger for expanded markets, coupled with a domestic recession, drove US businessmen to seek opportunities beyond the nation's borders, especially in Asia and Latin America. Mexico was attractive because it was rich in natural resources and easily accessible from the United States. If the United States did not act quickly, some feared, European nations would dominate Mexico's commercial and financial markets as they had in the past. As Albert Kimsey Owen, a civil engineer with plans to build a railroad to Topolovampo, a community he had established on Mexico's Pacific Coast, said, "When we fail to move, that moment our destiny is closed. When we fail to meet the demands of our continental situation and seize every rising opportunity of expanding our commerce, that moment of halt is the moment of retrogression; retrogression is decay; and decay is death."[7]

Americans also believed US investment in Mexico might help to stabilize the country, thereby enhancing their own nation's security. Americans had long viewed the northern Mexican border region as a troubled and chaotic place, a haven for revolutionaries and bandits who repeatedly raided US borders, stole and destroyed property, and killed its livestock and citizens. As justification for intervention, they focused on Mexico's political instability and failure to develop a modern economy. Owen captured the prevailing sentiment when he asked,

"[I]s Mexico to be invigorated and renewed by a new life from this Anglo-Saxon race of ours? May not the mines of Chihuahua and Guanajuato be made to glisten again under our energy?"[8] Some even spoke of making Mexico a protectorate of the United States. Publishing magnate William Randolph Hearst reportedly declared, "I really don't see what is to prevent us from owning all of Mexico and running it to suit ourselves."[9]

In 1865, after the end of the Civil War in the United States and the victory of the Liberal forces of Benito Juárez in the Wars of the Reform in Mexico, US capitalists began to move beyond the realm of commercial trade to invest directly in mining, agriculture, industry, and railroad construction, strategies that had proved successful in the American West. Among those interested in becoming more involved in Mexico were entrepreneurs with connections to South Texas, including James Stillman, Charles's son, Richard King, and Mifflin Kenedy. They, along with others, were reluctant to do so, however, without a strong leader they could trust to protect their property rights and pursue policies favorable to foreign investors. Americans with existing interests in Mexico had grown increasingly troubled by the policies of Benito Juárez and his successor, Sebastián Lerdo de Tejada, between 1867 and 1875. Both had moved very cautiously to break up communal and church landholdings and convert them to private property. Lerdo had even cancelled all railroad contracts with US companies except one and rejected a bilateral trade pact between the United States and Mexico. So when General Porfirio Díaz, who had lost the 1875 presidential election, sought support for a coup against Lerdo, Stillman, King, and Kenedy agreed to provide funds and arms. Díaz launched his coup in early 1876, using Brownsville as his initial base of operations, and finally overthrew Lerdo in November 1876. He formally rose to power in May 1877.[10]

The alliance between Díaz and the Americans paved the way for US dominance of the Mexican economy. Díaz's primary goal was to modernize Mexico and bring it into the system of global capitalism. The only way he saw that that could happen was by integrating Mexico's economy with that of the United States. When he took office, Mexico's transportation infrastructure, banking system, and industrial base were almost nonexistent due to the lack of native capital.[11] Díaz offered favors and subsidies to foreigners who had access to substantial capital, such as Stillman's National City Bank, in order to lure them to invest in and build railroads and telegraph lines, mining operations, factories, and agricultural enterprises. Investors in the United States responded overwhelmingly, providing the vast majority of Mexico's much-needed capital during the

Porfiriato, much of which flowed into northern Mexico because of its proximity to the United States. As a result, northern Mexico transformed from a peripheral frontier region into the nation's industrial heartland, and the city of Monterrey became its industrial epicenter. By 1910, Americans owned and controlled approximately 81 percent of the Mexican mining industry, 80 percent of its railroad stock, and hundreds of thousands of acres of land. Stillman's National City Bank had financed the construction of most of the railroads as well as much of the industry in and around Monterrey.[12]

One of the first things Díaz did after his ascent to power, under pressure from the US government to stop the border raids, was to imprison Juan Cortina. He also cooperated with the US military to finally subdue the nomadic tribes who roamed from the Great Plains into northern Mexico and force them onto reservations. Their lifestyle and constant raids had long posed substantial obstacles to capitalist development in the Texas-Mexico borderlands. After their defeat, the risks of settling in the region subsided, and railroad construction could safely begin.

Railroads across the Río Bravo/Rio Grande Borderlands

Díaz saw railroads as the key to Mexico's integration with the US economy, the expansion of its national market, and the development of its industries. In 1876, Mexico's railway system was minimal, consisting of only 400 miles of tracks. Mexico's first railroad, between the port of Vera Cruz and Mexico City, had opened just three years earlier, in 1873. Díaz offered concessions to major US railroad companies financed by J.P. Morgan and National City Bank and owned by Jay Gould, Collis P. Huntington, William K. Vanderbilt, and others to build the nation's railway network. These companies, in turn, were eager to construct new routes linking New York, Chicago, and San Francisco with Mexico City, Monterrey, and other strategic points in Mexico. They were already involved in massive railroad construction across the western United States. After the completion of the first Transcontinental Railway in 1869, the miles of railroad tracks increased from about 70,000 to 200,000 by 1900. In Texas alone, during the same period, tracks increased from 341 miles to well over 10,000. By 1910, the end of the Porfiriato, Mexico had more than 15,000 miles of track. Most of the lines ran north and south, connecting to the burgeoning railway network in the United States, where the bulk of Mexican exports were headed.[13]

The first rail lines to cross South Texas passed through the inland border towns of Laredo, Eagle Pass, and Del Rio rather than through Brownsville. The reasons for this were both regional and transnational. James Stillman, who owned the transportation rights across the Rio Grande at Brownsville, refused to grant any railroad company a right of way to build a bridge because he feared a railroad would boost the fortunes of the Americans' major competitors in the region, the European merchants of Matamoros and Monterrey. A railroad to Brownsville or Matamoros without access to the other side of the river was impractical. Moreover, Laredo, Eagle Pass, and Del Rio were closer to the growing commercial centers of Monterrey and Saltillo in Mexico, the mines of Sonora and Chihuahua, and existing rail lines in the United States, offering more direct routes between New York, Chicago, and Mexico City.[14]

Collis P. Huntington's Southern Pacific and Jay Gould's Missouri Pacific system became the major competitors to build the transnational lines that would penetrate the Texas-Mexico borderlands. The first railroad to reach the border, however, was a narrow-gauge line constructed by a local entrepreneur, the colorful Coloniel Uriah Lott. Born in Albany, New York, in 1842, Lott arrived in South Texas at the end of the Civil War. Never actually a colonel in the army, he lived near Port Isabel on Padre Island for a couple of years to apprentice as a sutler's clerk. In 1871, he moved to Corpus Christi, where he launched a commission and forwarding business, chartering ships to carry wool and hides to New York. Dissatisfied with the sluggishness of the existing overland and ocean-going trade, he sought the financial assistance of Richard King and Mifflin Kenedy to construct a railroad between Laredo and Corpus Christi. Despite a number of setbacks, the Texas Mexican Railway was finally completed in November 1881. The *Galveston Daily News* reported that in a couple of years there would be a line stretching from Chicago through St. Louis, Austin, San Antonio, Laredo, and Monterrey to Mexico City. The 2,200-mile trip from Chicago to Mexico City would reportedly take less than four days.[15]

Several rail lines eventually converged at Laredo, making it a transnational railroad hub. Jay Gould's International and Great Northern Railroad (I&GN), which connected to a Missouri-Pacific line running from San Antonio to St. Louis, reached Laredo by December of 1881. The Mexican National Railway extended from Mexico City through Saltillo and Monterrey and linked to the I&GN in Laredo in 1882, reducing the travel time from Monterrey through Laredo to San Antonio from eight days to eight hours. Upriver from Laredo, Huntington bought the Galveston, Harrisburg, and San Antonio Railway, whose tracks reached Eagle Pass in 1882. His interests constructed the Mexican International Railroad through Durango, Torreón, and Piedras Negras and through Eagle Pass to his

Southern Pacific transcontinental line, which traveled west to El Paso and then on to Los Angeles and east through New Orleans. Huntington also built a branch line to Del Rio in 1883.[16]

Plans for a railroad running through Brownsville/Matamoros were delayed but not defeated. Uriah Lott and the heirs of Mifflin Kenedy and Richard King played a key role. Lott had a vision of building a Pan-American railroad through Brownsville all the way to Mexico City and Yucatán. The King and Kenedy interests had long wanted a railroad line that would connect their ranches directly to major cities. The impetus for building the line between Corpus Christi and Brownsville, however, came from the region's potential for commercial agriculture. As Lott told the editors of the *Brownsville Daily Herald,* he believed the section "will soon settle up with a substantial farming class."[17] Robert Kleberg, John Kenedy, Francisco Yturria, Nueces County rancher John Armstrong, and other local merchants and ranchers contributed capital and land for the new railroad, the St. Louis, Brownsville and Mexico Railway, later known as the Gulf Coast Line. It was completed in 1904. The Mexican National Railway between Monterrey and Matamoros was finished in 1909, and a bridge was built across the river to Brownsville.[18]

Railroads were absolutely crucial for capitalist development in the Texas-Mexico borderlands. The absence of navigable rivers had impeded settlement and trade in the nineteenth century upriver from Brownsville/Matamoros and the few towns located on the navigable portions of the Río Bravo/Rio Grande. Transportation into the interior was difficult and inefficient. The 150-mile trip from Alice to Brownsville via stagecoach took forty hours in good weather through a "vast country sweeping for endless dreary miles" covered with cactus, mesquite, and blowing sand where livestock roamed widely. The land was desolate and a "brutal wilderness." If rain made the roads heavy with mud, it could take much longer. Oxcarts and mule trains filled with cargo moved even more slowly than the stagecoaches.[19]

Railroads solved the problem of transportation into the interior. They connected the Río Bravo/Rio Grande borderlands to a transnational transportation infrastructure, linking it more efficiently to industrial centers like New York, Boston, Chicago, Philadelphia, Pittsburgh, Monterrey, and Mexico City. Railroads overcame the barriers of weather, geography, and illness or injury, which had created obstacles to animal-powered transport. They vastly reduced time to market and the risks associated with shipment, thereby creating a cost-effective way to ship small quantities over long distances, which opened up opportunities for small traders. The railroads also reoriented the region away from the Atlantic trade with Europe via the Gulf of Mexico and toward US markets.[20]

The Evolution of the Border Towns

Railroads provided an impetus for trade, industry, and urban development in the border towns. The twin cities of Laredo/Nuevo Laredo, situated 136 miles north of Monterrey and 150 miles south of San Antonio, the largest city in Texas at the time, became a cosmopolitan trading center because of its location at the nexus of transnational rail lines. By the early 1890s, Nuevo Laredo had the largest volume of US goods flowing through its customshouse of any other location on the border and, in terms of the import/export trade, was second only to the port of Veracruz in all of Mexico. Commission merchants and wholesalers from Veracruz and Monterrey established branches in Laredo/Nuevo Laredo and, along with local merchants, became major suppliers of affluent northern Mexicans. A list of goods flowing into Mexico through Laredo/Nuevo Laredo in 1889 included cotton, linen, and woolen fabrics, silks, stone, earthen and crockery ware, machines, arms, munitions, paper, leather, drugs, metals, and notions.[21] A visitor from Indiana believed that Laredo "was destined to become one of the most important emporiums of trade in the whole Southwest" and predicted that it would become a major metropolitan city within a few years. Not surprisingly, James Saunders Penn, the owner and publisher of a new English language newspaper, the *Laredo Times,* coined the term "gateway of commerce" to promote Laredo as the center of the Mexican trade.[22]

Attracted by the possibilities of trade in Mexico, Anglo newcomers and European immigrants overwhelmed Laredo in a very short time. The population mushroomed from 3,811 in 1880 to 11,319 in 1890. The newcomers brought their own culture with them and began to change the character and appearance of the town. Construction began in 1890 on several new manufacturing establishments—a boot and shoe factory, a tannery, a woolen mill, a foundry, and machine shops. Between May and September 1889 approximately one hundred new residences "of the most substantial character, most of them of brick," adorned the "heights" above the river. Brick buildings became symbols of progress and American civilization as they replaced the adobes and *jacales,* emblems of the earlier Spanish and Mexican periods, viewed by Anglos as a more primitive time.[23] Stores, restaurants, and hotels opened, and an electric car line appeared. People around the United States began to take note. The city became more appealing to outside investors. For example, the Land Mortgage Bank of Texas, financed by Englishmen, loaned more than $50,000 to businesspeople in the town in the 1880s. Charles Silliman, manager of the Land Mortgage Bank, visited the town with two of the managing directors, Benjamin Brigg and Swire Smith of Yorkshire, England. Silliman reported that a building on which his company had loaned $5,000 sold for $14,000. He explained, "All the investments we had made were most satisfactory. . . . Laredo is very attractive and contains a population of very enterprising men."[24]

North of Laredo, similar changes were occurring. Some commerce from Mexico passed through the twin cities of Eagle Pass/Piedras Negras and Del Rio/Ciudad Acuña as a result of the railroad lines, but those towns grew more slowly than Laredo. They were relatively small and more remote from the main railways in Mexico, making them less attractive headquarters for the larger merchants. According to the *San Antonio Daily Express,* development in Eagle Pass was slow but steady. "Seldom a week passes but some new and stable enterprise is launched or a new business established. They are not temporary investments by wild-cat speculators from God knows where, but are permanently established by solid men, who, seeing the advantage of our location, determine to cast their lot with us . . . Where but three short years ago was but a barren prairie is now a forest of brick and mortar." By 1910, Del Rio had about 5,000 inhabitants, and Eagle Pass had 2,800. Maps of the towns reveal ongoing expansion of commercial and residential districts between 1894 and 1910.[25]

By contrast, Brownsville stagnated and actually lost population when bypassed by railroad construction in the late nineteenth century. Transportation in and out of the city was limited to the few small ships that could enter Port Isabel or the stagecoach trail, and a military telegraph line between Fort McIntosh in Laredo and Fort Brown provided the only means of rapid communication with the outside world. Although Brownsville had had brick buildings since the mid-1860s along its main commercial street, it had no electricity, no water supply, and no sewers. Kerosene lamps lit the dusty, unpaved streets. When the railroad reached the city in 1904, it transformed rapidly. By 1910, Brownsville had electricity, waterworks, a new bank, and plenty of drugstores. Scores of new lawyers arrived, the population boomed, and new houses were in short supply because of the demand (fig. 3). Across the river, the vacant commercial buildings in Matamoros began to fill with new businesses, and its population rebounded as well.[26]

The Transformation of the Countryside

The railroads began to transform the grasslands and open brush country of the Texas-Mexico borderlands into a fenced landscape dedicated to capital-intensive

FIGURE 3. Brownsville's commercial district around the turn of the twentieth century. Courtesy, Lower Rio Grande Valley Historical Collection, Library Archives and Special Collections, University of Texas–Pan American.

ranching and farming. Development was far more intensive on the Texas side, however. Most of northeastern Mexico remained devoted to ranching, and a pattern of communitarian land use persisted in places. Although developers had planned many agricultural projects for northern Mexico during the Porfiriato, few actually materialized. The situation was very different in South Texas, where dozens of private companies laid the groundwork for irrigated farming by clearing thousands of acres of brush and constructing miles of dirt-lined canals.[27]

In the United States, the range had begun to close even before the railroads reached the border, providing a greater impetus for railroad construction. During the days of the cattle drives, disease, excessive roaming of branded herds, and overgrazing fueled increased efforts to control and regulate the movement of livestock. Borderland cattle carried a tick-borne disease known as "Texas fever" or "Mexican fever." The hardy longhorns, a cross between the original Spanish cattle and breeds brought west from the US South, were essentially immune to the disease, which proved deadly to cattle on the Great Plains. In the 1860s, cattlemen in Indian Territory, Missouri, and Kansas organized vigilante committees to keep the longhorns far away from their herds and lands. Kansas imposed a statewide quarantine in the 1880s, and by 1890, Oklahoma Territory was requiring all cattle entering from the Texas-Mexico borderlands to be dipped in a mixture of oil and water. The US government created the Bureau of Animal

Industry in 1889, which set up vats and inspection stations in order to police the movement of diseased cattle across the US/Mexico border.[28]

Fencing followed closely on the heels of the quarantines. Fences kept stray and diseased livestock away and enabled pasture rotation in order to manage the problem of overgrazing. Richard King and Mifflin Kenedy began building wooden fences in South Texas as early as 1870, and more ranchers enclosed their land after the invention of the less expensive barbed-wire fence in 1874. By 1883, virtually all of the land in South Texas was fenced, making it extremely difficult for small *rancheros* with minimal access to water sources to sustain their livestock or drive them to market. Ranchers with substantial capital began buying up acreage from small operators, who often faced foreclosure, in order to sustain larger and larger herds. Similarly, the large cattle ranches in northern Mexico erected hundreds of miles of barbed-wire fences, enclosing thousands of acres of land once used by the local population as *ejidos,* or common lands.[29]

As the range closed, proximity to a railroad became critical for access to world markets. In order to ensure that access, several of the large Tejano and Anglo landowners in South Texas offered land subsidies to the railroad construction companies. Plácido Benavides, who owned one of the largest ranches in Duval County by 1880, donated land for the construction of a railroad depot, which became the center of the town of Benavides. Rancher Joseph Cotulla deeded 120 acres of his ranch to Jay Gould's International and Great Northern Railroad for the town of Cotulla. The Texas Mexican Railway purchased land from James Hebbron for a railroad depot and built the town of Hebbronville in 1883. Anglo rancher Ed Lasater convinced the owners of the San Antonio and Aransas Railroad to build tracks down to his ranch in 1904. The town of Falfurrias became the end of that line for many years. Towns like Benavides, Falfurrias, and Hebbronville became hubs for the distribution of livestock and ranching products and attracted small merchants who brought consumer goods into remote ranching regions.[30]

The arrival of the railroads and the fencing of the open range increased economies of scale in the ranching industry. Ranchers with substantial capital expanded their landholdings in order to sustain larger and larger herds. The consolidation of large tracts of land in private hands occurred on both sides of the border, throughout the American West and northern Mexico. Texas had sold virtually all of its public lands by 1880. Before 1900, the US government granted millions of acres of western lands to the railroads. Only a relatively small percentage went to homesteaders. Mining companies and ranching enterprises owned tracts of land consisting of thousands, sometimes millions, of acres. The XIT Ranch in the Texas Panhandle, for example, controlled more than three million acres. In Mexico the Díaz regime passed the *baldío* laws, which called for the identification, survey, and sale of public lands for development. Anglo-Americans, Europeans, and a few elite Mexican families bought up much of this land for ranches and farms.[31] In an effort to avoid an 1856 law that prohibited foreigners from owning land within sixty miles of the border, Americans and Europeans partnered with Mexican citizens or created Mexican corporations to hold the land. In the late nineteenth century, sizeable *latifundias* emerged all across the Mexican north. Stillman and a group of US investors acquired 819,000 acres between Matamoros and Monterrey, granted as a subsidy for the construction of a railroad. The 1,450,000-acre Rascon Hacienda, owned by Americans, sprawled across portions of Tamaulipas and San Luis Potosí. The Blocker brothers of San Antonio and their partner, William Henry Jennings, bought ranchland in South Texas and in the nearby Mexican state of Coahuila, where their Piedra Blanca Ranch encompassed 1,200,000 acres.[32]

In South Texas, the pattern of consolidation of large parcels of land into the hands of a few wealthy landowners, mostly Anglo-Americans, was especially pronounced in Cameron County. By 1892, twenty-four individual landowners with holdings in excess of 10,000 acres held 1,250,022 acres, or nearly 80 percent of the total in the county. Four Anglo families, the Kings, the Brownes, the Kenedys, and the Armstrongs, owned 851,061 acres, just over half of the county. Only five Hispanic landowners had estates over 10,000 acres. The largest belonged to the merchant Francisco Yturria, who had nearly 70,000 acres. José Fernandez and Ynocenia Portilla of Matamoros each had *ranchos* of just over 11,000 acres, and Feliciano San Román, a nephew of José San Román, the Spanish merchant, had a 13,000-acre estate. María Josefa Cavazos had the largest estate (29,524 acres) among the descendants of the original Tejano landowning class in Cameron County. Notably, seven out of the twenty-four largest landowners in the county were women. These women, most of whom were widows, collectively owned 447,282 acres. This is significant because it reveals that women had considerable economic clout, which gave them a crucial role as lenders in the community.[33]

By the early 1900s, farmland was beginning to replace ranchland in some parts of the Texas-Mexico borderlands. Plummeting prices for livestock products and several droughts had decimated ranching in the late nineteenth century, providing an impetus for the development of commercial agriculture, which was part of a larger expansion throughout the US/Mexico borderlands. In the United States, interest in farming the arid West had spurred innovations in irrigation technology, and the creation of the Bureau of Reclamation in 1902 made funds potentially available for western water projects. In northern Mexico, favorable policies by Díaz's government prompted US investors and Mexican elites to create large haciendas, such as the one controlled by the Anderson Clayton Company of Houston, in the irrigated cotton-growing region of the Comarca Lagunera in Coahuila and Durango.[34] South Texas developers followed a different model, patterned on California's land and water companies, which had platted and sold hundreds of small, irrigated farm tracts in the 1870s and 1880s in an attempt to reverse the state's trend toward agribusiness. The goal was to promote the family farm and create "a more homogeneous, virtuous, middle-class society" in keeping with American republican values, as historian Donald Pisani has argued. It was only during and after the Mexican revolution that some agronomists in Mexico, in the context of agrarian reform, pushed for private ownership of small farms in an effort to create a middle class of modern farmers.[35]

The process of laying the foundation for the expansion of commercial agriculture along the South Texas border occurred over the course of several decades, beginning with crop experimentation in the 1870s and 1880s and reaching its fruition in the 1920s. Two crucial technologies aided the rise of commercial agriculture along the South Texas border. One was the invention of the refrigerated railroad car in the 1870s, which enabled the shipment of perishable fruits and vegetables over long distances. The other was the development of irrigation. Because of inconsistent rainfall and the prevalence of drought, commercial agriculture initially developed in limited areas, in large part determined by the feasibility of irrigation. These included the lower Rio Grande Valley below Roma and an inland district northeast of Laredo centered in Dimmit and Zavala counties above a large underground aquifer. Smaller pockets emerged near Laredo, Eagle Pass, and Del Rio.

Forms of irrigated agriculture along the Río Bravo/Rio Grande predated the arrival of Europeans. Small indigenous bands of people who survived primarily by hunting and gathering periodically settled down during hot, dry months near water sources, where they built small ditches and canals to provide water for corn and squash plants. In the eighteenth and early nineteenth centuries, Spanish settlers built *acequias,* or earthen ditches, to divert water for corn crops and for livestock. Some of the Franciscan friars cultivated small orchards for the missions using water from the *acequias.* The *acequias,* like the river itself, tended to overflow during times of heavy rain, destroying fields and homes. Landowners built *acequias* in the mid-nineteenth century to water small plots of farmland. John McAllen successfully grew cotton, sugar cane, and corn on his Hidalgo County ranch using this method.[36]

Over time, these irrigation systems became more sophisticated. In nearby Cameron County, French merchants and landowners George Brulay and Celestín Jagou installed primitive but rather extensive irrigation works in order to grow sugar cane, bananas, cotton, vegetables, grapes, and almond trees. John Closner, the local sheriff and tax collector of Hidalgo County, was one of the first to use a pumping system. Where he lived, the banks of the river were deep and steep, making it difficult to get the water to flow out into the ditches. Closner therefore ordered a steam pump from New York in 1895. It successfully pumped river water into several miles of canals he built on his 45,000-acre San Juan Plantation. He irrigated approximately 200 acres and experimented with a variety of crops, including corn, figs, pecans, walnuts, and sugar cane.[37]

Lieutenant C. H. Chatfield was the first to publish a vision for a coordinated system of dams, pumping systems, and canals along the lower part of the river. Inspired by vegetable production in the Central Valley of California and the growing citrus industry in Southern California, he declared that the only thing the region needed to be "as fruitful as California" was a dependable water supply. In his 1893 publication, *The Twin Cities of the Rio Grande,* he estimated that one-quarter of a million acres of delta land was irrigable and that artesian wells could irrigate an additional one million acres. He foresaw one hundred settlers per square mile and farmhouses springing up everywhere.[38]

In the early twentieth century, B. F. Yoakum created the prototype for farm developments in the lower Rio Grande Valley based loosely on what he had seen in Southern California.[39] His vehicle was the American Rio Grande Land & Irrigation Company, which acquired 90,000 acres of land on the Texas side of the river directly from the heirs of Juan José Hinojosa and Rosa Hinojosa de Ballí. The company, incorporated in 1905, reflected the cooperation between elite Mexicans and Americans during the Porfiriato in the development of the borderlands. Investors included Americans James Stillman, Simon Guggenheim, James A. Baker, and Duval West (later a federal district judge in the area), all of whom had investments in Mexico, and Mexicans Yreno Longoria, Antonio Ballí, and members of the Cavazos family, all supporters of Díaz. Yoakum subdivided the land into 40- to 160-acre farm tracts to sell to individual families and then hired Mexican workers to clear the thick heavy brush and mesquite that still covered much of the land. He employed railroad engineer Sam Robertson, the labor contractor on the St. Louis, Corpus Christi, & Brownsville Railroad, to build irrigation works and canal systems to provide each tract with ample access to water. Pumping plants brought water from the river into the canals. One of the early purchasers was Democratic politician William Jennings Bryan, who also acquired real estate in Mexico.[40]

Yoakum's plan involved creating a farm community, not merely selling individual farm tracts. He established the town of Mercedes to function as the heart of the development. Towns like Mercedes were designed to meet the farmers' business, social, cultural, and educational needs. They contained facilities for warehousing, processing, packing, and distributing farm products as well as shops carrying the latest fashions. There were theaters, restaurants, and saloons. Most towns had at least one bank, a law office, a post office, and a doctor's office. They had schools and churches as well as places to gather for social functions, such as country clubs. Perhaps most important, they contained a section housing the farm laborers, virtually all of whom were ethnic Mexicans. Since most of the farms were small and lacked the facilities and space to house workers, this was the solution. These new towns, often called "Valley towns" to distinguish them from the older border towns, were almost always segregated, with the railroad dividing the Anglo section from the Mexican section. This spatial organization signaled the desire of the new class of migrants from the United States to remain socially and culturally separate from ethnic Mexicans and reflected their feelings of superiority toward them. Yet it also indicated their deep reliance on them.[41]

Other developers followed Yoakum's example, just as Chatfield had predicted, and farm colonies began springing up all over the area. By 1910, they extended from the mouth of the river to Mission in the western part of Hidalgo County. The westward expansion of farmland gave rise to the need for feeder lines to connect the new communities to the major railroad hub in Brownsville. Sam Robertson therefore raised funds to build the Rio Grande Valley Interurban Railway, more popularly known as the "Spider Web" because it was a maze of tracks going in every direction. The Spider Web remained in place until the 1940s and 1950s, when it was replaced by the farm-to-market roads.[42]

In the Anglo community, the land speculators became known as the "pioneers" of the Valley. These men came from a variety of backgrounds. Some were local ranchers and farmers, while others were businessmen and professionals making their first foray into real estate, and still others were railroad builders and entrepreneurs. One of the more colorful figures was Leonidas "Lon" Hill, a lawyer from central Texas who wore his hair long and claimed to have descended from the Choctaws. After partnering with John McAllen, his son James, and B. F. Yoakum to found the town of McAllen in 1904, Hill incorporated the Lon C. Hill Town and Improvement Company and the Harlingen Land and Water Company to begin a development just north of San Benito on property purchased from Henrietta King, Richard King's widow. Sam Robertson, the railroad engineer, planned the town of San Benito in western Cameron County and incorporated the San Benito Land & Water Company, San Benito Sugar Manufacturing Company, and San Benito Ice & Cold Storage Company. John Closner joined William F. Sprague, D. B. Chapin, J. R. Alamia, and Plutarco de la Viña to irrigate and colonize the area around present-day Edinburg. Rentfro Banton Creager, prominent Republican lawyer and head of the Republican National Committee in Texas from the early 1920s until his death in 1950, started the Alamo Land and Sugar Company in 1909 with a partner, C. H. Swallow. In addition, W. L. Stewart developed Weslaco and the surrounding area.[43]

Settlers began to move in and plant new crops. Great excitement accompanied the first shipment of vegetables on a train out of Brownsville on February 2, 1905. Residents decorated the cars with streamers proclaiming, "First car of vegetables ever shipped from Brownsville; from Buena Vista Truck Farm." The rapidity of the development was astonishing. In 1909, Cameron County had the most irrigated acreage of any county in Texas, 29,439 acres, and Hidalgo County had more than 20,000 irrigated acres. Between 1904 and 1910, virtually all of the towns that today sprawl along Highway 83 were established, including Harlingen, San Benito, Mercedes, Donna, Alamo, San Juan, Pharr, McAllen, and Mission.[44]

Many of the farm developments got off to a rocky start. They were all private business ventures, many of which were undercapitalized and financed with outside capital. Early developers borrowed from life insurance companies such as New York Life and Phoenix Mutual. A considerable number of Houston banks and finance companies were also involved. Increasingly, local banks like Merchants National of Brownsville and Valley State Bank loaned money to finance irrigation systems. Because of the heavy financing, sale of the land was crucial to make a profit, and this motivated a huge promotional campaign that did not pay off right away. Most of the land was not sold until the 1920s. Farmers experimented with cotton, rice, corn, and sugar cane, but only cotton was produced in significant commercial quantities prior to World War II. The flooding of land required to grow rice caused too much alkaline and salt to collect in the soil.

Sugar cane grew well in the fertile soil along the river, but sugar refining in the area proved unprofitable. Several sugar mills, including Sam Robertson's San Benito Sugar Manufacturing Company, ended up in bankruptcy. Sugar cane was therefore abandoned and was not commercially produced in substantial quantities along the Rio Grande until the second half of the twentieth century.[45]

Areas farther up the river and away from the coast developed farming more gradually alongside ranching. These areas did not experience the rampant speculation of the lower Rio Grande Valley. Instead, ranchers who had suffered from drought and depression in the late nineteenth century started converting ranchland to farmland and sold it piecemeal in the hopes that they could pay off debt. The discovery of a large underground aquifer, now known as the Carrizo-Wilcox Aquifer, hastened this process. A rancher drilled the first artesian well in Dimmit County near Carrizo Springs in 1884. Farther east, in 1900, King's son-in-law, Robert Kleberg, successfully drilled artesian wells on the King Ranch property, tapping into the extensive Gulf Coast Aquifer. Using water from these artesian wells, Kleberg and other ranchers experimented with the growing of winter vegetables. The most of important of these was the Bermuda onion, first produced in the region in commercial quantities on T. C. Nye's farm near Cotulla in 1898. Profits proved to be phenomenal, as much as $1,000 per acre. When Nye later moved to Laredo, the Bermuda onion became the first major commercial crop grown in Webb County and in nearby Dimmit and Zavala counties, the core of what would later become known as the Winter Garden.[46]

Several of the large South Texas ranchers diversified into farm development. Colonel J. S. Taylor, who owned 3,500 acres in Dimmit County, built a dam across the Nueces and divided the land into farm tracts for sale. Asher Richardson converted a portion of a 100,000-acre ranch into smaller tracts of 40 to 160 acres and founded the town of Asherton.[47] Ranchers in Webb, Maverick, and Val Verde counties shifted to truck farming in some areas. In Val Verde County, there were a number of grapevines and the development of an incipient wine industry. The sons of former sheriff and local rancher James G. Browne, A. Albert Browne, and James A. Browne formed the Santa Helena Improvement Company in the early 1900s and sold small plots of farm land out of their million-plus acres in Cameron County. The heirs of Richard King and Mifflin Kenedy saw planned agricultural development as a way to attract a railroad through their land and on into Brownsville. King's son-in-law, Robert Kleberg, and King's widow, Henrietta King, along with Kenedy's son John, organized the town of Kingsville and subdivided nearby grazing lands into small farm sites irrigated by artesian wells. Ed Lasater created the Falfurrias Farm and Garden Tracts, which he sold to both Anglos and Tejanos. He planned a town and invested in several businesses, including a local state bank, the Falfurrias Mercantile Store, a power company, the Falfurrias Machine Shops, which built windmills and pumps and repaired wagons and harnesses for local farmers, and Falfurrias Creamery Company, where he processed butter and milk products from his dairy cows.[48]

Inland areas such as the northern portions of Starr, Hidalgo, and Cameron counties, which lacked substantial groundwater sources and access to the Rio Grande, remained devoted primarily to ranching, although Tejanos developed dry-farming techniques to raise cotton in some places. Portions of Starr and Zapata counties gradually transitioned to a mixture of ranching, stock farming, and cotton planting. Farm colonizers had targeted lands along the Rio Grande in Starr County for development in the early 1900s because the county already had two towns, Roma and Rio Grande City, which could serve surrounding farm communities. Plans for a railroad circulated when the developers began construction near Rio Grande City. They abandoned the project in 1909 after floods destroyed the pumping plant and most of the earthen canals and left a layer of sand on the soil as the floodwaters receded. A rail line to Rio Grande City was not completed until 1925, but even then commercial agriculture never boomed the way it had farther to the east because of the uneven and rolling land. Similarly, Zapata County lacked a railroad, and its lands were more marginal. It therefore remained a rural ranching county dominated by Tejanos, many of whom also grew cotton and corn using dryland farming techniques.[49]

By the late 1910s, Texas land developers had turned their attention southward. Newspapers began to predict that "the next great land movement will be in Mexico." San Antonio rapidly became the center of interest in land development in Mexico. Companies dealing in lands in South Texas and in northern Mexico began advertising in Texas newspapers for lands located primarily in Coahuila and Tamaulipas. The International Land & Investment Company, owned and managed by Judge T. M. Paschall, L. Villarreal, Madero, and J. L. Hill, offered lands in both Mexico and Texas. Woods & Paschall, a partnership based in San Antonio, dealt in South Texas lands as well as lands in Tamaulipas. Their Mexican lands included "grazing and timber lands, irrigated farms and large colonization tracts." One advertisement for land in a 32,000-acre tract in Tamaulipas promised that an investor could triple his or her money within a year. Brownsville-based O. C. Hillebrandt Company advertised both unimproved and irrigated lands in the lower Rio Grande Valley as well as raw land in Mexico. Lands in Mexico were cheaper, sometimes selling for as little as $1 an acre.[50]

Mexico had had difficulty attracting immigrant farmers, but the government decided to make a few colonization grants in thinly settled portions of northern Mexico. These farm colony developments were somewhat similar to those along the north bank of the Rio Grande, although they were farther south. The Mexico-US Land Immigration Corporation organized a colony at Ciudad Valles near San Luis Potosí. George Blaylock formed the Blaylock Company of Tamaulipas and created a farm colony in southeastern Tamaulipas at Atascador. Five hundred Americans settled there, mostly farmers from the Midwest like those in South Texas. James Stillman and the Texas Company, a major US oil company, were among those who invested in a project begun in 1906 to irrigate and colonize portions of La Sauteña, a large hacienda in Tamaulipas outside of Matamoros. The owners of La Sauteña contracted with the state of Tamaulipas to build irrigation works and clear 100,000 hectares of land to prepare for sale to potential colonists, who would come mainly from the United States and Europe. Plans included a pumping station at Camargo and canals from that station, as well as a pumping station near a dam on the San Juan River near China, Nuevo León, about 100 kilometers southwest of the Río Bravo. Cotton would be the main crop, just as it was in the Laguna. The town of Río Bravo, just east of Reynosa, became the headquarters of the new settlement. The project generated resistance from local *rancheros,* whose families had used the land for generations for raising livestock. The Mexican Revolution halted construction, and massive loans could not be repaid, forcing the project into bankruptcy before it even got started.[51]

Before the Mexican Revolution broke out, however, irrigation projects like the one in La Sauteña represented the last phase of the transformation of the Texas-Mexico borderlands that held out great promise for future business. By 1910, Mexico's national railway network had connected Monterrey and Matamoros to San Antonio, Corpus Christi, St. Louis, Chicago, and New York. The border towns of the Río Bravo/Rio Grande had boomed as millions of dollars' worth of imports and exports flowed through them. Smelters, textile mills, breweries, cement works, tile manufacturers, and steel mills framed Monterrey's skyline, less than 150 miles from the Texas-Mexico border. Not far away, new and revived copper, gold, and silver mines were scattered across the mountains of Chihuahua and Coahuila. Oil wells dotted the landscape near Tampico. Within a few hundred miles of the Río Bravo/Rio Grande on either side, enormous commercial ranches, private cotton enterprises, intensive farm colonies, and new towns had emerged.

The Creation of the Border Labor Market

Throughout Mexico and the American Southwest, the privatization of land, the rise of commercial agriculture and ranching, and the surge in land values that followed displaced thousands of people who had previously subsisted on the land. In southern and central Mexico, hundreds of small, rural villages lost their *ejidos* and sufficient access to water sources, making it virtually impossible to continue their traditional ways of subsistence farming. Legislation abolishing debt peonage further loosened ties to the land and moved Mexico toward a modern, free-labor system. These policies spurred thousands to move north in search of wage-paying jobs on large *ranchos* and haciendas and in Monterrey's factories. Some of the small farmers in the Texas-Mexico borderlands who lost their land joined the immigrants from central and southern Mexico, swelling the ranks of the migratory workers. Competition between northern Mexican capitalists and American businesspeople in the Southwest over these workers became fierce as the demand for labor increased, creating a border labor market. The workers performed the necessary labor that was crucial for economic development throughout the entire region.[52]

The creation of the border labor market was one just example of how rapid capitalist growth in the Río Bravo/Rio Grande borderlands during the late nineteenth and early twentieth centuries generated both opportunity and loss. It brought new technologies, new opportunities, and substantial profits for some but also created deep economic and social inequalities, especially south of the border. In Mexico, President Díaz's policies had strengthened foreign capitalists and an upper class of wealthy Mexican businessmen at the expense of thousands of poor countrymen and women. Virtually every industry was an oligopoly, resulting in considerable barriers to upward mobility for most of the population. Wages had remained stagnant while prices of food and consumer goods skyrocketed. Although the middle classes grew somewhat during Díaz's tenure, their numbers and standard of living never reached those of their neighbors to the north. In the words of Friedrich Katz, the middle class "seemed to garner only the crumbs of Mexico's economic boom."[53] Economists have estimated that during the Porfiriato in Mexico about 1 percent of the population consisted of wealthy financiers, merchants, and industrialists, more than 90 percent of the nation's citizens were unskilled laborers, and only 8 percent could be classified as middle class. (This was in contrast to the United States around the turn of the century, which had a working class consisting of just over 50 percent of the population with the broad middle, made up of urban white-collar workers, professionals, artisans with their own businesses, small store owners, and farmers, constituting roughly 48 percent.[54]) Díaz's efforts to rein in some of the *caudillos* in the north and replace them with politicians loyal to him alienated a number of elite families. Resentment grew, and anti-Americanism spread as people perceived that most of Mexico's wealth was going to line the pockets of US bankers and investors.[55]

A failed uprising along the lower Río Bravo/Rio Grande in 1891 led by Catarino Garza, a border businessman and newspaper editor, foreshadowed a wider conflict. Many people on both sides of the border joined his movement, most of them Mexican day laborers and small *rancheros*. He received backing, however, from some of the elite businessmen of the border region such as Antonio Bruni of Laredo. Garza advocated economic development but resisted the form it was taking in northern Mexico and South Texas. Like Cortina several decades earlier, he resented Anglo-American greed for land and profits, which often resulted in the manipulation and exploitation of ethnic Mexicans. He blamed Díaz for economic policies that concentrated wealth in the hands of Anglo-Americans on both sides of the border. Although his insurrection failed in the short term, it planted seeds that erupted nearly twenty years later in a much more extensive movement in Mexico that would also affect South Texas.[56]

THE IMPACT OF THE MEXICAN REVOLUTION (1910–1917)

The Mexican Revolution of 1910 began in South Texas, where Díaz had originally launched his own coup. Francisco Madero, son of a wealthy, hacienda-owning family in Coahuila, fled to San Antonio in October 1910, shortly after losing the Mexican presidential election, allegedly as the result of fraud and corruption. There he wrote the Plan of San Luis Potosí, calling on all Mexicans to resort to arms in order to restore representative government. Díaz reportedly said, "Madero has unleashed a tiger. Now let's see if he can control it."[57] Díaz resigned on May 25, 1911, and supporters of Victoriano Huerta, an ally of Díaz, assassinated Madero in February 1913. Almost immediately, Venustiano Carranza of Coahuila, Francisco "Pancho" Villa of Chihuahua, Álvaro Obregón of Sonora, and Emiliano Zapata of Morelos rose up in opposition to Huerta, and a political revolution became a social one, permanently changing Mexico and deeply altering the broader context of commercial activity in the Texas counties along the Río Bravo/Rio Grande.

The Revolution marked a turning point in the economic history of the Texas-Mexico border region. It decimated the northern Mexican cattle industry, thereby reducing the stock available to South Texas ranches, disrupted cross-border commerce, and led to heightened security and control of the border itself. For a few years, it halted economic expansion in parts of South Texas but ultimately benefited the north side of the border. The south side took years to fully recover and rebuild. The United States' rapid progress toward domination of the global economy furthered prosperity in South Texas, whereas the revolution hindered growth in northeastern Mexico, causing it to fall behind and leading to greater disparities in the business environments north and south of the Río Bravo/Rio Grande.

Resentment over Anglo-American domination of the economy played a key role in the coming of the Revolution and affected its course. The cry "Mexico for Mexicans!" reverberated through the next few decades.[58] For years, roving bands of armed men targeted properties developed with foreign capital, including railroads, ranches, haciendas, and mines, tearing apart the transnational connections forged with businesses and investors in the United States. Hundreds of Americans who had bought farm tracts or operated businesses in Mexico during the Porfiriato fled, hoping the situation would be temporary, but most would never return. Attempts to regain control of property during temporary lulls in the violence proved to be a losing proposition. As one South Texan reported, "Americans are going back to get their shattered properties in place again, but they are all very dubious."[59] Brutal attacks on Americans and their belongings continued through the 1920s. People were beaten and killed, and their livestock, horses, and homes were confiscated and burned.[60]

The Mexican Revolution spawned political and legal instability, economic chaos, and violence, creating a climate of uncertainty that paralyzed business enterprise in Mexico and hampered transnational trade and investment for several years. The destruction of railroad tracks and telegraph lines throughout Mexico dealt a severe blow to the transportation and communication infrastructure upon which the nation's developing economy relied. Hunger and disease spread as food shortages increased, and prices skyrocketed. The Mexican banking system collapsed along with the peso. Both foreign- and native-owned capital fled the country. Mexicans shifted their deposits to US border banks, and US-based insurance companies cancelled their policies in Mexico. The circumstances made

it especially difficult for small businesses, the backbone of the economy, to survive. Hundreds of small businesspeople, the core of Mexico's new middle class,
left for a new life in the United States and crossed over the border at Laredo.[61]

During the bloodiest phase of the Revolution, between 1914 and 1917, the
border itself became a combat zone as different factions struggled for control of
the key points of entry from the United States into Mexico. Villistas and Carrancistas battled over control of Matamoros, Nuevo Laredo, and other border
towns as Americans watched from across the river. They destroyed many of the
few irrigation works in Tamaulipas, particularly on the large hacienda of La
Sauteña, which had received financing from Stillman interests. They repeatedly
raided border *ranchos* and farms belonging to Americans and suspected Díaz and
Huerta sympathizers and sold the livestock in US markets to fund purchases of
arms and ammunition.[62]

The cross-border sale of cattle and their products by the Villistas and Carrancistas contributed to heightened vigilance along the border. The United
States increased tariffs on imported cattle to protect the interests of ranchers
on the northern plains. When tick fever and foot and mouth disease began to
spread among the beleaguered Mexican herds, the US Bureau of Animal Hus-
bandry imposed new quarantines on live cattle crossing the southern border. In
order to avoid the quarantines, Villa, who controlled most of the border entry
points, set up slaughterhouses and sold the meat and hides in the United States
instead. The US government sometimes resorted to capricious enforcement of
sanitary restrictions on both live cattle and meat products to prefer one faction
over another. Villistas, Carrancistas, and Mexican and US cattlemen in Mexico continually evaded checkpoints and inspections, smuggling cattle and their
products across the border anyway.[63]

Revolutionary violence spilled over into South Texas, raising fears of a race
war. Terror struck the hearts of Anglo-Americans when a document of unknown
origin, the Plan de San Diego, surfaced in Hidalgo County in January 1915,
calling for an armed uprising in February against the United States and the
murder of all Anglo-American males over the age of sixteen. In the midst of a hot
July, the raids and killings began. Although apparently instigated by Mexican
citizens, the raids morphed into a wider Tejano rebellion that mirrored what
was happening south of the border in response to the dislocating effects of rapid
capitalistic development. The *sediciosos,* as they were often called, killed Anglos involved in local development and targeted wealthy Tejanos like Florencío
Saenz, who owned more than 40,000 acres in Hidalgo County. They threatened

and stole from merchants, tore up railroad tracks, demolished railroad bridges, smashed irrigation works, and raided trains. One report accused two bandits of attacking a farmhouse and shooting and wounding a woman who ran out to protect her children, who were playing in the front yard. Most of the violence was confined to Cameron and Hidalgo counties, but fear spread throughout South Texas and beyond that there would be similar uprisings, hardening Anglo attitudes toward ethnic Mexicans.[64]

The US government increased troop levels on the border to police the movement of people and animals, but it was the Texas Rangers who responded to the violence with brutal fury, indiscriminately killing hundreds, perhaps thousands, of innocent Tejanos. A band of Texas Rangers and local deputies showed up at the Flores Ranch near Harlingen in August to search the property. They killed Desiderio Flores, unarmed and standing on his front porch, along with two of his sons. When the Rangers retaliated for the attack on the Norias division of the King Ranch, they left the bodies of the Mexicans strewn across the fields. Vigilante violence became commonplace as some Anglos took the law into their own hands.[65]

The violence and disruption of the Revolution temporarily slowed parts of the South Texas economy. Fighting in the border towns led to embargoes on traffic over the international bridges. Stores closed as their customer base shrank. The import/export trade between Laredo and Monterrey suffered because of the damage to the city and along the railroad line. In early 1920, an American traveling from San Antonio to Monterrey noticed burned and dynamited houses immediately after crossing the border at Laredo. The Monterrey railroad depot lay in ruins.[66]

Farm development came to a virtual standstill in the lower Rio Grande Valley between 1913 and 1916. Few new farmers arrived to buy the land for sale, and many of those living in the area stopped paying water fees and taxes altogether. All but one of the private water companies suffered extensive losses and sought court protection under state receivership laws, paving the way for their replacement with public irrigation districts. James B. Wells, local land lawyer and Democratic political boss, faced a prolonged inability to make the regular payments on his outstanding debts. More than one of the new farm colonization ventures failed. Sam Robertson and Lon C. Hill both filed personal bankruptcy cases. Robertson tried to stay afloat by pledging stock in one company to secure new loans to other companies, but eventually this scheme collapsed. After he filed for bankruptcy, he lived in a tent in Amarillo for time, working for the Amarillo Petroleum and Refining Company while his wife took care of their home in San Benito. Lon Hill, who had borrowed in excess of $135,000 from New York life insurance companies, Houston banks, and individuals, could not repay his debts. The Lon C. Hill Town and Improvement Company lost its charter for failure to pay the state franchise tax, and Lon Hill's other companies had difficulty paying taxes and notes in 1916 and 1917. John Closner could not avoid financial problems, either; creditors filed state receivership cases against Closner and his partners when they defaulted on their debts.[67]

Tejano merchants and ranchers suffered more than Anglos. They were often caught in the middle during the time of the "border troubles." They not only faced possible attacks from the *sediciosos* but also lived under a cloud of suspicion that they might be their allies. They lived in constant threat of confrontations with the Texas Rangers. Many fled to Mexico with all of their household belongings, depopulating large sections of the ranching areas of northern Hidalgo and Cameron counties. Those who stayed, like Eutiquio Pérez, sometimes experienced business failure because of the loss of customers as well as property.[68]

Despite the short-term pain, the Mexican Revolution actually helped to boost the South Texas economy over the long term. During the war, a few South Texas merchants found ways to profit, especially local hardware merchants who sold arms to the revolutionaries in direct violation of US neutrality laws. Frank Rabb, for example, whose ranch stretched along the Rio Grande near Matamoros, sold arms to his friend Lucio Blanco, one of Carranza's generals. Still others profited legally by selling to the US troops stationed along the border in areas such as McAllen.[69]

The influx of refugees from all walks of life increased the availability of cheap labor, enhanced the local consumer market, and enlarged the pool of entrepreneurial talent. The violence, hunger, disease, and chaos of the revolutionary years accelerated the migration of people out of Mexico, which continued through the 1920s. It is estimated that nearly one million people left Mexico between 1910 and 1929. Many crossed the border into South Texas. Hundreds were small businesspeople fleeing for the safety and stability of the United States. The vast majority, however, were unskilled workers who provided the necessary pool of cheap labor that created the final impetus for an economic boom in South Texas. Although some had left during the final years of the Porfiriato, many more came as a result of the Revolution. They were willing to do the hard, physical labor required for the growth of the South Texas economy—clearing brush, laying railroad ties, picking cotton, harvesting fruit and vegetables, and packing crates for very low wages, approximately $1 a day. Some served local businesses as clerks or salespeople. Even though immigration restrictions increased after the passage of the Immigration Act of 1917, exemptions that were applied to Mexican workers allowed most to enter the country.[70]

The Revolution disrupted but did not destroy the transborder ties built up during the Porfiriato. The Mexican economy, damaged as it was during the most violent years (1914–1917), actually emerged remarkably intact. As had been typical of the borderlands for most of the nineteenth century, elite businessmen and large industrial enterprises in northern Mexico weathered the crisis fairly well. The Monterrey business leaders were among the most successful because they had generally avoided political activity both before and after the Revolution, and they were able to resume cross-border trade with the Laredo merchants fairly quickly. Between 1920 and 1940, South Texans benefited from ongoing trade with Mexico. The absence of many items in their own country motivated many of the more affluent Mexicans who were living in the northern borderlands to shop in US border towns. This trade continued despite enhanced border security by both nations.[71]

The Revolution complicated cross-border ranching and farming. Mexico's Constitution of 1917 created a climate of uncertainty; it designated private property as a privilege, not a right, granted by the government and revocable at any time. Land-redistribution policies, designed to break up the huge landholdings of the Porfiriato and to create *ejidos,* were implemented on a local basis at first and later on a national basis by Lázaro Cárdenas, resulting in considerable losses for wealthy Mexicans and Americans alike. Elites and foreigners lost an estimated 150 million acres as a result of the Revolution, just over a quarter of Mexico's total land.[72] In a 1921 letter, Moray L. Applegate, the manager of a large American hacienda in Baja California, recommended to his board of directors, "These are times when it is best not to have too much land in Mexico, and it would seem to be wiser to subdivide and sell off the surplus land before we were forced to do so through radical legislation."[73] In the late 1930s, a Del Rio rancher told a reporter, "After running cattle 15 years down in Coahuila, I have quit there for good. So have many other families. We couldn't stay in Mexico, conveniently, because of the expropriation policy and agrarian reform laws."[74]

The Revolution created opportunities for US land investors in South Texas even as it destroyed them in Mexico. John Shary, a Nebraska farm boy who became a wealthy real-estate developer, capitalized on the plunging property values along the Rio Grande during the revolution. Shary had had some interests in Mexico through his International Land and Investment Company, but he shifted his focus to South Texas after war broke out. Beginning in 1913 and continuing until 1922, he bought land near the Rio Grande in Hidalgo County from John J. Conway, J. W. Holt, James B. Wells, and John J. Closner, whose properties were completely underwater after the "border troubles" began. Out of this acreage, Shary formed the core of his new farm colony, Sharyland, which became one of the most prosperous in the entire Valley.[75]

While the Revolution raged, Shary quietly investigated innovative ways to generate profits. He had worked as a traveling lumber salesman in California in the 1890s. While there, he had observed firsthand the burgeoning citrus industry around Los Angeles. Southern California farmers had recently organized a cooperative, the California Fruit Growers' Exchange ("Sunkist"). Their marketing strategy involved converting oranges "from the class of luxuries to that of staples and necessities" in order to create a steady demand.[76] By the time he arrived in Hidalgo County, people all over the United States were beginning to eat oranges and drink orange juice for breakfast, but Shary realized that South Texas growers would have to market something new and different from anything he had seen in California if the region were going to compete in the national market. His solution was to develop new varieties of grapefruit. In 1914 he established the first commercial grapefruit orchard in Hidalgo County. Shary's efforts in developing and marketing citrus, promoting the Valley, and selling land made him one of the most important and successful Anglo-American entrepreneurs of the 1920s and 1930s.[77]

ECONOMIC GROWTH AND THE URBANIZATION OF THE SOUTH TEXAS BORDER REGION (1917–1940)

As northern Mexico struggled to recover from the Revolution, John Shary and other entrepreneurs set the stage for a tremendous boom in the South Texas economy that lasted until the early 1930s. Stimulated by the growth of commercial agriculture, oil and gas exploration, and the resumption of transnational trade, the border increasingly became an urbanized zone of commerce and nascent industry. As one promotional pamphlet proudly proclaimed, "Citrus fruits and farm products made possible these banks and modern buildings which rose as temples of prosperity out of the cactus and brush."[78] The resulting demographic growth stimulated a need for a wide array of businesses, creating new opportunities for small entrepreneurs, which later chapters explore in greater depth. The macroeconomic picture improved substantially.

Irrigated commercial agriculture in particular expanded, especially in the lower Rio Grande Valley, which became the most highly developed and populated area in the entire South Texas border region (map 2). Local newspapers proclaimed that a "gold rush" was taking place between 1922 and 1930; land developers in the "Magic Valley" sold most of their farm tracts after 1920.[79] These developers took advantage of the disrupted and delayed development of irrigation on the south side of the Río Bravo/Rio Grande. By 1929, they had siphoned off approximately 70 percent of the river's flow. In 1910, irrigated lands in Cameron and Hidalgo counties totaled about 50,477 acres and increased to 385,610 acres by 1929. The number of pumping plants along the river in the two counties increased from thirty-three in 1920 to eighty-nine in 1930.[80]

Farmers cultivated grapefruits, oranges, beans, cabbages, peas, squash, carrots, beets, turnips, cauliflower, lettuce, tomatoes, onions, and spinach and exported their produce to grocery stores from Alberta, Canada, to Ames, Iowa. Citrus in particular increased in the Valley in the 1920s; at the beginning of the decade, there were 135,153 citrus trees and 6,001,101 by 1930. Farm values, especially in or near irrigated areas, skyrocketed through the 1920s before falling in the early 1930s. By the end of the 1930s, they were once again trending upward (table 1). The profits from the farms flowed into bank savings accounts and into local businesses, boosting the entire economy.[81]

Other developing areas of South Texas followed similar patterns. The Winter Garden region, which was relatively undeveloped in 1919, boomed in the 1920s. In 1919, businessmen from Asherton, Big Wells, Carrizo Springs, and Crystal City formed the Winter Garden Chamber of Commerce in order to promote the area. Farmers constructed new artesian irrigation systems that resulted in a sizeable expansion of cultivated acreage. Zavala County, for example, had 532 irrigated acres in 1919 and 23,384 irrigated acres by 1939, dedicated mainly to onions, spinach, cabbage, and lettuce. In this period, farmers in the Winter Garden shifted from planting cotton to cultivating vegetables; in 1928, 96,300 acres of cotton had shrunk to 1,020 acres.[82] Because large growers owned a greater percentage of the land in the Winter Garden region than they did in the Valley, growth there was not as rapid or as large, but it was steady. Carrizo Springs and Asherton in Dimmit County became hubs for the marketing of Bermuda onions, and Crystal City in Zavala County became an important spinach distribution center. Farmers planted onions and fruit trees near Laredo. In the Quemado Valley of Maverick County and in parts of Val Verde County, farmers cultivated a variety of winter vegetables, grew grapes,

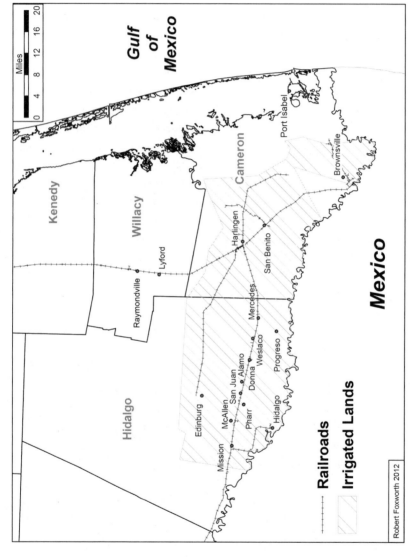

MAP 2. The towns of the lower Rio Grande Valley, railroads, and irrigated farmland, c. 1935. Map by Robert Foxworth.

TABLE 1. Farm values in the South Texas border region (selected counties)

COUNTY	1900	1910	1920	1930	1940
Cameron	$9,787,533	$9,184,783	$21,721,426	$48,006,482	$21,368,831
Hidalgo	$2,740,364	$10,992,746	$41,568,389	$70,335,234	$40,312,799
Starr	$2,187,879	$5,737,719	$1,902,742*	$2,302,369	$1,854,310
Zapata	$636,846	$930,820	$1,009,185	$1,656,619	$1,994,855
Webb	$2,724,250	$6,646,355	$8,746,719	$13,213,411	$7,949,237
Maverick	$2,826,498	$1,155,178	$1,222,439	$2,389,963	$4,111,389
Val Verde	$3,059,344	$5,332,392	$9,876,775	$19,211,028	$19,043,098
Dimmit	$3,089,333	$3,686,986	$5,428,765	$5,183,885	$3,390,289
Zavala	$1,211,849	$3,606,541	$7,119,913	$8,623,419	$8,876,182

Notes: Farm values include land and buildings as reported by the farmer.

* Starr County was divided into Starr and Brooks counties in 1911, with much of the valuable land going to Brooks.

Sources: US Bureau of the Census, *US Census of Agriculture, 1920,* vol. VI (Washington, DC: Government Printing Office, 1946), 667–746; US Bureau of the Census, *US Census of Agriculture, 1930,* vol. II, part 2 (Washington, DC: Government Printing Office, 1932), 1425–47; Zellmer R. Pettet, *Agriculture, Texas, First Series, 16th Census of the United States* (Washington, DC: Government Printing Office, 1941), 18–69.

and established wineries. Cotton expanded in Starr, Jim Hogg, Brooks, and Duval counties.[83]

The rest of the countryside remained devoted primarily to commercial ranching. Land ownership in ranching areas became highly concentrated in the hands of a few owners. In 1930, for example, Val Verde County had 205 ranches with average landholdings of 7,589 acres. Hidalgo County, by contrast, had 4,321 farms with an average size of eighty-seven acres. Land values in counties dominated by ranches, such as Val Verde, Maverick, and Webb, experienced rising values as well, although they were not as dramatic (see table 1).

In the 1920s, agricultural development in South Texas rapidly outpaced that of northern Mexico. The entire state of Tamaulipas had little more than 2,000 acres of irrigated farmland.[84] As Casey Walsh points out, "northern Tamaulipas was still a vast expanse of thorn forest with scattered settlements connected by footpaths and wagon trails."[85] Hundreds of people without formal title to the land continued to inhabit and use it in a communal fashion. By the late 1920s, some of the land was being cleared and planted in cotton. Some of these people were small farmers without clear title to the land, while others, like Juan Fernández of Brownsville, owner of Las Rucias hacienda south of Matamoros, built a pumping plant to irrigate more than 2,500 acres and signed contracts with local sharecroppers to plant and harvest the cotton. Local merchants from Matamoros financed much of this cotton production.

State plans to develop irrigated farming in northern Mexico emerged after the Revolution. In the 1920s, the Partido Revolucionario Institucional (PRI), Mexico's revolutionary political party, as well as President Álvaro Obregón and President Plutarco Elías Calles, had envisioned a society of small farms owned and managed by individuals, mostly drawn from the class of *rancheros* in the north, as a way to promote democracy, expand the middle class, and keep Mexican citizens from migrating to the United States. Calles saw the state taking an active role in creating this kind of society and actively promoted state-funded and -constructed irrigation zones. The creation of the Comisión Nacional de Irrigación (CNI) in 1926, a government agency, was intended to provide funding for these projects, much like the Bureau of Reclamation in the United States, but its lack of sufficient capital meant that few were established. Moreover, neither Obregón nor Calles was willing to engage in large-scale agrarian expropriations. That changed during the tenure of President Lázaro Cárdenas, whose administration expropriated substantial amounts of land across northern Mexico, especially in the Laguna and Mexicali in the Colorado River Valley, for the purpose of developing small irrigated cotton farms owned and managed by repatriated Mexican citizens.[86]

In Tamaulipas, shortly after the election of Cárdenas, efforts to turn *latifundias* into colonies of small farmers accelerated. In 1935, emboldened *agraristas* attempted to seize lands for *ejidos*. Shortly thereafter, the Tamaulipas government decided to expropriate almost three thousand acres of Juan Fernández's hacienda, Las Rucias, in part to pacify the *agraristas*. Fernández, a US citizen, was a target of resistance because he had violated Mexico's laws prohibiting foreign ownership of land too close to the border. At about the same time, the Cárdenas government began negotiations with the company that owned La Sauteña over completion of the old, unfinished irrigation canals and a process for turning its vast lands into small farm tracts for repatriated citizens. By the late 1930s, the Cárdenas administration had begun construction on new flood-control works along the Río Bravo. The long-term plan behind these efforts was to induce about half a million Mexican citizens (and even Mexican Americans) living in the United States, preferably those who had acquired knowledge and skill related to advanced agricultural technologies, to return to Mexico and cultivate cotton as owners and sharecroppers in the Valle Bajo Río Bravo zone near Matamoros. Settlement began in earnest in 1939, but it proved difficult to attract ethnic Mexicans who had built successful businesses or farms in the United States; most who returned were unemployed or unskilled.[87] Seemingly, the landscape of opportunity, at least before 1940, was better on the north side of the Río Bravo/Rio Grande for more skilled and educated businesspeople and farmers.

Oil and gas exploration began to take off in South Texas in the 1920s as ranchers signed mineral leases with the Texas Company and others. The discovery of a large oil field in 1908 around Tampico, Tamaulipas, approximately 225 miles away from the border, which produced as much as a quarter million barrels a day, had piqued an interest in oil exploration in South Texas. Wildcatters and oil and gas companies poured substantial sums into drilling wells in Starr, Zapata, Webb, Jim Hogg, McMullen, and Duval counties. New oil boomtowns like Oilton and Bruni, sprang up, and Hebbronville in Jim Hogg County became a leading oil town. Some of the land developers, including Nick Doffing and Rentfro Banton Creager, began to invest in oil. Natural gas fields in Starr, Webb, and Duval counties supplied San Antonio, Houston, Corpus Christi, and other local towns as well as Monterrey and towns in northern Mexico. Smaller fields in Maverick, Uvalde, Zavala, and Dimmit counties supplied energy for local markets.[88] Laredo boasted two refineries in 1926 and claimed that the "vast extent of the Laredo district oil fields offer rich reward to the developer."[89]

The expansion of commercial agriculture, the consolidation of ranchlands, and oil and gas exploration made it increasingly expensive to survive on the land without substantial capital. The result was a shift of population from rural to urban areas between 1920 and 1940 (table 2). This movement from country to city paralleled similar developments in the rest of the United States and accelerated during the Great Depression. Prior to 1913, farm development and town growth were roughly comparable. After 1913, farm development remained fairly constant until the end of the 1930s while town growth increased. Along the South Texas border, urbanization occurred more rapidly than in the state as a whole. One reason was that the laboring population, which consisted of ethnic Mexicans, tended to live in *barrios* in the towns and cities, a pattern typical of other parts of the Southwest.[90]

Urbanization occurred most rapidly in the lower Rio Grande Valley, where developers had established dozens of new farm towns as well as in the older towns that had arisen in 1848. In 1940, Brownsville's population was about

TABLE 2. Urban population, South Texas border region (selected counties)

COUNTY	1900	1910	1920	1930	1940
*Cameron (Brownsville)	6,305 (39%)	10,517 (39%)	16,861 (46%)	44,898 (57%)	59,677 (72%)
*Hidalgo	0	0	12,592 (33%)	37,830 (49%)	70,834 (68%)
*Starr	0	0	0	0	8,562 (64%)
Zapata	0	0	0	0	2,740 (70%)
Webb (Laredo)	13,429 (61%)	14,855 (62%)	22,710 (78%)	32,618 (77%)	41,744 (91%)
Maverick (Eagle Pass)	0	3,536 (62%)	5,765 (78%)	5,059 (82%)	8,429 (84%)
Val Verde (Del Rio)	0	0	10,589 (83%)	11,693 (78%)	13,926 (90%)

Notes: "Urban" is defined as living in towns with a population of at least 2,500.

* Lower Rio Grande Valley

Sources: US Bureau of the Census, *Thirteenth Census of the United States, Population,* vol. III (Washington, DC: United States Government Printing Office, 1913), 804–50; US Bureau of the Census. *Fifteenth Census of the United States, Population,* vol. III, part 2 (Washington, DC: United States Government Printing Office, 1932), 975–90; US Bureau of the Census, *Sixteenth Census of the United States, Population,* vol. II, part 6 (Washington, DC: United States Government Printing Office, 1943), 793–806.

22,000, Harlingen and San Benito both had populations of more than 10,000, and McAllen, Mercedes, and Mission each had a population in excess of 5,000. The other railroad Valley towns, including Donna, Alamo, San Juan, Pharr, Weslaco, and, Edinburg, had each grown to between 1,000 and 5,000 in population.[91] The recovery of trade with Mexico as well as heightened demand for consumer services spurred urbanization in the border towns. By 1930, Laredo handled more exports to Mexico than did all of the other cities along the Mexican border combined, and its population approximated 39,274. The slightly more remote cities of Del Rio and Eagle Pass handled less trade and therefore remained smaller. By the end of the period, Del Rio's population totaled about 13,343, and that of Eagle Pass was just over 6,000. Urbanization along the border, coupled with the growth of the agricultural economy, contributed substantially to the creation of a landscape of opportunity in the South Texas borderlands in the 1920s and 1930s by generating new demands for a wide variety of businesses, both large and small (fig. 4).[92]

FIGURE 4. Mercedes, c. 1938. Typical view of a new farm town in the Lower Rio Grande Valley. Courtesy of the Margaret H. McAllen Memorial Archives, Museum of South Texas History, Edinburg, Texas.

•   •   •

Urbanization and the expansion of specialized agriculture reflected the incorporation of South Texas borderlands into the global system of industrial capitalism. The integration of the US and Mexican economies during the Porfiriato laid the foundation for modern capitalist development, and the arrival of the railroads linked the region more effectively to world markets, dramatically improving the environment for business enterprise and commercial agriculture. The Mexican Revolution disrupted but did not destroy the ties forged in previous decades. In its aftermath, however, the wealth gap between the United States and Mexico widened and became increasingly apparent in the border towns. As Mexico continued to struggle to stabilize and develop its economy, the Texas side of the border boomed. The tide of refugees that swept into the region as a result of the Revolution helped to stimulate the South Texas economy in the 1920s by bringing a cheap labor pool, more consumers, and more business owners. One of the more dramatic changes of the period was the movement of the population from rural areas to towns and cities, which gave rise to the need for hundreds of new consumer-oriented businesses. The landscape of opportunity shifted as more capital was required in the countryside. Not everyone, however, was equally able to access the opportunities in this new landscape, as subsequent chapters show. Individual access to capital, credit, and markets, influenced heavily by class and ethnicity, played a significant role, as did personal creativity, drive, and ability. The next three chapters explore the nature of the business class in this changing commercial environment, which emerged in the South Texas borderlands between 1880 and 1940, as well as the opportunities individual entrepreneurs both seized and created.

PART II

TEXAS BORDERLAND ENTREPRENEURS

3

SEIZING OPPORTUNITY

"THE SECRET OF BUSINESS SUCCESS is knowing when to seize opportunity. Invest Now!" "Bigger business is attracted to those who seize opportunity vigorously." These early twentieth-century advertisements in the *Laredo Times* capture the spirit of the age and the essence of capitalist culture in the United States. The Anglo-Americans who followed the railroads into South Texas after 1880 hoped to seize the opportunities presented to them by local promoters and establish successful, enduring enterprises. They changed the way business was conducted and Anglicized the society in a relatively short period of time.[1]

To the native residents of South Texas, the new Anglo migrants displayed a noticeably competitive and acquisitive outlook. Jovita González referred to an "invasion of fortune-seeking Americans" in the lower Rio Grande Valley. Alonso Perales, president of the League of United Latin American Citizens, emphasized the need for resident Tejanos to keep up with the "harddriving [*sic*] Anglo-Saxon."[2] Like Alexis de Tocqueville in an earlier generation, González and Perales recognized the deep-rooted emphasis in Anglo-American culture on business success and entrepreneurship. According to de Tocqueville, Americans had "a restless disposition, an unbounded desire of riches, and an excessive love of independence . . . What we should call cupidity, the Americans frequently term a laudable industry; and they blame as faint-heartedness what we consider to be the virtue of moderate desires."[3] Americans, more than members of most other societies, valued innovation, individual ambition, competition, self-reliance, and business success, which they believed could be realized through hard work. They were optimistic about their chances for upward mobility and actively sought out new opportunities, which often took them to far, remote corners of the nation and the globe. Risk taking, acceptance of change, the willingness to innovate, and a strong work ethic were all essential parts of the American national character and its predominantly middle-class identity, which persisted despite inequities.[4]

The roots of this middle-class identity lay in the early Republican period, when American colonists rejected the ways of feudal, aristocratic Europe as they built a new nation. The idea of a merit-based society, revolutionary at the time, gave rise to laws and policies designed to eliminate aristocratic privilege, promote free enterprise, and create opportunities for small farmers and business-people. Ordinary people could suddenly change their destinies in ways previously unimagined. As a result, according to historian Joyce Appleby, American society resembled a "tomato with a rich slice at the top and a broad middle narrowing only gradually" more than the traditional pyramid. This was true, however, only among native-born white Americans; nearly every group of immigrants that came to the United States had to struggle for acceptance into this middle class, and the struggle lasted far longer for those who were not white. Most Anglo-Americans chose to treat people of color as invisible or inferior and viewed them as best suited to manual labor.[5]

Anglo-Americans brought this middle-class outlook with them to the border. Threatened by the rise of big business in the eastern United States, they saw the region as a place where small business could still thrive. They reshaped the region's economy into one that was more competitive, individualistic, and profit oriented. In the early twentieth century they also brought an emphasis on consumption and leisure, which was becoming an important aspect of middle-class culture in the United States. The desire to achieve a high standard of living, now a part of the "American Dream," increasingly motivated the pursuit of business success.[6]

THE PROMISE OF OPPORTUNITY—
THE PROMOTIONAL CAMPAIGN

The developers of South Texas, in their desire to further their own interests by selling land, drew on the wellspring of American middle-class tradition as they promoted the region. They faced fierce competition for potential settlers. The railroads had opened up hundreds of new areas in the western regions of the United States, Canada, and Mexico to settlement, and towns from the Great Plains to the West Coast were all trying to attract the same middle-class Anglo-Americans from the eastern United States, especially the more prosperous farmers and entrepreneurs of the Midwest. They directed less effort toward the South, which remained an impoverished region for many decades after the Civil War. South Texas promoters set about designing a new image of the border region, demonstrating that it offered more and better opportunities than its rivals as well as a unique quality of life.

The South Texas campaign began during a second period of Western booster literature, from the late 1890s through the 1920s, which saw the transformation of the United States from an agrarian society into a modern, urban, and industrial nation. After the Civil War, the middle class in the United States increasingly associated the American West with opportunity and individualism. Yet images of the violence of the Indian Wars and border conflicts as well as the difficulties of homesteading still lingered in the public mind. Western boosters therefore sought to convince people that the risks and hardships of pioneer life had vanished, but its benefits had not.[7] They described "western frontiers as 'closing' not 'closed,' with the wellspring of opportunity fast running out but not yet dried up." Besides, they argued, leaving the more developed areas of the country no longer meant abandoning all vestiges of civilization; western towns had the conveniences and amenities of any modern city in the East or Midwest, including good schools, churches, recreational facilities, and nice homes. South Texas promoters described a place where Anglo-Americans had chased away Indians and "border ruffians," converted a wilderness of cactus and mesquite into "a veritable winter garden," and built a modern, progressive society with a myriad of new business opportunities.[8]

Eliminating the perception of the "Wild West" in South Texas meant deemphasizing much of the existing Mexican culture, deemed primitive and backward by Anglo-American standards. Captain John G. Bourke had popularized images of Texas border residents as dirty and poor in articles published in *Scribner's* and the *New York Times* in the 1890s: "[T]hese Mexicans will sleep on the earthen floors of their hovels arrayed in the garments of the day, and these are changed only once a year, at Saint John's Day, in June, when whole villages may be seen on the river-bank taking the annual bath." Promoters resorted to similar descriptions in order to justify Anglo-American dominance in the region. Ethnic Mexicans had failed to develop the full potential of the land by allowing their cattle, goats, and sheep to range haphazardly across the landscape with no real planning or thought for the future. They were the opposite of the American entrepreneur—idle, unprogressive, unstable, and prone to lawlessness, living in a "God-forsaken" place filled with "cactus crowned hills and plains, with water only at the end of a day's journey."[9]

In contrast, "Anglo-Saxons," with their energetic and enterprising outlook, were beginning to transform the terrain and unleash its full productive capacity. Brownsville had changed from a "dead little town of 9,500 inhabitants, chiefly 'peon' Mexicans and a few wealthy, unprogressive citizens" into a "thriving town that bids fair to be a large city in a small number of years."[10] "[I]nstead of *sinderos* wending their tortuous and circuitous ways through the underbrush, there are these wonderful highways lined on each side by beautiful homes, stately orange groves which bending under their rich burden, the golden fruit among the green leaves, presents itself to the traveler as a veritable gold mine."[11]

The boosters interpreted the proximity to the Mexican border as a positive and unique aspect of the region. Mexican homes, buildings, and institutions that Anglos did not want in their own communities could be interesting and exotic places to visit when they were located south of the border. Interest in the exotic, whether overseas, across the border, or in a local Chinatown, was another characteristic of Anglo-American culture at the time. Matamoros, Reynosa, and Nuevo Laredo in "Old Mexico" were quaint and interesting spots for dinner and, during Prohibition days, a place where they could buy wine, beer, or whiskey. There, Anglos could shop in open markets and stores in Mexico for goods they could not easily acquire in the United States or witness a bull fight. The mountains of Mexico were not much farther away, "only a night's ride," and Monterrey and Saltillo were places where many "Valley folk spend vacation-time." Mexico City was billed as the "Paris of America" in the 1920s and readily accessible by rail. In the 1930s, the Mexican government had supposedly "awakened to the urge of tourist opportunities" and started constructing highways from the border into the interior so that Anglos could drive their own cars to different places.[12]

Proximity to the border also meant a constant source of cheap labor, and this became a major selling point that differentiated South Texas from other places. Mexican laborers were described as the "most skillful of humans in the mere use of [their] hands" and as hard workers. The willingness of ethnic Mexicans to work for low wages made it possible for middle-class Anglo-Americans to avoid sole reliance on family labor on their farms. They were also able to hire ethnic Mexican women as domestic servants, a luxury that they would have found difficult to afford in other parts of the country.[13]

   Photographs and flowery language evoked the romantic imagery of a "semi-tropical paradise" forged out of a wilderness, following a common theme of creating a garden in the desert, which irrigation had made possible. In an effort to address concerns over the region's aridity, promoters claimed that Texas droughts were virtually over; the rain had followed the plow. "There used to be a saying that it never rained southwest of San Antonio. One never hears it now. The rainfall has kept pace with the immigrant, and for years all the region lying along the border stream from Del Rio to the mouth of the river has had ample moisture for the raising of crops."[14]

   South Texas promoters borrowed the semitropical metaphor from Los Angeles–area boosters, who had rejected it in favor of the image of a Mediterranean paradise. The multiple comparisons to California throughout the regional literature leave no doubt that the promoters were always conscious of their major competitor. The South Texas climate was similar to "that of the much sought Southern California in winter."[15] South Texas was the new "'California' of the Southwest, the climate delightful for the diversified farmer."[16] Midwesterners would "enjoy life down here in these semi-tropics, away from the rigors of cold winters, with expensive coal bills, and the attendant ills of the North."[17] Theodore Plummer, writing for *Gulf Coast Magazine,* claimed that the weather in South Texas was actually superior to that of Southern California, where "in mid-Summer blankets are necessary and the nearness of mountains and sea causes heavy and damp fogs and mists nightly that are not dispelled until about 10 o'clock in the morning. These daily, sudden changes make rheumatism, colds and *lagrippe* much more prevalent in California than sickness of any kind in Southwest Texas."[18]

   The literature helped to create two new "perceptual regions" in South Texas, the "Magic Valley" and the "Winter Garden." Developers set about constructing a semitropical paradise in these places by lining streets in the new farm towns with palm trees and planting tropical plants and flowers. Architects designed many of the first buildings in the new Valley towns in the Spanish mission style of Southern California. The adoption of this architectural style was only one way that Anglo-Americans created a new identity and heritage in South Texas that was similar to that of Southern California. South Texas builders continued to follow California designs in the 1920s and 1930s, adopting both the Spanish Mediterranean and the Monterey styles. Local residents borrowed other elements of Hispanic culture, particularly during annual festivities like Charro Days in Brownsville, in order to feel that they were participating in its

Spanish past while at the same time rejecting modern Mexican culture, people, and institutions as inferior.[19] *Texas Geographic Magazine* suggested that visitors would "flock to South Texas to familiarize themselves with the interesting and strange customs of our Spanish-American cousins living on the border and eager to contribute their part to a fuller Texas life."[20]

Other border towns used different images to promote themselves but followed similar themes. Laredo called itself the "gateway to Mexico and center of a rich farming and oil district, [which] sits in the garden of South Texas, on a high bluff, looking across the shining waters of the Rio Grande to old Mexico."[21] Del Rio sold itself as one of the state's main centers of wool and mohair and promoted its wine industry. Eagle Pass emphasized its commerce with Mexico, social clubs, and modern amenities.[22]

The developers clearly targeted members of the middle class. Photographs, personal testimonies, and statistics sought to convince Anglo-Americans "of modest means" that they would find ample opportunities for business enterprises, a good education for their children, culture, and community life. Paralleling similar statements in literature about New Mexico and Arizona, references to modern amenities like waterworks, paved streets, and electricity signaled that the region was no longer a "primitive" Mexican place but had become a "progressive American" region. A Southern Pacific Railroad publication made explicit the gendered approach of the promoters, which reflected the "separate spheres" of men and women in US industrial society. "A man naturally considers investment and financial possibilities above other things. A woman reckons upon the basis of a proper environment for the rearing of her children, the servant problem, and the chances for a measure of a congenial church, civic, and social affiliation, either rural or community."[23]

"Opportunity" was perhaps the most common word appearing throughout the promotional literature. Brochures contrasted the availability of opportunities in South Texas with stagnation in overdeveloped parts of the country. South Texas was "a place of genuine opportunity for people of modest means to live happily" in contrast to the "limited opportunities in the large mills and factories of the crowded cities" of the Northeast and Midwest.[24] A farmer could expect better returns because he was not limited to one growing season. He could be confident that he was making a good investment. Local farm towns were busy twelve months out of the year, unlike those in the North, which essentially shut down in the winter. Farm profits would easily support local businesses throughout the year.[25]

Stories about men who had worked their way up from humble backgrounds reinforced the idea of South Texas as a land of opportunity. James Sullivan, a major Bermuda onion seed distributor in Asherton, "started out on a very small capital, [but] his business ability coupled with foresight and attractive personality has made for him many friends and an enviable record in the business he chose." A brief biography of Royle K. Mims described how he started out as a bank runner, sweeping floors, washing windows, and running errands and gradually moved through the ranks to become a cashier, a vice president, and finally the president of First State Bank & Trust Co. of Laredo. Personal testimonies about success filled the pages of promotional pamphlets. In one, Claude Macy certified that his orchard had produced more than $600 an acre in revenues.[26]

Business was not the only concern of potential migrants; they also desired a better quality of life. Brochures promoting South Texas therefore included photographs of beautiful homes complete with electricity and indoor plumbing, suggesting refined and comfortable but not extravagant living. This was a veiled reference to the "standard of living" people could expect to achieve with the profits they earned. The "standard of living" changed rapidly and constantly as the US economy supplied an increasing array of diverse and innovative consumer goods. The desire for these goods provided a major connection between the borderlands and the wider commercial society in the United States because it was through commerce that "the standard of living was defined, disseminated, and perceived."[27]

Publications also included pictures and descriptions of schools, churches, clubs, and recreational activities. Churches filled spiritual and social needs and provided moral guidance. Good schools offered the necessary training for one's children to maintain middle-class status. "The citizenship of the Valley takes much pride in its splendid educational advantages," proclaimed one article, "and points with pride to the . . . affiliation its schools have with the universities and higher schools of the country." With the rise of leisure time among members of the middle class in the twentieth century, promoters promised a myriad of recreational options, including golf, hunting, fishing, swimming, and county fairs.[28]

In addition to promoting the region through pamphlets, magazines, and newspapers, a few developers sent agents to talk directly to potential buyers, especially in Missouri, Kansas, the Dakotas, Minnesota, Iowa, Indiana, and Illinois. They set up "homeseeker excursions" to give people a chance to see the land for themselves (fig. 5). This personal touch was highly effective. John Shary partnered with railroad companies, arranging for his two Pullman cars to be

FIGURE 5. Farm excursion, Lower Rio Grande Valley, c. 1918. Midwesterners regularly rode trains down to the border and were escorted around the area in the hopes that they would purchase a farm tract in one of the new developments. Courtesy, Lower Rio Grande Valley Historical Collection, Library Archives and Special Collections, University of Texas–Pan American.

attached to trains heading down to the Valley. Potential customers paid a small fee to travel to the "Magic Valley," but Shary subsidized most of the costs. He scheduled regular tours for the first and third Wednesday of the month, leaving from Chicago, Minneapolis, Des Moines, Sioux City, Columbus, Milwaukee, and a few cities in Kansas. Although the excursions were geared to people interested in buying farmland, some of the people who bought tickets were more interested in starting businesses in the towns and cities. Sam Perl, for example, joined his brother, Leon, on an excursion and decided to move to Brownsville from Houston in 1926 to open a dry-goods store.[29]

On the trains, people were entertained with music and treated to delicious meals. They listened to lectures about new farming and irrigation methods. One man recalled, "[W]e went on a special excursion train, when the air was full of land boosting influences night and day, with songs in the air from the enclosed booklet of the 'Excursion to the Lower Rio Grande Valley of Texas,' and it simply made everybody thinking and dreaming that there could be no better place on earth."[30] Once they arrived in the Valley, a number of the land developers restricted what the visitors could see, carefully escorting them around so that they would be unable to talk to anyone unaffiliated with the developers. Reportedly, on some of these occasions, land agents would show prospects a recently planted field at the beginning of the trip. At the end of the trip, they would return to the same field, where ripe cabbages, hurriedly dug into the loose soil by the agents, had supposedly grown like magic.[31]

The promotional campaign continued into Mexico for a few years prior to the Mexican Revolution as US colonizers of Mexican lands advertised and brought prospective settlers to their farm colonies. The US Land Company sponsored trips from Wichita, Kansas, to Tampico for potential purchasers. The *Laredo Times* reported on a large homeseekers' excursion to San Luis Potosí, sponsored by the Mexico-US Land Corporation, which was scheduled to pass through the city on March 23, 1908. All of this promotional activity in northern Mexico ceased abruptly with the onset of violence, however. Even after the violence subsided, unrest and uncertainty plagued the countryside of northeastern Mexico, and most foreign real estate developers avoided the region for years afterward.[32]

THE ANGLO-AMERICAN MIGRANTS

The effectiveness of the promotional campaign became apparent as the twentieth century progressed. Thousands moved to South Texas, especially the "Magic Valley." As one Tejano put it, the "Nordic cloud appeared in the north, and slowly but unremorsely [*sic*], grew into monstrous proportions."[33] The changing demographics were quite remarkable. In 1880, most of the counties were over 90 percent Hispanic, while by 1930, in some areas nearly half of the population consisted of Anglo-Americans.[34]

The Anglo-American migration into South Texas was part of a larger stream flowing into the western United States. Many came from the South, following a well-entrenched pattern of movement. Southern farmers had often pulled up stakes, traveling west along the same latitude through Alabama, Mississippi, Louisiana, and East Texas. By the late 1800s, the scourge of the boll weevil forced many to seek a fresh start in the borderlands. Substantial numbers also migrated from the Midwest and Great Plains states. This was the beginning of what would later be called the shift from "Snowbelt to Sunbelt," which would continue through the twentieth century.[35]

People came for different reasons. Some sought a fresh start, others saw better opportunities to make money, and some simply wanted to join family and friends. When Mildred Fagg's parents lost their house in Oklahoma to fire, they moved to the lower Rio Grande Valley to live with her grandparents. Franklin Ewers' family, originally from Ohio, became familiar with the region through trips to visit his father's sister, whose husband was the depot agent and telephone operator in San Juan in the early 1900s. The train excursions subsidized by the land companies played a significant role in many families' decisions to relocate. The desire to escape the long, harsh winters and the perceived health benefits of the Southwestern climate motivated families like the Griffiths and the Reeds, who had family members suffering from rheumatism and tuberculosis.[36]

The Anglo migration to the border after 1900 was largely a middle-class phenomenon. Almost all of the migrants were independent businesspeople, professionals, and farmers who could afford the costs of transportation, land, equipment, inventory, seeds, livestock, or whatever was necessary to start the business of their choice but still needed a regular income to survive. Because the availability of cheap Mexican labor had a downward effect on wages and status, few Anglo-American and European laborers moved to South Texas, preferring instead to seek higher-paying jobs in mining in the intermountain West. The migrants generally came as families, which meant that few would be looking for wives among the existing population. The pattern of family migration was another feature that set the new Anglo migrants apart from earlier ones, many of whom had come as young, single males and married into local Tejano families. It also meant that they had less incentive to adapt to Hispanic culture.[37]

The vast majority of the new Anglo migrants concentrated in the areas developed and promoted by local entrepreneurs, especially the lower Rio Grande Valley. The towns and surrounding farmland of the Winter Garden region attracted fewer Anglo settlers; the counties of Dimmit and Zavala grew in population between 1900 and 1930 by about 18,000 people, but the majority consisted of migrant farmworkers. The Winter Garden counties had only about one-sixth of the population of the lower Rio Grande Valley, and much of the land was in the hands of a few large landowners, some of whom were absentee speculators. The border towns of Laredo, Eagle Pass, and Del Rio attracted Anglo settlers throughout the period. Except for a few years between 1907 and 1910, Anglo-American migration ended at the border. Revolutionaries drove out most Americans who had settled in the farm projects of northern Mexico during those years, and most lost their property in the aftermath of the revolution. Few Anglos settled in less developed parts of the region such as Zapata and Starr counties.[38]

Most of the new Anglo-American migrants appear to have identified themselves as middle class, as the following column from the *Laredo Times* indicates:

> In this country of opportunity a man with ability doesn't have to have an A-1 social background to succeed. Most of our great men have come out of middle-class homes. It is in these families that healthy bodies, honest characters, driving ambitions are moulded [*sic*]. Clean blood is better than blue blood. The young man rising up from the middle class is mightier than the young man leaning against a background that forbears have built for him.[39]

The new Anglo migrants sought to recreate a familiar world of Main Street America on the border by remaining apart from the local residents. Few had ever had any experience with ethnic Mexicans. Their knowledge of Mexican culture derived largely from what they had read or heard from those who already lived in South Texas. Midwesterners came from relatively homogeneous, white communities, where they rarely encountered people of color. Southerners brought their racial attitudes toward African Americans and generally viewed ethnic Mexicans through the same lens. Most saw no need to accommodate to the existing Hispanic society, as earlier Anglo migrants had done, because the numbers of Anglos in the region had grown large enough that they could basically stay within their own communities. Few learned Spanish, converted to Catholicism, married ethnic Mexicans, or engaged in business partnerships with them. They lived in segregated white neighborhoods, a practice that became common throughout the American Southwest as well as wherever they settled in Mexico. They tended to consider all ethnic Mexicans, regardless of class, background, or occupation, as "foreigners," "nonwhite," and manual laborers, words that were often synonymous in their minds.[40]

Anglo-American influence was most pronounced in new farm towns. Anthropologist Paul Taylor, as he journeyed through South Texas in the 1920s to interview local residents, found some of the most racist attitudes and extreme segregation in the Winter Garden, an area that had been part of Indian Country in the nineteenth century and lacked a long history of Tejano settlement. Closer to the border, in places where Anglos, ethnic Mexicans, and Europeans had interacted for several decades, class and capital continued to play an important role in relations between the different ethnic groups. Anglos generally differentiated between "Spanish-type Mexicans" or "Spanish *mestizos*" and "peon Mexicans." A greater degree of cooperation occurred in those border towns, more so in business than in social life.[41]

Many of the new Anglo migrants resented the power of the old Anglo elite, including the lawyers, wealthy merchants, land developers, and large ranchers, believing that they were exercising undemocratic control over the region through their manipulation of local ethnic Mexicans with whom they had cultivated a paternalistic relationship to remain in power. Democratic boss James B. Wells reportedly held large barbecues right before elections to try to influence voters. He allegedly paid poll taxes and marked ballots for illiterate voters, recruited noncitizens to vote, and stuffed ballot boxes. The new Anglos saw themselves as the champions of democracy and freedom against an unenlightened old order. They formed "good government leagues" to challenge the machines run by Wells in Cameron County and by A. Y. Baker in Hidalgo County. These challenges were similar to other ones around the country and were consistent with the American middle-class concern over the concentration of wealth at the top, class conflict, and the growing influence of "special interests" over government. The "Magic Valley" and the "Winter Garden," where challenges to the old order were successful, however, effectively disenfranchised many ethnic Mexicans. The boss system survived longer in places like Starr, Zapata, and Duval counties, where there were fewer Anglo migrants.[42]

FINDING OPPORTUNITIES AND DOING BUSINESS

As more and more Anglos arrived in the region between 1880 and 1940, they moved into and dominated virtually every sector of the border economy. With the exception of a few who became extremely wealthy, most became small farmers and small business owners, playing a vital role in the border economy and in its emerging social structure. Far from being unimportant because of their size, these small entrepreneurs carried on most of the economic activity in the region during this period and constituted the core of the middle class. As the previous chapter notes, making a living in the countryside as an independent landowner increasingly required more starting capital, while at the same time urbanization created a plethora of new opportunities in the towns and cities that required less capital. Anglo-Americans were more likely than other groups to have access to substantial resources, and therefore they increasingly dominated the countryside. Regardless of whether they operated a ranch, farm, or small business, they generally shared a common entrepreneurial outlook.[43]

In the Countryside

Few of the new migrants became ranchers. The closing of the open range, the expansion of industrial capitalism in the United States, and the Porfirian program of modernization in Mexico in the late nineteenth century had completely transformed border ranching into a capital-intensive enterprise. New technologies, including refrigeration and refrigerated railroad cars, barbed wire, windmills, and advances in veterinary medicine and scientific agriculture, coupled with the expansion of transportation systems, enabled ranchers to produce better breeding and feeder stock and thereby reach a wider range of consumers. The changes necessitated sizeable landholdings that most of the recent Anglo migrants could not afford; circumstances favored the heirs of nineteenth-century Anglo ranching families such as the Kings, Kenedys, and Armstrongs, who continued to expand their ranches in the twentieth century.[44]

Ranching in South Texas was part of a much larger transnational network of cattle operations that spanned most of the US/Mexico borderlands. By the 1880s, industrial packers like Armour and Company and Swift & Co., based in Chicago, had effectively utilized refrigeration technology to process and transport beef quickly and efficiently across the United States, where demand for beef was high and growing. By contrast, Mexico's urban beef market remained underdeveloped despite efforts by the *científicos,* the Porfirian administrative elite, to import refrigeration technology; Mexicans generally retained a preference for fresh meat. Therefore, the large border ranchers became more heavily invested in US markets, supplying breeding stock and feeder cattle to ranches and stockyards from St. Louis to Chicago.[45] In the early twentieth century, cattle exports by US and Mexican owners of large ranches in northern Mexico were substantial. Between 1906 and 1909, exports from northern Mexico totaled approximately 150,000 head of cattle, and between 1911 and 1912, northern Mexican ranches sent 95 percent of their cattle to the United States. The situation reversed somewhat after the Mexican Revolution, when the decimation of northern Mexican cattle herds created a heightened demand for cattle from the United States.[46]

Ed Lasater was one of the few Anglo-Americans with limited assets who, through access to credit, built a ranching empire during this period of rapid change. Born near Goliad, Texas, north of the Nueces River, he abandoned his goal of becoming a lawyer at age twenty-three and started working as a cattle buyer to support his widowed mother and sister after his father, a small-time rancher, died in 1883. After he established his creditworthiness, he was able to borrow enough money to buy land in 1895 in Starr and Duval counties at rock-bottom prices from several Hispanic families devastated by the drought. He eventually acquired 350,000 acres. He started with a herd of beef cattle acquired from the Kenedy Pasture Company and eventually diversified into dairy farming, farm development, town building, mercantile operations, and banking. This diversification paid off when he faced foreclosure and receivership proceedings in the 1920s. Lasater was able to expand because of his creditors' willingness to lend him huge sums of money, which often turned out to be more than he was able to repay.[47]

Along with other border ranchers, Ed Lasater worked to improve cattle breeds. Imported cattle from England and the northeastern United States that produced superior beef often fared poorly in the semiarid landscapes of the borderlands. Border ranchers faced the challenge of developing a crossbreed that could survive the climate and diseases of the region and still produce high-quality beef. The Mexican Agricultural Society, formed in 1879, promoted transnational cooperation in the industry by hosting livestock exhibitions in the United States and Mexico to showcase English and American breeds such as Herefords, Jerseys, and Holsteins and discuss how to breed them with Mexican stock. South Texas ranchers experimented with a variety of crossbreeds beginning in the early 1900s. Ed Lasater crossed Brahmans with Herefords and Shorthorns to create the Beefmaster. Robert J. Kleberg, son-in-law of Richard King and manager of the King Ranch after his death, began a program of breeding Shorthorn cattle with Brahmans to produce the famous Santa Gertrudis breed.[48]

Lasater embraced a business model of ranching. He believed that ranchers needed to adopt an entrepreneurial mindset and concern themselves "with improvement and innovation rather than with ordinary problem-solving."[49] When Lasater became the president of the Cattle Raisers' Association (CRA; now known as the Southwestern and Texas Cattle Raisers' Association) in 1911, he promulgated his philosophy to other ranchers. Originally formed in 1877 to prevent cattle rustling, the CRA became a transnational association representing "the progressive cattleman of Texas, Mexico, New Mexico, Oklahoma, Kansas and Neighboring States" during the Porfiriato, although its membership was almost exclusively Anglo-American. It advised ranchers that their operations needed to be "as thoroughly systematized as the merchant's store or the banker's bank" in order to compete effectively in global markets.[50] The CRA engaged in lobbying on issues of concern to ranchers, such as high freight rates and tariffs. Its primary publication, the *Cattleman,* carried articles on range-management practices, cattle breeding, cattle markets, vaccinations, the credit system, and the beef-making process. They encouraged better range-management practices to address the problem of overgrazing, the use of silos to store winter feed, and reseeding the grasslands with a variety of imported grasses. Increasingly, ranchers began to rely more on crops for feed and less on pasture lands.[51]

In an effort to promote a spirit of cohesiveness and cooperation, the CRA published a book in 1914 about prominent Texas ranchers, including South Texans William Henry Jennings, Richard King, Mifflin Kenedy, and John R. Blocker. Notably, there was not one biography of an ethnic Mexican in the entire volume, making it clear that they were excluded from the inner circle of the ranching elite. CRA publicized a new image of the border stockman as urban entrepreneur. He "was no longer marked out in a crowd by a frontiersman type of dress, boots, spurs and such like, but looked as he had become, a substantial and progressive American businessman, a leader in every phase of thought and in every branch of human industry." These ranchers had abandoned the old dugout in the country and had moved to the cities, where they lived in "elegant town mansions, rode in fancy autos, and invested in real estate, tall buildings and insurance companies."[52] They were full participants in the global capitalist economy.

Anglos moved into sheep and goat ranching across southwestern Texas in the first few decades of the twentieth century. An Anglo-Hispanic sheep industry had boomed on the Rio Grande Plain in the first couple of decades after the Civil War but declined in the 1880s. By 1900, sheep and goat ranching in Texas was basically restricted to Edwards, Val Verde, and Kinney counties on the Edwards Plateau, where the ethnic class structure was highly stratified; sheep ranchers there were almost exclusively Anglo-Americans, and the *pastores* and laborers were ethnic Mexicans. Sheep ranching, like cattle ranching in this period, became more capital intensive. Anglo sheep raisers fenced in their lands, managed overgrazing on their pastures, and engaged in scientific breeding programs. The use of mesh-wire fencing, which was fairly effective at keeping out predators like wolves and coyotes, reduced the need for reliance on ethnic Mexican *pastores* to protect the sheep. Imported Merino, Cheviot, and Rambouillet sheep replaced the rugged *chaurros,* which had produced mutton but not very fine wool. New breeds like Corriedales and Delaines adapted well to the arid southwestern Texas landscape and also yielded high-quality wool that satisfied the New England buyers and woolen mills. Around 1900, Del Rio ranchers imported Angora goats from Turkey and sold mohair for use in upholstery and carpets. Ranchers in the area formed the Texas Sheep and Goat Raisers' Association, an organization very similar to the CRA, and cooperative marketing associations. They made Texas the leading sheep producer in the nation by the 1930s.[53]

In contrast to ranching, farming had fewer barriers to entry, at least prior to the 1930s. Farming required less land and fewer expenses. While ranchers had to continue to care for livestock through hard times, farmers could temporarily stop commercial production and resort to subsistence farming without incurring huge expenses. A farm also did not require as much acreage to generate a profit, although farmland was more expensive than ranchland. Many of the new Anglo migrants, who usually had some but not a lot of capital, became farmers. On the whole, with the exception of large growers, they were not considered part of the elite. Within the state as a whole and in South Texas specifically, a divide developed between ranchers and farmers around the turn of the century because of the changing economies of scale in ranching. An "agricultural ladder" existed even among smaller farmers, with owners at the top, tenants in the middle, and sharecroppers near the bottom, just above wage laborers. Anglo farmers in South Texas who did not own land were generally tenant farmers because they usually owned their own tools, tractors, or animals, while landless ethnic Mexicans were either sharecroppers or wage laborers.[54]

Anglo farmers settled primarily in the "Magic Valley" and the "Winter Garden." Some scattered throughout the rest of the region, establishing cotton farms and stock farms, which usually combined the raising of some livestock with the growing of feed crops like milo. In the 1910s and 1920s, land developers in Cameron and Hidalgo counties sold hundreds of small farm tracts, averaging from ten to forty acres in size. Many of the buyers had owned farms or businesses elsewhere that provided enough capital to make a down payment on land, build a house, and invest in seed, animals, and equipment. Local lawyer Franklin Ewers estimated that most of the Valley farmers arrived with somewhere between $5,000 and $20,000 and paid approximately $250 to $300 an acre for irrigated land. Although sales slowed during the 1930s, people continued to move to the area and purchase the tracts. After an excursion to Sharyland between May 31 and June 3, 1931, Jim Luthi of Gage, Oklahoma, put down $500 in cash and signed a promissory note for $1,500 and a vendor's lien note for $2,500 for ten acres. W. A. Carlisle, from Nebraska, put $4,000 down on twenty acres and signed a promissory note for $2,500 and vendor's lien note for $7,500.[55]

Valley farmers practiced diversified farming, often raising hogs, dairy cows, cattle, and chickens alongside cotton, feed crops, vegetables, and fruit trees.

Elma Krumdieck Koch and her husband, Otto, had a farm in Hidalgo County, on which they grew corn and cotton in the summer and cabbage and onions in the winter. They also planted a small orchard. They had sixteen horses and some chickens. In Sharyland, W. L. Bradbury owned 167 acres, on which he grew broom corn and raised hogs, milk cows, and a few horses and mules. Alby Richard Juby raised vegetables and citrus trees on thirty-two acres of land near Donna, Texas. Over the course of the 1920s, more and more farmers devoted most or all of their land to citrus because of its profitability. George Hackney bought 115 acres from American Rio Grande Land & Irrigation Co. near Weslaco in 1919. By 1929, he had planted vegetables on forty acres and devoted the rest to an orchard (fig. 6a–c).[56]

The Winter Garden followed a different pattern as evidenced by average farm size, which, in the lower Rio Grande Valley, was between 46 and 87 acres in the 1920s. By contrast, the average farm in the Winter Garden was more than 1,000 acres, indicating that large agribusinesses owned much of the land. Small farms in the Winter Garden were larger than those in the Valley because of the types of crops grown. Jacob Vincent moved to Dimmit County with his wife and children in 1911. There he purchased 320 acres of land and built an artesian well, pumping plant, and reservoir to irrigate his own land as well as shacks for his temporary Mexican workers. He grew a variety of vegetables, including tomatoes, spinach, onions, peppers, beets, radishes, turnips, and carrots. James Braden of Uvalde raised corn and cotton along with a number of feed crops, including maize, milo, sorghum, and oats.[57] Tension existed between the big and small farmers. One of the largest growers of Bermuda onions, J. G. Sullivan, complained, "The small farmers are carried along on the skirts of the big farmer. We get the labor." Then, because they feared losing the laborers to the large operations, the small farmers would pay workers more, driving up prices.[58]

Although most Anglos wanted to own their own land, many were unable to do so. A considerable amount of land in South Texas was in the hands of absentee owners as well as wealthy merchants. In Hidalgo County, for example, in 1930, there were 1,520 owner-operated farms compared to 857 in 1920, 1,854 tenant farms compared to 549 in 1920, 719 farms operated by partial owners compared to 694 in 1920, and 289 farms operated by managers compared to 32 in 1920. In the farm colonies of the Valley, owners typically would not rent to ethnic Mexicans, so tenant farming by Anglos was relatively common. Some Anglo farmers could buy only small tracts of land, so they rented larger tracts to add to their income. Still others got a start by renting exclusively.[59]

Anglo tenant farmers came from the South as well as the Midwest. Howard Millen's family moved to the Valley in a Model T Ford truck with all of their belongings covered under a tarp in the back. His father rented a farm, bought three mules and a cultivator, and grew cotton in the summer and cucumbers in the winter. Ira Ragsdale, originally from Indiana, planted onions and hay and raised chickens on rented land near Mission in the 1910s. William Duncan owned a half interest in land on which he built his home and then leased an additional thirty-eight acres, where he grew corn and cotton. Peter Bentsen, grandfather of

FIGURE 6. Three Anglo-American farmhouses in the Lower Rio Grande Valley: (a, facing top) farm home with orange orchard, c. 1915. Courtesy of the Margaret H. McAllen Memorial Archives, Museum of South Texas History, Edinburg, Texas; (b, facing bottom) young girls in front of their farm home, c. 1920. Courtesy of the Museum of South Texas History, Edinburg, Texas; (c, above) farm in eastern Hidalgo County, c. 1922. Courtesy, Lower Rio Grande Valley Historical Collection, Library Archives and Special Collections, University of Texas–Pan American.

Senator Lloyd Bentsen Jr., who had arrived in the Valley with limited resources after driving for more than sixteen hundred miles, started off as a tenant farmer. He rented a place in Mission, ran a nursery business, and worked as a land agent for John Shary. By saving money over the course of the 1920s, Peter and his two sons, Lloyd and Elmer, were able to profit from land development when values plummeted in the mid-1930s.[60]

Farming was a predominantly male domain. In 1930, 3,390 men were operating farms compared to 855 women in Hidalgo County and 3,008 men compared to 83 women in Cameron County. Women rarely bought farms and usually became farmers only after receiving an operating farm as an inheritance from a parent or spouse. Ed Lasater saw an opportunity to pitch farm tracts to single women as an investment when he began dividing some of his ranchland into farms and platted the town of Falfurrias in the early twentieth century. Ella Hockaday bought one of those tracts before she moved to Dallas, where she founded a private girls' school in 1913.[61] Martha Furman and Alice Furman, two sisters, operated a seven-acre orange and grapefruit orchard near Donna.

Ethel McManus, a widow, had owned a ten-acre orchard of Valencia orange trees and Marah grapefruit trees since 1925. By the mid-1930s, the income from the orchard was not sufficient, so she went to work as a salesperson in Edinburg. Another widow, Mrs. Annie Penry, ran a twenty-two-acre general farm near Weslaco for several years until her death in 1941.[62]

Although many Anglo farms were family owned and operated, they were, in essence, small, commercially oriented businesses. Farming, like virtually every other field of endeavor at this time, was conceived in business and industrial terms. Farms were "factories in the field." As B. F. Yoakum said, "Now, our soil is a . . . factory whereon we manufacture the products which subsequently make the stock and trade of hotels and restaurants and of the home kitchens. There is no reason why we should not apply to the soil the same principles that we do to the factory."[63] Railroads and land developers partnered to assist farmers in enhancing their productivity. They brought in speakers from places like Texas A&M College to give lectures to groups of up to 150 farmers about scientific farming techniques, including the use of fertilizers, seasonal crop rotation, and pest management. These lectures occurred in "community houses" designed to bring farmers together for business and social purposes. Farm demonstration trains taught about how to grow winter vegetables and citrus.[64]

Small farmers were not exclusively individualistic. They formed organizations in order to help with the growing costs of farming, one of the largest of which was the processing, packing, marketing, and distribution of their crops and produce. Following the example of Southern California, where orange growers had devised the first local coops, in 1923 John Shary and a group of growers organized the first cooperative in the Valley, the Texas Citrus Growers Exchange, which adopted "TexaSweet" as its trade name. Advertisements for the TexaSweet grapefruit appeared in newspapers across the country, in Iowa, Kansas, Ohio, Michigan, Pennsylvania, and even Alberta, Canada, revealing the reach of their marketing efforts.[65]

Farmers in the Valley, resentful over having to pay high water costs to the land developers, also joined together to form municipal irrigation districts, approved by the Texas legislature in 1905, to take over local canals and pumping plants from private companies. These municipal entities could float bonds and tax local farmers to raise the necessary finances and therefore had an advantage over private companies. The farmers could then agree to a flat water-rental rate. In some areas, ranchers resisted the formation of these municipal districts because they had to pay taxes to support them even though they did not benefit from them. In other places, private companies like John Shary's United Irrigation Company retained control of the water.[66]

The American business-oriented mindset transformed labor relations in borderland farming. While Tejanos and earlier Anglo settlers had relied on a patriarchal structure that had considered workers as part of an extended family, many newly arrived Anglos rejected those paternalistic arrangements in favor of voluntary, arms' length business contracts more consistent with their republican, free-labor principles. Their approach to labor corresponded with that of the capitalists in northern Mexico, who had already helped create a migratory work force that worked for wages mainly on a temporary basis. Relations between most Anglos and their ethnic Mexican workers thus became more formal and impersonal. There was also little reciprocity and an unspoken assumption that the workers should remain in their place and show deference to Anglos. More and more of the workers lived in segregated spaces in the towns rather than in shacks on the farms. Anglo restaurant owners often refused to serve ethnic Mexicans at tables, and store owners restricted the hours when they could shop. The groups rarely mixed socially, although Anglos had the freedom to go into bars, restaurants, and movie theaters on the Mexican side of towns.[67]

The movement of farm laborers to the towns was not the only close tie between rural and urban South Texas. Farmers supported many of the local businesses by using their revenues to buy new farm equipment and tools, seed, automobiles, clothing, and appliances from store owners in the towns and cities. Disc cultivators, disc harrows, plows, corn planters, and rakes were common purchases. Farmers bought feed for their mules until tractors began to replace them in the 1920s, and then they needed services, supplies, and fuel. Almost every farmer owned an automobile in the 1920s and 1930s. They paid for rugs, pianos, sofas, and dining suites for their homes and bought clothing from local stores. They also purchased a variety of appliances such as sewing machines, Victrolas, and electric refrigerators and stoves. In 1918 W. L. Bradbury even acquired an "Edison talking machine," or phonograph. Frank Barfield and his family owned a General Electric refrigerator, a Crosley radio, an electric stove, and two Chevrolet cars in 1936.[68]

The relationship between country, city, and the rise of urban businesses is evident in the 1930 census. The lower Rio Grande Valley, which had the largest number of commercially oriented small farms, had the most diverse economy and the greatest number of small businesses. Most workers were not employed in agriculture. In Cameron County, just over one-third (9,828) of all gainfully employed workers were in agriculture, and of those, about two-thirds were farm laborers. There were 3,091 farm owners and tenants. The rest (19,524) worked in a wide variety of businesses, including wholesale and retail trade, hotels, automobile-related services, construction, banks, laundries, and insurance companies. Hidalgo County had a higher proportion involved in agriculture, 48 percent, although it was still not the majority of employed persons in the county. There, too, approximately two-thirds of the people employed in agriculture were farm laborers. By contrast, Tejano-dominated counties where there had been no farm developments supported fewer and less specialized business enterprises. In Starr County, more than 67 percent of the population was employed in agriculture, and the numbers of laborers and farm owners were roughly equal. Similarly, agriculture accounted for 75 percent of all workers in Zapata County.[69]

In the Towns and Cities

Anglos were responsible for beginning many of the new enterprises in the Valley and the Winter Garden (table 3) (see appendix 1 for the total numbers of businesses listed in the R. G. Dun Reference Books and the approximate percentage of non-Hispanic-owned businesses). Anglos dominated almost every sector of the urban economy as they had the rural economy. In addition, they established a wide variety of organizations similar to those in others parts of the country, such as Chambers of Commerce, Rotary Clubs, Masonic Lodges, Kiwanis Clubs, and Elks Clubs, to facilitate networking and business deals. Like the Texas Cattle Raisers' Association for ranchers, these groups provided a source of identity and shared association for members of the urban business class. Some were exclusive, with membership reserved primarily for affluent Anglos, while others, such as the Masonic Lodge, were open to a wider range of participants.[70]

In the 1890s, Brownsville and Laredo served the largest geographic markets and could therefore support the most diverse array of businesses. Customers from northern Mexico, small towns nearby, and surrounding ranches traveled to these border cities to shop for items they could not acquire elsewhere. Advertisements for Brownsville and Laredo businesses in the *Texas State Gazetteer* included general stores, grocery stores, meat markets, saloons, drugstores, liquor stores, cigar shops, saddlery makers, millineries, dressmakers, jewelers, and hardware dealers. Outside of Laredo and Brownsville, however, towns could not support more than a general store or a couple of groceries and meat markets until after 1900.[71]

TABLE 3. Types of non-Hispanic businesses, South Texas border region, 1930

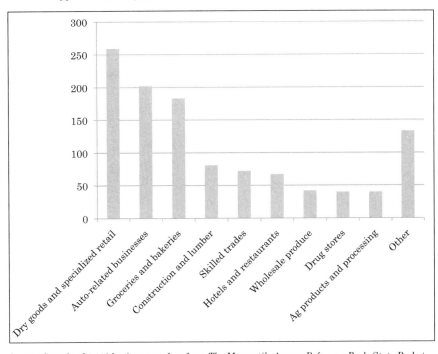

Source: Sample of 1,119 businesses taken from *The Mercantile Agency Reference Book*. State Pocket Edition. Texas. New York: R. G. Dun & Co., 1930.

After 1900, proprietors specialized as the population grew and as the region became more integrated into the US economy. In 1901 R. G. Dun & Co. listed a total of fifty-three businesses in Brownsville, thirteen of which were general stores. By 1938, 369 businesses were listed, only two of which were general stores. The change was even more dramatic in Crystal City in the Winter Garden. In 1910 R. G. Dun listed only two businesses in Crystal City, a grocery store and a planing mill. By 1938, R. G. Dun reported on ninety-five businesses, including bakeries, confectioneries, restaurants, women's ready-to-wear stores, gents' furnishings, furniture and hardware stores, and automobile dealerships. Automobile-related businesses constituted one of the largest growth areas in the region in the 1920s and 1930s. As in other parts of the nation, members of the middle class began buying automobiles in significant numbers during this decade, creating a huge demand for new filling stations, garages, car dealerships, and auto repair shops. Brownsville had one car dealership in 1910. By 1925, it had at least twenty-one automobile-related businesses and sixty-eight by 1935

FIGURE 7. Patteson Motor Company, Brownsville, c. 1920. The proliferation of automobile dealerships and auto-related enterprises reveals the growing importance of the
automobile along the border, especially among the growing Anglo-American middle
class. Courtesy, Robert Runyon Photograph Collection, 08569, Dolph Briscoe Center for
American History, University of Texas at Austin.

(fig. 7). Entertainment-oriented businesses like hotels, restaurants, and movie
theaters also sprang up around the region. Saloons were ubiquitous until Prohibition forced them south of the border in 1920.[72]

Industry along the border was limited prior to the 1960s. With the exception
of a few somewhat primitive oil-refinery operations, most involved agricultural
processing or construction, like brick-making factories. Canning and packing
plants, flour mills, grist mills, and cotton gins dotted the area. They were often owned by only a few individuals, and many were not very large. Palm Valley Canning Company was a partnership operated by George William Russell,
George Barber Russell, and Emery Russell in Raymondville, whose most valuable assets consisted of machinery and equipment worth approximately $6,500.
Lumber yards and brick-making operations existed to provide the materials for
the construction of new homes and businesses.[73]

Although Anglo-owned businesses steadily rose in value prior to the 1930s,
most of them remained rather small. Small is, of course, a relative term. By the
standards of New York City or Chicago, virtually every business along the border

was small. At the height of the region's prosperity, in 1930, only five businesses in all of the key border towns, Brownsville, Laredo, Del Rio, and Eagle Pass, had a value in excess of $1,000,000 (see appendix 2). Sixty-six percent of non-Hispanic-owned businesses had a net worth of less than $10,000 that same year. Values plummeted during the Depression; 48 percent of non-Hispanic-owned businesses had a value of less than $3,000 in 1938 (see appendix 3). Although the region actually had more large businesses, most of them were sizeable corporations based elsewhere that had opened branches in several towns.

Most of the bigger businesses were located in more heavily populated border areas, in Brownsville, Laredo, Del Rio, and Eagle Pass. No one type of business appeared to have paved the way to wealth; high net-worth enterprises included general stores, dry-goods stores, hardware stores, lumber companies, furniture stores, automobile dealers, and wholesale and retail grocery stores. Over time, corporations rather than individuals dominated this category, many of which were based outside the area. Notably, few businesses could continue to grow or even maintain their net worth for more than ten years through boom-and-bust cycles, and many did not outlast the death of their founders. As compared to Jews, Italians, Spaniards, and other European immigrants, Anglo-Americans were actually underrepresented in the category of urban businesses valued at more than $20,000 identified by R. G. Dun & Co. This suggests that the wealthiest Anglos in the area were the land developers, ranchers, and large growers. In fact, R. G. Dun & Co. listed real-estate developer John Shary as the richest Anglo in the region, with a net worth of more than $1,000,000 in the 1920s and 1930s.[74]

Class relations in the towns were somewhat more complex and fluid than in the countryside. The urban business class along the border as a whole was far more diverse than the farmer class and, as the next chapters show, included Europeans, Middle Easterners, Mexicans, and Tejanos in addition to Anglo-Americans. The majority of the newly arrived Anglo business owners and professionals, whose income and assets remained at moderate levels, probably identified with the broader American middle class. Descendants of nineteenth-century Anglo merchants, prominent lawyers, and ranchers still constituted an "old elite" in the region and were joined by a newer elite group of land developers, bankers, wealthy merchants, and industrialists. At the lower end of the middle class were the owners of extremely small shops, usually less than $500 in value (between $4,500 and $5,500 in today's dollars compared to the 1920s and 1930s), and self-employed skilled artisans, like carpenters, painters, tanners, saddlers, wheelwrights, plumbers, and blacksmiths. These skilled artisans were listed in R. G. Dun because they had their own businesses.[75]

Anglos who moved to the towns found the greatest number of opportunities in consumer goods and services. Demand for the ever-increasing array of products mass-produced by industries in the United States increased over time as the population expanded. Everyone was a consumer, from the poorest workers to the wealthiest developers. In a place where even foodstuffs had once been scarce, South Texas merchants brought America's growing culture of abundance to the border.[76]

Merchants in South Texas had three markets in which they could participate. One was the transnational market, which was essentially a continuation of nineteenth-century patterns of cross-border trade with Anglos, Europeans, Tejanos, and Mexicans who lived both north and south of the border. The partnership of A. Schmidt & Co. provides an illustration. William Pfeffer of Louisiana started a furniture business in Laredo with A. Schmidt in 1893. To open a new branch of the business, Schmidt moved to Mexico City, where he sold liquor and furniture. Pfeffer stayed in Laredo but sold furniture to customers primarily in Mexico. Roy Lowry had a furniture store in Del Rio and sold to Anglos and ethnic Mexicans in the area, including residents of Ciudad Acuña. Henry Dewey Tobias, a merchant in Brownsville in the 1920s, did most of his business with other merchants in Matamoros and Monterrey.[77]

The *1926 Standard Blue Book, South Texas Edition,* reveals the ongoing importance of cross-border business relations and activity in the first few decades of the twentieth century. It included descriptions of Matamoros and Nuevo Laredo and biographies of Mexican businesspeople from those towns in the Who's Who section. Anglos viewed the potential of cross-border trade as important for the growth of new Valley towns, not just the older border cities. Plans were in process to build a bridge across the Rio Grande to Reynosa, only ten miles from Pharr, "thus making it a port of entry, and over which the Southern Pacific will also enter Mexico, thus contributing to the material growth and prosperity of Pharr."[78]

Tariffs complicated cross-border trade, however, deterring some from pursuing it. During the Porfiriato, tariffs were a major source of government revenue for both nations and an important tool for protecting the development of local industries. The United States and Mexico had to balance these interests against the desire to promote international trade. In general, both nations engaged in protectionism to varying degrees in an effort to stimulate industrial expansion.

Merchants looked for ways to circumvent the regulations and fees in order to maximize their profits. The willingness of large US companies like Florsheim Shoe Company of Chicago to hire brokers to assist them in smuggling products into northern Mexico evidences how acceptable and widespread the practice was. After 1910, tariffs and customs regulations continued to be a permanent feature of the business landscape, but issues of border security began to take precedence. Income taxes replaced tariff revenues as the primary source of federal revenue in the United States, and there were fewer prosecutions for smuggling in South Texas, causing illicit trade to flourish even more.[79]

For those who did not want to deal with the complications of international commerce, the Anglo-American middle class constituted a large, new market. These Anglos had more disposable income than the typical Mexican consumer. As the Anglo population along the border expanded, it appears that most Anglo business owners preferred dealing primarily with other Anglos. European, Jewish, and Hispanic merchants were far more likely than Anglos to engage in cross-border trade.[80]

A few Anglo merchants sold almost exclusively to Mexican laborers. In the Winter Garden counties of Dimmit and Zavala, the wages received by agricultural laborers supported most of the groceries and general stores because large growers, rather than small farmers, dominated the area. In some cases, the large growers entered into special arrangements with merchants to provide necessities for their workers. The workers would buy on credit, and the growers would pay the merchant, receiving a discount or "kickback" in return. In other cases, the local consumer market was so small that merchants would readily sell to anyone who was willing to buy, regardless of ethnicity.[81]

Most of the border businesses Anglo-Americans started were small operations organized as individual proprietorships or partnerships. Many of these people, like James Hockaday, who ran a drugstore in Port Isabel, leased space and kept a simple set of books, one to record customer purchases, the other for checks. Some, like Lee Reader, a grocer in San Benito, spent additional money on adding machines and cash registers and displayed their wares in glass cases. They relied on family members and Mexican workers to serve as clerks, stock shelves, and haul boxes. Like small businesses of today, most had minimal profit margins and were prone to fail. The enterprises of Monty Colvin and Robert Jeffreys were fairly typical. Colvin moved from Oklahoma to Harlingen in 1929 and set up a small dry-goods store. When that business went bankrupt during the Depression, he and his wife started a tiny confectionery that remained in business through the rest of the decade but had an estimated value of less than $500. Robert Jeffreys opened a small bookstore and printing shop in Mission that was worth about $500 in 1918. The shop generated enough income to enable him to buy a house and a 1936 Chevrolet Town Sedan DeLuxe but failed in 1939.[82]

Prior connections and a preexisting asset base enabled some businesses to expand more rapidly than others. August Richter, who founded a department store in Laredo, started out with a medium-sized business and became quite wealthy. Richter's father, Charles A. Richter, was a German immigrant who had become a successful merchant in San Antonio. Because of his father's connections, August was able to work as an apprentice for two of the leading mercantile establishments in the city. He moved to Laredo in 1888 and partnered with Mr. D. Stumberg before opening his own store in 1898. In 1901, his net worth was somewhere between $10,000 and $20,000, not an insubstantial business, but by 1925 it had grown to over $200,000, or approximately $2,000,000 in today's dollars. His success was attributed to "the large and varied stocks constantly carried coupled with business methods which make friends of all their patrons, and every year the goods of the store go into a wider territory."[83]

Most border businesses acquired and maintained customers primarily through personal relationships during this period, although those who could afford it advertised in local newspapers. Typical advertisements were fairly simple, with few or no designs. Clothing and department-store advertisements became more elaborate in the 1920s and 1930s in order to compete with the chain stores and mail-order companies. Local advice columns indicated, however, that most small businesses believed that the best they had to offer their customers was a fair price and knowledge of their needs. The mail-order catalogues perhaps offered a larger and more intriguing array of products, but the local merchant "sells more besides goods; he sells service, courtesy and accommodation." Chain stores were bland, impersonal, and uniform, unlike the colorful and lively neighborhood store, where one might hear the latest gossip and drink a cup of coffee with the owner before shopping.[84]

While most of the Anglo business owners in the towns and cities of South Texas were men, a few Anglo women found opportunities as well (see appendix 4). Most of their businesses remained comparatively small; in 1938, sixty-three out of eighty female proprietorships owned by non-Hispanics had a value of less than $1,000. Yet there were exceptions. As early as 1892, Miss A. Lorber, a single woman, a seamstress who was reportedly very hardworking, honest, and wealthy, was one of sixteen women listed among sixty-two individuals in Brownsville in 1892 who had property valued in excess of $5,000.[85]

Female entrepreneurs were not a new phenomenon along the border. Since the Spanish period, women had owned and managed their own property. Most women seemed to have started businesses to support themselves or their families. Most female proprietors were widows like Lula Bonnett de Bona, Mrs. A. Siros, and Mrs. E. V. Sprowl, who managed dry-goods stores, hardware stores, and automobile shops long after their husbands had died. The frequency with which women outlived their husbands led one man to comment, "I believe every man should put into his wife's hands some property to manage for herself, since life is very uncertain and death is very certain. If he should die, why then she knows something about handling business."[86] Women also supported husbands whose businesses did not provide enough income. Lee Dillon's wife rented out rooms above her husband's store to schoolteachers in the area; the store produced little revenue. Similarly, Joseph Netzer's wife took in boarders during a period when his business was failing. The number of female proprietors increased substantially in the 1930s, providing further evidence that income was a primary motivator.[87]

Yet for some, starting a business was more than simply a source of income; it represented autonomy and provided an outlet for their talents. A Mrs. Koneman seems to have been motivated by more than money. She was the manager of a women's clothing corporation with four female stockholders, all of whom were married. She had previously owned her own dress shop in Crystal City and a novelty shop in Carrizo Springs before starting the Crystal City Dress Shop. She lived apart from her husband, although they were not separated, in order to manage the business. She owned five rental houses that provided sufficient income to pay the couple's living expenses, and the dress and gift shops actually lost money.[88]

The most common types of female-owned businesses along the border were millineries and ladies' dress shops, which paralleled the situation in the rest of the country (table 4). Some women crafted dresses and hats by hand while others sold the new "ready-to-wear" clothing manufactured in large cities in the United States. Demand for fashionable clothing increased with the growth of the population, and most towns had at least one or two of these female enterprises. A notice appeared in the *Brownsville Daily Herald* on March 2, 1909, advising readers that Mrs. Scrivener had opened a millinery shop in the Aschenberger Building. She "is experienced and solicits the patronage of ladies throughout the

TABLE 4. Types of women-owned businesses, South Texas border region, 1938

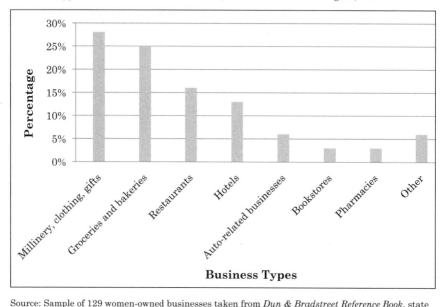

Source: Sample of 129 women-owned businesses taken from *Dun & Bradstreet Reference Book,* state pocket edition (Texas) (New York: Dun & Bradstreet, 1938).

Valley."[89] In the 1920s, Mrs. Berdelle Harris ran "The Frock Shop" in the Franklin Building at the corner of Salinas and Hidalgo streets in Laredo.

Sisters Marie Miller and Katherine Miller's "The Justine Shop" and Dorothy Haas's millinery and dress store were both in the commercial district of Edinburg. In 1920 Miss Eva Preuss, a dressmaker, advertised several times a month in the *Brownsville Herald,* promising "quick service" and "reasonable prices." As department stores started carrying more and more ladies' ready-to-wear clothing, smaller shops found a niche by continuing to supply custom-made dresses. They advertised by participating in style shows hosted by local ladies' clubs.[90]

Women were also successful in opening and operating boardinghouses, small hotels, restaurants, bakeries, and grocery stores. In the small town of Winter Haven, Mrs. Sudie Knoblauch, a widow, had a general store that catered mainly to ethnic Mexicans. She and her two daughters lived on the top floor of a two-story frame building and operated the store on the first floor. Her inventory included Folgers and Maxwell House coffee, Jell-O, apple butter, canned vegetables, Hershey's cocoa, canned vegetables, Palmolive dishwashing liquid, asbestos stove rings, rainproof lanterns, combs, hairbrushes, curling irons, work shirts and gloves, Mexican hats, and a variety of pharmaceuticals, including camphor oil and "Grandma's Liniment," which she placed on shelves and in glass display cases. She carried both life and fire insurance. In her home, she had an electric range and a Frigidaire, among her other home furnishings, and a set of twelve books. She owned a cow and a 1932 Ford sedan.[91]

The experiences of Donna Hooks Fletcher reveal the range of business endeavors that Anglo women who were entrepreneurs could pursue along the border, given the motivation and the right circumstances. Donna Fletcher was a divorcée, which carried substantial stigma at the time, but as the daughter of Thomas J. Hooks, a merchant and one of the founders of the town of Donna and the La Blanca Agricultural Company in Hidalgo County, she did have some advantages that others lacked. She became the first postmaster of Donna and its first notary public, opened the town's first boardinghouse, and built its first office building. Her father gave her one hundred acres of land in Hidalgo County in 1908. She borrowed money to clear the land, cultivate and plant crops, and construct a small house, a "shack," as she called it. In her words, "Astride my pony, I daily went forth with a gang of Mexican laborers into the wilderness . . . We commenced chopping out the mesquite, cactus, *huisache,* cat claw, etc. and after a while had hewed out a clearing large enough for a garden and flowers and the site for a small house." She bought some Jersey cows, began a dairy operation, and sold sweet cream butter. In the early 1920s, she opened a department store, "a sort of cross between an elegant general store of that day and a high fashioned ladies and gentlemen's specialty shop." She referred to herself as an "imaginative merchandiser." As a later chapter explores more fully, she, like many others, had to cope with reversals of fortune as a result of her own mistakes and the waxing and waning of the boom cycles.[92]

· · ·

It was the promise of economic opportunity that lured many thousands of Anglo-Americans like Donna Fletcher's family to the South Texas borderlands around the turn of the century. They followed the railroads, which were part of a larger wave of US investment in northern Mexico during the Porfiriato. Promotional campaigns endeavored to convince them that this region, once described in US newspapers and magazines as foreign, exotic, and volatile, was really just another corner of the American West that offered bounteous prospects along with all of the amenities they were used to in their own communities. Regardless of whether they recognized it, they functioned within larger transnational networks of commodity, produce, and crop distribution, and their success and survival depended at least in part on Mexico.

Few of the Anglo-Americans who came lived a transnational lifestyle; instead, as they settled down, they sought to make the region look and feel more familiar, like the parts of the United States from which they had come. They brought with them the entrepreneurial values that permeated US culture and society and created a more competitive business environment. They quickly dominated many areas of the borderland economy, especially agriculture. They also brought with them American middle-class culture and set a new standard of living by decorating their homes and buying cars and appliances. Some became wealthy, but most were ordinary middle- to lower-middle-class Americans trying to live the American dream. In the areas where irrigated agriculture predominated, they contributed to the creation of a more ethnically stratified society due to their dependence on Mexican labor. Yet they did not completely change border society; they became part of its multicultural mosaic, adding a new dimension but never completely erasing its past. The next two chapters explore other facets of the expanding business class in the South Texas borderlands.

4

SEARCHING FOR THE
AMERICAN DREAM

O N OCTOBER 22, 1907, the *Laredo Times* reported, "Nine tongues are represented among the several travelers who are today Uncle Sam's guests at the Immigration Department of the city. And a queer mingling of strange sounds and incomprehensible voices filled the Hall this morning as these men of many strange lands and many strange tongues endeavored each to motor the car of conversation in their midst."[1] The "men of many strange lands" included Syrians, Russian Poles, Slovaks, and Croatians.

Despite the images created by the promoters favoring settlement by middle-class Anglo-American families, hundreds of foreign-born immigrants from countries other than Mexico arrived in the border region, driven by the search for greater economic opportunities than they could find in their home-lands. The Texas-Mexico border had long attracted immigrants from Europe who came to trade in Mexico and forged business partnerships with Americans and Mexicans in the area, and this pattern continued in the twentieth century. The presence of a cosmopolitan business class made up of Germans, French, Irish, English, Scots, Italians, Spaniards, Mexicans, and Americans created a somewhat fluid society that was more open to immigrants from southern and eastern Europe, Jews, and Syrians than that of other parts of the United States.

Foreign immigrants made their way to the South Texas borderlands through Ellis Island in New York City, the ports of New Orleans and Galveston, and Mexico. Hundreds disembarked at Veracruz and moved into northern Mexico and over the river into South Texas. They settled in Brownsville, Laredo, Eagle Pass, and Del Rio as well as the Valley farm towns. In 1930, the foreign immigrant population, excluding those from Mexico, totaled 1,068 in Cameron County and 1,164 in Hidalgo County. Webb County, where Laredo is located, had 327, while Eagle Pass and Del Rio had 87 and 130, respectively. Fewer traveled to the interior border region. Only 38 non-Mexican foreigners were living in Starr County, and 1 took up residence in Zapata County. Capitalist development and urban growth brought greater diversity.[2]

Anglo-Americans from places like Iowa, Indiana, Nebraska, or Oklahoma did not always fully accept the foreigners they found in their midst. They shared the attitudes of Americans in other parts of the country. As historian John Higham notes, "By western European [and hence US] standards, the masses of southern and eastern Europe were educationally deficient, socially backward, and bizarre in appearance."[3] Local newspaper articles almost always noted whether a person was a Syrian, an Italian, or a Pole. The *Laredo Times* reported that the "nationalities which furnish the greatest percentage of our foreign criminal class" included Italians, Poles, Syrians, and Lithuanians. They were "ignorant" and lacking in any "concept of liberty and freedom."[4] During Prohibition, the *Laredo Times* printed an article declaring that "The immigration of low-class Europeans is a far greater menace to our country than the whiskey traffic ever was."[5] Evidence of prejudicial attitudes among Anglo-Americans from the larger region exists as well. In an interview by Paul Taylor, the county superintendent of schools in Gonzalez County, said, "We don't like the Sicilians, or the Austrians, Bohemians, Poles . . . we have here." Another man referred to Greeks as "white Mexicans."[6]

Prejudicial attitudes may have precluded Russian Jews, Italians, Spaniards, Syrians, and others from interacting socially or intermarrying with Anglo-Americans but generally did not affect their ability to engage in business; Jews, Italians, and Spaniards in particular ranked among the wealthiest businesspeople in the South Texas borderlands. The immigrants' foreignness may have actually enhanced their capacity to cultivate contacts in both the Anglo and Tejano communities and thereby expand their businesses. Whether they were interacting with Mexican nationals in Matamoros or Anglos in Harlingen, they were operating in an alien context. The adaptability this required seemed to have made many of them very adept at navigating the cultural and social frontiers of borderland society and also at nurturing relationships in diverse communities. Moreover, the fact that these immigrants were not Mexican, Indian, or black opened a door for them to be accepted, to varying degrees, into Anglo society.[7]

EUROPEANS AND CANADIANS

The majority of non-Mexican immigrants, roughly 75 percent, came from western Europe and Canada. Among the western Europeans, Germans, Swedes, and Danes predominated. Western Europeans and Canadians successfully assimilated into Anglo-American border society because they shared a similar ethnicity, culture, and Protestant faith and, in the case of Canadians and immigrants from the British Isles, the same language. They were more likely than other foreign immigrants to buy farms. George Federolf from Germany had a dairy farm north of Brownsville in 1917. Near Edinburg, J. W. Petrie had moved from Canada to raise corn and cotton on a small six-acre farm. John Waldorf, another German, planted citrus trees on sixteen acres near Los Fresnos in the Valley in the 1930s. Julius and Kate Johnson of Norway grew cotton, corn, sorghum, potatoes, tomatoes, and cabbage on seventy acres near Rio Hondo. Some had settled elsewhere before moving to South Texas, such as Clara and Peter Dicken from Germany, who were living in Chicago when they heard about the sale of farm tracts in the Valley. They bought twelve acres in 1930 and planted an orchard of orange and grapefruit trees.[8]

Others established businesses in the towns. Joseph Netzer, who was born in Frankfurt, Germany, in 1863, moved as a boy of sixteen to the United States, living in New Jersey and Philadelphia for a time before enlisting in the army. He fought the Apaches in Arizona and New Mexico and then moved to Laredo in 1889. By 1900, he had set up a plumbing and hardware business, following an established pattern of Germans in Mexico, who dominated the hardware industry. His store was on the first floor of a two-story brick building on Lincoln Street, and he lived with his family on the second floor. Netzer served customers in Laredo and Nuevo Laredo as well as Monterrey and Victoria in Mexico. John Buenz, who left Denmark as a young man, originally settled in New Braunfels. He moved to Laredo in 1881, where he started a lumber business with George Pfeuffer, worth at least $75,000 in 1918.[9]

Southern Europeans, although less accepted in other parts of the United States, fit in well along the border, where Catholic Spaniards and Italians had long been part of the elite. Spaniards dominated the small Hispanic professional class, which included lawyers like Emilio Forto and Agustín Celaya of Brownsville. They and their descendants continued to rank among the wealthiest within the Spanish-speaking community. Francisco Yturria's estate had a value in excess of $1,000,000 in 1918, six years after his death. Celestino Barreda was the only individual entrepreneur in Brownsville whose businesses were valued in excess of $1,000,000 by R. G. Dun & Co. in 1930, and he had the highest possible credit rating. Celestino Barreda's uncles had started a mercantile house in Matamoros in the 1830s and later moved to Brownsville. He left his birthplace of La Penilla in Santander, Spain, in 1871 at the age of thirteen to join them. Celestino Barreda started his own dry-goods store when he came of age. He eventually bought up ranchlands and town lots in the area and invested in sugar plantations in Cuba. He became a vice president of First National Bank of Brownsville in 1920 and organized the Texas Bank & Trust Company. He lost much of his fortune when he filed for bankruptcy in 1935.[10]

Juan Armengol of Laredo was another wealthy Spaniard in the region who became an important supplier of local ethnic Mexican merchants. Originally from Cataluña, Spain, he engaged in business in Havana, New York, and Torréon, Coahuila. For a time, he owned a ranch in Chihuahua but moved to Laredo in 1899, where he set up a very profitable wholesale grocery business. He later bought a farm near Laredo, where he planted fifty thousand citrus trees. Between 1918 and 1930 R. G. Dun & Co. reported a net worth of approximately $200,000. Upon Armengol's death in 1930, his nephew Antonio inherited his estate, but due to difficulties during the Great Depression, he faced heavy losses.[11]

Italians and their descendants had been an integral part of the business class in the border towns since the mid-nineteenth century. The Campione brothers, for example, who had arrived in the 1840s, started out as petty merchants. As they became more and more affluent, their descendants owned land and businesses in the lower Rio Grande Valley. Once Anglo-Americans became dominant in the early twentieth century, they changed their name to Champion, indicating some possible concern over their ethnicity in the new environment.[12]

Miguel Volpe, born in Italy, had moved to Matamoros with his parents in the 1860s. He made his way to Guerrero, Mexico, opening a store there in the 1870s. He became a wealthy merchant and purchased extensive ranchlands in the border region, including a 150,000-acre ranch near Monterrey, Mexico and a 22,000-acre ranch in Laredo. He, his Mexican wife, and his children moved to Laredo permanently during the Mexican Revolution. He died there in 1913. Three of his sons, Arturo, Martin, and Ludovico, identified as Mexicans in the 1930 census, formed a partnership and established an extensive wholesale and retail grocery business, a coffee-roasting plant, and a pastry plant in Laredo, with an estimated value of between $200,000 and $300,000. Their sister, Alicia Volpe de Theriot, lived across the river in Nuevo Laredo.[13]

FIGURE 8. Joe Collavo and Butch Stutzenbaker, McAllen meat market, c. 1922. Courtesy of the Margaret H. McAllen Memorial Archives, Museum of South Texas History, Edinburg, Texas.

Italians and Greeks continued to migrate to South Texas after the railroads arrived. Population growth, mechanized agriculture, high tariffs, and industrial growth displaced peasants and artisans in rural villages throughout Italy as well as neighboring Greece in the late nineteenth and early twentieth centuries, spurring ongoing emigration. Most ended up in the industrial cities of the United States, but a few made their way to the Texas-Mexico border. Organized efforts brought some, such as a recruitment initiative by Governor Jim Hogg and Italian ambassador Baron Mayar des Planches to convince Italians to settle and plant vineyards, raise grapes, and make wine near Del Rio. Others came alone. Few had much capital; like Joe Collavo, who owned a meat market in McAllen, they set up small businesses scattered throughout the towns of the region (fig. 8). In Laredo, James Margas and Santiago Pappas both operated confectionaries, an industry dominated by Greeks throughout the United States. Gus Marinos ran a cigar store in Eagle Pass, and Spiro Allis opened a Greek restaurant in Brownsville in 1917.[14]

Some became wealthy. Frank and Rocco Caffarelli built a wholesale grocery operation that supplied retail stores all over South Texas, including a number owned by ethnic Mexicans. According to R. G. Dun & Co., in 1930, they had a credit rating of B+1, which meant their creditworthiness was excellent, and their business was worth between $300,000 and $500,000, or between $3.2 and $5.4 million in today's dollars. They developed a reputation as generous philanthropists.[15] Like the Caffarelli brothers, Rocco, Pasquel, and Leonardo de Bona emigrated from Italy to San Antonio, where they set up a fruit and confectionary business. However, in the late nineteenth century, San Antonio was a thriving city with a considerable amount of competition. In the 1890s Rocco and Leonardo saw an opportunity to advance by moving to Eagle Pass, where they set up a major grocery business and a dry-goods store in a large brick building on Main Street in the heart of the commercial district. They also had a business across the border in Piedras Negras. Rocco married into a local banking family, the Bonnets. When the brothers died, their wives, with the help of their sons, managed the stores for many more years. In 1936, local Anglos honored them as "pioneer citizens" and "progressive business men," phrases that signaled acknowledgement of their place at the top of border society.[16]

Probably the most remarkable story is that of Antonio Bruni, an orphan who left Italy in 1872 at the age of sixteen to live with his uncle and work as an apprentice for A. B. Frank Co. in San Antonio for five years. He moved to Laredo in 1877 to start a small grocery and dry-goods business with his brother, Luigi. His business expanded substantially after the arrival of the railroad in 1880, enabling him to set up a second store in Nuevo Laredo. He invested his profits in land and livestock on both sides of the border. The *Laredo Times* reported in July 1897 that he had imported 950 head of cattle. He kept substantial herds of cattle and sheep on his 200,000-acre ranch, which spanned Webb and Zapata counties. He was also a significant player in the Laredo real estate market, purchasing, leasing, and selling hundreds of town lots during his lifetime. By 1918, he was the wealthiest man in Laredo. He became active in local politics, serving as tax assessor, county commissioner, and county treasurer. He was also a director of Milmo National Bank. In 1930, shortly before Bruni's death in August 1931, R. G. Dun & Co. reported a net worth of more than $1,000,000.[17]

Many of the southern and eastern Europeans remained on the edges of Anglo society. Their occupation, income, and consumption patterns resembled those of elite and middle-class Anglos, but their culture and ethnicity made it difficult for them to fully integrate socially, except in a few places like Laredo, where there was considerable mixing. Some moved more comfortably in circles of elite Mexicans and Tejanos. Antonio Barreda of Brownsville was still unable to speak English very well in the 1930s and had to use his sons as interpreters. Barreda's son had married into a Tejano ranching family. An Anglo-American lawyer referred to customs among "your people" when he was questioning him, revealing that he did not consider him part of the Anglo community. Others sought to differentiate themselves from Mexicans even though they regularly did business with them. Paul Taylor interviewed a Greek factory owner in Eagle Pass who had lived for some time in Mexico City. He had lost his business during the Mexican Revolution and moved to Piedras Negras. In 1926, he decided to cross over to the Texas side of the border. He explained that Greeks had fully embraced the entrepreneurial values of the United States. "The Mexicans don't get ahead while the Greeks do because the Mexicans haven't the ambition—they spend all or more than they make—the Greeks spend less." The experience of these groups was not unique to South Texas; it occurred throughout the US-Mexico borderlands during this period as people struggled over the definition of who was an American and who was not.[18]

JEWS

First- and second-generation Jews of both Ashkenazi and Sephardic heritage settled in the South Texas borderlands as they did in other parts of the American West. Around the latter part of the nineteenth century, American Jewish culture merged the image of the western frontier as a place of unlimited opportunity, openness, and bounteousness with the biblical concept of a "desert promised land" to create a unique vision of the possibilities of life for Jews in the West, according to historian Bryan Stone.[19] The West's pluralistic and relatively amorphous society offered potential for greater economic mobility and social integration than many other places in the United States. Attracted by this potential, Jews migrated to hundreds of western towns as mining and agricultural booms sparked growth. In 1880, San Francisco's Jewish population was second only to that of New York in the United States. By the turn of the century, thousands of eastern European Jews were residing in the multicultural neighborhood of Boyle Heights in Los Angeles.[20] As they settled down and formed communities in this new environment, Jews nurtured cross-cultural relationships while maintaining their own distinctiveness. They became prominent in the region's commercial and civic life.[21]

The first wave of Jewish migrants to the Texas-Mexico borderlands had come from France and Germany in the early to mid-nineteenth century. They and their descendants had more or less assimilated into Anglo-Hispanic borderland society by the turn of the century. A new wave of Jews from Russia and various parts of eastern Europe arrived in the border region after 1900, a small part of a much larger stream of Jews fleeing violent pogroms and intense discrimination in their homelands. Unlike the earlier migrants, the Russian and eastern European Jews assimilated more slowly; they spoke Yiddish and continued to practice their Orthodox Jewish faith. Most initially traveled through Ellis Island and settled in New York City, the center of Jewish life in the United States, or in the nearby cities of Philadelphia, Boston, and Baltimore, which also had heavily populated Jewish neighborhoods. Anglo-American attitudes toward Jews in these cities steadily worsened as more and more arrived.[22] An editorial in the *Boston Herald* called for "a restriction on Jews, allowing them a single quota for the whole body; intelligent Jews know that nothing could be more unfortunate for the Jews than the Judaizing of America, at which many short-sighted Jewish leaders aim."[23] The economic development of the South Texas borderlands provided an opportunity to escape the congestion of the northeastern ghettoes, growing anti-Semitism, and stagnating prospects.

Jewish migration into Texas increased between 1890 and 1940. In 1878, there were only about 3,300 Jews in Texas; by 1900, that figure had grown to 15,000 and 49,196 by 1937. Most congregated in the larger urban centers of Dallas, Houston, and San Antonio, but others moved to more remote areas, creating a widespread presence throughout the state. San Antonio, the largest urban center in South Texas, had a Jewish community numbering about 8,000 by 1927 and therefore became a base for many families and individuals who did business in the lower Rio Grande Valley and the border towns of Laredo, Eagle Pass, and Del Rio. Some Jewish migrants came on their own, while others were part of organizational efforts. Jacob Schiff, a prominent Jewish banker in New York City, organized the Galveston Plan, which operated from 1907 until about 1914 and helped move about 10,000 Jews to Texas. Similarly, the Hebrew Immigrant Aid Society encouraged Jews like Morris Davis to move to South Texas by claiming that they would experience a healthier climate and more business opportunities.[24]

The establishment of Jewish institutions along the border revealed the presence and expansion of the Jewish community in the region. Jews arrived in Laredo/Nuevo Laredo with the railroads. Morris Hirsch held Rosh Hashanah services for the small cross-border community in his home in October 1881. The *Laredo Times* often included a calendar of the Jewish holy days, and local Jewish merchants typically closed their businesses on Yom Kippur and Rosh Hashanah.

Laredo had a Jewish cemetery by 1907 and a Young Men's Hebrew Association and local congregation, B'nai Israel, by 1916. Albert Granoff organized a Hebrew school in 1919, and the community began gathering for services on the High Holy Days in the Western Union building on Flores Street. With the arrival of more eastern European Jews in the 1920s, the community split into Reformed and Orthodox congregations. In part because of this Reform/Orthodox divide, Laredo did not have a synagogue until 1938. Its Jewish population totaled about 128 in 1927 and 175 in 1937. About sixty Jews lived in Nuevo Laredo during the same time period.[25]

Despite the presence of Jewish merchants in the Matamoros/Brownsville area since the early nineteenth century, for many years the only evidence of Jewish community life in the Lower Rio Grande Valley was the Hebrew Cemetery, founded in 1868 on a plot of land purchased by the Hebrew Benevolent Society from Charles Stillman. In 1882, the Matamoros/Brownsville Jewish community had established a Hebrew school. The Bollack family of Brownsville held High Holy services in their homes from the 1870s to the 1920s. In the 1920s, merchant Sam Perl began serving as a lay rabbi to a diverse congregation of Orthodox, Reform, and Conservative Jews when he saw that a number were attending Episcopalian and Catholic services for lack of a better alternative. Brownsville's first synagogue was erected in 1931.[26] Mercedes became the center of the eastern European Jewish community of the Valley in the 1920s. In the 1920s and 1930s, it had the largest Jewish population of any town along the border, numbering about 250 in 1927 and 315 in 1937. Jews in Mercedes constructed a synagogue in 1936 that drew from the surrounding towns. After 1940, Jews moved out of Mercedes as its commercial district declined and into the rapidly growing cities of McAllen and Harlingen. Both towns opened synagogues in the early 1950s.[27]

Jews who moved to the border region participated in a variety of endeavors, but in the 1880 to 1940 time period, most were dry-goods merchants, a reflection of their dominant ownership of the garment industry in the United States. This pattern had its roots in Russia and other parts of Europe where Jews had moved into urban areas to pursue trade and artisan work because they were often prohibited from owning land. Jews carried on this commercial tradition in the United States. In 1880, Jews in New York City owned 90 percent of the wholesale clothing dealerships. They developed extensive cross-country distribution networks through which they supplied Jewish merchants operating small stores in remote, rural areas throughout the American South and West. Despite their overrepresentation in the retail trade, a few Jewish families acquired farms and ranches in the West and continued a tradition of cultivation of the land that was deeply rooted in ancient Jewish culture.[28]

Throughout the American West, many young Jewish men advanced economically by starting out in very tiny enterprises and then using their revenues to gradually expand them in different geographic locations. They would peddle wares in one town and move once they had enough profits to open a store. As they pursued socioeconomic advancement, they moved to more heavily populated urban areas, where they could serve a larger market. They also often moved when they experienced failure in one location.[29] The lives of Sam Greenfield and Esidor Pupkin in the border region illustrate this pattern of geographic mobility. Greenfield, a Lithuanian immigrant, left his family in Baltimore in the late 1890s, while he migrated from place to place, trying to start businesses that could support them. He first moved to Cincinnati for three years. In 1903, he started a business in San Antonio, which he operated for eight years before it failed. He then traveled to Mission in 1915 to open another store with a couple of hundred dollars and $1,700 worth of stock.[30]

Around 1880, when he was in his early twenties, Esidor Pupkin emigrated from Poland to New York City. In 1885, he moved to Tennessee, where his first son, Benjamin, was born. There he opened a small dry-goods store in the town of Ripley, located in the far western part of the state, not far from the Mississippi River. By 1909, he had moved upriver to the larger city and major western wholesale distribution center of St. Louis, where he opened a second store. He operated Pupkin Brothers Dry Goods Business in St. Louis for only two years before filing for bankruptcy in 1911. Pupkin then decided to move south and try his luck there. He and his son, Ben, opened a store in San Benito, a new farm town near Brownsville, drawing on suppliers he had probably used in St. Louis. Esidor filed for bankruptcy in Brownsville in 1915 after the San Benito store suffered losses. By then, his son, Ben, was old enough to start his own store with his brothers and help his father out. Ben later started another dry-goods shop in Harlingen with his brothers Milton, Joe, and Alex.[31]

Jews owned most of the clothing and department stores in the Texas-Mexico borderlands, which made them central to local communities because it was through these retail establishments that American consumer capitalism most deeply penetrated the region. By the turn of the century, fashion had become the primary vehicle through which ordinary middle-class men and women could experience glamour, luxury, and the exotic. The fleeting nature of fashion trends provided a source of constant demand. Cosmetics, perfumes, and home decorations followed fashion as objects of desire, and Jewish merchants carried all of these products.[32]

The Jewish border retail community was transnational; many Jews moved in and out of the United States and Mexico, making them adept at doing business with both Anglos and ethnic Mexicans. Morris Hirsch moved to Brownsville at a young age to work for local Jewish merchant Solomon Schwartz as a clerk. He started a dry-goods business in Nuevo Laredo in 1874 and became a prominent rancher in Webb County in the 1890s. Because of his wealth, he was an important source of loans for other ranchers. In 1908, he served as vice president of First State Bank in Benavides. His son Isaac was involved in City Drug Co. of Laredo and later became director of Union National Bank. Ben Freudenstein grew up in Parral, Chihuahua, a mining town, and El Paso, Texas. At the age of thirty-six, he moved to Brownsville to open the Valley Wholesale Dry Goods Business. Brothers Solomon and Ephraim Block, born in France, started one of the longest-standing mercantile houses in Rio Grande City, S. Block & Co., where they sold to customers in Mexico and the United States. Ephraim's three sons, Pierre, Gaston, and Robert, started a customs brokerage house in Laredo and Nuevo Laredo in 1928 along with several prominent Tejanos. Pierre's ability to speak four languages was advertised as of great benefit to his customers. Brothers Israel and Nathan Goldberg, immigrants from Lithuania, worked as traveling salesmen in Nuevo Laredo in the late 1920s. Israel became a Mexican citizen and opened a business in Nuevo Laredo in 1929, while Nathan started an army and navy surplus store in Laredo. In the mid-1940s, Israel immigrated to the United States and took over his brother's business. In order to expand the store's customer base, Israel renamed it "Casa Raul," and he became known as "Don Raul."[33]

Although some came only temporarily to get a start and move elsewhere, others stayed. Some operated small, local storefronts, while others ran large department stores. Michael Riskind owned the major department store in Eagle Pass for many years. Born in Russia, he moved with his family to Chicago as a child. He left Chicago as a young man in his twenties after he lost everything in the Panic of 1907 and moved to Eagle Pass, where he started out as a peddler. Although Eagle Pass had a population of only 5,000, Piedras Negras enlarged the potential market because its population was 15,000. By 1910, Riskind was successful enough to start a store and move into a new brick building on Main Street. The store became widely known throughout Coahuila; Mexican governors, generals, and prominent ranchers all shopped there in the 1920s and 1930s. One of the largest and longest-lasting department stores along the border, Bollack's, was owned and operated for many years by Pauline Bollack, the widow of Henry Bollack. She was the only woman along the border whose business lasted for more than fifty years and had a value approximating $100,000.[34]

Members of the Stool family became the most prominent Jewish dry-goods merchants in Del Rio. Max Stool immigrated to Chicago in the late 1800s. In 1905, he left, planning to go all the way to California. He never made it to the West Coast, stopping after he traveled through Del Rio, where he opened Guarantee Dry Goods Store. David Stool, who knew Russian, German, and Yiddish when he moved to Del Rio in 1921, reportedly learned to speak Spanish and English in a matter of weeks. There, near an irrigation ditch he set up a small store that lasted through the difficult times of the 1930s and maintained a value between $10,000 and $20,000.[35]

In Laredo in the 1920s, Jews owned five out of eleven major department stores, Shapu and Frelich, Franklin Brothers, M. Joseph, Rubinstein Mercantile Company, and Aaron Schwartzman. Dozens of others, like Isadore Goodman, who had a shoe store in the 1920s and 1930s, ran small shops: the Torchin brothers from Russia, Henry Ladabaum, Sam Sbarr, Leon Daiches, who had a jewelry company, and Sam Scherr. After the passage of laws severely restricting immigration to the United States from eastern Europe in the early 1920s, Jewish families began to settle in Nuevo Laredo. There they could serve customers in both towns and mingle with people in Laredo. Some later crossed over into Laredo.[36]

Jews also became successful merchants in the new Anglo farm towns of South Texas. One of those was Solomon Freed. Born in Russia in 1891 near Minsk, he followed his family to the United States in 1904, when he was thirteen. He moved to Laredo after visiting his sister and brother-in-law in 1910. After a couple of business failures in Laredo, the family moved to Crystal City in the 1920s, and Sol set up stores in Dilley and Crystal City. In the 1930s, with the help of a bank loan, he started a canning and packing company, which became the largest employer in Zavala County until the arrival of Del Monte Foods in the 1940s. He bought three thousand acres of farmland and four thousand acres of grazing land, where he ran about two thousand head of cattle.[37]

Not all Jews started off or remained in retail trade. Some ventured into media and entertainment. Morris Stein purchased the *Brownsville Herald* in 1916 and owned it until 1934. At the age of seven, Adolph Dittman of Germany originally moved to Salt Lake City with his family. He left to seek his fortune on the vaudeville circuit, becoming a magician. He arrived in Brownsville in 1907 and bought the Electric Theater. In 1910, he built the Dittman Theater where he started showing silent movies and became famous for producing films about the Mexican Revolution. Sam Schwartz opened two movie houses in Eagle Pass, the Aztec Theater in 1915, which showed movies in English, and a Spanish-language drive-in theater. Others moved into various aspects of the agricultural economy. Louis and Sam Hausman of Vancouver owned a packing company from 1923 until the mid-1930s. Ferdinand and Julius Wormser of Germany moved to Laredo in 1892 to open a dry-goods store. They eventually established a large farm and raised Bermuda onions and winter vegetables. In 1883, Don and Soffie Pfeiffer settled in Carrizo Springs, where they opened a general store. They later purchased farmland and grew strawberries.[38]

Jews were among the most upwardly mobile entrepreneurs in South Texas, as they were elsewhere in the United States. Morris Edelstein's life story provides an illustration. He moved from Lithuania to Brownsville in 1906 at age sixteen. With two suitcases full of items for sale, he peddled in local neighborhoods until he could save enough to buy a horse and wagon. His yellow delivery wagon became familiar to Brownsville citizens (fig. 9). He rented space in the business district, where he initially sold ready-to-wear clothing but quickly shifted into furniture. In 1920, he bought a building that had once belonged to the US Customs and Immigration Office. He opened branches of Edelstein's Furniture and House Furnishings in Harlingen and McAllen in 1925 (fig. 10). By 1930, he owned thirteen stores in a variety of locations on both sides of the border, including Matamoros, Piedras Negras, and Eagle Pass. He found innovative ways to profit in different areas of retail. When Studebaker exited horse-drawn vehicle operations in 1920 to focus on automobiles, Edelstein bought some of their remaining buggies, wagons, and harnesses at a fire-sale price and for several years sold them in northern Mexico, where there was still a market. He was also known for his ingenuity in advertising. One time he had a woman sleep overnight on a Simmons mattress in the front of the store. On another occasion, he borrowed a large python to place in the main display case, which proved to be quite a draw until the snake disappeared. It was later found sleeping in the elevator shaft. Edelstein used his store profits to buy farmland in the lower Rio Grande Valley and a small ranch near Kerrville, Texas. His net worth in 1918 was between $10,000 and $20,000 and had grown to somewhere between $75,000 and $125,000 by 1930. His store was one of the few in the region that outlasted the death of its founder.[39]

FIGURE 9. Edelstein's furniture truck. Courtesy, Robert Runyon Photograph Collection, 08717, Dolph Briscoe Center for American History, University of Texas at Austin.

Because of their success, Jews found a place as civic and business leaders within the Anglo community. They both participated in and led local organizations such as the Masons, Rotary Club, and the Chamber of Commerce. They regularly served in city government and on school boards. When Morris Hirsch died in 1925, he was honored as "one of the pioneer residents" of the Texas-Mexican border. Benjamin Kowalski served as mayor of Brownsville from 1912 until 1914. Leon Daiches, a jeweler who came to Laredo in 1891, was recognized as one of the "real pioneer merchants of Laredo"; he was a civic worker, member of the school board and the Rotary Club, and owner of one of the leading jewelry businesses of the Southwest. Ben Freudenstein was appointed to liquidate a number of the major failed banks in the Valley in the 1930s, including Merchants National. He was elected president of the Brownsville Rotary Club in 1934 and 1935. Louis Franklin of Laredo served on the town's city council. Ben and Louis Alexander both became presidents of Laredo National Bank.[40]

Although Jews were admired for their success, they still faced subtle forms of anti-Semitism from the Anglo-American community. According to Ruthe Weingarten, who interviewed a number of Jews living in South Texas, "[W]e know from

FIGURE 10. Edelstein's furniture advertisement, *Mission Times,* 1926. Advertising became more common in the 1920s and 1930s and reflected the growing consumer culture along the border. Courtesy of the Margaret H. McAllen Memorial Archives, Museum of South Texas History, Edinburg, Texas.

whispers in the Jewish community that there were certain clubs, neighborhoods, and places that Jews were not permitted." Jews only sporadically appeared in local business directories. There were rumors that the Ku Klux Klan was active in Mercedes, and as a result, many Jews moved west to McAllen in the 1930s.[41] Octavío García, a Tejano surgeon from a prominent local ranching family, observed that his wife, a Russian Jew, experienced as much discrimination from the Anglos of McAllen as he did, if not more. Anglos refused to mingle socially with McAllen's Jews despite their wealth and commercial prominence. Buddy Freed realized that he was "different" when he was growing up in Crystal City. He said, "I had my share of anti-Semitic remarks and my share of fights over them."[42]

Mid-nineteenth-century Jewish immigrants from Germany and France had dealt with Anglo attitudes by assimilating almost completely into Anglo-Hispanic society, nearly erasing their Jewish identity. Many had intermarried with Protestant Anglos or Hispanic Catholics. Later Jewish immigrants from Russia and eastern Europe retained their distinctiveness by continuing to speak Yiddish and read Yiddish newspapers, by cooking and eating their traditional food dishes, and by practicing their orthodox religious beliefs. When Eva Silberman arrived in Brownsville in the 1930s, she found the Jewish community to be somewhat insular. Its members had formed their own networks through Hebrew benevolent associations and branches of international Jewish groups, including Zionist organizations. They did not fear comparisons with ethnic Mexicans, however, because "in looks and lifestyle," the Jews were European.[43]

Jews interacted with ethnic Mexicans regularly. Selig Deutschman, an attorney from Brownsville, married a Hispanic Catholic woman. When she died in 1915, he created a stir in the local Jewish community by insisting that she be buried in his family plot in the Agudas Achim Cemetery on Palmetto Street. Deutschman regularly cultivated relationships with businessmen from Mexico. A lieutenant colonel in the Texas Guard, F. A. Chapa, wrote, "He is considered in Southwest Texas as the best friend of the Mexicans. He speaks their language fluently and has been their friend and advisor for many years. In fact he has been raised among them . . . He loves humanity and has done a great work among the middle and poorer classes of the Mexican people, in helping to elevate their position, so much so that he has perhaps more influence with the best element than any man outside their race."[44] Oscar Sommer, a Romanian immigrant with stores in Brownsville and Matamoros, became a much-loved figure in Tamaulipas. He would ride around on a horse with a serape on his shoulders, visiting his customers to collect their installment payments. He spoke English, Spanish, and German with the same fluency as Yiddish and Romanian. In McAllen, Dr. Octavío García found the Jewish community to be far more accepting of ethnic Mexicans than were most Anglos.[45]

Jewish merchants actively sought out ethnic Mexican customers not only in the more racially fluid border towns but also in the highly segregated farm towns of the lower Rio Grande Valley. They attracted customers from all over northern Mexico. Some served ethnic Mexicans almost exclusively; customer lists suggest they sold goods on credit for very small amounts. Albert Granoff, who migrated from Ukraine to Laredo, said in his memoirs that Mexican families made good customers. Sam Greenfield supplied a number of ethnic Mexican merchants in the area. During the Depression, Morris Edelstein decided to try to sell mattresses in the *barrios*. He would have his salesmen take the mattresses to people's homes so they could see them firsthand.[46]

Since most Jews of the border region were not natives of either the United States or Mexico, they faced the challenge of negotiating their status between the Anglo, Tejano, and Mexican communities while at the same time determining how to hold on to their own ethnic identity. They had to navigate cultural, social, and linguistic borders on a daily basis even as they also often crossed the literal border to do business.[47] As they assimilated certain features of Anglo culture, they also incorporated aspects of Mexican culture, especially as it facilitated their business endeavors. Perhaps because of their presence at the economic center of the Anglo community while simultaneously on its social margins, Jewish merchants may have functioned to some extent as intermediaries between the Anglo and ethnic Mexican communities. They benefited from the presence of a cosmopolitan business class in the border towns, which they found to be more open than many of the Anglo farm towns.

Not all Jews in the border region chose to settle permanently in the United States. Once the Mexican state stabilized under Lázaro Cárdenas in the 1930s, many eastern European Jews, along with Syrians, decided to pursue their entrepreneurial ambitions exclusively in northern Mexico. There they engaged in the retail trade as well. A number accumulated enough capital to establish small textile mills. Thus, the owners of Mexico's newly emerging textile industry almost all bore Jewish and Syrian names.[48]

SYRIANS

Most Lebanese Christian immigrants, called Syrians at the time, arrived in the South Texas borderlands around the turn of the twentieth century. At that time, Syrians faced persecution under the rule of the Ottoman Turks, whose attitudes toward non-Muslims fluctuated between openness and repression. Syrians turned to European immigration agents for assistance to travel to the United States through New York as well as to Mexico through the port of Veracruz. Many settled in northern Mexico near the Texas border in the late nineteenth and early twentieth centuries. Almost all of them were members of the educated merchant class in their homeland. During the late Porfiriato and the Mexican Revolution, as life became increasingly unstable, hundreds attempted to cross into the United States. Laredo became known as the major US port of entry for emigrants from the Ottoman Empire, rivaled only by New York City.[49]

Although the border was relatively open at the time, Syrians were often unwelcome in the United States because many of them suffered from trachoma, a highly contagious eye disease that could cause blindness. The US immigration laws barred the entry of people who had "loathsome or contagious diseases" and also shut out anarchists, Chinese workers, and people who might become dependent on the public welfare. According to one paper, "Mexico has long been the stamping ground of Syrians and other foreigners who go to that country because they have been denied admission to the ports of the United States because they are victims of the disease. Heretofore they have been permitted to enter, and to go to all parts of Mexico unmolested, and thousands of them have gathered at the border cities, with the ultimate object of effecting an entrance into the United States."[50]

The fear that erupted over Syrians' attempts to enter the United States seemed out of proportion to their actual numbers. Most newspaper articles at the time identified Syrians as the ones most likely to be detained. Camps were set up along the border to house Syrian, Greek, Japanese, and Chinese individuals trying to enter the country illegally. People were stopped even while they were escaping for their lives. One episode occurred during the battle for Nuevo Laredo in 1914. About twenty-nine men, women, and children from Syria, living in Nuevo Laredo at the time, fled across the river to avoid being killed in the crossfire. Local authorities detained them when they discovered that several had trachoma. Nuevo Laredo officials initially refused to allow them to return, but as soon as the permit was issued, "they were rushed to Nuevo Laredo without delay." Syrians continued to enter the United States regardless; the length of the border and the number of shallow river crossings allowed many to slip by unnoticed.[51]

Syrians who managed to enter the United States faced even more obstacles because, for a time, their ability to become citizens was uncertain. Although US citizenship was not a requirement for doing business, for those from countries other than Mexico, it was a requirement for owning real estate, usually a prerequisite to developing a large business. Naturalization laws prior to 1952 prohibited nonwhites other than those of African descent from becoming US citizens. Court decisions about whether Syrians were "white" and therefore could become naturalized citizens were inconsistent. Some determined they were white; others ruled that they were Asians and therefore nonwhite. In 1914, Syrians achieved a victory in a court case filed in Fort Worth when Judge Meek opined that Syrians were members of the white race and therefore entitled to all prerogatives of citizenship. The Syrians' loyalty was questioned later as tensions heightened during World War I. One court refused to approve the naturalization papers of several Syrians because of their potential ties to the Ottoman Empire, an ally of Germany and Austria-Hungary. Citizenship of Syrians living in South Texas varied. Some had become naturalized citizens, whereas others were aliens.[52]

The Syrian community in the Texas-Mexico borderlands remained small and somewhat insular. Syrians tended to live in cultural enclaves and maintained their own benevolence societies and clubs. San Antonio, which lay outside of the immediate border region, had the largest Syrian community, large enough to support a Maronite Rite Catholic congregation. The city had one of only three Maronite Catholic priests in the United States. Construction of St. George's Maronite Catholic Church was completed in 1932, a congregation that had existed prior to that time. Services were held at least partly in Aramaic.[53] None of the border towns had enough of a Syrian population to sponsor significant institutions like St. George's.

Syrians along the border typically started small businesses, often beginning as peddlers because they had no capital. Their wives assisted them, frequently carting goods from their husband's stores around the countryside. George Sahadi, who immigrated with his family at the age of sixteen, got his start that way. He, along with his father and brothers, borrowed money to buy about 152 acres of land in San Patricio County near Taft, Texas, in 1919. Shortly thereafter, he opened a store in Harlingen. Matilde Karam, born in Chihuahua, Mexico, in 1908, accompanied her family to the Valley during the Mexican Revolution; there she met Aziz Showery. They later married and peddled goods together until they had enough income to open a store on La Calle Diez y Siete, now Guerra Street in McAllen, in the early 1920s. The store, Showery Dry Goods, catered to ethnic Mexicans. Syrian women occasionally opened their own stores as well. One of these was Julia Shahady, who had a women's clothing store in Laredo in 1930.[54]

Syrians, like the Jews, established cross-border communities such as the one in Laredo/Nuevo Laredo. They moved back and forth across the Río Bravo/Rio Grande to visit relatives and establish different branches of their businesses. Unlike the Jews, however, the Syrians seemed to be identified more with ethnic Mexicans, particularly in the lower Rio Grande Valley, and, for the most part, they were not as wealthy or as upwardly mobile. They lived in the *barrios* and sold almost exclusively to the ethnic Mexican community. Emil Ayoub, for example, started a dry-goods and grocery store in San Benito, where virtually all of his customers had Hispanic surnames. Prior to the Depression, he was fairly successful, accumulating an estimated $12,000 worth of city property as well as a 1929 automobile.[55]

Some Syrians, like members of the Kazen family in Laredo, moved into the mainstream business class. Abraham Kazen and his brothers, Antonio and Joe, arrived in the United States in the 1880s, moved to Laredo, and peddled dry goods between Laredo and San Antonio and later all along the Rio Grande. In due course, they established a profitable mercantile house. Abraham's son Philip became a prominent attorney in Laredo, served as district attorney between 1938 and 1942, and represented a number of bankrupts during the course of his practice. Antonio Nassar was the only Syrian to appear in the 1931 publication *The Lower Rio Grande Valley and Its Builders.* He owned a warehouse in McAllen and conducted a wholesale business in Reynosa, Mexico. The experiences of Nassar and Kazen illustrate that Syrians, like other immigrants, could participate in the Anglo-American community by becoming successful entrepreneurs. Entrepreneurship then provided a foundation for their children and grandchildren to eventually become full participants in US society.[56]

· · ·

The lives of people like Antonio Nassar, Morris Edelstein, and Rocco de Bona seem to embody the essence of the American dream. They risked more than any of the Anglo-Americans who arrived in the border region around the turn of the century by leaving their countries and moving across the ocean to a completely alien land. With relatively little capital, a number set up small businesses, bought homes and cars, and educated their children in the local public schools. Some became very successful. Their ability to rise was due to many different variables, including personal ingenuity, but one reason they generally fared well was that they started businesses rather than working for a wage. For immigrants, the path to upward mobility in US society was independent entrepreneurship. Laborers simply did not have the opportunities to make money that a self-employed person had; if someone could start a business that offered something that people wanted or needed, he or she could potentially make substantial profits. Of course, the path to upward mobility was not always smooth, and immigrants, like everyone else, faced the uncertainties of the capitalist system.

Another advantage, for nonwestern Europeans, was that the South Texas border region had not completely become "Iowa on the border." It remained part of *México de afuera,* or "outer Mexico," a place with long-standing connections to the nation of Mexico, its people, and its culture. The Texas-Mexico borderlands had long had a cosmopolitan business class in the towns and cities that was made up of people with many different backgrounds and varying degrees of wealth and who engaged in transnational trade and business deals. This class was in effect a continuation of the nineteenth-century accommodation structure between elite Anglos, Europeans, and Tejanos, although it expanded to include more people of middling income and assets as the population grew. Americans had become an increasingly important part of this group during the Porfiriato, but they by no means composed all of it. The Revolution had convinced many businessmen in Mexico that they were better off in the United States, contributing to the expansion of this group in South Texas in the 1920s. Spaniards, Italians, Greeks, Jews, and Syrians could live and move relatively comfortably in this world. They could also do business in northern Mexico, and some chose to live there. In a sense, the American dream for this group meant pursuing opportunity in the "Americas," not in the United States alone.[57]

5

NAVIGATING CHANGE

I N 1922, THIRTY-SIX-YEAR-OLD ALONSO ANCIRA was operating the
Rialto Clothing Store in downtown Laredo, Texas, on Hidalgo Street. He
still owned a house in Nuevo Laredo, where he had been born, but lived in
rented quarters in Laredo. He also owned some land near Sabinas Hidalgo, Mexico, where he and his wife had lived for a few years after they married. He was
in the process of applying for US citizenship. In addition to the clothing store,
he operated a cigar stand and a barber shop owned by his wife. He sold merchandise to customers in Laredo as well as in Tampico, Saltillo, Nuevo Laredo,
and Monterrey. His recent purchase of a 1921 Oldsmobile touring car evidenced
participation in the American consumer economy and a desire to achieve the
standard of living it represented.[1]

Ancira's life illustrates how ethnic Mexican businesspeople pursued success by using proximity to the border to their advantage as they navigated the
changes brought about by the rise of industrial capitalism. Whether they migrated north from Mexico or already lived in South Texas, they were more likely
to have a transnational lifestyle than Anglo South Texans, who "lack[ed] a com-
pelling economic need to cross the border, learn Spanish, or become familiar with
Mexican culture." Ethnic Mexican entrepreneurs searched for customers among
the Spanish-speaking population on both sides of the Río Bravo/Rio Grande.
They cultivated and nourished social and business contacts in Mexico based on
shared language and culture and on familial ties, which helped to sustain them

economically. They participated in the US economy not only as businesspeople but also as consumers. Many learned English in order to improve their chances of success in Anglo-American entrepreneurial society.[2]

During and after the Porfiriato, as American investors and businesses penetrated *México de afuera,* the lives of people in the lower Río Bravo/Rio Grande borderlands changed forever. Those changes led to the emergence of an urban class of ethnic Mexican entrepreneurs (of which Ancira was a part) in South Texas between 1880 and 1940. Trends contributing to the growth of this business class included the ongoing displacement of Tejano landowners and the immigration of Mexicans into South Texas. Anglo-Americans, however, did not entirely dislodge property-owning Tejanos from the countryside. A few made a successful transition to commercial ranching, acquired substantial landholdings, and maintained properties on both sides of the border. Hundreds of Tejanos in places like Starr, Duval, and Zapata counties held on to small tracts of land and transitioned into the new economy by growing cotton or winter vegetables and raising livestock, supplementing their income with day jobs here and there. Whether they lived in the towns or remained on the land, ethnic Mexican businesspeople had to navigate not only economic change but also the political and social changes brought about by the influx of both Anglo-American farmers and migratory Mexican farmworkers. Particularly in the new farming areas, rigid patterns of segregation, identification of all ethnic Mexicans as "Mexican" regardless of their nationality, and the accompanying discriminatory actions and attitudes of the new Anglo migrants generated obstacles in the pathway to success for many aspiring ethnic Mexican entrepreneurs.

NAVIGATING CHANGE IN RURAL SOUTH TEXAS

"Off the beaten track of the main roads of the Lower Rio Grande lie many old ranches," begins an article published by the *Brownsville Herald* in 1942. "Some are in a fair state of preservation, some have been cut into small tracts and sold to homeseekers, and some are ghost ranches—just names to conjure pictures of what has been. In a number of instances the owners have the original grant from the Spanish king tucked away in a chest or in their bank box. A goodly number have retained small holding and will the title to their children."[3] This description suggests the presence of both continuity and change in South Texas. In a few small corners, the Tejano ranching society survived well into the twentieth century, providing a link to the Spanish past, but in most places Tejano landowners either transitioned into some form of commercial agriculture or lost their land altogether.

Rural Tejano society centered in five counties, Cameron, Hidalgo, Starr, Webb, and Zapata, the core of the original Spanish and Mexican land grants. According to the 1887 census, the population of those counties approximated 40,679. "Mexicans" (which in the census meant those of ethnic Mexican origin, not necessarily Mexican nationality) totaled 35,945, or 87 percent, and "Spaniards" totaled 208. Hispanic ranching had moved north beyond the core counties in the boom years after the Civil War. In 1887, 93 percent of Duval County's population was of Hispanic origin, with 5,615 residents listed as Mexican and seventeen as Spanish.[4]

Significantly, ethnic Mexicans made up a lesser percentage of the overall population and never owned much land in the areas north and west of Laredo, which had been controlled by Kickapoos, Comanches, and Lipan Apaches through the 1860s and where there had been no Hispanic settlements dating to the Spanish and Mexican periods. Therefore, after Anglos arrived, class and ethnic relations in these places developed differently from the way they evolved in the heart of the Tejano region. When the threat of Indian raids subsided in the 1870s, Anglo-Americans rapidly acquired most of the land as they moved westward onto the Edwards Plateau. Most ethnic Mexicans who migrated into the area worked in subordinate positions. Mexican *pastores* routinely crossed the border in the spring to graze sheep in Texas and returned to Mexico for shearing in the fall. In the 1880s, other Mexicans moving north out of Mexico worked on the railroads in and around Eagle Pass and Del Rio or in general construction. Some searched for work on Anglo-owned ranches. By 1887, about 1,534 ethnic Mexicans lived in Maverick County, mainly in Eagle Pass, which had a total population of 2,223. Del Rio and its environs had a total population of 2,020, which included 990 ethnic Mexicans. The development of irrigated commercial agriculture, especially in Dimmit and Zavala counties (the "Winter Garden"), attracted thousands of Mexican migrant farmworkers in the late 1910s and 1920s.[5]

Before 1900, in the core Hispanic counties outside of Brownsville and the areas near the Gulf Coast, where Anglos and Europeans had taken over much of the land, Tejanos lived a predominantly rural lifestyle in a society governed by traditional Hispanic values and patriarchal kinship networks. Elite Tejanos sent their children to schools in Mexico, spoke the Spanish language, read Mexican newspapers, attended Spanish Catholic services, used Mexican pesos, shopped,

FIGURE 11. *Jacales* on a Tejano *rancho* in the South Texas countryside, c. 1916. Courtesy of the Margaret H. McAllen Memorial Archives, Museum of South Texas History, Edinburg, Texas.

dined, traveled, and did business in Mexico. A number owned properties on both sides of the Río Bravo/Rio Grande.

Rural Tejano society revolved around *ranchos,* which were essentially small villages. The patriarch of the family typically lived in the main house, the *casa mayor,* which was made of stone or *sillar* and had a flat wooden roof supported by *vigas,* huge wooden beams. It almost always had a covered patio. Other members of the family often lived in nearby *jacales,* thatched-roof homes of upright mesquite logs held together by mud or clay (fig. 11). *Jacales* had one or two rooms furnished with wooden benches and beds and animal fur rugs, and the walls were whitewashed with a mixture of sand and lime. The larger *ranchos* had a central plaza framed by *tendajos,* small general stores, and *jacales* housing a variety of artisans such as blacksmiths, carpenters, wheelwrights, and saddlers. The main business of the *ranchos* was to care for and raise cattle, sheep, and goats. According to the 1880 manuscript census, Hidalgo County was composed entirely of *ranchos,* the majority of which were owned by Tejanos.[6]

The arrival of thousands of Anglo-Americans after 1900 shattered the isolation of this rural society. Jovita González described the Tejano elite as a "landed aristocracy, impregnable in their racial pride" and living "in a world of their own, sincerely believing in their rural greatness" until "the development of the Rio Grande Valley brought hundreds of foreigners to their doors," dealing a blow to their material circumstances as well as their spiritual well-being.[7] Few Tejano families fit this image, however, and they were actually the ones most likely to navigate the changes with relative ease. Most Tejanos owned relatively small *ranchos* and lacked the resources to compete with the incoming migrants. Capitalism's dislocating effects were geographically uneven, affecting some areas more rapidly and completely than others.

Tejano land loss was highest in areas developed by Anglo-Americans. The *ranchos* of Hidalgo County were virtually all gone by 1920. Approximately 499 Tejano landowners in Hidalgo County owned 208,747.20 acres, or about 18 percent of the total. Tejano landholdings were relatively small; 425 owned fewer than one hundred acres of land, and only fifty-seven owned more than a thousand acres. Of those, only Francisco Yturria's 136,000-acre estate and the 20,000-acre Chihuahua Ranch west of Mission owned by Ramón Vela of Reynosa, Mexico, were very large; most of the rest (forty-six) owned fewer than five thousand acres.[8]

The inability to pay property taxes, which were beginning to skyrocket due to rising property values, was often the culprit behind land loss, especially in portions of the rapidly developing lower Rio Grande Valley, where farmers were utilizing irrigation technology. Failure to pay property taxes could result in what appeared to be an egregious miscarriage of justice. Texas real estate law allowed the foreclosure of a lien or mortgage for the amount of the outstanding arrearage or indebtedness even if that amount was far less than the value of the property. The law did not require the property to be auctioned for market value. This meant that a taxing entity could foreclose a piece of property worth $10,000 based upon a tax arrearage of $1,000 and resell the land for $1,000, the amount of the arrearage. The buyer in such a case received a windfall. Land-rich, cash-poor Tejano landowners became victims of this process. Anglo-American businessmen with access to both cash and credit were usually the beneficiaries, and they acquired hundreds of acres at minimal cost to themselves. Tejanos saw this as a form of theft sanctioned by the Anglo-American legal establishment.[9]

In contrast to the lower Rio Grande Valley, Laredo was the hub of a region where ethnic Mexicans held on to more land and maintained substantial economic as well as political power throughout the period.[10] Around Laredo, in parts of Starr, Zapata, and Webb counties, hundreds of Tejano families continued to own *ranchos* and seemingly lived much the way their ancestors had. In 1942, an Anglo-American visitor to the area reported the following in the *Brownsville Herald:*

"Coming down from Roma one sees signs but no habitations to speak of but if he will take the road that leads off into seeming brushes he will soon come to thickly settled communities that are as picturesque as any from the old country. Adobe houses nestle close together and their thatched roofs portray the architecture of Spain, France, and England. Crooked winding streets delight the artist's eye . . . Spend a night in one of the ranch houses where every courtesy is extended but not a word of English spoken and you will feel like some disembodied spirit and ask yourself: 'Is this the United States?'"[11]

In 1938, the town of San Ygnacio in nearby Zapata County was a small village with adobe and stone houses "built close to the street with patios enclosed and to the sides and back of the home predominating. Telephones are rare; no railroad comes nearer than Laredo, which is thirty-six miles away."[12]

These newspaper descriptions cannot be completely trusted because of Anglo bias toward romanticizing Hispanic culture and viewing ethnic Mexicans as primitive and uninterested in modernity, but they likely contain some element of truth. Tax rolls and census records reveal how little the counties of Starr and Zapata had changed in comparison to neighboring Cameron and Hidalgo counties. Starr and Zapata both lacked fertile soil, irrigation facilities, and proximity to major transportation routes. The majority of residents lived in rural areas rather than in the towns. The population of Zapata County remained relatively constant between 1910 and 1940, 3,809 to 3,916, with some loss of population in the intervening years. Starr County had a population of 13,151 in 1910 and 13,312 in 1940. Most residents in both counties were Tejanos, and there were far fewer aliens, suggesting that migratory Mexican workers felt little incentive to move there. In 1919, the *Galveston Daily News* reported that of 9,000 people living in Starr County, only forty-five were "Americans," and nearly all the land was owned by "Mexicans."[13] The 1920 census reveals that most of these were native-born Tejanos.

The only way to get to Rio Grande City prior to 1925 was by oxcart, mule wagon, or truck from the nearest railroad, eighteen miles away. Zapata never did get a railroad and had to wait until the 1940s for a paved state highway. The railroad built into Starr County in 1925 did not change life appreciably right away, perhaps because it came just a few years before the Depression. Also, none of the land developers found it feasible to plant a farm colony there.[14] The lack of development meant that land was cheap. On average, in 1930, a peak year for land values, undeveloped or grazing land was worth approximately $38 to $47 an acre in Cameron and Hidalgo counties, while irrigated lands sold for around $200 per acre. By contrast, land in Webb and Starr counties was valued at $3 an acre.[15] The lower valuations would have made it easier for Tejanos to hold on to their land because property taxes would have remained relatively low in contrast to the skyrocketing taxes in neighboring Hidalgo and Cameron counties.

Land loss continued, however, even in these areas that were not intensely developed by Anglo-Americans. One reason, as historian Armando Alonzo has noted, was the manner in which land was passed down through families. With a few notable exceptions, Tejanos generally acquired their land through inheritance rather than purchase. In most Tejano families, when the patriarch died, all of the heirs, not just the eldest son, obtained "joint and several interests" in the land. Since owning land in common was often unwieldy and problematic, Texas courts allowed the land to be partitioned so that individuals could sell or use their portion however they wanted. This promoted commerce in land but hurt families' ability to maintain large estates over several generations. Instead, the land was typically subdivided into smaller and smaller plots that could not support a family, creating a pattern of fragmentation among Tejano landowners at the very time that Anglo landowners were consolidating their landholdings through purchase. This pattern paralleled similar trends in much of rural Europe during the nineteenth century, which had forced countless people off the land.[16]

Starr County, where Tejanos owned virtually all of the land in 1880 as well as the largest ranches, provides an illustration. According to county tax rolls, Gregorio Villarreal, Pablo Ramírez, and Felipe Hinojosa Guerra each owned more than 40,000 acres in 1880. A number of other Tejanos possessed between 2,000 and 10,000 acres of land. There were only twenty-two Anglo landowners who together owned about 11 percent of the land in the county, or 129,306 acres. John P. Kelsey, a merchant who had moved to Rio Grande City shortly after the US/Mexican War, owned the largest Anglo ranch, approximately 23,000 acres. By 1910, everything had changed. A significant drought in the area in the early 1890s, coupled with extremely low wool prices, had contributed to the problem, wiping out many of the smaller *rancheros*. With a few exceptions, most Tejanos had tracts of fewer than 1,000 acres, while Anglos had consolidated substantial landholdings and owned approximately 53 percent of the land in the county. Of the twelve ranches in excess of 20,000 acres, Tejanos owned only three. Manuel Guerra had the biggest ranch among the Tejanos (39,008 acres). The largest landowners in the county included W. W. Jones (139,613 acres), James B. and Pauline Wells (71,799 acres), Ed Lasater (69,486 acres), and A. C. Kelsey (48,216 acres). These numbers changed in later years with the redrawing of county lines. Frustrated by Manuel Guerra's iron grip on county politics, in 1911 Ed Lasater successfully pressured the Texas state legislature to form a new county, Brooks, out of Starr, which included his ranch as well as some of the larger Anglo-owned operations. A couple of years later, ranchers in the area challenged Lasater's control, and the legislature created Jim Hogg County out of western portions of Brooks.[17]

The effects of fragmentation among ethnic Mexican landowners had become particularly apparent in Starr County by 1930. Even though ethnic Mexicans owned the majority of land in the county, 80 percent of them had tracts of fewer than 100 acres. Overall, 1,640 ethnic Mexicans owned 434,638 acres of land compared to 227 Anglos who owned 310,818 acres. This situation remained constant through the decade of the Depression. In 1940, more than 90 percent of 2,745 property owners in Starr County were ethnic Mexicans, but most owned fewer than 100 acres of land; only a couple of dozen owned more than 1,000 acres. Seven of the ten largest landowners in the county were Anglos, but the Guerra family continued to own the most acreage. A partnership run by Manuel Guerra's sons, M. Guerra & Son, controlled more than 40,000 acres, and Manuel Guerra's wife's estate comprised 21,219 acres. Anglo ranchers seemingly suffered more during the Depression. They lost nearly 60,000 acres in Starr County over the course of the decade, reducing their share of the land to 30 percent. In neighboring Zapata County, Anglos lost 123,628 acres. In all likelihood, the high land loss by the Anglos was due to more aggressive financing, an inability to pay back the loans after the Depression hit, and resulting foreclosure.[18]

Within the Tejano community in the South Texas borderlands, land loss and fragmented landholdings were the visible signs of the impact of the intrusion of global capitalism. Few had the resources to modernize in order to keep pace with the new demands and innovations required in the rapidly changing livestock industry. Some coped by focusing on basic survival and by withdrawing into their families and cultural enclaves in those areas where it was still possible to do so. They chose "to measure their humanity and purpose in life by more than their material achievements," refusing to assimilate to Anglo-American culture.[19] Still others embraced US entrepreneurial values, adopting a market-oriented outlook and cooperating to some degree with the Anglo establishment, cultivating business and political ties. Most blended elements of both Mexican and Anglo business culture and values in order to succeed in the multicultural borderland environment. There was a definite trend, however, away from the land and to the towns and cities.

Throughout this period, some members of the Tejano elite maintained residences in the river towns of Camargo, Guerrero, Mier, Reynosa, and Nuevo Laredo and operated ranches that spanned the border. Children of these families might be either Mexican or American citizens, depending on where they were born on their parents' property. Esteban García, who lived in Rio Grande Valley, explained that he was a Mexican citizen, having been born in Camargo, but that he had brothers and sisters who were US citizens because they had been born on property his father owned in Brooks County.[20]

The Tejano elite who remained successful into the twentieth century diversified into mercantile operations as well as commercial ranching and agriculture. They also continued to engage in business in Mexico as much as possible. Manuel Guerra of Starr County, a descendant of Don José Alejandro Guerra, recipient of a land grant from the Spanish Crown in 1767, was one of the few Tejanos who held on to and significantly expanded his family's ancestral lands in the twentieth century. Manuel was born in Mier, Mexico, in 1856. He moved to Corpus Christi when he was fourteen years old to work for an American merchant and learn the English language. When he was twenty-one years old, he moved to Roma, across the river from Mier, opened a general store, and managed the Guerra holdings in Starr County. He ranched and farmed cotton and acquired land from other Tejanos. He and his family controlled the Democratic political machine in Starr County from the late 1800s until the 1940s.[21]

The García family still owned vast lands in Starr and Brooks counties as well as in Nuevo León and Tamaulipas in the early twentieth century. In the eighteenth century, the García family had received a royal land grant that comprised more than a quarter million acres of land on the north and south banks of the Rio Grande. One of the descendants of the García family, Esteban, made a successful but difficult transition to commercial ranching in the twentieth century. Esteban was born on December 2, 1896, in Camargo, Tamaulipas, ancestral home of the García family. In 1913, his parents moved their children to their ranch in Starr County after the Carrancistas confiscated most of their land in and around Camargo because they had supplied food and munitions to the resistance. Shortly thereafter, Esteban dropped out of school when his father fell ill. He worked for a number of Anglo ranchers in the area to try to save his family's land. He took over management of the ranch when he was twenty-three years old. In the late 1920s, he and his brother had enough money to add to their holdings. In 1936, he bought a ranch in Nuevo León between Monterrey and Reynosa. He also invested in breeding better cattle, and he and his brother Eligio developed the Mexican Brahman. Esteban was one of the few Tejanos to join the Southwest Cattle Raisers' Association and was honored in 1981 as "a master of the breed."[22]

Between 1875 and 1892, Manuel Benavides Vela bought 30,436 acres of land in Webb and Duval counties. He also owned a ranch near his native town of Guerrero, Mexico. When he died, his sons, Servando and Ygnacio, inherited the land, and they maintained the ranches as well as businesses in Laredo and Nuevo Laredo.[23] Servando lived in Nuevo Laredo until the Mexican Revolution. Carrancistas confiscated his ranch and attacked and burned Nuevo Laredo in April 1914, forcing him to escape across the international bridge at night with his family. He remained in Laredo for the rest of his life, working with his brother, Ygnacio, in a variety of ranching and real-estate ventures. He did not lose all of his Mexican properties, however, because he owned a 25,000-acre ranch not far from Monterrey in the mid-1930s. He became one of the major creditors in Laredo, along with his sister-in-law, Rosa Vela de Benavides, who had continued managing Ygnacio's properties after he died.[24]

Other large Tejano landowners included men like Eusebio García, who had not inherited land. Eusebio was born in Guerrero, Mexico, in 1859. He worked for his uncle, Ramón Alvarado, foreman of the King Ranch, for a few years beginning at the age of thirteen. He later moved to Laredo to establish a mercantile business with his brother but sold his interest in 1903. He married Josefa Guerra, daughter of Dionisio Guerra, owner of Los Ojuelos Ranch in Webb County. His wife inherited a portion of that ranch, and Eusebio bought more land, eventually acquiring more than 50,000 acres. His son, Amador, eventually took over management of the ranch. Amador, like Esteban García, was one of the few Tejanos to participate in the Southwest Cattle Raisers' Association.[25]

The Mexican Revolution complicated the situation of Tejanos who owned cross-border ranches and made it more difficult for them to retain all of their landholdings. Mexico had restrictive alien land laws that only became more so after the Mexican Revolution. The Mexican Constitution of 1917 prohibited non-citizens from owning land in Mexico in a zone extending one hundred kilometers from the border or fifty kilometers from the coast. It also generally prohibited noncitizens from owning land in the rest of Mexico unless they received specific approval of the Mexican government and agreed not to invoke the protections of their own governments in any matters relating to the property. Owners of cross-border ranches, many of whom lived in Texas but were still citizens of Mexico, could not become US citizens without risking the loss of their Mexican properties. Texas laws were more lenient with regard to land owned by "[a]liens who are natural born citizens of nations which have a common land boundary with the United States." Resident Mexican aliens in South Texas could own land as long as they filed a Report of Alien Ownership in the county deed records even if they never became citizens of the United States. Esteban García said he never became a US citizen for fear of losing his properties south of the Rio Grande. Some Tejano families eventually lost their lands in Mexico as a result of land redistribution and agrarian reform policies.[26]

As descendants of these original landholding families moved away from the land, they often became successful professionals and businessmen in urban areas. Octavío García, for example, was born and raised in Mier and attended school in Saltillo at the age of ten. Once the revolution began, his father, a friend of Francisco Madero's, sent for him to join the family on their 12,000-acre ranch in Brooks County. During his teen years, he lived on the Texas ranch and attended St. Louis College in San Antonio. He matriculated at St. Louis University in Missouri to study medicine. He received a medical degree with a specialty in surgery and returned to South Texas to open a practice in McAllen. A direct heir of José Narciso Cavazos, M. D. Cavazos, who was born on Retama Ranch in Hidalgo County on November 12, 1887, became a soft-drink manufacturer and opened Mission Bottling Works in the 1920s.[27]

Some heirs of the Tejano elite moved into politics and cooperated with Anglo-Americans to maintain their socioeconomic position. Juan de la Viña, son of Don Manuel de la Viña y Moran and Doña Carmen Amador, a prominent Tamaulipas ranching and political couple who had acquired substantial lands in Texas and Mexico between 1820 and 1860, became a local judge in the 1880s by associating with the political machine of Hidalgo County, run initially by John Closner and later by A. Y. Baker, a former Texas Ranger. His son, Plutarco de la Viña, served as a justice of the peace and deputy sheriff in Hidalgo in the 1910s and, along with his brother Juan, participated in the founding of Edinburg. Plutarco left politics in the 1910s to pursue his business and ranching interests, including the founding of the first open-air theater in Edinburg. He joined several Anglo associations, including the Masonic Lodge and the Rotary Club.[28] Plutarco's brother-in-law, Melchor Mora Sr., son of a ranching family in South Texas who had emigrated from Mexico in 1848, served with the Texas Rangers between 1879 and 1883. After his father died in 1884, Melchor Sr. installed irrigation canals and pumps on the family's land and farmed cotton. In 1906, he sold some of the land to the American Rio Grande Land and Irrigation Company. He worked for a while as their labor agent, recruiting hundreds of Mexican workers to help build thirty miles of canals. In the 1930s, Melchor Mora's son and Plutarco de la Viña both filed for bankruptcy. Members of the de la Viña family continued to remain active in local politics through the end of the twentieth century.[29]

Members of elite Tejano families were important because they continued to provide leadership and, in some cases, resources to the Tejano community, but they constituted only a very small percentage of the ethnic Mexican landowners in the region. The largest group consisted of those who owned relatively small tracts of land. Some combined working for wages with raising cows, pigs, and chickens and planting vegetable gardens to feed their families. Others, however, transitioned into various forms of commercial agriculture, usually a combination of raising livestock and growing corn, feed crops, and cotton. One of these was Feliciana Cisneros de Rotge. After the death of her husband, Domingo, in 1929, once a fairly prominent rancher, and a subsequent bankruptcy case, she cultivated cotton and managed livestock with the help of her two sons.[30]

Ethnic Mexican farmers were among the first to grow cotton experimentally in the region, using dry-farming methods, and cotton continued to be the primary commercial crop they cultivated. Counties where ethnic Mexicans owned the most land had the highest amount of acreage dedicated to cotton. In 1910, Duval County had 17,478 acres devoted to cotton production, and Starr County had 14,339 acres. There were several operating cotton gins in Starr County in the 1920s, and Ildefonso Ramírez opened a cotton gin in San Ygnacio to serve farmers in Zapata County. By contrast, Cameron and Hidalgo counties, where Anglo-American farmers dominated, had only 3,598 acres and 3,334 acres, respectively, planted in cotton in 1910. By 1930, a majority of the farms in Starr, Zapata, and Webb counties, where ethnic Mexicans still owned a sizeable amount of the land, were cotton farms.[31]

Irrigation was cost prohibitive for most Hispanic farmers, but a few were able to borrow the money to implement it. Juan Acevedo, a farmer near Laredo who had emigrated from Mexico in 1913, bought 150 acres from the De Lachica family and acquired pumps, engines, pipes, and conduits to use for irrigation. He grew spinach, onions, beets, and carrots. In 1928, he purchased another

747 acres, on which planted additional vegetables and pastured his livestock. Francisco Farías owned a farm consisting of 1,435 acres along the Rio Grande near Laredo, which he improved with fences, barns, irrigation canals, and houses for his tenants and laborers.[32]

Tejanos unable to hold on to their land often turned to leasing rather than wage labor. Tenancy rates in Starr County increased dramatically in the 1920s, from 16 percent of all farms in 1920 to 42 percent in 1930, whereas the corresponding percentage of owner-operated farms declined. In Zapata County, tenancy rates jumped from 11 percent in 1920 to 28 percent in 1930.[33] By 1930, nonresidents owned more than half of the land in Zapata County. Some of these absentee owners included oil companies and wealthy merchants in nearby Laredo, like Antonio Bruni (62,000 acres) and the Volpe family (26,278 acres). The majority, however, were individuals with Spanish surnames who owned tracts of fewer than 1,000 acres. These individuals lived in Laredo, Corpus Christi, Mission, Hebbronville, and Brownsville. The 1940 census for Starr County and Zapata County showed a similar group. While some of these owners may have purchased the tracts as an investment, hoping to capitalize on the oil discoveries in the area, it is more likely that most of them had inherited the land and moved to the towns in search of work or to start a business. The numbers of both tenant- and owner-operated farms declined in Starr and Zapata counties during the 1930s. Small farms simply could no longer support a family.[34]

One way that Tejanos endeavored to either avoid or cope with land loss was by starting a small business. They opened grocery stores, meat markets, general stores, and saloons. In 1919, Donato Saldivar, a rancher in Mexico, relied on his general store in Brownsville for income after he could no longer sell his cattle. He regularly carted goods to Matamoros to sell to the people who lived there. Domingo Benavides, born in Texas in 1860, owned a few acres out of the Espíritu Santo grant in Cameron County, where he ran some cattle and also operated a general store in Brownsville with his two sons, Antonio and Simon. Eutiquio Pérez raised sweet potatoes, corn, and cotton as a tenant farmer on 350 acres at the Jesús María Ranch, owned by Juan Fernández. Pérez had owned some ranch land previously but had sold it to Antonio Barreda in payment of a debt. He ran a grocery business and owned a few head of cattle and some horses, which he pastured on leased land. The Yznaga brothers, who had grown up on a large ranch in Cameron County, opened a dry-goods and grocery store in Harlingen. Their father had to sell most of the land to his brother to pay off debt that he owed. In the 1930s, members of the Salinas family, who shared ownership of

4,500 acres of land in Starr County, supplemented their income by operating a beer garden and meat market. Surviving on small plots of land increasingly became so difficult that some Tejanos probably sold their land in order to raise a small amount of capital to put into a new business.[35]

Starting a small business provided a path for Tejanos to avoid falling into the laboring class even as they faced accelerating land loss. They joined in the general migration from country to city, which, as we have already seen, was occurring throughout the region at the time as well as in other parts of the United States. These small businesses required far less capital to start and maintain than ranches and farms, and as discussed in the next chapter, it was usually easier to obtain credit for them. This transition to urban life marked a significant change in the core of the ethnic Mexican community in South Texas.

NAVIGATING CHANGE IN URBAN SOUTH TEXAS

The arrival of hundreds of Mexican immigrants during the late Porfiriato and the Mexican Revolution created a new potential market for ethnic Mexican entrepreneurs. The number of ethnic Mexicans living in the entire state of Texas tripled between 1887 and 1910, and about 37 percent of those resided in South Texas. By 1930, about 683,681 ethnic Mexicans were living in Texas. Approximately 371,486 of these lived in counties south and west of San Antonio and Victoria. Although the vast majority of these immigrants were unskilled migrant workers who received very low wages, they still needed to purchase food and other necessities in order to survive. Smaller numbers of middle- and upper-class Mexicans, who had the disposable income to purchase more expensive products such as automobiles, appliances, fashionable clothing, and fine furniture, also fled Mexico. Importantly, these new immigrants were not really foreigners in the sense that immigrants from Europe and the Middle East were. Most came from the border of Tamaulipas, Chihuahua, Coahuila, and Nuevo León, part of a larger region that had long encompassed South Texas. The presence of these new consumers from all income levels contributed substantially to the expansion of an ethnic Mexican business class in the towns between 1880 and 1940. Historians have often dismissed this group as unimportant because they constituted a very small percentage of the overall ethnic Mexican population in the region. They were not, however, an insignificant part of the business class. In some places, they constituted more than 40 percent of local business owners (see appendix 1).[36]

In the towns within a few miles of the border, Spanish-speaking businesspeople had a significant advantage because of their intimate knowledge of the language and culture of many potential customers in the surrounding area. They reached out to affluent Tejanos and Mexicans on both sides of the border. In the 1920s, the Brownsville Spanish language newspaper, *El Cronista del Valle,* contained many advertisements for stores with locations in both Matamoros and Brownsville. Laredo merchants advertised in Nuevo Laredo. Ethnic Mexican merchants also continued to find opportunities for business deeper in Mexico, exporting furniture, clothing, and gourmet foods to customers in Monterrey or Saltillo and importing Mexican products for customers in the United States.[37]

Ethnic Mexican entrepreneurs moved back and forth across the border, depending on revolutionary activity, politics, and available opportunities. The main restriction they faced was the tariff policy; the border remained relatively open to the physical movement of businesspeople throughout the period. Hijinio Salinas and his cousin Jesús Salinas moved from Monterrey to Brownsville in 1908 to start a general merchandise store, but both later returned to northern Mexico. Alfonso Sierra, a large landowner in Tamaulipas, fled the Carrancistas in the summer of 1913 after they confiscated his livestock, furniture, and clothing and sacked his general store in Río Bravo. Sierra temporarily set up a general store across the river in the town of Hidalgo but eventually returned to Mexico. His partner, Elías Castillo, decided to remain in the United States. A visitor to Eagle Pass in 1930 observed, "This American town is made up mostly of Mexican people who have, at various revolutionary times, fled to the north side of the river for safety if their views did not coincide with those of the current faction in power. Many of them remained to live, and the business and commerce is now largely carried on by Latin Americans."[38]

Class and capital continued to influence the place of ethnic Mexicans in towns close to the border, where a business class composed of middle- and upper-class Tejanos and Mexican citizens, Anglo-Americans, and European immigrants had forged a cosmopolitan society born out of economic partnerships and intermarriage. This was especially true of Laredo.[39] As J. G. Sullivan, an Asherton grower, told University of California economist Paul Taylor in 1929, "On the border, you can do business with the Mexican—they call themselves Spanish—you can't be quite so rough with them." He compared the Texas-Mexico border to California, "where the line [between the races] isn't so sharp."[40]

Even in the lower Rio Grande Valley, although Anglo-Americans distanced themselves socially from the ethnic Mexican community, they adopted a somewhat more inclusive stance when it came to business. According to *The Standard*

Blue Book, 1929–30, a local business directory, the people responsible for the dramatic economic growth of the "Magic Valley" were "from the best blood of the citizenship of our nation as well as of Spain, and the romantic LAND of the MONTEZUMAS, our Sister Republic. They are cultured, refined, brainy, and progressive." The *Blue Book* entries in the "Who's Who" section included fifty-two businessmen and professionals of Mexican or Spanish descent, but the Social Register contained only two. Ethnic Mexicans participated in the local Chambers of Commerce, Masonic Lodges, and Woodmen of the World organizations, but they were excluded from country clubs and the Rotary Club.[41]

The more affluent ethnic Mexican merchants usually did some business with Anglo-Americans. They leased or purchased space in the main commercial districts, which provided access to the Anglo population. They had sufficient income to purchase homes, cars, furniture, appliances, and fashionable clothing as well as life insurance. Their business success and adoption of a consumer-oriented lifestyle similar to that of the Anglos paved the way for Anglos to accept them on some levels. Their lifestyle mirrored that of members of the business class in Mexico, who were also purchasing American-made cars, clothing, appliances, and other products as they became increasingly available in the 1920s. Even ethnic Mexicans of more modest means owned businesses, homes, and automobiles (fig. 12).[42]

The emerging ethnic Mexican business class along the border included immigrants from Mexico as well as Texas-born Mexicans. A number had been born in towns on the south side of the river, such as Matamoros, Mier, and Camargo. They included men like merchant Leopoldo Cantú, a resident of McAllen, Ygnacio Garza, owner of a hardware store in Brownsville, and Moisés García, a merchant in Mercedes who predicted that the Valley would "surpass California in 25 years." Santos Lozano was one of the first merchants in Harlingen. Born near Monterrey, he moved to South Texas as a child with his parents and reportedly worked as a "Texas cowboy" for several years. His store was in a brick building on Jackson Street in the center of town. Matías de Llano, a native of Monterrey and descendant of some of the earliest settlers in Nuevo León, moved to Laredo, where he established Mexican Products Co. and Harvest Hat Co. There were also Texas-born Mexican entrepreneurs such as Alberto Gutiérrez Jr., who owned an auto-supply business in Rio Grande City, and Raul Dominguez, who managed an undertaking business in Brownsville.[43]

Although most of the ethnic Mexican entrepreneurs were men, a few Tejanas operated their own businesses. Most Tejana enterprises involved food in

FIGURE 12. F. Pérez & Bro. General Merchandise, a typical ethnic Mexican enterprise, c. 1920s. Courtesy of the Margaret H. McAllen Memorial Archives, Museum of South Texas History, Edinburg, Texas.

some way and included groceries, bakeries, and restaurants. Few operated millineries and dress shops, some of the more common female enterprises among Anglo women. The numbers of Tejana businesses, like those of Anglo women, increased in the 1930s. Married women occasionally operated their own shops, probably to supplement the family's income. Widows took over operation of their husbands' businesses temporarily or permanently after they died. Aurelia de Treviño, for example, managed her husband's store in San Diego until the business failed in the depression of the early 1920s. She then moved to San Antonio and bought a house. By 1930, her oldest son, Leopoldo, was able to work and support the family as a shoe salesman. Guillermina Marques, whose husband died when she was in her thirties, opened a shoe shop. Although she had inherited a fair amount of real estate, including nine town lots and ninety-three acres of ranch land, apparently these did not generate sufficient income for her family.[44]

Despite the success of some, the segregation of the ethnic Mexican community throughout much of the region circumscribed the opportunities of most aspiring ethnic Mexican entrepreneurs, men and women alike. Disproportionate numbers of their businesses were valued by R. G. Dun & Co. at less than $500. For example, in 1930, about 49 percent of the total number of businesses with Hispanic owners fell in that category, compared to only 17 percent of non-

Hispanic businesses. Another 28 percent of Hispanic businesses were valued between $500 and $3,000, compared to 25 percent of non-Hispanic businesses (see appendices 2 and 3). In the Winter Garden and Valley farm towns, most ethnic Mexicans had to set up their businesses in the "Mexican" part of town, or the *barrio,* where the residents were unskilled, low-paid workers. Many of the *barrios* lacked paved roads and running water. The residences were little more than shacks. In Del Rio, a border town, ethnic Mexicans lived in an area separated from the center of the town by San Felipe Creek. Amid the adobes and wooden frame houses were bookshops and print shops. On the plaza stood one of the only brick buildings on that side of town, a large drugstore, and next to it was a movie theater.[45]

The poverty of the *barrios* resulted from the low wages paid to Mexican workers, which in turn meant a very limited market for most small businesses run by ethnic Mexican entrepreneurs. The consumer market of northeastern Mexico, where the incomes of the vast majority of residents were even lower than in South Texas, was similarly limited. It was virtually impossible for those whose businesses were in the *barrios* to find customers among the more affluent residents of the region, which represented the only path to growth and expansion. Thus, the majority of ethnic Mexicans operated very small groceries and general stores that carried basic food items, inexpensive dishes, tools, clothes, and canned goods (table 5). They generously offered credit because their customers were chronically short of cash. Outstanding accounts frequently remained unpaid, making it difficult for many to sustain their enterprises.[46]

Anglos used the buying habits and supposed consumer tastes of ethnic Mexicans as justifications to pay their workers extremely low wages. According to many Anglos, Mexican workers lacked ambition and had "few wants." They were willing to live in shacks and uninterested in modern amenities and appliances. An American pamphlet about potential consumers in Mexico suggests similar attitudes about those south of the border as well. They "wear no shoes—only native, tanned sandals. They wear no civilized clothes, only white cotton woven at home. They wear only home-made hats, the raw material the fiber of palm trees which grow wild. They have no need for culture, for house, for travel."[47] Anglos often accused ethnic Mexicans of spending the small amount of money they had unwisely. One man told Paul Taylor in an interview, "The Mexicans buy all kinds of nick-nacks. They buy everything except what they should buy. They buy flour and beans but just as little as they can get along on. They buy canned goods. They spend a lot on shoes and hats. They spend all they make. They leave

TABLE 5. Types of Hispanic businesses, South Texas border region, 1930

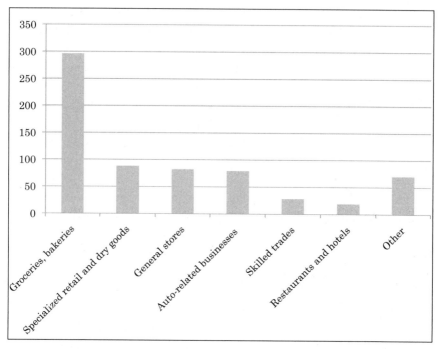

Source: Sample of 655 businesses from *The Mercantile Agency Reference Book*. State Pocket Edition. Texas. New York: R. G. Dun & Co., 1930.

here about as poor as they came."[48] One complaint about the farm-labor camp set up by the Resettlement Administration near Crystal City, Texas, was that its budget had been based on "experience with Anglo-American families" and was therefore "out of proportion for a Latin-American family."[49]

Along the border, the increasing availability of consumer goods from the United States added to the growing divide between Anglos and ethnic Mexicans. Consumption patterns became important signs of civilization, modernity, and middle-class status.[50] Many Anglo-Americans and European immigrants could afford to buy the available products, whereas the majority of ethnic Mexicans, both north and south of the border, had more limited incomes and therefore experienced greater difficulty in acquiring them. This resulted in inconsistency in their perceived standard of living; someone might live in a tin shack but own an automobile. The small businesspeople of the *barrios* were more likely than anyone else to be able to afford American products. Américo Paredes captures the pursuit of material goods among ethnic Mexicans as they struggled to adapt to Anglo dominance in his novel *George Washington Gómez,* situated in Depression-era South Texas:

> Feliciano felt he could be justly proud of the house his family lived in. It was not a brick mansion like those downtown, but except for the López-Anguera house, it was the best in the whole Dos Veintidós area. Now it was a house with several rooms. It had glass windows and linoleum-covered floors. Even more, it had running water and electric lights and a water toilet inside the house. There was also space for a shower stall, but they still took their baths in a washtub because they had no hot running water. But soon, perhaps.[51]

Segregation and Anglo prejudice limited lifestyle choices and social standing of ethnic Mexicans of all income levels. Anglos in general viewed Mexicans as unprogressive, passive, lazy, dishonest, and profligate, qualities that were the opposite of what they considered to be crucial for entrepreneurship. Segregation limited the actual business opportunities of the smaller ethnic Mexican business owners; they generally lived and worked in the *barrios,* where most of their customers were poor. Wealthier ethnic Mexicans were more successful in reaching out to Anglo customers and expanding their businesses but did experience forms of social discrimination, the effect of which is difficult to quantify.[52]

The Winter Garden region was particularly divided between the Anglo land-owning class and the ethnic Mexican working class. In an interview on April 9, 1929, the owner of City Drug Store in Carrizo Springs told Paul Taylor that he did not serve Mexicans at the soda fountain but instead gave them bottles of Coca-Cola or ice cream cones to take outside the store. "We just tell them it's our rules." One time, an "educated Mexican" from Eagle Pass came in, and the owner refused to serve him. "It's not a question of cleanliness or education [i.e., social class] but race." Yet even in these areas, class differences led to ambivalence in Anglos' attitudes. In nearby Big Wells, the owner of Hale's Restaurant said that Mexicans ate there occasionally, sometimes at the same time as the Anglos. Morris DuPree, from a farm near Asherton, said, "No, I wouldn't object to my children's marrying educated, cultured Mexicans; that is, if they weren't so dark in color so there would be any suspicion of Negroid ancestry." An aging cattleman from a ranch near Carrizo Springs said, "I feel sorry for the high-class Mexicans, who are sometimes refused at hotels and restaurants." He went on to say he would "do business with them but have no social contact with them."[53]

In many of the Valley farm towns, Tejanos found themselves shut out of restaurants, swimming pools, and neighborhoods. When prominent rancher

Esteban García moved his family to the "Anglo" side of McAllen, he was infuriated when his children were prohibited from swimming in the local pool. He demanded an explanation and threatened a boycott by Mexican Americans. The city leadership relented and allowed his children to swim there. He said that by and large his family had a good experience living in McAllen, and his children had friends of all ethnicities. Ramón Guerra was the only Mexican American to serve on the McAllen City Council between 1931 and 1941. Both Guerra and García are examples of the few ethnic Mexicans who were somewhat grudgingly accepted on the margins of Anglo society.[54]

Octavío García, a highly trained surgeon, faced enormous barriers when he tried to practice medicine in McAllen. After finishing medical school in St. Louis and obtaining his Texas medical license, García settled in McAllen in the 1930s to be near his widowed mother, who lived in Mier, Mexico. Local doctors initially refused to allow him to practice in the hospital. One even suggested that he "settle in Mexican town and deliver babies in the shacks." He was later permitted to use the hospital basement, but his patients had to enter through a back way. Eventually, through persistence and professional competence, he gained the trust and respect of many members of the Anglo community, but it took a long time.[55]

Anglo prejudice created tension within the ethnic Mexican community as members of the elite and middle classes sought to differentiate themselves from migrant farmworkers. Frustration appeared on the pages of Mexican American periodicals. As one article protested, "Who is the Latin-american [sic]? Who is this 'liability' so often spoken of by some of the 'fire-eaters' that do not even try to understand us, and whose dealings have been with a few cotton picking 'drifters'?"[56]

Ethnic Mexicans responded differently to their situation in South Texas. Some remained oriented toward Mexico, particularly those who still had land and investments there, which included many of the affluent refugees of the Mexican Revolution. They were less likely to adopt US citizenship, in part because it may have meant permanent forfeiture of some of their properties. Some members of the middle class who had left during the Revolution actually returned to Mexico in the 1930s, lured by the Mexican government's efforts to repatriate its citizens and colonize newly irrigated lands in Tamaulipas. The Comisión Nacional de Irrigación actively promoted settlement of its new projects throughout the towns of the lower Rio Grande Valley to Mexican workers and businesspeople. Francisco Salazar, the Mexican consul in Laredo, reported in early 1931 that forty-six families and five single persons "took with them all their personal belongings, wagons, autos, and farm equipment, to settle on the farm lands recently opened up at the San Carlos and Don Martin irrigation projects."[57]

Yet most ethnic Mexicans who had purchased homes and started businesses in the United States were unwilling to pull up stakes and leave. They had invested too much. Despite the segregation and discrimination they often experienced, hundreds of small shopkeepers, grocers, and other businesspeople from Mexico who chose to become US citizens and live permanently in South Texas must have seen the possibility of a better life north of the border than in Mexico. Along with descendants of native-born Tejanos, they formed the core of the urban Mexican American middle class. They began to use their resources to improve their status and position within US society while continuing to draw on cross-border contacts to maintain their livelihoods.

THE RISE OF THE MEXICAN AMERICAN MIDDLE CLASS

Small business made the rise of the Mexican American middle class possible, which, in turn, made possible the formation of the League of United Latin American Citizens (LULAC), one of the first ethnic Mexican civil rights organizations, formed in Corpus Christi in 1929. Like the ethnic Mexican middle class, LULAC was based in urban, not rural areas. By 1932, LULAC councils were active in Brownsville, McAllen, Mission, Encino, Edinburg, Falfurrias, Laredo, San Diego, Crystal City, Del Rio, Uvalde, Eagle Pass, Rio Grande City, Roma, and Hebbronville, in addition to the larger cities of Corpus Christi and San Antonio. LULAC was essentially the organizational expression of the ideology and values of a segregated and marginalized Mexican American middle class, which largely consisted of small business owners (predominantly men) seeking to participate fully in American society. They directly challenged the marginalization of the ethnic Mexican community in South Texas, which, among its many consequences, had curtailed their own business success.[58]

The founders of LULAC wanted to expand opportunity for ethnic Mexicans, mainly through education, so that they could compete as the equals of Anglos in the twentieth-century economy. Improving the lives of ethnic Mexicans generally would enhance their status and their economic opportunities by increasing the overall wealth of the community. Moreover, as evidenced by the promotional pamphlets about South Texas geared to Anglo-Americans as discussed in chapter 3, education, along with consumption patterns and certain values, were significant markers of middle-class status in Anglo-American society. The goals of LULAC included developing US citizens, pursuing equal rights and equal protection under the law for ethnic Mexicans, promoting English-language skills, eradicating racial prejudice, and eliminating segregated schools. LULAC limited membership to US citizens, a requirement that created considerable controversy within the ethnic Mexican community. In pursuing these goals, however, the members of LULAC did not seek to deny their heritage or relinquish their traditions. Instead, they sought to adapt to US society in certain ways while maintaining aspects of their Mexican past. In essence, they promoted biculturalism. They demonstrated how the efforts of their ancestors equaled or surpassed the contributions of the Anglo-Americans. "As a matter of absolute record, it was the Latin-American (Mexicans) who first braved and tamed the Texas wilderness. They were the first white race to inhabit this vast empire of ours." They were political leaders, intellectuals, and artists, not simply manual laborers.[59]

Members of LULAC accepted US capitalism because it worked to their benefit. They adopted a discourse of achievement, even "progress," that mirrored that of the Anglo community, although its source was not purely Anglo-American. Northern Mexican capitalists had held similar views since the beginning of the twentieth century.[60] In a letter to Ben Garza, lawyer Alonso Perales succinctly described the problem in the Mexican American community as he saw it: "Are we going to continue in our backward state of the past, or or [sic] we going to get out of the rut, forge ahead, and keep abreast of the harddriving [sic] Anglo-Saxon?" LULAC members believed the exclusiveness of Anglo-American society prevented ethnic Mexicans from fully realizing the opportunities American capitalism had to offer. They lobbied for change while promoting hard work, perseverance, thrift, and wise money management. These virtues mirrored those advocated by the Anglo-American middle class of the early twentieth century and echoed the small-town culture of many communities across the United States.[61]

During the 1930s, the *LULAC News* published brief biographies of Mexican American leaders. These biographies typically described their humble beginnings, their paths to success, and their patriotism. The life story of Ben Garza, who died at the age of forty-four, "read like one of the old Horatio Alger books." Ironically, Garza's success did not depend on education but rather on his entrepreneurial abilities. He quit school at fifteen when his father died to work at odd jobs to help the family survive. He moved to Corpus Christi, worked as a waiter in a local café, and returned after service in World War I to purchase the Metropolitan Café. The profitability of his restaurant provided the basis for his entry into the middle class. He later became a leader in LULAC. The story of the life of Ramón Longoria, elected president of LULAC in 1937, was similar. Although he left school in the sixth grade to support his family, he later returned, studying and taking classes at night while working during the daytime, eventually earning his law degree.[62]

In addition to these brief biographies, the *LULAC News* contained articles advising young men about how to succeed in business. One article discussed how to acquire the skills of a salesman. It emphasized the need for "selfconfidence [*sic*], perseverance, courage, poise, honesty, tact and a good appearance." Another article described the need for every businessperson to master the art of sales.[63] Other articles implied that business success was important to achieve a middle-class standard of living as defined by Anglo-American society. One story that Alicia Dickerson Montemayor, associate editor of the *LULAC News* in the 1930s, recommended for publication provides an illustration of an "ideal LULAC family." The father worked, the mother stayed at home, and the children attended public school and saved their money for college. They lived in a three-bedroom home with "quality" furniture. The children learned to play musical instruments, and the oldest daughter studied at a music conservatory in New York and married an Anglo-American. The son became a lawyer, and the youngest daughter taught home economics in high school. This story suggests the degree to which some middle-class ethnic Mexicans had adapted to aspects of middle-class Anglo-American culture.[64]

LULAC was significant because it had a vision for a Mexican American middle class that transcended South Texas. Although some participants in the 1960s' civil rights movements would later challenge that vision as not being sufficiently radical to bring about necessary change, it was progressive in the context of its time and location. Through LULAC, the urban-based ethnic Mexican businesspeople of South Texas eventually influenced the entire United States. They saw possibilities beyond the harsh realities of racial segregation. They were among the first to envision and articulate a transnational, multicultural American dream, that is, that the United States could offer a chance for racial and ethnic minorities to achieve a better life without sacrificing their heritage. Although, as historian Cynthia Orozco emphasizes, they remained in touch with the concerns of the working class, their goals were essentially those of a rising business class that desired success within the capitalist system. They therefore combined strategies of both resistance and accommodation and became influential voices for greater acceptance of all ethnic Mexicans in US society as they sought social, economic, and educational parity with Anglo-Americans.[65]

. . .

The emergence of a new core of ethnic Mexican leaders in urban areas that accompanied the loss of economic dominance in the countryside evidenced the substantial dislocation that ethnic Mexicans throughout the Texas-Mexico borderlands faced between 1880 and 1940 as a result of the deep penetration of capitalism into the region. With the rise of capital-intensive ranching and the expansion of irrigated commercial agriculture, it became less and less viable to make a living on the many *ranchos* scattered across the landscape, which led to land loss and migration to urban areas. Despite the barriers to upward mobility they faced, ethnic Mexican entrepreneurs who stayed or settled in South Texas found ways to navigate and adapt to the competitive and often discriminatory Anglo capitalist economy. As the twentieth century progressed, some managed to continue their ranch and farm operations while others started and sustained hundreds of business enterprises in the old border cities and the new farm towns. They took advantage of cross-border ties and sold goods and services to the thousands of migratory workers crossing back and forth across the border. As they integrated more and more into the greater US economy while at the same time retaining their cultural values and ethnic identity, a group of them developed a sense of themselves as Mexican Americans and created a lasting vision for a national Mexican American middle class.

PART III
THE ELUSIVENESS OF SUCCESS

6

ACCESSING CREDIT

I N 1930 DONATO MUÑOZ and Antonio Garza, two men in their mid-thirties, became partners in a retail grocery store in Del Rio, Texas. Both were Mexican citizens, Muñoz having emigrated from Mexico with his parents in 1905, when he was a child, and Garza arriving just a year before they went into business together, in 1929. They reportedly had "no money or property" to start with and did not borrow any from relatives. They were able to open their business because, according to Muñoz, "the wholesale houses gave us merchandise to work with." Those wholesalers included, among others, Hormel, Tucker Coffee Co. of San Antonio, Magnolia Macaroni Manufacturing Co., Swift & Co., and the Panama Vinegar Company.[1]

The experience of Muñoz and Garza reveals that credit was becoming increasingly available as the US credit system expanded into the Texas border region, following on the heels of the railroads. Credit was crucial for the rise of small business along the border and the development of a middle class. It unlocked potential opportunities by enabling people with little or no capital to purchase the land and buildings, inventory, equipment, and supplies necessary to start and operate their own businesses.

The wide availability of credit was a distinguishing feature of American society. Ever since colonial days, the credit system, a complex web of obligations that financed the creation, delivery, and consumption of goods and services, had developed alongside the market economy. In the antebellum period the United

States cultivated a strong financial and manufacturing base in New York City to support the growing web of credit. New York also served as the nation's gateway to commerce with Europe and its wholesale distributing center. Canals, railroads, and telegraph lines facilitated the distribution of goods and capital from New York into the nation's ever-growing hinterland. After the Civil War, US industrial growth exploded and expanded inland. Both the federal government and the states passed laws to protect creditors' rights, facilitate interstate commerce, and enable the growth of a decentralized banking system. Mexico, by contrast, lacked the requisite native capital, financial infrastructure, and the legal framework necessary to build a strong financial and manufacturing base, crucial for making credit widely available to its population. The situation changed little under Díaz; wealth remained concentrated among a few wealthy entrepreneurs and large businesses, and the lack of legal protections for creditors hindered the growth of a modern credit system. The border therefore divided two very different credit regimes.[2]

Greater availability of credit in South Texas, however, did not ensure equal access or equitable distribution; it simply offered more possibilities to a greater number of people to improve their situation. Class, capital, and possibly ethnicity played a role in how much credit a person could acquire. Furthermore, the most accessible forms of credit favored small enterprises in the towns and cities as opposed to farms and ranches, contributing to the ongoing movement out of the countryside.

THE EXPANSION OF MERCANTILE CREDIT

Mercantile credit, which financed the delivery and purchase of goods for resale to consumers, was one of the oldest forms of credit in the border region. For most of the nineteenth century, it was confined to the coast and remained expensive and out of reach for all but the largest merchants. The modernization of the physical and legal infrastructure supporting mercantile credit, including construction of railroads, standardization of credit reporting, expansion of federal court jurisdiction, and the passage of a permanent federal bankruptcy law, facilitated its flow into underdeveloped regions. It became one of the more readily accessible forms of credit in South Texas after 1900.

Mercantile credit was central to the functioning of the market economy. Importers, customs brokers, jobbers, wholesalers, manufacturers, factors, country storekeepers, department store owners, and retail grocers all depended on some form of mercantile credit to operate their businesses. It involved lending goods in exchange for a promise to pay at a later date, usually twenty to thirty days, but sometimes as long as four to six months in agricultural areas. Typically, these obligations were unsecured by any form of collateral other than a right of redemption in the actual goods that were shipped. Retail grocers, hardware stores, and dry-goods establishments were able to offer credit to their customers because of the availability of mercantile credit.

Railroads enhanced the availability of mercantile credit by dramatically reducing the time and risks of transport across the interior of the continent. Railroads enabled the growth of inland wholesale and manufacturing centers, shortening the distance between suppliers and retail borrowers. Chicago became the gateway for western commerce, and cities like Cincinnati, St. Louis, Louisville, and Kansas City became important intermediate distribution centers. Railroads made the shipment of small inventories more cost effective. Suppliers became more willing to deal with small traders who could not purchase large amounts, and merchants could order fewer products when they anticipated fewer sales.[3]

While the railroads reduced some of the risks of extending credit, they increased others. Economic expansion had introduced a significant element of impersonality into the commercial sphere. Nineteenth-century border merchants had often had direct and personal ties with suppliers in New York and London. The small twentieth-century trader did not. Suppliers were therefore more likely to be unaware of the character and circumstances of their borrowers. They were also more likely to be dealing with marginal businesspeople, thereby enhancing the possibility of nonpayment. A borrower's failure to pay could disrupt the cash flow of the wholesaler and sometimes force him out of business. Some of the larger wholesalers employed their own traveling salesmen to collect information about potential borrowers, which often proved to be less than ideal. These salesmen were not always very skilled credit reporters, and they tended to focus on their primary jobs of advertising and selling goods or collecting delinquent accounts. In 1914, one bankruptcy trustee asked a traveling salesman employed by Central Shoe Company of Kansas City, "Why did you ask a man who you understood was a refugee from Mexico, and busted—if he wanted to buy shoes—a man that you had met casually on the street?" The salesman replied, "Because I have known of many men who came from Mexico and went into business who had backing."[4]

Not all wholesalers had enough funds to hire traveling salesmen, and many wanted to rely on a more systematic investigation into the affairs of a potential borrower to avoid situations like the one that confronted Central Shoe Company.

Thus, analyses produced by mercantile agencies such as R. G. Dun & Co. and the Bradstreet Company became crucial for creditors who were doing business with people in remote and relatively unknown parts of the country. By the late nineteenth century, R. G. Dun had replaced its earlier approach of impressionistic reporting with a systematic method of rating potential borrowers based on a variety of factors, including net worth, patterns of debt repayment, competence, and length of time in business as well as "character, habits, ability, and responsibility." Potential borrowers were assigned a combination of letters and numbers to represent net worth and creditworthiness. In addition, R. G. Dun stopped relying on local attorneys to supply information about area merchants and started hiring internal credit reporters stationed in branch offices. These credit reporters interviewed local attorneys, bankers, and area businesspeople, in addition to the debtor, and obtained financial statements. As a result, R. G. Dun began to move away from exploring the details of borrowers' personal lives. "[W]hen we attempt to uncover the seamy side of life in the character of any one we are treading on dangerous ground and should try to avoid it."[5]

Along with its major rival, the Bradstreet Company, R. G. Dun & Co. contributed to improved access to credit in South Texas and the rest of the American West by making it possible for distant creditors to reasonably evaluate potential borrowers whom they did not know. Solid credit ratings, however, were no guarantee against insolvency. Even seemingly prosperous businesses might experience a fire, the illness of their owners, or some other difficulty that would make it impossible to repay their debts. Moreover, in the increasingly competitive environment, wholesalers and jobbers often dealt with merchants who had less than stellar ratings. The need was growing for an updated legal infrastructure to deal with increased lending across state lines and the mounting problem of unpaid debts.

The nineteenth-century state debtor/creditor laws governing collection and insolvency had failed to keep pace with the changes in wholesaling and transportation. In the 1870s and 1880s, suppliers dealing across state lines faced a maze of debt-collection laws that differed from state to state. They often experienced discrimination as outsiders when they filed lawsuits to collect debts in state or county courts, where judges tended to protect local residents. Most lacked the resources to hire lawyers in multiple states. To make matters worse, competition among creditors had accelerated. In the antebellum period, most merchants had dealt with one large wholesale house; by the late nineteenth century, retail merchants were often doing business with as many as twenty or thirty different specialized suppliers. This made it far more likely that any one supplier would lose the "race to the courthouse" to file suit and get a judgment lien on the merchants' remaining goods before anyone else. The possibility of inequitable and inefficient liquidations therefore became more pronounced. The difficulty of collecting unpaid debts actually increased the costs of credit, reducing some of the benefits of railroad transport.[6]

Faced with these obstacles, some manufacturers and wholesalers began to agitate for a new federal bankruptcy law that would provide creditors with a way to systematically liquidate and dispose of a failed merchant's assets on a *pro rata* basis. Such a system increased the possibility that each one would realize at least something on his outstanding debt. The formation of a national organization, the National Representatives of Commercial Bodies, provided a vehicle to lobby the US Congress. Creditors also sought to expand the jurisdiction of the federal court over their disputes so that they could avoid the bias of local courts. Massachusetts senator George F. Hoar took up their cause and argued that "the new frontier agricultural communities," like those that would later emerge in South Texas, would benefit the most from a permanent bankruptcy law. "Why is it that these millions hoarded [by] the capitalists in New York or Boston waiting to be loaned out do not pour out their fertilizing streams to the most distant borders of the country? It is because of the doubt whether the creditor will have his fair share of the estate, if the debtor happens to be unfortunate." He went on to say that the "desire for a bankruptcy law . . . is one which is almost a measure of the progress of civilization and of business, and of wealth and prosperity."[7]

Congress slowly began to act to update the legal infrastructure for interstate commerce in order to facilitate the flow of credit and goods into the West. First, it passed the Federal Judiciary Act of 1875, which expanded federal court diversity jurisdiction to cover disputes between residents of different states. This meant that out-of-state creditors could sue to collect a debt or file for breach of contract in what was supposed to be a more neutral and objective forum. Commercial claimants filed hundreds of cases, causing the federal caseload to double between 1875 and 1885. In order to handle the burgeoning dockets in South Texas, the federal judiciary added four new courts between 1879 and 1912. San Antonio acquired a federal court in 1879, Laredo in 1899, Del Rio in 1906, and Corpus Christi in 1912. Prior to that time, a federal court established in Brownsville in 1851 served virtually all of South and West Texas, while courts in Austin and Galveston handled the more populated eastern parts of the state.[8]

Twenty-three years later, after extensive debates, Congress finally passed the Bankruptcy Act of 1898, which became the nation's first permanent bankruptcy law. In addition to creating a framework for equitably distributing the assets of a business in case of financial failure, it incorporated fairly liberal debtor provisions, such as prohibitions against the filing of involuntary cases against farmers. In most of the cases, creditors received less than a 20 percent dividend on the amount of their outstanding debt. Yet, the law did have its advantages. Creditors could more readily assess their risk by evaluating the debtor's total assets and debts and calculate the possibilities in the event of a bankruptcy. They also had a tool for preventing one creditor from taking everything out of the estate. Finally, all bankruptcy cases were to be filed in the more outsider-friendly federal courts. The combination of the railroads, the establishment of new federal courts, standardized credit reporting, and the creation of a national bankruptcy system all served to make mercantile credit more readily available in South Texas.[9]

Mercantile credit began flowing into South Texas more freely as early as the 1890s. Harry Stein, who operated a small general store in Juno, Val Verde County, in the mid-1890s, bought goods on an open account from C. H. Henderson and Butler Brothers, both based in Chicago. Louis Lindheim, a general merchant in Del Rio in 1900, had dealings with suppliers in New York, St. Louis, Louisville, Boston, and New Orleans. Guadalupe Cuevas, a Laredo merchant, borrowed from wholesalers in New York, Tennessee, and New Orleans before 1907. The habit of borrowing from distant suppliers continued throughout the period despite the expansion of local wholesalers because the local dealers often did not carry the items that a particular merchant needed. For example, José Martínez of Brownsville, owner of a Brownsville pharmacy, turned mainly to suppliers in Tennessee, Kansas City, New York, Missouri, and Boston.[10]

Some connections with distant suppliers arose out of personal relationships or kinship-type networks. Jews in particular sustained cross-country supply networks. Major garment wholesalers remained in New York, where they had more direct access to fashionable clothing and luxury goods coming out of Europe. They shipped directly to large department stores, ladies' ready-to-wear stores, and gents' furnishing shops owned by Jews across the country. In the 1920s and early 1930s, for example, Franklin Brothers of Laredo purchased merchandise from Edelstein Clothing Co., Feifer Brothers, M. Finklestein & Sons, J. B. Hirshfeld & Co., and Markel Brothers, all based in New York. Jews also established intermediate dry-goods wholesale businesses, some of which were in Texas. They included M. Halff and Brothers in San Antonio, owned by Adolphe,

Mayer, and Solomon Halff, brothers from Alsace-Lorraine, and Sanger Brothers, a Dallas-based enterprise started by German Jews. Solomon Halff later became the president and controlling stockholder in A. B. Frank Company, another major supplier of South Texas retail merchants.[11]

The railroads led to the emergence of more and more Texas-based wholesalers in the major cities of San Antonio, Dallas, Houston, and Galveston. The majority dealt in wholesale dry goods or groceries and, by the 1920s, in automobile supplies. The largest wholesale grocers in the South Texas borderlands included Desel-Boettcher, Walker-Craig Company, which had a huge warehouse in Brownsville, and Caffarelli Brothers (fig. 13). Smaller border wholesale grocers included Manuel Samano and Antonio Barreda of Brownsville and Juan Armengol and J. Villegas & Bros. of Laredo. Most small retail grocers in the area did business with these local firms. Eustalio Peña's situation was typical. A grocery merchant in Mission in the 1920s, he had acquired most of his stock from Caffarelli Brothers in San Antonio. Other major suppliers included Sam Greenfield and the Mission Commission Company, both based in Mission, and A. B. Frank Co. of San Antonio.[12]

The R. G. Dun Reference Books for the first four decades of the twentieth century reveal the ever-growing numbers of people along the South Texas border who were participating in the market economy and the credit system. In 1881, R. G. Dun & Co. opened a branch office in San Antonio and another in Monterrey shortly after the establishment of its Mexico City office in 1897. By the late 1910s, the company had a reporter traveling around every week or so in the lower Rio Grande Valley acquiring financial statements from merchants. However, R. G. Dun & Co. did not limit its reporting to large firms; in fact, most entries for South Texas towns were very small businesses operated by individual proprietors. The company reported on these marginal firms because of competition among suppliers for customers of any size. It did not report on every business in the area, nor did it rate every business about which it collected data. Usually, if R. G. Dun listed a business and gave it no rating, either it lacked sufficient information to form a definite decision about its value and creditworthiness, or the business had recently filed a bankruptcy case.[13]

By providing an opinion about creditworthiness, the credit ratings provide a general indication of who was able to borrow money and how much they could borrow. Some of the questions they raise include the following: (1) how creditworthy were businesses in general in the South Texas border region? (2) were Anglo-Americans and Europeans generally deemed more creditworthy than eth-

FIGURE 13. A distribution center for Caffarelli Brothers Wholesale Grocers, one of the major suppliers in the South Texas border region, December 21, 1912. Courtesy, Robert Runyon Photograph Collection, 02458, Dolph Briscoe Center for American History, University of Texas at Austin.

nic Mexicans, therefore giving them an advantage in obtaining credit? (3) how important was a good rating to obtaining credit? (4) how do the credit ratings for men and women compare?

In the R. G. Dun ratings, business size and strength played a major role in determining creditworthiness. Credit ratings ranged from "high" to "good" to "fair" to "limited." Those valued at $1,000 or less could not receive more than a "fair" credit rating, and most received the lowest rating: "limited." The highest rating a business valued between $1,000 and $10,000 could receive was "good." Samples of South Texas credit ratings from 1901, 1930, and 1938 reveal that the majority of enterprises, whether operated by Anglos or Hispanics, men or women, received only a "fair" or "limited" credit rating. The percentage of businesses with a "high" or "good" credit rating increased during the 1920s, but during the Great Depression, the percentage with only a "limited" credit rating rose dramatically (see appendix 5).

We have no evidence to indicate that wholesalers as a group actively discriminated against Tejanos and Mexicans on the basis of ethnicity. The fact that so many were included in the R. G. Dun Reference Books indicates that, to the contrary, wholesalers were actually eager to do business with them. More-

over, R. G. Dun's decision to keep branch offices in Mexico reveals that wholesalers continued to do business across the border after the revolution. If an
entire category of people had been excluded from the credit system on the basis
of race or ethnicity, R. G. Dun would not have bothered to report on them.[14]
Hispanic-owned businesses had more limited access to credit, however, because
most were very small (see appendices 2 and 3). Over the course of the first
three decades of the twentieth century, the credit ratings of non-Hispanic businesses improved significantly, while an increasing number of Hispanic-owned
businesses received the lowest credit rating. In 1901, when the population of the
region was still predominantly of Mexican descent, out of a sample of 222 enterprises (141 non-Hispanic and 81 Hispanic), 44 percent of Hispanics compared
to 36 percent of non-Hispanics had a "limited" credit rating. By 1930, at about
the height of prosperity in South Texas and right before the region felt the influence of the Great Depression, the numbers and overall percentage of Hispanic
businesses had increased, but their credit ratings were lower when compared to
those of non-Hispanics. Fifty-two percent of Hispanic-owned businesses received
a "limited" credit rating, whereas only 20 percent of non-Hispanic businesses did.
The Depression affected all business owners, but again, a substantial disparity
existed between Hispanic and non-Hispanic businesses (see appendix 5).

   Throughout the period, Tejanos and Mexican citizens living in the United
States bought goods on credit from both in- and out-of-state wholesalers, such
as Mission Supply Co. (fig. 14). Lists of their creditors were comparable to
those of Anglo-Americans and Europeans who had similar businesses. Eustaquio Vallejo operated a grocery store in Mercedes in the 1920s. In 1929, he
had outstanding open accounts with suppliers totaling about $4,000. Most were
local, including J. Armengol of Laredo and Rio Grande Coffee Co. of Brownsville, but he had also done business with suppliers in San Antonio, Houston,
and New Orleans. In addition, D. C. Decker, who had a slightly larger grocery
business in nearby Mission, had outstanding debts of about $3,000 to various
suppliers, most of whom were located in Mission, Harlingen, Brownsville, and
other Valley towns.[15]

   A low credit rating did not preclude a person from obtaining credit because
there was intense competition among suppliers for customers. In the early 1900s,
Galveston Dry Goods Company, for example, shipped goods to Guadalupe Cuevas, a Mexican citizen living in Laredo, on an unsecured basis despite the fact
that a Bradstreet report stated that he had several accounts past due, was "found
generally slow and unsatisfactory in his dealings," and had probably inflated his

FIGURE 14. Mission Supply Co., one of the early local wholesalers, c. 1906. Courtesy of the Margaret H. McAllen Memorial Archives, Museum of South Texas History, Edinburg, Texas.

assets. In 1902, Nicéfero Buitrón, a general merchant in Laredo with a "limited" credit rating and a small store worth less than $500, had borrowed between $30 and $250 from each of several suppliers located in Baltimore, New Orleans, Chicago, St. Louis, and San Antonio. In San Ygnacio in 1930, Zaragosa Domínguez had a similar type of store that was not rated and reportedly had a value of less than $500. He was still able to purchase at least $600 worth of goods on an open account from Galveston Dry Goods. The rest of his merchandise came from wholesalers in Laredo and San Antonio, including Volpe Brothers and M. Halff & Bro. Oscar Sommer, a Jewish immigrant from Romania who sold primarily furniture, had a business with a value of about $1,000 and a limited credit rating in 1918, which he built up to one worth between $5,000 and $10,000 with a fair credit rating by 1925. He was listed but not rated in the 1930 R. G. Dun Reference Book for Texas. In 1932, he had almost $14,000 in unpaid accounts to more than thirty suppliers from around the country.[16]

Local creditors did not need to rely on the R. G. Dun reports because they knew people personally or by local reputation. Thus, one's credit rating was more

important for obtaining "outside" as opposed to local credit. The lending relationship between a couple of the major wholesale grocery companies in Brownsville
and G. W. Cook's cash grocery store in the early 1920s illustrates how local credit
often worked. According to William Craig, the general manager for Walker-Craig
Company, the decision to lend to Mr. Cook was based on character and a general
understanding of his assets, not on any formal investigation of his affairs. Mr.
Cook had started his business in a frame house in San Benito with about $1,500
in capital. Walker-Craig did not request an inventory either at the beginning or
on an ongoing basis. When asked whether he knew of any property Mr. Cook
owned outside of his store, Mr. Craig replied, "No, but I knew if he bought for
cash and sold for cash he had made a success of it before, and it was a very good
account; he had been doing a good business; paid his bills promptly, taking care
of what we credited him, and as long as he run that way, he was all right." Similarly, Walter Roberts, a salesman with Ullman, Stern, & Krause, did not take
any inventories or request financial statements from Mr. Cook. He simply looked
around the store and glanced at the books. The primary basis for giving him
credit was trust. He knew Cook's capital was very limited, but he found Cook to
be "honest and reliable," and he had "a great deal of confidence" in him to manage
his business well. Unfortunately for Walker-Craig and Ullman, Stern & Krause,
Cook started taking credit, the customers were not always able to pay, and he
ended up filing for bankruptcy.[17]

The vast majority of credit came from the United States, but occasionally
merchants dealt with suppliers in Mexico on a credit basis. This was especially
characteristic of the Laredo-Monterrey trade but extended to transactions with
merchants in Saltillo and the border towns. Oscar Sommer, for example, purchased furniture from a dealer in Monterrey and mattresses from a store in
Nuevo Laredo, giving liens on his customer accounts in exchange for credit
offered. Romulo Martínez, who ran a novelty shop in Laredo, borrowed small
amounts from suppliers in Guanajuato and Monterrey.[18]

Women appear infrequently in the credit reports. Like most ethnic Mexicans, most female entrepreneurs had very small businesses and therefore limited credit ratings. In 1901, out of a sample of 197 businesses, 13 were owned
by women; 8 had a "fair" credit rating, and 5 had "limited" credit ratings. Little
changed over the next thirty-seven years except for the number of women in
business. In 1938, out of 129 women in a sample of 1,176, 71 had "fair" or "limited" credit ratings, and 80 were not rated at all. Despite these low or nonexistent
ratings, these female entrepreneurs were still able to borrow. A few examples

are illustrative. Mrs. Louis Pasco, who ran a small millinery shop in Laredo, was listed without a credit rating in the 1901 R. G. Dun Texas Reference Book. Her bankruptcy schedules in 1902 revealed that she had purchased most of her stock on credit from James G. Johnson & Co. of New York and three suppliers in St. Louis. In the 1920s, Mrs. D. P. Stoner, who had a millinery and gift shop in Laredo, was listed without a credit rating in 1925, the year she filed for bankruptcy. Her schedules revealed that she had $13,079.06 in debt, $2,929.06 of which was owed to suppliers in New York, St. Louis, Chicago, Cincinnati, and Dallas. In addition, Mrs. M. L. (Guillarmina) Marques, a widow, operated a shoe shop in Brownsville. In 1925, while her husband was still alive, the business had an estimated value between $5,000 and $10,000 and a "fair" credit rating, but by 1930, the business was listed without any estimate of worth or a credit rating. In 1932, she had nearly $7,000 in outstanding debt to suppliers in Dallas, Boston, New York, Chicago, and St. Paul.[19]

A couple of notable women in the region managed to expand their businesses and thereby increase their credit ratings substantially. In Brownsville, Mrs. H. Bollack's dry-goods and clothing store was valued between $2,000 and $3,000 in 1900 and had a "fair" credit rating. By 1918, the Bollack Store was worth over $75,000 and had a "high" credit rating. It sustained that value and high credit rating after Mrs. Bollack's death and throughout the Great Depression. Also in Brownsville, Mrs. L. Thielen had a bakery and confectionery that she built up over the course of twelve years from a $5,000–$10,000 business with a fair credit rating to one worth over $20,000 with a high credit rating. And in Laredo in 1930, Mrs. A. Siros had a hardware store worth $10,000 to $20,000 with a "high" credit rating.[20]

Mercantile credit both opened and restricted opportunities. It enabled a diverse group of people with little or no capital to start hundreds of new small enterprises, including general stores, dry-goods stores, clothing stores, filling stations, groceries, drugstores, and restaurants. These small businesses became a path to middle-class status for the foreign born as well as a way for Tejanos to avoid moving into the laboring class. Yet these small enterprises could borrow only relatively small amounts unless they happened to produce substantial profits, something that did not happen very often. Limits on the capacity to borrow inhibited the possibility of growth.[21]

Mercantile credit was insufficient to meet all of the region's needs for capital. It was of little value for purchasing store buildings, warehouses, or heavy equipment. It did not help farmers and ranchers who needed funds to purchase land, equipment, and livestock. In order to flourish, the border economy needed a reliable banking system.

COMMISSION FIRMS AND THE GROWTH OF THE BANKING SYSTEM

The border region was dependent on outside sources of capital throughout the nineteenth century and into the early twentieth century. Outside of mercantile credit, commission firms, life insurance companies, and eastern banks provided much of this capital. Individual entrepreneurs, including ranchers and farmers, had difficulty accessing these sources unless they had substantial operations. By the late 1910s, however, the expansion of the banking system was providing needed credit for people of more modest means to buy land, homes, storehouses, and office buildings, thereby greatly expanding opportunity in a wide variety of areas.

Banks had been scarce throughout the Texas-Mexico borderlands in the nineteenth century. Mexico had little financial capital, and the Anglo-Americans who had settled Mexican Texas in the early nineteenth century had an antipathy to banks in general. Many had fled there to escape their creditors. The Panic of 1837 and the losses resulting from widespread bank failures made them even more wary. As a result, once they gained their independence from Mexico, the authors of the 1845 Constitution of the new Republic of Texas prohibited state-chartered banks. This ban survived the rewriting of the constitution during the Reconstruction era and was not lifted until 1905. Unfortunately, this antibanking prejudice inhibited the growth of native capital, which might have facilitated more opportunities for an entrepreneurial middle class at an earlier stage. By fostering dependence on eastern sources of capital, it had the opposite effect desired by its proponents; it contributed to elite control over the economy.[22]

Due to their access to mercantile credit and dominance over the import/export trade out of northern Mexico, a few wealthy merchants controlled available credit on both sides of the Río Bravo/Rio Grande prior to the arrival of the railroads. Some, like Francisco Yturria, acted as private bankers. Yturria founded a private bank in Brownsville in the 1850s, the largest and for many years the only bank in the lower Rio Grande Valley. It remained in business for nearly a century. Private banks like Yturria's could be less restrictive in their lending practices because they were not closely regulated by either the state or federal government. They had no minimum capitalization or reserve requirements. On the other hand, since their owners were local merchants, they had an interest in keeping out the competition and thus refused to lend to people who might threaten their own enterprises. Yturria's bank was frequently accused of restricting access to credit. The lack of regulations also meant that private banks made risky loans and were therefore more vulnerable to failure, putting deposits at risk. Louis Lindheim & Co., for example, was the only bank in Del Rio in 1900. In 1903, Lindheim, who was also a general merchant, filed for bankruptcy. Despite some of their defects, private banks continued to be an important source of credit even after the establishment of state and national banks in the region. Their numbers declined after 1923, when the Texas legislature passed a law prohibiting the creation of any new ones.[23]

Merchants and private banks served the basic credit requirements of the town residents and the local ranchers for many years. Smaller ranchers relied heavily on merchants for basic supplies as well as food and clothing. In Duval County, Margarito, Pedro, Francisco, and Jesús Lopez all had open accounts with José Vaello in San Diego, who had emigrated from Spain in the 1860s, as well as smaller accounts with a number of other local merchants.[24]

Merchant lending, however, became insufficient for the rapidly commercializing ranching industry in the 1870s and 1880s. After the fencing of the open range, ranchers increasingly needed funds to buy land, livestock, and feed and to build fences, stables, barns, windmills, and artesian wells. Commission firms filled the gap before the establishment of a network of banks in the region. They specialized in the livestock industry and served as advisors as well as lenders. They brokered loans backed by mortgages on land and provided cash in exchange for consignment of cattle headed for the stockyards. The commission agents could often negotiate better prices for the cattle than the ranchers. These commission firms, however, served as brokers mainly for British investors, furthering local dependence on outside capital.[25]

The major local commission firm in South Texas was H. P. Drought & Company, organized by Francis Smith, a young Scot who saw the great potential of ranching in the counties along the Rio Grande. Smith began as an independent agent negotiating loans for a number of British companies during the height of the cattle drives from 1865 until 1875, when British firms were investing in ranches all over the American West. In 1877, Smith moved to San Antonio and started his own commission firm, Francis Smith & Co., and hired a young Irish lawyer, Henry Patrick Drought, to assist him. Drought took over the firm in 1900 and renamed it H. P. Drought & Co. The company continued to act as an agent for British investors such as the US Mortgage Co. of Scotland, but its portfolio included a growing number of American mortgage and life insurance companies as well.[26]

Like virtually all commission firms, H. P. Drought & Co. focused on financing the large, commercial ranches in South Texas and in Mexico, at least prior to the revolution. Its borrowers included Asher Richardson, Manuel Guerra, and Ed Lasater. The company actually saved Ed Lasater from near bankruptcy by loaning him $200,000 to pay off a mortgage owed to Henrietta King, Richard King's widow, who had indicated she was planning to foreclose on his land. Moreover, H. P. Drought would carry these ranchers for a long time when they fell behind on their debt payments. Lawyer and Cameron County political boss James B. Wells remained in arrears for several years in the 1910s, but Drought refused to foreclose. He reasoned that Wells's properties would be hard to sell because of the recent raids along the Rio Grande as well as a persistent drought, which would preclude leasing out the lands.[27]

Creditworthiness in the ranching industry, as in merchandising, became associated with size; the large ranches not only provided creditors with more ongoing business but were also less vulnerable to the boom-and-bust cycles of the ranching industry. As Tom Lea said of the King Ranch, its "very size . . . gave it an economic momentum, a credit when it need cash, which was a built-in power to bridge a bad season or even a series of bad years. In adding to the ranch's lands during hard times, Manager Kleberg used the ranch's credit to borrow the cash required; the lenders found no fault with the soundness of the ranch's paper or the way it always paid off."[28] The greater availability of credit to large commercial ranches contributed to the ongoing consolidation of land in the hands of a few elite ranchers, most of whom were Anglos. It also set up high barriers to entry into ranching.

Few Tejanos appear in the H. P. Drought records, primarily because most of their ranches were relatively small and therefore more prone to failure in difficult times. They did not provide sufficient collateral for Drought's clients to willingly assume the risks of lending and lacked adequate capital to acquire the technology that might make them more profitable. Drought appeared to be far more willing to foreclose on its few Tejano borrowers. On July 3, 1891, Antonio and Lázaro Peña borrowed $10,000 at an interest rate of 10 percent, secured by 11,060 acres of pasture land in Starr County. Drought foreclosed in July 1898. Toribio Guerra of San Diego borrowed $4,000 on March 5, 1892, secured by his 3,835-acre ranch. Drought foreclosed on his land in November 1894. In another case, Drought foreclosed on approximately 11,000 acres in Starr County owned by Juan Acebo. The reason for the foreclosure became apparent when the trustee sold the property to a couple of Anglo-Americans and informed Francis Smith that the company was now in a much better position. The pair had improved the land and installed a couple of "magnificent artesian wells."[29]

The Mexican Revolution and the ensuing concern over the maintenance of a civilized society conducive to modern business enterprise south of the border may have played a part in Drought's apparent reluctance to lend to Tejanos north of the border. In a letter dated January 13, 1915, Drought told some Scottish investors, "The present condition is in reality the normal condition of Mexico. The long term of peace under Díaz was abnormal. From the time Mexico became independent up to the present time with the exception of the Díaz regime, there has been nothing but insurrection."[30]

In the 1910s and 1920s, H. P. Drought continued to make a few loans to Tejano ranchers, sometimes in relatively small amounts, such as the $2,500 loan in March 1913 to Julio Rodriguez. Rodriguez, who owned a 1,280-acre ranch in Encinal County, paid 8 percent interest on the loan, which was fairly typical for the period. Resendo Martínez of Starr County borrowed $5,000 on January 17, 1928, and he, too, paid 8 percent in interest. Drought did not vary its interest rates based on the ethnicity of the borrower, but it did sometimes charge a slightly lower rate for larger loans. Several loans Drought brokered for the US Mortgage Co. of Scotland in 1910 and 1911 illustrate this practice. Drought charged 8 percent on a $30,000 loan to L. R. Ortiz, a breeder and dealer in cattle, horses, and mules and owner of 28,000 acres of land in Webb County. Similarly, Drought charged 8 percent for a $30,000 loan to rancher Amado Garza, who owned 14,444 acres in Brooks County, and 8 percent for a $29,000 loan to J. M. Dobie of Cotulla, who owned a 25,439.5-acre ranch in Webb and La Salle counties. John Armstrong, however, received a 7¼-percent interest rate for a $62,000 loan secured by approximately 35,800 acres in Cameron and Hidalgo counties.[31]

The commission firms continued to provide capital for ranchers throughout the period, but after the railroads arrived, the options expanded to include national banks. Congress had passed a National Bank Act in 1863 to help finance the Union military effort during the Civil War. During the Reconstruction era, due to the need for development capital in depressed postwar Texas, a few national banks were established in the major cities of Houston, Dallas, and San Antonio. The minimum capital requirement of $50,000 made it difficult to open one along the Rio Grande, however, until it became clear that it would be profitable. The integration of the US and Mexican economies during the Porfiriato provided the necessary impetus, and northern Mexican capital made the establishment of the first border national bank possible. Milmo National Bank, founded by Patricio Milmo, the cotton magnate and son-in-law of Santiago Vidaurri, opened its doors in Laredo in the early 1880s, not long after the arrival of the railroad. Other national banks soon followed. William Kelly, who took over King and Kenedy's steamboat operations after they went into the ranching business, opened First National Bank in Brownsville with the help of some Galveston businessmen in 1891. Brownsville's second national bank, Merchants National Bank of Brownsville, opened the same year as the railroad arrived, in January 1904, with $100,000 in capital. Del Rio did not have a national bank until after 1900. Eagle Pass had two national banks established in the late 1800s, but one of them, Woods National Bank, failed shortly after its creation.[32]

Like the commission firms, national banks generally catered to larger concerns. They became important sources of development capital after 1900. While eastern banks, especially Stillman's National City Bank, had financed most of the railroads and the first farm colonies in the region, local national banks provided substantial sums for later developments. Rentfro Banton Creager, Al Parker, and Celestino Barreda, for example, all borrowed from Merchants National in Brownsville to fund farm colonies and subdivisions built in the 1910s and 1920s.[33]

National banks slowly began to loan to ranchers and eventually became the primary source of credit for the large ranches seeking to expand operations or enhance liquidity. The larger ranchers often sat on the boards of the banks and had strong personal relationships with the owners, managers, and loan officers. Banks such as Stockmen's National in Cotulla catered almost exclusively to local ranchers. Personal relationships provided the basis for lending money; local banks did not need to resort to credit-reporting firms because their borrowers were in their communities. These relationships were extremely important not only to the bankers but also to the ranchmen because of their long-term dependence on loans due to the unstable, boom-and-bust nature of the ranching industry.[34]

The presence of national banks in the border region did not facilitate the growth of smaller enterprises. Although national banks occasionally made loans to small farms and ranches, they generally avoided them because of the high rates of default. National banks also did not meet the needs of the vast majority of South Texas residents, whose primary asset was their land. Nineteenth-century national banking laws highly restricted the use of land and buildings as collateral for loans because these were deemed too illiquid and difficult to sell in the event of a default. National banks could and did take land as supplemental collateral, but laws prohibited direct mortgage lending until 1914. Even after 1914, banks often loaned against livestock rather than land, obtaining chattel mortgages in exchange. They then could readily order the sale of some of the livestock if they felt the repayment of the loan was in jeopardy.[35]

By the early twentieth century, it was apparent that the existing network of private banks, merchant lenders, and national banks did not meet the needs of the bulk of the population. Many rural areas lacked sufficient capital to establish a national bank, leaving people at the mercy of the unregulated, often arbitrary and unstable, private banks. The Texas legislature therefore finally passed a law in 1905 allowing the incorporation of state-chartered banks and setting up a state agency, the Department of Insurance and Banking, to supervise them. This law had a dual purpose: to encourage the creation of more small banks and to further decentralize banking in Texas in order to keep the national banks from controlling most in-state credit. State banks had lower capitalization require-ments than national banks and could lend up to 25 percent of their capital to one entity, whereas national banks could only lend 10 percent. They could also loan more freely against different types of collateral, including real estate. Although these rules allowed capital to flow with fewer restraints to local businessmen, they also contributed to the shaky financial structure of the time. State banks were more stable than private banks but not much more so.[36]

Following the passage of the law, state banks sprang up along the border. Their expansion was particularly rapid and dramatic in the lower Rio Grande Valley, where, fortuitously, the law had coincided with the arrival of the rail-road and the development of the farm colonies. In 1903, there had been only two banks, Yturria's bank and First National; by 1913, four national banks and eighteen state banks had opened their doors. Virtually every new farm town had its own bank. Farther upriver, Laredo and Eagle Pass each had a state bank by 1910, and Del Rio had one by 1918. Rio Grande City also had a state and a na-tional bank. Notably, many towns dominated by ethnic Mexicans lagged behind in terms of the establishment of banking institutions. Roma still did not have a bank in 1925, nor did San Ygnacio in Zapata County. San Diego had one state bank with a capital of $35,000. This meant that residents of these areas had to travel farther to see whether they could take out a loan and, depending on where they lived, might have been less likely to have personal connections with the bank's officers, which was often crucial for borrowing money.[37]

The passage of the state banking law spurred the growth of an entrepreneurial middle class in South Texas by making bank loans more readily available to small businesses and farmers. Capital was no longer restricted to the elite, who were able to cultivate ties outside the state. Unlike the national banks, the state banks immediately accepted land as collateral. They provided funds to buy homes, stores, town lots, farmland, automobiles, and equipment. The presence of a bank was an important drawing point for a new farm community. Local banks promoted themselves through advertisements as well as personal relationships. A local advertisement published by Brownsville Bank & Trust in the *Brownsville Daily Herald* in 1913 stated, "When you have a bank account, you have a bank connection. Your CREDIT is better. You have more confidence and self-reliance. It will help you in every way."[38]

In the 1910s and 1920s, the credit options for ranchers and farmers began to grow. During this period, even the national banks and life insurance companies made riskier loans to smaller enterprises because of the increasingly competitive lending environment. Competition aided borrowers by lowering the costs of credit. Correspondence from 1918 in H. P. Drought's files reveals the company's growing concern over the incursion of life insurance companies, federal land banks, and the joint stock banks into its territory. Federal land banks, created by Congress in 1916 to improve the availability of loans at lower interest rates for farmers and ranchers, made loans at an interest rate as low as 6 percent. In general, H. P. Drought charged 8 percent, but by 1918, there was some discussion about whether it would have to reduce the rate to 7 percent to keep its customers.[39] In addition to the competition from the banks, Drought also faced rival commission firms and cattle loan companies such as the Strahorn-Hutton-Evans Commission Company of Kansas City, the Chicago Live Stock Commission Company, the National Cattle Loan Company of St. Louis, and the Stock Raisers' Loan Company. These firms, many of which had ties to the large meat packers in Chicago, advertised in regional newspapers such as the *San Antonio Daily Express* that they offered "liberal loans . . . on cattle in feed lots and pastures."[40]

The experiences of individual borrowers provide a glimpse into the changing credit landscape in the 1910s, 1920s, and early 1930s. The debts of Eleanor Jennings, a widow managing a ranch encompassing 117,000 acres in Val Verde and Terrell counties, were typical of the large ranchers. In 1923, her two largest debts, secured by a first and second lien on her land, included a $150,000 loan from American National Insurance Company of Galveston and a $135,000 loan from the National Cattle Company. She also owed $15,000 to Lubbock State

Bank. Bub and Frank Davenport, who owned approximately 30,000 acres in Uvalde County, had borrowed from Sabinal National Bank, Commercial National Bank, the National Cattle Loan Company of St. Louis, the Stock Raisers' Loan Company, and Commerce Farm Credit Company.[41] Tejanos who owned large ranches also borrowed from similar sources. Eusebio García's son Amador took over management of the 48,000-acre Los Ojuelos Ranch in 1929. Together they took out a $95,000 loan from Frost Bank in San Antonio and a $25,000 loan from Laredo National Bank, using ranch land as collateral. The Treviño brothers, who leased most of their land in Webb County, borrowed $23,962.62 from Laredo National Bank, secured by a chattel mortgage on 704 cattle.[42]

With the rise of state banks and the increasing competition for loans, even smaller Tejano ranchers and farmers had greater access to credit. On June 27, 1914, T. T. Margo, who had fifty-two and a half acres of land in Starr County, borrowed $2,000 from First State Bank of Rio Grande City. In the early 1930s, Juan Acevedo, who engaged in mixed ranching and farming, borrowed about $5,000 from Laredo National Bank, secured by 100 head of cattle. Francisco Farias borrowed over $26,000 from the Federal Land Bank to refinance his 1,435-acre irrigated farm near Laredo. José Solis, who farmed fifty four acres of land in northern Cameron County inherited from his mother, borrowed about $3,000, secured by livestock, from First State Bank of Raymondville and another $1,000 from Merchants National Bank. José María Guerra owed $532 to First State Bank of Rio Grande City, secured by his forty-seven-acre farm.[43]

Mortgage statistics from the period suggest that Tejano farmers borrowed less than Anglos. The numbers and percentages of mortgaged farms in Starr and Zapata counties, where Tejanos were the majority, were far lower than they were in the Anglo-dominated areas. This suggests that either banks chose to loan less often to Tejanos or that Tejanos were more reluctant to borrow money and pledge their land for fear of losing it. It is virtually impossible, based on the documentary record, to determine definitively whether Tejano farmers had less access to bank credit than Anglos, but it is a reasonable inference. Tejano-dominated rural areas had fewer banks, and their operations were usually smaller and less profitable. José Salinas's profile may have been typical of small Tejano landowners. He owned 1,659.7 acres, where he grew cotton and pastured some cattle, horses, and mules. His debt totaled $3,330, most of it owed to individuals. He had an outstanding debt of $135 to First State Bank & Trust Co. of Rio Grande City and $150 to Zapata County Bank.[44]

In contrast to Tejano farmers, Anglo farmers borrowed more frequently and had better access to bank credit. The larger numbers of state banks in Anglo-dominated areas made this possible and gave Anglos an advantage in terms of expanding their farms and upgrading their equipment. According to local attorney James Ewers, most of the Anglo-American farmers who moved to the Valley had solid credit ratings and arrived with some capital acquired from the sale of their lands and homes in the Midwest. They usually made a down payment for their new orchard or vegetable tract and then financed the rest directly through the land company. After the first year, the farmers often ran out of money and then had to rely on local credit for operations and supplies. They then borrowed from the local state banks and gave land, crops, mules, cows, pigs, and horses as collateral. For example, Walter Wade McClain, a farmer from Indiana, bought forty acres in the Alamo tract in about 1915. In 1921, he borrowed $1,700 from San Juan State Bank & Trust Company and in 1922 took out an additional $800 loan from First State Bank of Alamo, secured by a chattel mortgage on his pigs, horses, and crops. William Duncan, who owned twenty-two acres in the La Blanca tract near Donna, gave Farmers State Bank a mortgage on his mules and his automobile in exchange for a loan of approximately $800.[45] In the 1920s, Anglo farmers also began to take out loans to buy automobiles and farm equipment, sometimes directly from the manufacturer. For example, H. O. Berset bought a tractor on installment for $450 from J. I. Case Tractor Co. in Alamo. Steve Pfeiffer, who was farming fifteen acres near Alamo, signed an installment contract in 1930 with General Motors for the purchase of a Pontiac sedan. He also bought tractors from International Harvester and John Deere Plow Company.[46]

The apparent disparity between Tejanos and Anglos in obtaining bank credit for small and medium-sized enterprises was less pronounced in the towns than it was in the countryside. One reason for this is that the banks were located in the towns and tended to cultivate relationships with as many businesspeople as possible in their community, regardless of citizenship or ethnicity. Cristóbal Rodríguez, a general merchant in Mission, borrowed $2,300 from First State Bank & Trust Co. in McAllen sometime in 1919. The partnership of January & Hill, which operated a gents' furnishing store in McAllen, borrowed $2,600 from the same bank at about the same time. The two businesses had comparable assets. Local bankruptcy records show that ethnic Mexican businesspeople in the towns borrowed from local banks to buy town lots, store buildings, houses, and automobiles. They also took out unsecured loans to fund operations when cash reserves were low. This was especially common in the lower Rio Grande Valley, which had more state banks. Although ethnic Mexicans suffered segregation and more prejudice in this Anglo-dominated area, those who started businesses had an advantage over Tejanos in more rural areas, where there were fewer credit facilities.[47]

The state banks had their limitations, of course. Local elites did tend to control them, which could be a problem in areas that had one or two banks. Bank credit, however, was far more accessible in the first half of the twentieth century along the border than it had been in the nineteenth century. Also, more small businesses and middle-class, white-collar workers and professionals had access to credit in South Texas than they did in Mexico. Credit in Mexico was restricted mainly to those with political connections, leading to a highly concentrated industrial and business structure that diminished opportunities for small, emerging, middle-class entrepreneurs.[48]

In stark contrast to the decentralized system of banking developing in the United States around the turn of the twentieth century, the financial sector in Mexico was dominated by two major banks, El Banco de Londres y México, owned by British investors, and the government supported Banco Nacional de México (Banamex). Government regulations privileged Banamex and erected barriers to the creation of new banks, mainly to protect the government's primary source of credit. In 1909, Mexico had only forty-one chartered banking institutions, compared to 18,723 banks and trust companies in the United States.[49]

Then, between 1910 and the early 1920s, Mexico's banking system virtually collapsed as a result of the Mexican Revolution. Violence and political instability led to insolvency and bank closures. High debt threatened the nation's financial infrastructure. Even the Banco Mercantil de Monterrey, which managed to survive the revolution relatively intact, shut down all of its branches outside of the city. Along the border, affluent Mexicans shifted their assets into banks in Brownsville and Laredo.[50]

The contrast between the two banking systems of the United States and Mexico highlights the very different opportunities available for up-and-coming entrepreneurs. South Texas had the credit facilities to promote the growth of an ethnic Mexican small-business class while northern Mexico did not. Even though ethnic Mexicans had some disadvantages in accessing the credit available in South Texas, they were not barred. A few ethnic Mexican entrepreneurs in South Texas borrowed from banks in Mexico, but this seems to have been relatively rare.[51] The improving situation for credit for small business in the United States compared to Mexico may have enticed some middle-class Mexicans to immigrate and settle north of the Río Bravo.

Banks in the United States had their own problems and limitations, of course. They experienced boom-and-bust cycles, threatening the savings of border residents as well as their ability to borrow. The undercapitalization of many of the state banks became evident during economic downturns. The Federal Reserve Bank of Dallas, founded in 1914, served South Texas and provided a source of stability for banks in its system. It operated branches in El Paso, Houston, and San Antonio. Very few South Texas banks were eligible to participate in the Federal Reserve System, however, because of the $25,000 minimum capital requirement. The expansion of state banks came to a virtual standstill during World War I, and the state banking system almost collapsed during the postwar recession of the early 1920s. Hidalgo and Cameron counties were hit especially hard because of the prevalence of crop loans and the severe decline in crop prices. Banks foreclosed on land worth far less than loans against it and incurred severe losses. Lawyer James Ewers said his father's bank failed in McAllen at this time. Those banks that survived the crisis enjoyed record profits as the economy boomed in the mid- and late 1920s.[52]

Scandal rocked the First State Bank & Trust Co. of Laredo in 1928. Rafael Martínez, the cashier for First State Bank & Trust Co. of Laredo, was caught embezzling large sums of money from the bank and investing them in his dry-goods business, La Bella Jardinera. Along with the bank president, Royle K. Mims, the vice president, Luis Lafón, and the assistant cashier, Serapio Vela, Martínez was accused of misappropriating bank funds to speculate in cotton and Mexican gold mines. The bank had to close its doors, and all four men went to jail.[53]

The Great Depression affected banks along the border as it did others around the country. Credit dried up as they began to fail. The largest bank failure involved Merchants National Bank of Brownsville, which closed its doors on March 24, 1932. Other smaller banks folded, resulting in bank deposit losses for hundreds of people.[54] After the bank holiday on March 5, 1933, several of these institutions, including the First State Bank of Mission, did not reopen. The Security State Bank of Weslaco, First State Bank of Lyford, Farmers State Bank of San Benito, Valley State Bank of Harlingen, Arroyo State Bank of Rio Hondo, the First National Bank of Pharr, and Texas Bank and Trust Co. of Brownsville all failed during the decade. Other banks limited their loans drastically, decimated by the inability of many to pay back loans. Foreclosure was not a solution because of the surplus real estate, livestock, and inventories for which there was no market. Ramón Guerra of McAllen recalled his father asking friends for loans to keep buying and selling cattle because all of the banks in his area had closed. One of Guerra's brothers ended up traveling all the way to Oklahoma to borrow enough money to buy feed for the cattle.[55] By 1938, Brownsville had only one bank, First National. Laredo, Eagle Pass, and Del Rio each had two banks.[56]

With the drying up of other sources of capital in the 1930s, South Texans turned to the federal government for help. South Texas farmers in particular increasingly relied on funds borrowed from New Deal agencies rather than on private loans. More than three hundred farmers in Maverick County alone applied for emergency crop loans in 1935. Many farmers also turned to the land banks for assistance but quickly learned that federal assistance was limited. Ninety-eight farmers in the La Feria District of Cameron County applied for loans in the mid-1930s, but the Federal Land Bank in Houston rejected all but thirty-eight of them because of inadequate drainage on the lands and delinquent taxes.[57]

The Great Depression revealed the limits of the US banking system's ability to provide capital to up-and-coming entrepreneurs. The creation of the Federal Deposit Insurance Corporation (FDIC) did the most to restore confidence and capital to the banks along the border as elsewhere in the country. The implementation of the FDIC and the restoration of the banks took time, however. Since many of the state banks had failed, people were forced to temporarily fall back on friends and family, who had always been an important part of the credit network in South Texas.

FAMILY AND COMMUNITY

When other forms of credit were either too expensive or unavailable, family and friends filled in the gaps. They often charged little or no interest and sometimes allowed the strength of the personal relationship to outweigh concerns they might have over the risks of the venture.[58] Individuals of means within a community also loaned money or sold property on credit to local residents, often for investment purposes. Many of these individuals were women, widows left to manage their husbands' estate or wives who owned separate property, often inherited from parents. They played a key role in financing businesses in the border region. Their collective impact as creditors was more significant than as entrepreneurs because the numbers of women loaning money to local businesses far exceeded those who operated them.

Texas community-property laws, adopted from Spain, facilitated the role of women as creditors because they allowed married women to buy, sell, and own property separate from their husbands.[59] Wives often loaned money or leased property that they had acquired as gifts or inheritances from their parents. David Chapa's wife, Petra Garza de Chapa, had received some cattle from her mother. She sold the cattle for $1,500 and loaned her husband the money for his mercantile business. Gregorio Sosa also borrowed money from his wife to operate his business. She had inherited about $3,000 from her father when he died in Spain. She purchased two lots with some of the money and loaned $600 to Gregorio. Mauricio Zertuche's wife loaned him money for his store in Del Rio, but when he started having difficulty paying his creditors, she refused to lend any more until he gave her some security. Oscar Kessler, a twenty-five-year-old merchant just starting out in business, obtained loans from his wife to invest in town lots and pay some debts of the business.[60]

Community-property laws enabled women to shield assets acquired prior to the marriage or through a gift or inheritance from their husbands' creditors. A wife's separate property could be a source of security in the event her husband squandered the couple's jointly owned community property. Husbands sometimes attempted to use these laws to circumvent their creditors by putting property or even entire businesses in their wives' names.[61]

Dozens of widows around South Texas lived on income derived from leasing and selling property and lending funds out of their estates.[62] In the 1930s, Rosa Vela de Benavides and Teresa Salinas de la Chica were two of the most important lenders in Laredo, especially within the Tejano community. Rosa was the widow of Ygnacio Benavides and the sister-in-law of Servando Benavides, brothers who had inherited substantial town and ranch properties from their father. Oil was discovered on some of the Benavides' ranch lands in the 1920s, making them even more valuable. Teresa Salinas de la Chica was the widow of D. C. de la Chica, a native of Monterrey, Mexico, who had moved to Laredo in 1880 at the age of fourteen to work for Antonio Bruni. In 1905, he bought Laredo Brick Manufacturing Company, which became very profitable. He invested those profits into real estate around Laredo, including the Robert E. Lee Hotel. After D. C. de la Chica died in February 1932, his wife, Teresa, took over management of the properties. Rosa Vela de Benavides and Teresa Salinas de la Chica sold farmland and town lots on credit to many businesspeople in the area.[63]

Widows also loaned money or property to help struggling relatives. Forty-year-old M. A. García, a merchant in San Benito, felt deeply indebted to his aunt, Mrs. Lafargue, of Rio Grande City. "I was educated by her and she sent me to school, she has been more than a mother to me." In addition, Mrs. Lafargue provided $3,000 for the initial down payment to buy his mercantile business and loaned additional sums thereafter. Edward Sisk leased space for his drugstore in Laredo from Mrs. Arthur, his mother-in-law.[64]

Despite the increasing availability of impersonal forms of credit, much lending continued to depend on personal relationships and the trust they created. Those with access to wealthy family members, kin-based or ethnic networks in particular industries, and personal connections with local bankers and wholesalers had a substantial advantage over those who lacked those kinds of associations. This became especially apparent during down times, when national credit institutions faltered or collapsed.

•   •   •

The expansion and contraction of credit throughout the United States in the late nineteenth and early twentieth centuries contributed to a pervasive ambivalence about its use in South Texas as it did elsewhere. Credit seemed to be beneficial when the economy was prosperous, and people were able to repay their loans. Credit had a dark side, however. It involved dependence, the opposite of self-reliance. It potentially weakened moral character, leading to extravagance rather than thrift and dishonesty rather than integrity. It could destroy close relationships when loans went unpaid. Debt could also be coercive. In Laredo in the 1920s, there were allegations that several influential bankers threatened to call the loans of those opposed to their political stands. Lawyer J. T. Canales asserted that the "banks and money lenders instead of being helpful to humanity are in reality the leeches and parasites of our civilization."[65]

On the other hand, many believed that, without credit, there could be no progress. "The mortgage system has carried the south and west to their present state of industrial progress and their various communities have been most prosperous when borrowed money was most plentiful and the greatest number of mortgages was being filled with corresponding application of intelligence and energy to productive and gainful enterprises. Men as a rule do not borrow money to squander."[66] Overall, acceptance of debt was growing, particularly business debt. Many people differentiated between "productive" credit, which was acceptable because it produced more value, and "consumptive" credit, used for items that quickly depreciated or lost their value, such as clothing or appliances. Yet consumer credit was growing as well, particularly to buy automobiles, which was apparent in South Texas in the 1920s. More and more, credit became the way to achieve a middle-class standard of living.[67]

In the South Texas border region, the expansion of mercantile credit and the banking system were undoubtedly crucial for the development of small business and a middle class, thereby expanding the business class beyond just the elite. Credit enabled more and more people to acquire the necessary capital to become independent entrepreneurs and pursue success as defined by evolving notions of the American dream. Its availability may have even lured businesspeople out of Mexico and into the United States. Credit, however, was not equally available to everyone and limited opportunities even as it expanded them. It also rendered its recipients more vulnerable to financial failure, exacerbating the uncertainty of their status and livelihood, as the next chapter explains.

7

FACING FAILURE

J OSEPH NETZER FILED FOR BANKRUPTCY in the summer of 1917. When asked about his future plans, he said, "I hope to go back into business. If I had a year's time, I would pay out dollar for dollar, but I was too pushed. I do not know just now what my present intentions are with regard to engaging in business; I am in the hands now of the creditors, I do not know what to do, I do not know where to turn. I am dazed, really, I have not been myself."[1] Joseph Netzer expressed the feelings common to those facing failure—a sense of disorientation and deep discouragement. His experience revealed how the pursuit of opportunity inevitably carried with it the possibility of loss.

Failure, or business insolvency, which Scott Sandage artfully calls "an entrepreneurial fall from grace," is the downside of the risk that entrepreneurs undertake in starting and carrying out various business enterprises. An innate feature of capitalism, failure accompanied the expansion of the market economy and the credit system into South Texas, hovering as a threat over every enterprise. It became a common experience along the border between 1880 and 1940; it did not discriminate among its victims, affecting a wide range of people regardless of their ethnicity, gender, class, or capital. Smaller enterprises, however, were more vulnerable to failure because they had fewer assets to summon and fewer connections with creditors to rely on during a business downturn. Since so many of the border enterprises were small, insecurity and uncertainty about the future permeated the society.[2]

VULNERABILITY TO FAILURE

Credit paradoxically enhanced vulnerability to failure even as it increased the possibility of gain. The greater one's dependence on credit, the greater one's exposure to failure during times of disaster or difficulty. The difficulty of gauging potential markets and future prices made the choice to borrow as well as how much to borrow to some degree a shot in the dark. Consequences were not always foreseeable and were often influenced by circumstances beyond one's control. The threat was a condition known as "equitable insolvency," or the inability to pay debts as they came due, caused by lack of cash, liquid assets, or access to additional credit. Even people with substantial net worth could experience equitable insolvency if their resources were illiquid, and they could not get new loans. On the other hand, business owners whose debts exceeded their assets could stay afloat if they could continue borrowing.[3] A person could avoid equitable insolvency by refusing to borrow or by borrowing only small amounts. Yet the refusal to borrow carried risks as well, limiting the possibility of growth.

Extending credit to others compounded the dangers of personal reliance on credit. Border merchants typically sold on credit because of the scarcity of cash in the local economy. Profit margins were thin. Customers delayed payments when droughts, insect infestations, and low prices affected the local agricultural economy, exposing local storekeepers to the risk of collection suits and asset seizures by creditors. Recognizing these risks, suppliers often extended lenient terms. Reportedly, grocery wholesalers customarily allowed retail merchants in South Texas to give postdated checks. Yet, if a supplier's terms were too lenient, and enough retail merchants failed to pay, then the supplier might face insolvency. The web of interrelated obligations made everyone vulnerable.[4]

The case of Sam Greenfield illustrates how the interrelationships between suppliers and customers could lead to failure. Greenfield had a general retail store in Mission, and he also acted as a wholesale supplier for other shops in the area, mostly operated by ethnic Mexicans. Prospects looked encouraging in 1920, so he bought about $140,000 worth of merchandise. Although he sold some of it, he noticed that prices were beginning to decline, and he tried, without success, to return the remaining amounts to the wholesalers. He paid some of his outstanding debts but was unable to sell enough merchandise to pay all of them, forcing some of the wholesalers to take deep losses. He had no sympathy for them, however, because, in his words, "You take the wholesalers that lost. I lost too." The deepening postwar recession hurt some of his own customers to the extent that they could not pay him, further hastening his downward slide toward bankruptcy. Refugio Garza, who ran a store in Pharr stocked with about $5,000, had always paid promptly, but business had slowed, and he now "owe[d] lots of money." Cantú Brothers in Hidalgo had an outstanding account of about $1,200. Greenfield said they could not pay because they owed the commission wholesalers too much money and could not sell the cotton they had taken from their customers as collateral. When asked whether any of these men had tried to offer him security, he responded, "What kind of security can you get? If they get money, they will bring it in and get some more goods. If you don't give them some more goods they don't bring the other money."[5]

Merchants who catered to the ethnic Mexican community were especially vulnerable to customer nonpayment. As Alfonso Sierra reported, most of his customers were "floating laborers, hence have no permanent address, working in work camps."[6] The migrant workers purchased groceries and other necessities from local merchants, usually in small amounts on credit. Frequently, these outstanding accounts ranged between $2.00 and $6.00, and the individuals who owed them lived in both Texas and Mexico. The amounts owed were difficult to collect because the workers had very little money or assets and sometimes moved away from the area in pursuit of work. In the bankruptcy case of Luz González de Balderina, the bankruptcy trustee decided not to try to collect any of the outstanding customer accounts because they were against "Mexican people, most of whom have no property exempt from execution and are of little value."[7] Eutiquio Pérez, who operated a store on the Santa Maria Ranch along the Rio Grande near Brownsville, reported in his bankruptcy schedules that he had little hope of recovering money from customers who had not paid. "Many of these debtors, thru loss of crops have abandoned farms and moved away. Some have gone to Mexico on account of the recent bandit troubles along the border."[8]

Even when times were prosperous, merchants faced stiff competition. The railroads had provided many benefits to small proprietors, including the expansion of opportunities, but this expansion led more and more people to do business in a local area. No one had a monopoly anymore and therefore could not keep prices artificially high. The trend toward larger businesses in the United States affected retail sales as well, and the rise of mail-order companies and chains, such as Piggly Wiggly and Howard E. Butt (H. E. B.) grocery stores and the J. C. Penney department stores, further threatened the position of local proprietors. The chains often sold on cash, which meant they could undersell the individual proprietors who typically sold on credit. When asked what caused his grocery store in Del Rio to fail, Antonio Garza responded simply, "We had a lot of competition."[9]

In addition to the difficulties inherent in the commercial economy, fire was a particular hazard in the towns because so many of the stores and warehouses were made at least partially of wood. Also, wooden boxes were often used as crates. Stories about fires filled newspaper headlines. The day after Christmas 1902, the *Laredo Times* proclaimed, "Fire Record: Big Fire at Laredo," which destroyed, among other businesses, Eduardo Cruz's dry-goods store. A few years earlier, fire had destroyed Mrs. Louis Pasco's millinery shop, which she had operated in Laredo for more than fifteen years. In 1919 Mr. Marroquín, a wholesale produce dealer, lost $18,000 worth of goods and sustained $8,000 in damage to the building in a Laredo warehouse fire. Pedro Zavaleta of Los Fresnos lost his merchandise as the result of a fire. Isadore Goodman's store in Harlingen burned in 1931, just as the Depression was beginning to hit South Texas. Fires frequently led to failure because, although fire and casualty insurance was available, most merchants either did not purchase it or lacked adequate coverage.[10]

Injury or illness of the merchant or a member of the merchant's family usually affected business adversely and often led to failure. Besides the added debt burden of medical bills, the time away from work contributed to financial difficulties. Guadalupe Medrano and Manuel Muñoz, merchants in Del Rio, had been ill for four or five months prior to their bankruptcy cases. When asked what caused his financial failure, Rafael Rangel, a Mexican merchant in Laredo, said that, in addition to "general hard times," the "long illness of my wife, who is still sick," was responsible. The root of W. P. Strawbridge's bankruptcy case was attributable, at least in part, to a four-month illness. His wife wrote a letter to the court official presiding over the case, expressing her appreciation for his helpfulness in securing a moratorium from creditor action during the time her husband was sick. August Linnard had a stroke in 1930 and suffered substantial losses in memory and physical strength. His son, Elmer, assisted him with his affairs, but he filed for bankruptcy in 1934. Max Tavss, who had had a shop in Mercedes, became totally disabled as the result of an automobile accident. His inability to work thereafter eventually led to the failure of his business.[11]

Sometimes a business owner died, leaving wives and children to sort out the tangle of debt. Flavio Vargas, a Laredo druggist, died on June 1, 1921, leaving a wife and four children. Narciso Alanis, a butcher in Laredo, died on February 28, 1922, about two years after filing a voluntary bankruptcy case. He had purchased about four lots in Laredo in 1916, 1917, and 1919 and had given a vendor's lien to M. A. Hirsh. Alanis had built a home and a store on the property. Hirsh was anxious to recover his collateral throughout the case. Alanis's widow, Amelia López de Alanis, tried to raise the money to keep her home, but, unfortunately, the court finally ordered the sale of the property and evicted Amelia and her four children, Guadalupe, Amelia, Alberto, and Alfredo, in December 1923.[12]

Ranchers and farmers were even more vulnerable to insolvency than merchants, largely as the result of unpredictable forces beyond their control. Agricultural and livestock prices usually fluctuated widely, depending on international demand and production. Weather patterns in any given year could jeopardize their ability to make payments on outstanding debt incurred to care for livestock or expand their operations. Unlike merchants, ranchers and farmers had little access to unsecured credit and usually had to pledge their property as collateral in exchange for loans.

Drought was one of the greatest perils in the region. From 1915 through 1917, a major drought struck South Texas. It was so severe that even the King Ranch suffered losses, $77,266.63 in 1917 and $144,475 in 1918.[13] An Anglo-American rancher in Hidalgo County, S. M. Hargrove, lost most of his cattle, more than one thousand head, because of the inability to find good pastureland. He burned prickly pear cactus to feed them. He kept begging his main creditor, Merchants National Bank, to allow him to move the cattle to better grass near San Antonio, but it was too late to save most of them. Merchants National foreclosed on the ones who survived the drought. Alonzo Yates of Webb County filed for bankruptcy in 1917 primarily because of the drought, but he was not the only rancher in the vicinity who was struggling. Virtually all of them were "in hard circumstances, and their time [was] practically all taken in trying to take care of their cattle." Lee Dillon started a farm near Asherton in 1925, but climate forced him out of business by 1928. When asked whether he considered himself a farmer, he replied, "I don't know what I am, I am a man out of business. I don't consider farming at present—it is too dry down there, not enough rain."[14]

Diseases affecting livestock and cattle could also strike without warning. Texas fever, the tick-borne disease, remained prevalent throughout the US-Mexico borderlands and periodically devastated cattle herds, especially the newer breeds that had not yet developed immunity. Flare-ups occurred during the Mexican Revolution when American ranchers pulled their cattle out of Mexico, most of whom carried the disease. About eighty of Salvador Armstrong's cattle died of Texas fever in 1918, probably contributing in part to his bankruptcy filing a few years later. In the early 1900s, ranchers in Oklahoma and Texas had developed a method of dipping cattle in crude oil to kill the fever ticks. Robert Kleberg, manager of the King Ranch, constructed the first dipping vats in South Texas; cattle were herded through chutes filled with the mixture. Sometimes the cure proved worse than the disease; Salvador Armstrong lost some of his cattle that had survived the tick fever to this form of treatment.[15]

Pest infestations were among the greatest challenges for farmers. The boll weevil crossed the border from Mexico in the early 1890s and could destroy entire fields of cotton. Each female insect laid hundreds of eggs in the cotton bolls, and when the creatures hatched, they would eat the immature bolls. They were extremely difficult to kill and had been found alive in cotton bales after the cotton had passed through the ginning process. In the early 1920s, campaigns were waged in the lower Rio Grande Valley to eliminate the boll weevil with pesticides. Other pests such as red scale, black scale, and rust mites attacked fruits and vegetables. "Blue mold" decimated the crops of spinach farmers in Zavala County, and reportedly nearly half of the region's farmers left as a result.[16]

Farmers and ranchers were also deeply affected by price fluctuations. One particularly devastating period came after the First World War, when the European economy began to recover, reducing demand there for US farm exports. Prices fell, and farmers across the United States struggled to survive. Cattle markets were hit especially hard. When asked why he filed for bankruptcy, Bub Monroe Davenport of Uvalde County responded, "Well, just hard luck, I guess." When pressed, he admitted, "We bought a lot of high-priced steers. . . . I think about seven hundred."[17] He later had to liquidate them at rock-bottom prices to pay his loans. He and his brother Fred lost 13,571 acres of ranchland in Uvalde County. Ed Lasater lost $205,000 in 1921 and had another net operating loss of $165,000 in 1922. His problems extended beyond cattle; the boll weevil had attacked his cotton crop. Two of his creditors forced him into receivership in 1923, and several of his properties were auctioned to pay outstanding debts. He struggled throughout the 1920s; H. P. Drought foreclosed on some of his property in 1928. The advantage a big rancher like Lasater had over the smaller ranchers is that he had other lands that were not mortgaged that he could keep from his creditors. Many small farmers lost all or most of their land through bankruptcy or foreclosure.[18]

Although it was true that smaller concerns were more vulnerable to failure than larger ones, failure could affect anyone under the right combination of circumstances. Many people who failed had good credit ratings, sometimes the year prior to filing for bankruptcy. One of the wealthiest men on the border,

Celestino P. Barreda, who had the highest rating possible in 1930, AAA1, filed a bankruptcy case just five years later. Saul Cohen, who had a small shoe store in Harlingen, had received a "good" credit rating in 1938, the year before he filed for bankruptcy. In 1925, Franklin Brothers received an "excellent" credit rating, which was downgraded to only "good" in 1930, the year they filed for bankruptcy. Morris Edelstein had a "good" credit rating two years before he filed a bankruptcy case.[19]

Although rarely acknowledged, this vulnerability to failure pervaded border society as it did all of American society. The complexity of situations in which people found themselves unable to pay their debts coupled with a strong American belief in personal responsibility created ambivalence and uncertainty about the causes. Were they structural or individual? Was sin or risk the cause of insolvency? Did the fault lie with the debtor or with forces beyond the debtor's control? Was the failure to pay one's debts an economic or a moral failure?[20]

RESPONSIBILITY FOR FAILURE

Although external circumstances might make success more difficult at times, the sense that character defects or poor choices contributed to failure persisted. Bankruptcy trustees, who were responsible for collecting, organizing, and distributing the assets of bankrupt estates, frequently probed debtors with questions designed to ascertain how their actions led to their plight. The trustees discovered and exposed instances of mismanagement, inexperience, profligate spending, and greed. Sometimes they found that people had become victims of wrongs perpetrated by others through fraud or outright embezzlement.

Small businesses were not always run in an efficient and careful manner. Their operations were informal, and their methods of tracking sales and purchases were often haphazard. Many were family owned and operated and failed to keep personal finances separate. Some business owners were unaware of the extent of their financial problems until creditors began demanding payments and filing lawsuits. Guadalupe Medrano of Del Rio reported that he never took an inventory of his goods, never kept track of what he sold, and "never kept any memoranda, books or accounts showing how much [he] owed." Don Lázaro Champion of Mercedes told the bankruptcy trustee in his case, "I never made inventory or balanced my accounts for 2 years until February of this year, and I found out then I was in very bad condition financially, and took the matter up with M. Halff & Brother, in the hopes they would help me." George Cook's once-profitable grocery store in San Benito collapsed after he helped his sons establish a second store. Cash continually "leaked" from the first store to the second store, and ultimately both went out of business.[21]

Inexperience also often led to financial problems. Promotional materials about the huge profits possible in truck farming or citrus probably contributed to the decision of many to abandon their stores or professional positions to buy land in South Texas. These moves were not always successful. When asked why he moved from Kingsville, Texas, to Edinburg in 1933, Arthur Chaney, a painter by trade, replied, "Well I thought it would be easier for me than painting and paper-hanging. An easier life to grow and buy fruit." His attempt to make a living operating a small orchard proved disastrous, and he ended up in bankruptcy court. After Richard Masters' general mercantile business failed, he decided to go into farming. Unfortunately, he failed at that as well.[22] Moving from farming into retail trade could also lead to financial difficulties arising from inexperience and may have contributed to the failure of Chapa Mercantile, owned and operated by David Chapa, whose primary occupation appeared to have been farming and ranching.[23]

The lure of a consumptive lifestyle ensnared more and more Americans as options for leisure increased and American industry produced a greater and greater array of products for personal use. Spending too much on these items or borrowing money to acquire them could contribute to business failure. A number of bankrupts, for example, had recently purchased new automobiles on credit. In the case of a failed automobile dealership in Uvalde, the bankruptcy trustee pointed out that the debtor had taken frequent trips to San Antonio. "The expenses on these trips were very heavy, due to the fact that Mr. Saylor and his wife always dressed very well and he would spend money very freely at all times." Guadalupe Cuevas made two trips per month to Monterrey and spent money "going around having a good time." Yet, ethnic Mexicans were often unfairly suspected of using money unwisely. The bankruptcy trustee in Gregorio Sosa's case kept asking him whether he had gambled, played roulette, or bet on chicken fights in Matamoros.[24]

The loss of reputation due to moral turpitude or crime was extremely difficult to overcome and often led to a downward spiral. Mauricio Zertuche, a merchant in Del Rio, was convicted of a federal crime, possibly smuggling, and went to jail for thirty days during the Christmas season in 1920. He left his father and sister in charge of the business, but "they all got scared, thinking about [him], and never look[ed] after the business right." They failed to sell much merchandise during the most crucial time of year for sales. Although Zertuche did not

stay in jail for very long, he was never able to make up for the lost business. Moreover, his customers had lost confidence in him. He reported at the meeting of his creditors, "The reason why the business didn't get good results, Mr. Hirshberg, is, as a matter of fact, you know, as long as people knew I went broke, why, the majority of people that owed me, they didn't try to get around, they didn't try to see me anymore, and really, I lost all the way through,—neither, they didn't care to go by even the store."[25]

Sometimes it was not an individual's own actions but the actions of others that led to failure. William Pfeffer, member of the partnership of A. Schmidt & Co., filed for bankruptcy in Laredo in 1900 because of his partner's fraud. Schmidt, who ran the partnership's office in Mexico City, had embezzled money from Mexican customers instead of putting the funds back into the partnership.[26]

Perhaps the greatest con scheme of the period, which contributed to the failure of many of the newly arrived farmers, was the promotion of the lower Rio Grande Valley. The motivation, according to victims of the scheme, was greed. Approximately six hundred farmers signed a petition in 1921, arguing "that during the last five years certain land companies operating in this valley have been guilty of the most gigantic fraud that has ever been perpetrated in the United States in the exploitation of its lands, and that through these fraudulent representations and transactions they have received millions of dollars from hundreds and hundreds of farmers taken from various northern states to the Rio Grande Valley, some of whom are still here in a destitute condition, and some of whom have been able to get sufficient funds from their friends or relatives to return to their former homes."[27]

The farmers alleged that the companies failed to provide proper deeds or in some cases gave them no deed, showed them land that was far better than what they actually received, falsely represented the lands as well-irrigated, and falsely claimed the farmers could reap substantial profits from the land. They also said that land agents told them that there were no flies or mosquitoes in the area, and when they arrived, they discovered swarms of them. Another false statement related to the overflowing of the Rio Grande; land agents claimed the area had not flooded for sixty-four years when, in fact, floods had inundated the area as recently as 1909. The biggest complaint was the practice of selling the lands for a cash down payment plus a contract for deed. When the farmers were unable to make the payments, which they claimed was a direct result of inadequate irrigation facilities, which hindered their ability to produce crops in the promised amounts, the companies would foreclose and make a huge profit selling the land to another victim.[28] One attorney said the "northern farmer lasts about two years, after which time he is busted and the crops, when they are raised, remain to rot in the fields."[29]

People invested and lost their life savings. One letter summed up the feelings of many victims. "My clients entered into a contract to purchase 105 acres in June, 1919, which two months later was covered with water from an overflow of the Rio Grande River. The weather reports show that the river is subject to perennial overflow of the property sold to my clients and many others were found on investigation to be subject to overflow yearly. Barnacles were found on the trees and shrubs about three or four feet from the ground up. The railroad is wholly incapable of taking care of even a small amount of produce. The labor (Mexican) in the vicinity is wholly worthless, treacherous and engaged chiefly in robbing and killing. The property in question is in the same locality where the State troops were stationed on the border in 1916."[30]

The US Senate ordered an investigation into the matter. Targets included W. E. Stewart, Rentfro Banton Creager, C. H. Swallow, Al Parker, Nick Doffing, and John Shary, as well as their affiliated companies. Although it was never proven, Senator Heflin of Alabama accused the land companies of employing assassins to harass or murder anyone speaking out against them. As proof, he produced a long letter with a newspaper clipping from the March 20, 1924 *Weslaco News* stating that two land agents had beaten an attorney nearly to death because he represented a woman who had allegedly been cheated by one of Creager's companies. During the course of the investigation, Kansas and Ohio revoked the business permits of several of the land companies, banning them from soliciting buyers in their states.[31] Although the investigation resulted in only one indictment against W. E. Stewart, the existence of pervasive land fraud was evident in the number of successful court cases brought by buyers in the 1920s. Most of these cases involved claims of defective deeds or misrepresentations about flooding and irrigation.[32]

The land company investigation matter highlights some of the ways in which boosters and speculators could mislead people and ultimately cause their failure. Yet boosting was such a widespread phenomenon that others would place the blame on those who believed the boosters. Local residents sarcastically referred to the Midwestern farmers as "home suckers," who were ready to buy land as soon as they saw palm trees and oranges.[33] The apparent lack of due diligence on the part of the farmers themselves raises questions about who was truly responsible for their financial woes. Thus, even when failure was the fault of individuals rather than a result of structural problems, sometimes assessing blame among those individuals was a complex matter.

DEPRESSION ON THE BORDER

Although failure could strike at any time, it became more widespread during national recessions or depressions. The risk was particularly acute during the Great Depression. The hardest-hit areas included those that had experienced the greatest speculative expansion in the 1920s, particularly the lower Rio Grande Valley and the Winter Garden. The Depression forced people to come to terms with failure on a more massive scale than they had ever seen previously. Dozens of well-established businesses in every community failed, leading some to question the prevalence of opportunity and inevitability of progress in the United States.[34]

According to J. T. Wise, chief deputy tax assessor of Webb County, the Depression along the Texas-Mexico border began in Laredo during the Christmas season of 1929, "the time that the big row was had here about the president of Mexico coming here."[35] On Friday, December 13, 1929, local district attorney John Valls issued a warrant for the arrest of the president of Mexico, General Plutarco Elías Calles, charging him with conspiracy in the 1922 murder of General Lucio Blanco, one of Calles's political enemies. Calles was on his way back to Mexico from New York City and had planned to travel through South Texas. In retaliation, the Mexican government effectively closed the international bridge between Nuevo Laredo and the United States and shut down the Mexican consulate in Laredo for several weeks. The customshouse in Nuevo Laredo prohibited all US imports from Laredo, including small consumer purchases. Even after Mexico begrudgingly reopened trade over the bridge, it imposed customs duties of 10–50 percent on all imports, large and small, from Laredo.[36]

Because the conflict occurred during the Christmas season, when the merchants made most of their sales, a crisis erupted. Mose Franklin, owner and the manager of Franklin Department Store, said his sales losses approximated 50 percent for the year. "A great deal of trade comes from the interior of Mexico and we lost practically all of it as a result of the trouble." Carlos Otal also estimated his losses to be more than 50 percent. "The magnitude of the thing cannot be conceived by the people not directly concerned, but we in the business realize it is most serious." Even Richter's Department Store, the most substantial one in town, suffered declines of 25–33 percent.[37] The Laredo merchants took matters into their own hands, making several attempts to negotiate directly with the

Mexican government. The Chamber of Commerce in Monterrey also became involved because of the adverse impact on its members, who traded regularly with the Laredo merchants. The Mexican government refused to negotiate without the resignation of John Valls. Desperate to avoid bankruptcy, more than four hundred businessmen in Laredo signed a petition calling for Valls to resign. Valls refused but softened some of his rhetoric, and the consulate reopened in mid-January 1930.[38]

The Valls-Calles controversy, although it was a relatively short-term event, had long-term repercussions for the Laredo merchants. They faced competition from stores opened in Nuevo Laredo during the embargo. Sales prices declined, in some cases below wholesale costs, making it almost impossible to recover the losses from the winter of 1929–1930. As the Depression deepened in the surrounding area, consumer demand in general slowed, and merchants stocked fewer goods. Over the course of the decade, assessed values of merchandise in Webb County fell from $905,216 in 1930 to $517,687 by 1936, rising only slightly to $585,800 in 1940.[39]

Several well-established Laredo stores eventually had to close their doors. Franklin Brothers Department Store asked for extensions from its creditors in early 1930. Still unable to pay its debts a year later, the company, through its officers Mose, Louis, and William ("Wolf") Franklin, filed for bankruptcy, blaming the company's difficulties on President Calles. Franklin Brothers attempted to stay in business by proposing a reorganization plan that would pay the creditors 25 percent. Despite court approval of the plan, Franklin Brothers proved unable to maintain operations. In August 1932, several creditors forced liquidation of the store's assets. A couple of years later, Shapu & Frelich Department Store failed. Other well-regarded Laredo merchants, including Manuel Cruz and Francisco Ibañez, filed for bankruptcy at about the same time.[40]

Other businesses began to fail as the Depression persisted. In 1932, the grand new Laredo Robert E. Lee Hotel closed. The John O. Buenz Lumber Company, the largest lumber operation in Laredo, liquidated. A number of oil and gas operations were unable to avoid the impact of the Depression. James Kepley, an independent oil operator who lived in Laredo, filed three bankruptcy cases in the 1930s, two for his personal debt and one for his corporation, Kepley Production Company. Texas Gas Utilities, which supplied most of the power for homes and commercial buildings in the cities and towns of the Winter Garden District, faced a crisis caused by the depletion of its natural gas reserves. Unable to pay the interest on its corporate bonds, the company filed for bankruptcy reorganization twice during the 1930s.[41]

The bankruptcies of formerly wealthy ranch owners Eusebio García and Albert Urbahn revealed the pain in the countryside. Ranchers were hit hard by plunging prices and the need to borrow money to feed and care for their herds. Both Urbahn and García owned ranches in excess of forty thousand acres. Urbahn, in addition, owned dozens of town lots in Laredo. He had bought land in the area in the late nineteenth century and lost almost all of it as a result of his bankruptcy case.[42] Juan Armengol's heir, Antonio Valls Armengol, who was the first to ship citrus out of Laredo, filed a bankruptcy case in 1935. The foreclosure and liquidation of James G. Sullivan's commercial truck farm and seed distribution center in Dimmit County was symptomatic of the problems of farmers generally. Land returned to brush, and wealthy individuals or large businesses bought up the rest.[43]

Eusebio García, who was born in Guerrero, Mexico, had owned and operated the large ranch of Los Ojuelos for many years, which his wife had inherited from her father, Dionisio Guerra. According to J. Frank Dobie, "Don Eusebio García's people had owned the hacienda for generations. He owned it free of mortgage. He never speculated."[44] By the 1930s, that had changed. His son Amador took over management of the forty-eight-thousand-acre ranch in 1929. He borrowed money from Frost Bank, Laredo National Bank, and others and heavily mortgaged the ranch lands. Eusebio tried to borrow money from an insurance company to pay off some of the debts, but once the creditors learned that Frost Bank had filed suit and recovered a judgment against him, they stopped negotiating. In March 1935, Eusebio García filed for bankruptcy to stop a foreclosure. He told the court that he would pay off the liens on the land either by borrowing money, selling land, or making payments out of farm income. The year 1935 was a difficult one for him. His wife died, and he himself succumbed to a lingering illness a couple of years later at age seventy-eight. The family lost most of its real estate by 1940.[45]

The lower Rio Grande Valley suffered the most during the Depression years, in part because a destructive hurricane hit right after the low point of the Depression. Bankruptcy filings in the Southern District of Texas, Brownsville Division, exceeded all cases filed in the federal courts in Del Rio and Laredo combined. In the early 1930s, business in the towns gradually began to slow, hitting a low in 1932.[46]

The impact of the Depression was uneven across the region. Declines in taxable land values in the various counties give some indication of the degree to which local economies suffered. The citrus land boom, which had started in about 1922, ground to a complete halt in the early 1930s. Both Cameron and

Hidalgo counties saw dramatic drops in the land values. In 1930, taxable land values in Cameron County totaled $27,830,050. By 1933, they had plummeted to $18,215,320 and continued falling for the rest of the decade. In 1935, the tax assessors valued the land at $15,280,050, and by 1940, it was worth only $14,514,440. In Hidalgo County, declines were even greater. The 1930 tax rolls showed real estate worth $39,832,066. By 1933, those values had declined to $26,800,195. In 1935, they totaled $16,179,180, and by the end of the decade, taxable real estate in the county had a value of only $15,652,235. In neighboring Starr County, land values remained relatively constant because very little land development and speculation had occurred there in the 1920s. They were low and remained low throughout the period. Taxable land values in Starr County totaled $2,568,275 in 1930 and declined only slightly, to $2,247,100, in 1935. By 1940, they had shown some improvement, rising to $2,306,020. The decline in land values was significant because land sales had been a major driver of the economy in the 1920s.[47]

Farmers were struggling just to break even. Prices of fruits and vegetables were down 30 percent in August 1931 compared to a year earlier. The *Hidalgo County Independent* published long lists of delinquent taxpayers for the years 1930 and 1931, most of whom were farmers. The Edinburg School District collected at most 60–65 percent of its outstanding taxes during the entire decade. By 1938, in the La Feria Water Control & Improvement District, Cameron County No. 3, the average amount of taxes past due per acre totaled $101.00. Out of 32,533 acres of land in the district, 18,552 had outstanding taxes owed from past years. The Valley Gin Company, which owned cotton gins in several Valley towns, filed bankruptcy twice in the 1930s and suffered deep operating losses, including $45,348.87 in 1939, indicating the vastly reduced production of cotton in the area.[48]

As prices of fruits and vegetables continued to decline, farmers had trouble repaying debts. Loans incurred during the prosperous, inflationary late 1920s became a huge burden in the 1930s. Banks tried to be generous with repayment terms because farmland values had also decreased. Since there was virtually no market for real estate, the banks knew they would recover more money if the farmers made their payments even if they were late. Yet, as banks themselves faced a liquidity crisis, they often had no choice but to foreclose. When banks failed, they sold their mortgages, and farmers became subject to the whims of receivers and state banking commissioners or purchasers with whom they had had no prior dealings. Between September 1929 and December 1941, 156 Valley farmers filed for bankruptcy, and hundreds of others faced imminent foreclosure.

Some were even on the verge of starvation. Cash was virtually nonexistent, and people reverted to a system of barter and exchange. People paid for services with chickens, eggs, and other farm products and grew their own food.[49]

The farm crisis affected the land developers, who had relied upon increasing and rapid colonization of the land for their income. When colonization substantially ceased in the early 1930s, the land developers could not pay their debts, and several filed for bankruptcy. Al Parker, who had developed the area around La Feria in Cameron County, liquidated his land company and filed a personal bankruptcy case to eliminate his personal debt. All of the vendor's lien notes from people who had purchased the land were either sold or abandoned. Rentfro Banton Creager filed a personal bankruptcy case to discharge debts incurred as the result of his failed land dealings. He had had problems going back to the 1920s. Nick Doffing, the developer of Golden Groves near Mission, filed a case because of imminent foreclosure proceedings by one of his creditors, the Yturria Land & Cattle Company, from whom he had bought most of his land. He defaulted on his loans as the market slowed and was unable to sell his land to individual farmers. The court eventually dismissed both of Doffing's cases because he failed to demonstrate that he had any possibility of feasibly reorganizing his debts.[50]

According to the *Hidalgo County Independent* in 1933:

> We are facing a period of readjustment . . . Unless creditors are willing to meet their debtors in a spirit of fair play and readjust their claim on the basis of fair value and ability to pay, they are likely to find that they have pulled their house down on their heads. If there is to be a process of wholesale foreclosures and people are to be deprived of their homes and their property and the very means of making a living, then there is liable to be serious trouble ahead. There is a growing sullenness on the part of debtors who have found themselves caught in a vice [*sic*] that is squeezing them dry. Between the lack of markets and the demands of the insatiate creditor who requires that he be paid, the debtor feels the injustice of being forced to vacate his farm or his home and see it possessed by those who are amply able to extend leniency and await the time when the debtor can earn something to meet his obligations.[51]

Banks and other creditors, however, were not always able to be lenient because of the massive scale of defaults. Yet foreclosed properties had no market. As banks failed, credit began to disappear. The lack of credit coupled with slowing demand caused numerous groceries, clothing stores, jewelry stores, drugstores, filling stations, and garages to fail. The bankruptcy petition of the Rio Grande Valley Gas Company, filed in 1935, noted that the "depression which affected the business of the entire United States, and which resulted [sic] particularly disastrously for the Rio Grande Valley territory and industries therein," made it impossible for the company to meet its corporate bond obligations. The failure of the Valley Gin Company, which owned and operated cotton gins in several farm towns, made front-page news.[52]

Climate and weather exacerbated the consequences of the Depression. As Nick Doffing said, "The financial depression from 1929 on was enough to wreck a lot of institutions but if the elements had left us alone we would have come out on top and wouldn't owe a dime of money to anybody today. We can't control the elements and if you stop to think what nature has done to us the past four years I think all of you folks will agree with me that it is not our fault that we are in this position."[53] There were freezes in 1930, 1934, and 1935 that especially hurt the citrus crop. The most devastating blow, however, came from a major hurricane that hit the area in September 1933.

The hurricane "smashed through the full length of the Lower Valley" on Labor Day weekend, September 4–5, 1933. Forty-four people died, fifteen hundred were injured, and property damage totaled $16,900,000. Winds and water destroyed houses and buildings, uprooted trees, and downed power lines. A dozen inches of rain fell in less than eighteen hours, flooding US Highway 83 with water one to four feet deep between Harlingen and Mercedes and filling up ditches and canals. The Valley was isolated for several days. The flooding halted traffic on highways and railroads. Communication was cut off as the result of damaged telephone and telegraph lines. A San Antonio newspaper mistakenly reported that the streets of Harlingen were littered with the bodies of the dead and dying. A local reporter corrected the story:

[T]he streets WERE covered with hundreds of bodies, but that [sic] were the tired and worn-out bodies of sleeping Valleyites, exhausted from their 48- to 60-hour battle with Mother Nature's hurricane elements and totally spent from their fierce struggles with flying, falling and death-dealing debris, driven like spears before the 110-mile-per-hour winds. Forced from their homes that quickly became wrecked and sodden from wind and rain, they dropped where they could and rested as best they could.

Henrietta Kassabaum and her family, who lived in San Benito at the time, lost everything as a result of the hurricane. The house collapsed, and they piled into the car to drive to her father-in-law's home for shelter in the midst of the storm. She recalled that everyone had to get typhoid shots because of exposure to the floodwaters.[54]

The hurricane nearly destroyed the citrus crop. Large quantities of oranges and grapefruit fell onto the ground or floated in the floodwaters, and winds uprooted or damaged many of the trees. Howard Millen remembered that his family had to dig ditches to bury all of the grapefruit. It took several months for some orchards to fully recover. Peter and Clara Dicken, who filed for bankruptcy in 1937, reported that the hurricane had torn down their chicken houses, destroyed the roof on their home, and ripped 3,000–4,000 pounds of fruit off the trees in their orchards. They had not been able to fully recover their losses from that year.[55]

The hurricane damaged businesses in the towns as well. Near the end of 1933, Emmett Kasey, a merchant in Mercedes, wrote his main creditor, McKesson Drug Company, asking for more time to pay his debt. "I cannot pay any money since I have scarcely enough to live on through the winter and Mrs. Kasey is badly crippled and will be for several months. I have no work and no prospects of any. Had I continued to operate a store, I was headed for certain bankruptcy. The condition in the Valley is a despicable one since the hurricane. One in business, with few exceptions, will loose [sic] money and one out of business has little or no chance of employment."[56]

The hurricane had long-term effects on farming in the Valley. Land became waterlogged. There was inadequate drainage to begin with, and the hurricane only made things worse by creating a general rise in the water table. Furthermore, the hurricane increased soil salination, which had always been somewhat of a problem in the Valley. Large areas were designated as "waste land." It took two to three years for the Valley to recover from the immediate property damage the hurricane caused and far longer to recover from the effects on the soil.[57]

Farmers who had been successful all of their lives faced ruin during the Depression. Herbert Van Vliet, who had farmed for forty-five years, filed his first bankruptcy case in 1937. Originally from Minnesota, he had purchased a forty-acre tract from the Stewart Land Company in 1918 near Weslaco. He worked long hours and Sundays but could not get ahead of his debt. The farmers in the area had destroyed more crops than they sold as the result of efforts to reduce production and raise prices. James McClintock, a seventy-four-year-old farmer, had always paid his taxes and interest prior to the Depression. He had put almost all of his life's savings into twenty acres of land near Brownsville, which he tried to sell in order to avoid a foreclosure. He ended up in bankruptcy court. A merchant who lived nearby said, "Mr. McClintock is not extravagant or wasteful. He was always considered one of our prosperous farmers when he first came to the country and until the depression almost broke him."[58]

The Depression did not completely destroy the consumer society on the border, but it diminished for a time. In the midst of hardship, people tried to hold onto a few luxuries. The *Eagle Pass Daily Guide* noted that the "Depression's long arm has reached only a few radios and automobiles of the farmer. The department of agriculture has found that he still clings to these newly acquired advantages despite the hard socks of adversity."[59] Certainly the bankruptcy cases filed during the period bear this out.

The combination of a shrinking tax base and delinquent taxes began to have a deleterious effect on local water districts, which had issued bonds to construct canals and irrigation systems during the 1920s, when development was continuing at a rapid pace. As delinquent taxes rose, the districts were increasingly unable to pay the interest due on their bonds. A few attempted to initiate foreclosures, but since the market for real estate was virtually nonexistent, it was impractical to continue. Moreover, in most cases, the land was worth less than the taxes and debts against it. At least five of these districts from Cameron County became insolvent during the 1930s, six from Hidalgo County, and two from Willacy County. Additionally, eight of the Hidalgo County road districts, municipal corporations created to construct and pave highways and streets, became unable to pay their debts and filed for bankruptcy.[60]

Even more serious than the failures of the irrigation and road districts were the insolvencies of the cities, towns, and school districts of the Valley. Seven of the new farm towns filed for bankruptcy in the 1930s, including Edinburg, Lyford, Donna, Mercedes, Pharr, San Benito, and San Juan. Delinquent tax rates for San Benito had risen steadily over the course of the decade, from 14.81 percent in 1930, to 24.76 percent in 1933, to a high of 34.94 percent in 1938. Both the City of Brownsville and the Brownsville Independent School District filed bankruptcy cases in 1940 and 1941. The Brownsville Independent School District attributed its filing primarily to the decrease in market values of real estate caused by "an accumulation of circumstances, the depression, as well as poor crops and crop returns."[61] Brownsville had been able to keep its taxable values relatively constant until 1936 and 1937. Several other school districts in the Valley filed, including the Mission Independent School District, the Mercedes Independent School District, the Edinburg Consolidated School District, and the Tabasco Consolidated Independent School District in western Hidalgo County.

Virtually all of these municipal entities attributed their filings to the inability of farmers to make a profit.[62]

The pain suffered by farmers and businesspeople inevitably affected the predominantly ethnic Mexican working class. Some farmers and merchants kept their workers on, paying them with food and other necessaries, but others had to let them go. It is telling that most Anglos who discussed their memories of the Depression years later did not remember widespread unemployment and hunger, whereas most ethnic Mexicans who recalled those years did, whether they were from affluent or poor families.[63] Robert Ramirez recalled that the only time the poor received any kind of aid was shortly after the hurricane of 1933. The Red Cross arrived to provide clothes and food for the people with the greatest needs. The Ramirez family did not qualify since they owned their own business, but they, too, suffered, often not having enough to eat. Francisco Orneles' father, a construction worker, had jobs throughout the Depression, but the family just barely made it most days. Orneles recalled that the merchants who had small stores in their communities were "very difficult persons" and focused almost exclusively on their own businesses, rarely offering any help to anyone else. People bought on credit, making it difficult for the storeowners to keep their businesses going.[64]

Deportations of Mexican immigrants began as early as 1928 as the nativist forces in Congress began to prevail against growers and others who wanted to keep cheap Mexican labor flowing into the United States.[65] Deportations continued through the early years of the Great Depression, the result of fears that Mexicans were taking jobs away from unemployed Americans and collecting sizeable sums from local relief agencies as well as of repatriation efforts by the Mexican government. The deportations began to create a labor shortage on Valley farms. One newspaper reported that about fifty families consisting of 125 people, most of whom had lived in the United States for twenty-five years or more, returned to Mexico in one day. Esteban García remembered that there were "caravans" of people leaving the lower Rio Grande Valley.[66] As ethnic Mexicans left the area, unemployed Anglos arrived, roaming the region in search of work. The Southern Pacific chased a number off their trains in Del Rio, leading to numerous complaints by local residents about the "steady stream of back-door moochers" who were begging for food all around the residential areas of the city.[67]

The Depression coincided with and accelerated long-term trends of consolidation of land into the hands of agribusiness and the movement of people from country to city. Economies of scale were already making it difficult for the small

farmer to survive. Those who grew citrus, which was less dependent on mech-
anization and huge crop yields, could hang on longer than farmers who grew
staple crops, especially when they could continue to get cheap Mexican labor, but
even the small citrus farmers were eventually replaced by larger growers. Land
developers and large agribusiness bought land at cheap prices. Central Life of
Illinois acquired 524.58 acres of cotton land near San Benito through foreclosure
and was willing to sell it at almost any price. The Nick Doffing Company stepped
in to buy it.[68]

An estimated 4,906 farms in the Valley ceased operations. The average farm
size rose throughout the region. For example, in Cameron County, the average
farm in 1930 was only 46 acres. By 1940, it was 98.3 acres, and by 1945, it had increased to 111.1 acres. In Hidalgo County, the average farm size in 1930 was 87
acres and 134.9 acres in 1940. One of the most dramatic examples of agricultural
consolidation was in the Winter Garden County of Dimmit. There, the average
farm totaled 732 acres in 1930, 1,404.10 acres in 1940, and 1,537 acres in 1945.[69]

The 1940s marked the end of many of the individually owned dry-goods and
ready-to-wear stores along the Texas-Mexico border. Small businesses in the
towns continued to thrive, but they did not carry on as much of the overall economic activity as they once had. More and more children of the small businesspeople of South Texas moved to larger cities like San Antonio, Houston, Dallas,
and Fort Worth. The path to opportunity increasingly moved in the direction
of white-collar employment with large corporations. Chains, especially grocery
stores, continued to expand. Sales for independently owned stores dropped more
precipitously during the 1930s than for chains and mail-order houses. Sales in
Cameron County stores dropped nearly 50 percent between 1929 and 1935.[70]

Ethnic Mexican businesspeople were hurt more than Anglo-Americans.
Their percentage of overall businesses dropped substantially (see appendices 2
and 3). At the same time, the Depression began to level the playing field. Anglo
business values also declined precipitously. Lawyer J. T. Canales noted, "The
present depression has been another agency in the hands of the Almighty to keep
our people democratic, for our Anglo-Saxon brethren, who have heretofore believed in race superiority because they possess more wealth and more land than
their less fortunate brothers of Latin extraction, suddenly have awakened to the
realization that their vast, landed wealth is a liability, for they should have to
pay taxes and have no money with which to pay them and their products have
no market; hence they have become poor, just as poor as the Mexicans who they
have considered as their inferiors."[71]

People responded to the Depression in the same way they typically responded to looming personal insolvency—denial and an overly optimistic assessment of how to get out of the situation. The newspapers in the border towns participated in a national campaign of confidence, supported by the Texas press as a whole. At the end of 1931, the *Eagle Pass Daily Guide* proclaimed, "The time has come to forget about a depression that has never really bothered us; to wake up to the wonderful possibilities of our country and to 'do things in a big way.' "[72] By 1932, the local press was beginning to acknowledge the Depression and the difficulties people were facing. Newspaper articles urged people to stop hoarding cash, make bank deposits, pay off their debts, and buy from local merchants.[73]

· · ·

The Depression reminded people in the South Texas borderlands how elusive the pursuit of success really was. The American dream was not always as accessible as it seemed. Anyone could end up losing everything and fall out of the business class. As a result, attitudes about failure began to shift along the border and elsewhere in the country. People were not losers simply because they had lost a business. In a reversal of the rags-to-riches tale, the *Saturday Evening Post* told a story about a businessman who lost everything in the stock market crash of 1929 and ended up living in his car. He then decided to make a "come-back at age sixty" by buying an old, broken-down roadside inn, remodeling it, and opening it for guests.[74] Quitting, not insolvency, was becoming the mark of the loser. More significantly, the widespread presence of failure in society in the 1930s caused some to question the system of capitalism, which had seemingly led to so much destitution. Still others sought to find ways to better cushion the impact of loss in order to continue to encourage risk taking, innovation, and entrepreneurship, as the next chapter explores.

STARTING OVER

NOT LONG AFTER THE STOCK MARKET CRASHED in September 1929, the *Laredo Times* noted that "the gambling instinct is strong in the human breast. Life, the life of a nation or an individual, is a story of gains and losses. Indeed, it is a gamble from cradle to grave."[1] As those who faced failure realized, starting any kind of business was a gamble. The possibility of failure always lurked around the corner, even for the most seemingly successful enterprises. The awareness of the risk of failure increased exponentially during the Great Depression of the 1930s. Yet encouraging people to take risks to start new enterprises despite the possibility of failure was crucial for the functioning of the emerging capitalist economy in the South Texas border region. If the cost of failure was too high and uncertainty too great, people would not take the necessary risks, and the economy would stall and stagnate. On the other hand, complete elimination of risk was impossible. The solution was to find a way for entrepreneurs to start over again after failure without losing everything they owned and without carrying an impossible burden of debt.

Wealthy entrepreneurs have generally always had the connections and deep pockets necessary to gamble on a new venture and recover from failure without the assistance of the state. This is one reason that elites have typically dominated developing economies. Small business owners, on the other hand, have lived with uncertainty, constantly confronting the very real prospect of downward mobility if their enterprises did not succeed. The private insurance industry in the United States developed in part to allay some of those fears, but it had definite limitations, protecting against only a few defined threats.[2] Over the course of the nineteenth century, state legislatures and the US Congress struggled to design laws to manage and apportion the risks of failure among entrepreneurs, investors, and creditors. The state of Texas developed laws that exempted a considerable portion of a debtor's property from the reach of creditors. After a rocky start, a federal bankruptcy law had by 1898 become a permanent part of the nation's legal landscape. Its inclusion of generous discharge provisions combined with a choice to utilize state exemptions represented a substantial step forward in promoting small, individually owned enterprises. Passing generous bankruptcy laws favoring debtors was unique among the nations of the world and reflected the US penchant for promoting entrepreneurialism. Texas borderland entrepreneurs, with varying degrees of success, turned to the federal bankruptcy law to gain a fresh start after failure.

THE EVOLUTION OF GOVERNMENT SCHEMES TO MITIGATE RISK

Developing a permanent federal bankruptcy law in the United States took a long time despite the presence of a bankruptcy clause in the 1789 Constitution, partly because of the moral ambiguities inherent in designing such a law. Legislators engaged in heated discussions about the necessity, purpose, scope, and nature of federal bankruptcy relief, alternately passing and repealing short-lived laws: the Bankruptcy Act of 1800, repealed in 1803; the Bankruptcy Act of 1841, repealed in 1843; and the Bankruptcy Act of 1867, repealed in 1878. They had difficulty compromising on the balance between a bankruptcy scheme's dual roles of debt collection and debtor relief. Fault lay at the core of the debate. A strong belief in the obligation to repay one's creditors, otherwise known as the "moral economy of debt," prevented some lawmakers from agreeing to generous discharge provisions. Others feared that creditors would victimize debtors through forced involuntary bankruptcy. Still others acknowledged the need for bankruptcy in particular circumstances, such as a national depression, when many people were overburdened by debt they could never repay; this was one of the reasons that Congress passed the Bankruptcy Act of 1840 on the heels of the Panic of 1837 and the Bankruptcy Act of 1867 following the Civil War.[3]

For most of the nineteenth century, therefore, a diverse and evolving patchwork of state insolvency laws, stay laws, and exemption laws governed debtor/creditor relations. As the nation expanded and industrialized, acceptance of the failure that accompanied the risk taking necessary in an entrepreneurial society made Americans more and more open to liberal debtor relief. State laws requiring imprisonment for debt fell by the wayside.[4]

Debtor relief was a priority among the Anglo-Americans who settled Mexican Texas in the 1820s in the aftermath of the Panic of 1819. Small farmers fleeing aggressive creditors scrawled the words "Gone to Texas" on their abandoned farms and homes. Stephen F. Austin, who brought three hundred families to settle an *empresario* grant he had received from the Mexican government, had failed in business himself and was sympathetic to the debtors' perspective. He and his father, Moses, had financed a variety of business ventures, including lead mining, a mercantile house, farming operations, and a bank. They both struggled with inadequate cash in the aftermath of the War of 1812 on the frontier, frequently incurring new debt to repay old loans. Creditors sporadically sued both Stephen and his father, and on March 11, 1820, a Missouri sheriff arrested Moses Austin for nonpayment of debt. The Austins' entire lead mining operation, Mine à Bretôn, was sold at auction for a pittance to satisfy the debts. These experiences marked the younger Austin, and he worked to ensure that both his and others' fortunes would be preserved despite financial misfortune. As the result of his repeated petitions to the Congress of Coahuila y Tejas, the province passed a law in 1829 forbidding lawsuits based on prior debts for a period of twelve years after the acquisition of a land grant. The law permanently protected lands, farming tools, and other necessary items from seizure by prior creditors. Austin's approach to this issue set the pattern for the development of future Texas debtor-relief laws.[5]

After gaining independence from Mexico, Anglo-Texans borrowed heavily from Spanish and Mexican legal sources to craft property laws designed to protect assets from the reach of creditors. One of the most radical of these laws, the homestead exemption, originated on the Texas/Mexican frontier and from there gradually spread to the rest of the United States. It authorized the legislature to protect a rural family home of up to two hundred acres or an urban home valued at $2,000 or less from all creditors except those who held mortgages for purchase of the home, improvements, or property taxes. The exemption's stated purpose was to protect debtors and their families from destitution so that they did not become a burden on society and "to retain in pioneers the feeling of freedom and sense of independence which was deemed necessary to the continued existence of democratic institutions." One of its provisions, designed to prevent "drunken and worthless husbands [from] bringing their wives to want and poverty," prohibited a husband from selling the family home without the wife's consent. The 1876 Texas Constitution increased the value of an exempted homestead to $5,000 and added a "business homestead" exemption that protected a debtor's place of business located in the same urban area as the family home.[6]

Texas legislators also protected certain categories of personal property from seizure by creditors. Throughout the twentieth century, the Texas legislature continued to revise and expand those laws to address changes in the economy. The statutes in force during the 1910s and 1920s exempted all household and kitchen furniture, cemetery lots, farming implements, tools of one's trade or profession, a family library, family portraits, five milk cows and their calves, two mules, two horses and a wagon, one carriage or buggy (or an automobile), one gun, twenty hogs, twenty head of sheep, saddles, bridles, and harnesses, food and groceries, forage for livestock consumption, and current wages for personal services.[7]

Standing alone, the Texas exemptions were valuable to entrepreneurs taking risks in a new environment, but their scope was limited. When Congress finally passed the Bankruptcy Act of 1898, it turned out to be more of a boon to entrepreneurs than it was to the creditors who had lobbied for it. It assisted them as they navigated the process of "creative destruction" inherent in capitalism by offering the possibility of a fresh start and a second chance. The act combined broad federal discharge of debt provisions with state property exemptions. The discharge was crucial because it freed future income from the reach of creditors. (A discharge actually erased the obligation; the creditors received only a percentage of any assets remaining in the estate and had to bear the loss.) Fortuitously, the act immediately preceded most of the commercial development of South Texas, contributing to an improving business environment in South Texas between 1880 and 1940. Mexico, by contrast, did not develop a set of coherent, nationwide insolvency laws until the passage of the Ley de quiebras y suspensión de pagos in 1943. Both during and after the Revolution, creditors faced greater uncertainty in terms of debt repayment in northern Mexico, and debtors had no options for discharging debt. The Mexican state itself was insolvent, and its leaders made several attempts to work out debt-restructuring plans with its creditors in the 1920s. Then the Great Depression hit, making it virtually impossible for Mexico to honor any debt agreements.[8]

Bankruptcy decisions in federal district courts in South Texas tended to favor the debtor. Their decisions mirrored bankruptcy policy in most of the country, which had evolved from treating bankruptcy laws primarily as a method for distributing property equally and fairly among creditors to emphasizing their role in giving a debtor "a fresh start" or "a new opportunity in life." According to the US Supreme Court, bankruptcy laws served an important public interest in facilitating the rehabilitation of debtors so that they could continue to function as productive members of society rather than as homeless vagrants. That was not their only purpose, however, because a wide variety of social programs could also accomplish that objective. Bankruptcy laws were specifically designed to encourage entrepreneurs to restructure, innovate, and move back into the business arena to take new risks and contribute to economic growth. As legal historian Lawrence Friedman has pointed out, "Bankruptcy is part of the psychological and cultural underpinnings of a society of entrepreneurs . . . Failure is not total catastrophe. Would people put their savings into a pizza parlor or an internet start-up if they thought debtor's prison, or a lifetime of grinding poverty, was the price of failure? If you want many people to walk on your tightrope, you had better provide them with a net."[9]

Businesspersons or farmers could file under the Act, keep their exempt property, relinquish the rest for distribution to the creditors, and start over again with a slate wiped clean of virtually all of their debt. The Act allowed discharge of all debts except taxes, certain wages due to employees earned within three months of the bankruptcy filing, and debts incurred as the result of various dishonest or malicious actions. In the 1920s, Congress added alimony and child-support payments to the list of nondischargeable debts. Perhaps the most onerous aspect of the law was the requirement to submit a detailed account of one's assets and liabilities and to appear for examination at a creditors' meeting. Although the Act provided a way to arrange a settlement or "composition" with one's creditors, it required the consent of a majority of the creditors holding a majority in the amount of the outstanding indebtedness. Due to the difficulty in getting full cooperation from the creditors, most cases filed under the 1898 Act involved straight liquidations.[10]

The first major set of changes to the law occurred in response to the worsening plight of debtors during the Great Depression. In 1933 and 1934, Congress passed a series of emergency provisions allowing individual proprietors, farmers, municipalities, railroads, and corporations to reorganize their debts. According to Hatton W. Sumners of Texas, "The philosophy of the bill rests upon the assumption that it is better for all parties concerned that these various activities— farms, businesses and so forth—shall be kept intact than to break them up and undertake out of the junk to find something that shall go to the creditors."[11] The deepening economic distress of many businesses made it more plausible to argue that it was in the nation's interest to preserve them as going concerns, mainly to keep people employed. Congress modified and made permanent the reorganization provisions in the Chandler Act of 1938. In that Act, Congress also included reorganization provisions for consumers. This reflected the reality that more and more people were going into debt to buy consumer goods like radios, furniture, clothing, automobiles, and household appliances. It also suggested changing attitudes in society toward consumer debt and greater openness toward giving those who took on that sort of debt a second chance.[12]

AVOIDING BANKRUPTCY

Despite some of its potential advantages, filing a bankruptcy case was typically a last resort for those who saw no other way out of their predicament. It involved a very public display of personal failure. Local newspapers published notices of bankruptcy case filings, creditor meetings, and sales of assets by the bankruptcy trustees. In the relatively small communities along the border, most of the people who read the newspapers knew the filers. Some saw business failure as weakness and debt as evidence of an inability to function independently in accordance with American republican ideals of self-reliance. The influence of the old "moral economy of debt," which emphasized one's individual responsibility to repay one's creditors, also lingered. In a meeting with her creditors in Brownsville, Mrs. Elizabeth King emphasized that she was not trying to "take bankruptcy as the easiest way out," although she had had "many personal troubles in the last several years."[13]

People would often struggle for years, borrowing from one creditor to pay another, avoiding bankruptcy as long as they could. As one farmer said, "We are now in hard financial straits. I have no place to borrow money. I am just up against it. I think I have $8.00 left and that is all we have." At that point, he filed for bankruptcy. George Sutherland of Duval County, whose creditors filed an involuntary case against him, informed the court that he was "broke as a spirit," but he could not recall how long he had been in that predicament. "Well, I couldn't tell you, been fighting this thing along, didn't know whether I was broke or not. . . . I consider I have been broke ever since they took the ranch away from me." In many cases, an individual would not file for bankruptcy until forced to do so by creditor action, such as a foreclosure notice, a lawsuit, or a sheriff's sale.[14]

It was not only fear of failure that caused people to avoid bankruptcy but also the fear of loss. Even though exemptions protected some assets, they left others unprotected. People pursued a variety of strategies to prevent creditors from seizing those assets, both inside and outside of bankruptcy. Some moved across the border beyond the limits of the court's jurisdiction and the reach of process servers. Shopkeepers who were unable to pay their debts escaped to Mexico, just as Anglo-Americans had once fled to Mexican Texas to avoid their creditors. Laredo merchants Margarito Osuña and Carlos Otal crossed the Rio Grande to avoid aggressive creditors. Joseph Rosenblum, a Laredo produce broker praised for saving the town's onion industry in 1925, likewise disappeared after his creditors filed an involuntary bankruptcy case against him in 1929. A relative claimed that Narciso Alanis, a butcher and general merchant, had secretly shipped all of his goods across the river to Nuevo Laredo, where he was operating a large gambling house, in order to keep a creditor from collecting a judgment.[15]

Some people tried to hide property by giving it to family members, who were often subject to a secret promise to return it once the threat of creditor action had passed. This strategy could backfire, as in the case of Tomás Cantú, an immigrant from Mexico who engaged in a complicated set of land transfers to his son-in-law, wife, and children over a four-year period before he filed for bankruptcy in June 1899. Two of his sons, Juan and Cenobio, ended up with 1,920 acres of land in Duval County in December 1898. His other children, Valentina and Francisco, received all of his sheep, horses, cattle, and goats. The court decided that Cantú had transferred the property with the intent to defraud his creditors and denied him a discharge of his debts.[16]

Arturo, Martin, and Ludovico Volpe of Laredo conveyed forty thousand acres of land near Monterrey inherited from their father, Miguel Volpe, to three of Ludovico's sisters-in-law. Three creditors of the Volpe brothers filed an involuntary bankruptcy against them in the 1930s, but the court could not seize the land in Mexico to pay off the Volpes' debts because it lay outside the jurisdiction of the US court. The Volpes avoided liquidation, continued business operations in bankruptcy for almost three years, and finally settled with their creditors so that the case could be dismissed.[17]

A final reason for avoiding bankruptcy was the expense involved. Some people decided it was easier to simply close up shop and move to another town. Others abandoned farmhouses and struck out for Mexico or California, leaving little or no trace of their difficulties other than a foreclosure deed filed away in a county courthouse. More and more, however, over the first four decades of the twentieth century, residents of South Texas increasingly made use of the federal bankruptcy laws.

THE DEMOGRAPHICS OF BANKRUPTCY

Filing a bankruptcy case was not the same as failing; hundreds of people failed and never darkened the doors of a federal court. Paradoxically, it evidenced some degree of responsibility—an attempt to manage debt and a willingness to disclose one's assets and affairs to a court and creditors. Bankruptcy was primarily a tool of the middle and even the upper classes, not the impoverished, who lacked sufficient income and assets to take on the debt that forced people into bankruptcy court. Bankrupt debtors typically paid a filing fee and hired a local attorney to represent them. Voluntary bankruptcy filings (by the debtors) outnumbered involuntary ones (filed by creditors) by almost seven to one. Most of the filers (about 85 percent) were individual proprietors, farmers, or ranchers (table 6). Bankruptcy filings spiked during periods of recession or depression (table 7). Anglos and Europeans dominated the filings, but Hispanic entrepreneurs made up about 15 percent of the total. More than half were foreign immigrants, at least ninety-two from Mexico and five from Spain. The majority of the Mexican nationals, or sixty-five individuals, were not US citizens when they filed. A person did not have to be a US citizen to file for bankruptcy but simply had to own property or do business in the United States. Nearly 75 percent of the Hispanic cases involved merchants, a few of whom were also large landowners (table 8). There was one enterprising individual in Laredo, Pablo Chapa, who had started about nineteen gas stations and built his own oil refinery on the edge of town. A number of these Hispanic debtors did not speak English. In those cases, the courts brought in translators to facilitate the proceedings.[18]

Women also appear in the bankruptcy records as debtors, although less frequently than men. Forty-seven female-owned businesses filed during the period. Fifty-two women filed jointly with their husbands. Four businesses involved a combination of men and women, usually a brother and sister or cousins. The debtors were overwhelmingly literate, and most of them spoke English.[19]

Perhaps the best evidence of the importance of bankruptcy to the South Texas economy during this period was its frequent use by prominent businesspeople. They included Valley land developers Lon Hill, Rentfro Banton Creager, and Al Parker and famed trail driver Benjamin Borroum. Donna Fletcher, whose father founded the town of Donna and named it after her, filed a bank-

TABLE 6. Occupational and business categories, bankrupt debtors, South Texas border region, 1898–1941

Note: Counties included: Cameron, Hidalgo, Starr, Willacy, Zapata, Zavala, Webb, Brooks, Jim Hogg, Kenedy, Dimmit, La Salle, McMullen, Duval, Uvalde, Maverick, Kinney, Edwards, Real, and Val Verde.

Source: Bankruptcy Docket Books and Case Files, US District Court for the Southern District of Texas, Brownsville, Corpus Christi, and Laredo Divisions, US District Court for the Western District of Texas, San Antonio and Del Rio Divisions, in Records of the District Courts of the United States, Record Group 21, National Archives and Records Administration, Southwest Region (Fort Worth).

ruptcy case in 1921. Oilman Finley Ewing, Antonio Armengol, heir to his uncle's profitable wholesale grocery business in Laredo, furniture merchant Morris Edelstein, department store owners Moses and Louis Franklin and Leon Shapu of Laredo, Spanish merchant Antonio Barreda, and realtor Celestino Barreda numbered among dozens of well-known local entrepreneurs who filed for bankruptcy in the 1930s. Ernesto Urtusastegui, a Mexican lawyer living in Brownsville, filed a bankruptcy case in 1930, apparently due to liabilities arising from a lease-purchase agreement with Juan Fernández for Hacienda de las Rucias, the large cotton hacienda in Tamaulipas. In addition, J. B. Symonds, a druggist who had a full-length picture in the *Standard Blue Book for South Texas, 1929–30,* filed bankruptcy twice, once in 1914 and again in 1931.[20]

TABLE 7. Bankruptcy case filings, South Texas border region, 1898–1941

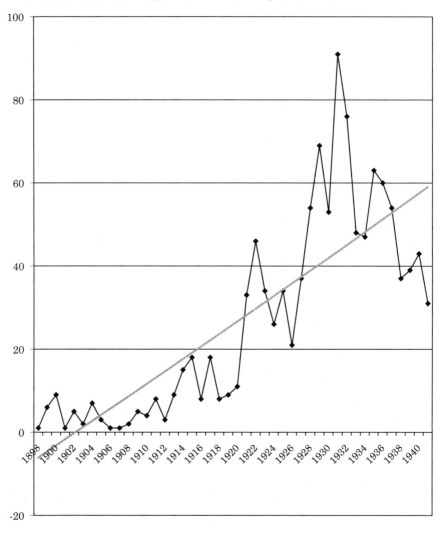

Note: Counties included: Cameron, Hidalgo, Starr, Willacy, Zapata, Zavala, Webb, Brooks, Jim Hogg, Kenedy, Dimmit, La Salle, McMullen, Duval, Uvalde, Maverick, Kinney, Edwards, Real, and Val Verde.

Source: Bankruptcy Docket Books and Case Files, US District Court for the Southern District of Texas, Brownsville, Corpus Christi, and Laredo Divisions, US District Court for the Western District of Texas, San Antonio and Del Rio Divisions, in Records of the District Courts of the United States, Record Group 21, National Archives and Records Administration, Southwest Region (Fort Worth).

TABLE 8. Occupational and business categories, Hispanic-surnamed debtors, South Texas border region, 1898–1941

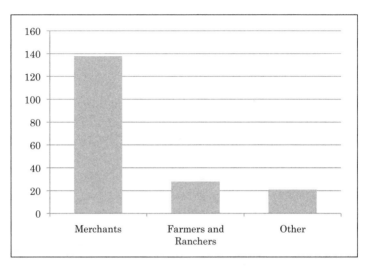

Note: Counties included: Cameron, Hidalgo, Starr, Willacy, Zapata, Zavala, Webb, Brooks, Jim Hogg, Kenedy, Dimmit, La Salle, McMullen, Duval, Uvalde, Maverick, Kinney, Edwards, Real, and Val Verde.

Source: Bankruptcy Docket Books and Case Files, US District Court for the Southern District of Texas, Brownsville, Corpus Christi, and Laredo Divisions, US District Court for the Western District of Texas, San Antonio and Del Rio Divisions, in Records of the District Courts of the United States, Record Group 21, National Archives and Records Administration, Southwest Region (Fort Worth).

A FRESH START?

Not everyone benefited equally from filing a bankruptcy case. In terms of protecting the property needed to start over again, small business owners in the towns and cities reaped the greatest advantages. They could typically protect both a residence and business homestead as long as they were within the value limitations, along with their clothing, furniture, household goods, and an automobile or horse and buggy. Although they had to relinquish any remaining merchandise and outstanding accounts receivable, they could start up business after bankruptcy by acquiring new inventory on credit, something that many of them were able to do, often by agreeing to repay certain creditors even though the debts had been discharged in the bankruptcy. Individuals who had substantial assets had more to lose. Corporations could not reap the benefit of state exemption laws; all corporate assets in a bankruptcy case were liquidated for the benefit of the creditors.[21]

Three cases help to illustrate the effect of bankruptcy on small versus large business owners. The first concerns M. M. Peña, who had operated a store under the name of Mission Commission Company and kept three town lots and a house in Mission worth about $3,000, along with household furnishings, clothing, and two life insurance policies. He relinquished three other lots burdened by mortgages and tax liens and his outstanding customer accounts. Leon Russell, who ran a small proprietorship called Russell's Pharmacy, did not own any real estate, but he kept all of his household goods and clothing, a De Soto Coach automobile, and three life insurance policies. He had to relinquish approximately $950 worth of merchandise and $1,400 worth of fixtures.[22]

Antonio Barreda, a formerly wealthy merchant and landowner, lost approximately $100,000 worth of real estate, including 1,554 acres of irrigated farm and pasture land near the Rio Grande and eighteen town lots. He also had to turn over $6,000 worth of merchandise and accounts receivable and about $2,600 worth of farm equipment. Barreda kept the building where he lived and operated his store in Brownsville, his home's furnishings, his family's clothes, the family portraits, five milk cows and their calves, two horses, a wagon, and three insurance policies. His wife still owned land in Mexico, so he was not destitute by any means, but he had lost most of his former wealth. Creditors fared much better in cases like Barreda's than in small ones, where they typically did not receive a dividend. In Barreda's case, the dividend for the creditors was 20 percent.[23]

After bankruptcy, businesspeople usually tried to return to independent entrepreneurship with all of the risks and uncertainties that entailed. Many saw no other choice. One frequent response to a bankruptcy case was to move to a new location to start over again, usually in order to leave the stigma of the filing behind. When James Underwood's drugstore in San Benito failed in 1920, he moved to Alpine in far West Texas to open another pharmacy. Similarly, Aaron Braunstein launched a new store in San Antonio after his Brownsville store failed. Morris Kaplan, a Russian immigrant, started his first business in Louisiana in May 1900 with several of his brothers. He launched other stores in Jefferson, Beeville, Corpus Christi, and San Antonio. When a store failed, he would file bankruptcy and move on. He ended up in Brownsville.[24]

Many former bankrupts, often because of deep-seated ties to an area, decided to remain in the same place. In the 1920s, Tomás Guerra reopened his grocery store in Pharr, and Guadalupe Cantú continued to sell groceries in Weslaco. After Emil Ayoub's dry-goods store failed in San Benito in 1931, he started a small grocery and confectionery. Bruno Rios, a pharmacist in San Diego, Duval County, filed a bankruptcy case in 1914. He continued his drugstore in the same town for at least twenty-four more years. Morris Edelstein remained in the Valley despite facing a series of difficult challenges in the 1930s. Along with many other merchants in the region, he filed for bankruptcy in 1932. As he was recovering, the September 1933 hurricane blew down his wholesale building, and he lost all of the furniture inside. He had no insurance, but he still managed to rebuild. In 1936, fire engulfed the building, and all of the merchandise was lost with 24 percent coverage. He rebuilt it again. Edelstein's Better Furniture Stores lasted well beyond the lifetime of its founder and were only recently sold by the family to a large Mexican company, the bankruptcy case filed during the dark days of the Great Depression having been long forgotten.[25]

Other former bankrupts sought the seemingly more secure path of working for someone else, which was difficult because high-paying, white-collar jobs were relatively scarce in South Texas before the 1950s. Some became real estate, automobile, or insurance salesmen. Some worked as clerks or bookkeepers for other small stores. After Merchants National Bank foreclosed on Robert Burdette's store, J. C. Penney hired him as the manager. He received a salary of $200 a month, plus a commission on the store's profits. His annualized base salary would be equivalent to about $36,400 today. Skilled workers usually found employment that utilized their expertise. John McGuire worked as a machinist after his garage failed. Ethnic Mexican store owners who failed typically did not become farm laborers. Those who did not return to proprietorship seemed to have worked as clerks or bookkeepers. These positions were not well paid, but they were better than most farm jobs.[26]

Starting over was more difficult for farmers and ranchers. Bankruptcy was a less useful tool for them, and again it was the small operations that benefited the most. Before banks started regularly taking land as collateral for loans, those who owned small farms and ranches of 200 acres or less could potentially benefit from a bankruptcy filing, as long as their debt was unsecured. For example, Margarito, Pedro, Francisco, and Jesús Lopez all filed for bankruptcy in 1900. Each kept his farm and ranch lands, which ranged in size from 80 to 200 acres, and discharged several hundred dollars in debt to local merchants. Around 1915, Walter McClain moved to the Valley from Indiana and bought a 40-acre tract of land from Alamo Land and Sugar Company. He took out a chattel mortgage to First State Bank of Alamo on his livestock, crops, and farm equipment in order to acquire the funds to start his new farming venture. He was able to keep the farm after he filed for bankruptcy in 1922 because he had not mortgaged the land. Similarly, W. C. Schultz exempted 130 acres of land near Pharr, Hidalgo County, where he raised cotton, along with his household furnishings, a cow, calves, hog, and horse, and a Ford touring car from his bankruptcy case. He discharged nearly $10,000 in unsecured debt.[27]

On the other hand, farmers who had mortgaged their land or owned more than 200 acres stood a good chance of losing most or all of it. The bankruptcy system did not strip creditors of their collateral, and exemption laws did not override mortgages on exempt property. Farmers faced with this scenario sometimes left farming altogether. William Knippa opened a store because of a drought that destroyed his crops and ruined his hopes for the future.[28]

Ranchers, who had to have more than 200 acres in order to sustain their operations, were hit the hardest in bankruptcy court. John W. Sullivan, an Anglo rancher who had acquired thousands of acres of land, mostly from Tejanos in Webb County, lost all of it in 1903. William Doyle, a cattle rancher in Zavala County, lost 3,100 acres in 1912, and Frank Stafford Weaver, a sheep rancher in Uvalde County, lost 35,000 acres in 1917. Albert Urbahn had heavily mortgaged his 53,142-acre Santos Tomas Ranch, his 5,314-acre irrigated Santa Rosa farm, and hundreds of town lots in Laredo. His debt totaled almost $500,000. Urbahn lost all of his property in a bankruptcy case he filed in February 1935. One rancher's misfortune created opportunity for others. In 1905, Charles Schreiner, who became one of the largest ranchers as well as a prominent merchant and banker in the area, bought 11,292 acres of land in Val Verde County formerly owned by Louis Lindheim for sixty-five cents an acre.[29]

Filing a bankruptcy case frequently meant downward mobility for a rancher. Some ranchers became ranch foremen or laborers because they were unable to gain the credit needed to begin over again. Charles Blair, who filed a bankruptcy case in 1921, was living as a boarder on a farm and working as a farm laborer in 1930. Still others found ways to make a living in white-collar jobs. After filing for bankruptcy in 1926, Osee Pope worked as a clerk in the sheriff's office in Camp Wood, Real County. Benjamin Borroum, celebrated trail driver of the nineteenth century who had ranched in both Texas and Mexico, filed for bankruptcy in 1904. He subsequently became a county commissioner in Del Rio and promoted town development for the rest of his life. Some used their skills to become cattle buyers or continued trying to make it as stock farmers. A few ranchers were able to maintain strong connections with friends and creditors willing to continue to lease land and lend money to them. Salvador Armstrong, for example, rebounded from a 1917 bankruptcy filing and built a large cattle operation once again by the late 1930s. Instrumental in his eventual success was his partner, Charles H. Hoyle of St. Louis.[30]

As mortgages on land became more common, bankruptcy was a less viable option even for small farmers prior to the mid-1930s. Concern over the plight of small family farmers in the midst of the deepening agricultural crisis of the Great Depression prompted Congress to pass a number of laws designed to assist them. One measure targeted their main problem, high mortgage debt, by amending the Bankruptcy Act to provide ways to restructure that debt. Section 75 prevented foreclosure, if the creditor would agree to it, while a farmer proposed a plan to extend the due date of mortgage payments or even reduce the amount of the debt. It identified farmers as "debtors" rather than as "bankrupts" to indicate that they were trying to pay, rather than discharge, the majority of their debts. Less than two years later, Congress passed the Frazier-Lemke Farm Mortgage Act of 1934. Conceived primarily by William Lemke, an outspoken congressional representative from North Dakota who championed farmers, it was far more radical than Section 75. It allowed farmers to reduce the amount of their outstanding mortgage to the value of the property. When the Supreme Court declared Frazier-Lemke unconstitutional, Congress revised it on August 28, 1935, to provide a way for the creditor to force a public sale of its collateral if it did not agree to the terms of the mortgage reduction. Congress also expanded the provision to cover cattle ranchers and dairy farmers in addition to traditional farmers. Special conciliation commissioners, rather than bankruptcy referees, managed the farm reorganization cases. In Cameron and Hidalgo counties, R. A. Rowland was appointed commissioner.[31]

Between January 1933 and December 1941, 109 out of 142 farming cases filed in the Brownsville Division of the US District Court for the Southern District of Texas were reorganization cases. Most were filed to stop an imminent foreclosure. Very few farmers actually filed a successful reorganization plan, however. Many used their time in bankruptcy to forestall creditor action long enough to negotiate with one or two major creditors and then dismiss the case once that was accomplished. A few did not even attempt to reorganize. Antonio Valls Armengol, for example, essentially gave up his irrigated onion farm in the mid-1930s.[32]

The case of Oliver and Grace Newcomer, filed in 1938, reveals how difficult it was for farmers to get a fresh start even with the help of the new farm-reorganization provisions. Grace and Oliver had moved to the Valley in 1917 and purchased a thirty-five-acre tract near Pharr. They planted an orchard on seventeen acres and used the rest to grow sugar cane and other crops. The orchard consisted of grapefruit trees and Valencia and navel orange trees. The Newcomers began to fall behind on their taxes in 1928. They did not pay any taxes that year or in 1930, 1931, 1932, or 1933. Another creditor sued them in 1933 and obtained a judgment lien. In order to avoid foreclosure, the couple turned to the Home Owners Loan Corporation to refinance their debt. They were unable, however, to make the monthly $53.79 payments on that loan and faced another foreclosure proceeding. They filed a farm-reorganization case in 1938. Unfortunately, they were unable to complete a plan because their orchard did not produce enough income for them to pay their debts and living expenses.[33]

The Newcomers' case shows that maintaining control of property and eliminating or restructuring debt aided but did not guarantee a fresh start. Former bankrupts also had to have a source of ongoing income and attract new credit in order to survive. This was much easier for proprietors of town-based businesses than it was for farmers and ranchers, who were in an industry prone to uncertain income where increasing economies of scale were driving out smaller operations. Creditors were reluctant to risk loss on these small enterprises. By contrast, despite consolidation within the retail and service sectors, small fashion shops, filling stations, auto repair and supply stores, corner groceries, restaurants, bakeries, and ice cream stores still had a place. The costs of operating these businesses remained relatively low, and the risk for creditors was far lower because their exposure in any one business was usually limited to a small amount.

Filing a bankruptcy case destroyed one's credit rating. Most former bankrupts received no credit rating in the R. G Dun Reference Books for a few years after they filed. Businesses like Armengol's wholesale grocery were affected the most. In 1930, Armengol's rating was C+1.5, which meant the business's value was between $125,000 and $200,000 and its creditworthiness was "good." In 1938, the business received an "L4" rating, which meant the business was worth less than $1,000 and its creditworthiness was limited. The example of Ancira's grocery illustrates how little bankruptcy filings affected the credit ratings of smaller businesses; it had no credit rating either before or after a bankruptcy filing.[34]

Creditworthiness, however, often was not the determining factor in whether a person could borrow money. Some former bankrupts, like William Pfeffer, turned to family and friends for loans, usually the best source of assistance immediately after bankruptcy. Pfeffer had originally filed for bankruptcy in 1900 as part of the partnership of A. Schmidt & Co. He blamed the filing on Schmidt's embezzlement of the partnership's Mexican accounts. Schmidt was hundreds of miles away, living in Mexico City and running a branch of the business there.[35] After the bankruptcy filing, Pfeffer started his own furniture business in Laredo with some money borrowed from his father and brother. His brother explained, "I knew that he had failed and that he had no credit at that time, and that William Pfeffer could not carry on a business without cash, also knowing that the first failure of William Pfeffer was through no fault of his, and knowing at the time that William Pfeffer had the reputation of being a good, sober, business man, I let him have the money to put in business, to start again, and my object in doing so was to give my brother william pfeffer [sic] commercial credit. I would not have loaned this sum of money to a person not a relation of mine, or a friend, immediately after he had been declared bankrupt."[36]

Honesty, consistency, and a history of paying back debts went a long way toward repairing credit relations after filing for bankruptcy, especially if the filing could be blamed on some external circumstance like a fire or unanticipated illness. The fact that people were actually able to continue in business after a bankruptcy filing suggests that creditors were willing to work with them despite low or no credit ratings. This was true for small as well as large businesses. James Ayoub went into business with William Ayoub after he filed a bankruptcy case in 1928. That may have helped him to reestablish credit. A list of creditors in the second bankruptcy case filed in 1930 reveals that at least two, M. Halff & Co. and Eli Feldstein Co. of New York City, were both willing to lend to James after his first filing. Robert Savage, whose general store had gone bankrupt in 1922, switched to wholesale groceries and formed a corporation. A 1930 bankruptcy case of that business shows he had no trouble borrowing money after his first case. He had more than $54,000 in unsecured debts. Although the amount of debt Savage incurred was unusual, similar scenarios played out in the lives of many former bankrupts.[37]

A true fresh start involved the restoration of not only one's business and credit but also one's reputation. Restoration of reputation is far more difficult to measure. In South Texas, bankruptcy apparently carried a stigma but did not mark a person as a permanent loser as long as he or she had overcome the failure. Stories about several prominent individuals provide insight into how the society dealt with bankruptcy. A 1930s' article praising Hill's efforts in developing the Lower Rio Grande Valley mentioned the failure of his first store in Manor, Texas, near Austin. Hill filed for bankruptcy and paid every creditor "even though according to the law he was not obligated to do so."[38] Neither that article nor many of the other articles about his pioneering spirit mentioned that he had filed a second bankruptcy case after he moved to South Texas and discharged more than $450,000 in debt.[39] Despite Joseph Netzer's bankruptcy filing five years earlier, as well as his ongoing failure to restore his credit rating, *Pioneer Magazine* described Netzer as a man of thrift and excellent business ability.[40] Similarly, Sam Botts, the mayor of Harlingen known for his compassion for ordinary people, was called a true "pioneer" even though he had filed a bankruptcy case shortly after he arrived.[41]

Salvador Armstrong stood six foot two and weighed in excess of 250 pounds. He was a jovial South Texas rancher who, for many, epitomized the legendary Anglo-American cattleman of the border region. He was "a breed of range riders fast passing into oblivion" and an "old-time cowpuncher." He had "the air of having just come from camp where, most likely, he squatted on his heels or drank black coffee with the fellows or stripped off chunks of barbecue with his pocket knife." None of the articles about him in the *Cattleman* or the *Fort Worth Press* hint at his personal financial difficulties or his bankruptcy case.[42]

Levi Snavely from Indiana moved to Corpus Christi and then to the lower Rio Grande Valley and became a substantial citrus grower and winter vegetable farmer. He also owned a number of packing plants and was seen as an expert in citrus. He ended up in bankruptcy court twice, once because a clothing merchant had foreclosed on his goods in 1915, and he filed voluntarily again in 1937. He had mortgaged virtually everything he owned except the farm where he actually lived. In between his two bankruptcy filings, his name and picture appeared in a 1930s' publication, *The Lower Rio Grande Valley and Its Builders,* which honored him as one of the important "pioneers" of the lower Rio Grande Valley.[43]

James Garfield Sullivan was a commercial onion grower who developed a successful business selling onion and spinach seeds around the region. He personified what many Anglo farmers aspired to in South Texas. He started out in Asherton in 1910 with very little capital. He developed a large farm of 597 acres, 300 of which were irrigated, and hired more than 150 Mexican laborers. He built a two-story brick building in Asherton to distribute seeds he had acquired from the Tenerife Island, part of the Canary Island chain off the coast of Spain. *Pioneer Magazine* quoted the president of the Asherton Chamber of Commerce as saying, "His business ability, coupled with foresight and attractive personality, has made for him many friends and an enviable record in the business he chose."

He held "in the palm of his hand the destiny of every crop of Bermuda onions and spinach" planted in Texas' Winter Garden District but still filed two bankruptcy cases, one in 1913 and another in 1931.[44]

. . .

Stories like that of James Sullivan highlight that this willingness to overlook failure and give people a second chance was as much a part of American culture as its embracing of success. Acceptance of failure on some level also meant embracing risk, an inherent feature of entrepreneurial capitalism. The adoption and use of the bankruptcy laws was part of this culture of risk taking, which was especially pronounced in the United States. The kind of safety net it provided required people to go out and take new risks again. By helping to smooth out the consequences of boom-and-bust cycles, bankruptcy became the "safety valve of capitalism."[45]

The choice by many borderland entrepreneurs to utilize the bankruptcy system reveals that they fully accepted the US culture of risk taking and second chances. The federal bankruptcy statutes in turn provided a way for them to preserve their status as members of the business class in the region by enabling them (in most cases) to avoid extreme downward mobility and start over. Yet, even though the bankruptcy system kept them from homelessness and permanent debt enslavement, it did not eliminate the ultimate insecurity of independent entrepreneurship. As the "free-market solution to bad debt," it simply established a floor on what they could lose, forcing them to move back into the economy in some capacity to take new risks in order to generate income to support themselves and their families. Although Congress did create new kinds of social safety nets in the 1930s as a result of the harsh realities of the Depression, the deep and abiding influence on US culture of free-market principles and entrepreneurial values of individual achievement, competition, inventiveness, and a willingness to venture into the unknown kept US lawmakers away from instituting more radical and socialist solutions to problems of failure and income inequality. Even today, the excitement and the uncertainty associated with starting and managing new enterprises that permeated commercial life in the South Texas borderlands between 1880 and 1940 continue to have an impact on borderland entrepreneurs.[46]

CONCLUSION

THE CONSTRUCTION OF RAILROADS during the Porfiriato marked a turning point in the history of the South Texas borderlands and facilitated the expansion of a diverse, modern business class. Ever since the drawing of the international boundary along the Río Bravo/Rio Grande in 1848, business in South Texas had had a transnational dimension. Proximity to the US/Mexico border, coupled with the relative social and cultural fluidity of the borderlands, had also long sustained a multicultural business class in the region. For most of the nineteenth century, however, that class consisted of a small group of elite merchants in Matamoros/Brownsville and Monterrey, who controlled commercial trade in silver, cotton, and manufactured products between Europe, New England, and northern Mexico after Mexican independence in 1821. Due to the risks and expenses involved in seaborne trade and the absence of adequate transportation routes into the interior, few small merchants could participate.

Beginning in the early 1880s, railroads built to expedite the flow of investment capital and raw materials in and out of Mexico broke the elite merchants' hold on the region's commerce by connecting South Texas more efficiently to US and Mexican centers of finance and industry. Credit, customers, and labor followed the railroads. The farm development and urbanization that occurred as a consequence created a greater need for consumer goods and services, especially after 1917. This demand, in turn, led to more business opportunities for people with little or no capital, thus giving rise to an entrepreneurial middle class. Hundreds of migrants—Anglo, Mexican, European, and Middle Eastern alike—converged along the South Texas border to pursue their version of the American dream. The process of "creative destruction" was at work in this period; even as capitalist development produced new opportunities, it displaced substantial numbers of Tejano *rancheros,* fragmenting the Hispanic ranching society that had persisted for more than one hundred years.

The Mexican Revolution of 1910 in many ways improved business conditions in South Texas as compared to northeastern Mexico. The influx of unskilled workers created not only a pool of cheap labor for both farmers and business owners but also a growing market for various kinds of retailers. The migration of members of the Mexican middle class added to the entrepreneurial talent in the region and augmented the customer base. Ranching and agriculture remained the mainstays of the local economy, but commercial activity in the towns became increasingly important. Moreover, as ranching and agriculture became more and more capital intensive and required greater economies of scale, fewer people were able to make a living on the land, regardless of their ethnic background. The Great Depression accelerated the shift of population from country to city so that, by the end of the 1930s, more people in the region lived in urban than in rural areas.

South Texas' business environment was part of the greater American Southwest, and it shared with the rest of that region some unique qualities. Proximity to the border meant an expanded consumer market and a constant pool of cheap labor. Diversifying one's operations across an international boundary also offered the possibility of mitigating the impact of varied business cycles and government policies in the United States and Mexico. Some business owners saw the border as a way to escape difficulties in one country or the other, especially if creditors were after them. Despite the outbreak of the Mexican Revolution in 1910, these features remained relatively constant in the immediate border zone.

Between 1880 and 1940, the business class of South Texas was multiethnic, more so in the cities and towns than in rural areas. Although it comprised both men and women, men dominated, and most women operated small enterprises. Particular ethnic groups tended to gravitate toward different economic sectors. The majority of Anglo-Americans who migrated to the border in this period were farmers or stock raisers with long family histories of living off the land; they moved to the border region with an intention of continuing those activities. They dominated farming and ranching in most parts of the region because of their superior access to capital and credit. They relied on ethnic Mexican labor; as a result, many rural areas along the border became highly stratified between a class of Anglo-American farmers and ranchers and ethnic Mexican workers. Ethnic Mexicans, however, continued to own farms and ranches, especially in Starr and Zapata counties, which had a long history of Hispanic settlement and limited access to transportation, and they, too, depended on ethnic Mexican workers.

The greatest diversity of business owners resided in the border towns, Brownsville, Rio Grande City, Roma, Laredo, Eagle Pass, and, to a lesser extent, Del Rio, all of which dated to the mid-nineteenth century. The composition of the business owners varied in the farm towns that sprang up after the railroad arrived in the lower Rio Grande Valley. These towns tended to be sharply divided between an Anglo and a Mexican side, but because they were close to the border, some had a fairly cosmopolitan mixture of Anglos, Mexicans, Jews, Tejanos, Italians, and Spaniards in their central business districts. Mercedes is probably the best example of this. In others, like Harlingen, Anglo-Americans overwhelmingly dominated. Similarly, the towns of the Winter Garden region, such as Carrizo Springs, Asherton, and Crystal City, were visibly divided between Anglos and Mexicans and had few non-Anglo business owners. The ethnic Mexican businesses there initially consisted primarily of small general stores and groceries in the *barrios;* in the 1920s, garages and filling stations began to appear.

Anglos were represented in every economic sector of the towns and cities. They were less likely than other groups to engage in cross-border business, focusing more on the local Anglo-American community. They brought to the border the values of US entrepreneurial culture, including a strong emphasis on individual achievement, competition, profits, consumerism, and the possibility of socioeconomic mobility, which influenced not only South Texas society but that of northeastern Mexico as well.[1]

Jews, Italians, and Spaniards, many of whom arrived in the region with little or no capital, numbered among the most successful urban business owners. Jews served an especially important role in bringing American consumer culture to the region and, as a consequence, helped to create the borderland middle-class lifestyle. As the dominant owners of department stores, jewelry stores, and specialty clothing and dry-goods stores, they brought fashionable and luxury goods from the US industrial heartland to its periphery, along with the necessities of everyday life. Syrians and Greeks usually had smaller businesses; Greeks tended to start confectioneries along the border, as they did in other parts of the United States. Members of these groups took advantage of proximity to the border to seek customers in northeastern Mexico in order to enlarge their businesses and profits.

Finally, ethnic Mexicans, who made up a sizeable proportion of the business class, served primarily the ethnic Mexican community. They, too, frequently engaged in cross-border business. Small grocery stores, general stores, and later auto repair shops and filling stations made up the vast majority of their establishments. They carried items necessary for basic survival because the limited incomes of the majority of the ethnic Mexican population allowed for few or no luxuries.

Members of the business class shared common business goals; that is, they wanted to attract customers, sell their products, goods, or services, and make a profit. Business owners cooperated with others as necessary in order to accomplish these goals. Therefore, issues of nationality, class, and ethnicity were less important in the commercial sphere than in the social one. On a certain level, therefore, the commercial realm served an assimilative function for those who were not Anglo-Americans, especially in urban areas, where people engaged in business tended to come from many different backgrounds. This was particularly apparent in the outlook of the Mexican American middle class. Organizations like the League of United Latin American Citizens stressed the need to retain Hispanic culture, values, and language, while at the same time they urged their members to embrace Anglo-American business practices, entrepreneurial values, the English language, and education in order to facilitate the rise of ethnic Mexicans within US society.

For most businesspeople, the ability to access credit was crucial to survival and expansion. The size and the nature of one's business became the primary factors in borrowing money; gender and ethnicity were relevant but secondary considerations. The relatively wide availability of credit in the United States gave people from many diverse backgrounds the opportunity to move into the mainstream of the American middle class by engaging in entrepreneurship. This was as true on the border as it was in other parts of the country. The wide availability of credit, however, does not mean that everyone was equally able to access it and start a new business. The fact remains that the overwhelming majority of ethnic Mexicans who worked as unskilled laborers had little chance of upward mobility. Although race played a role in this, class was also important. Few spoke English or had the skills necessary to start new business enterprises. This was also characteristic in this period of hundreds of unskilled laborers in other parts of the United States who had emigrated from Europe.[2]

Yet, the ability of middle-class and skilled ethnic Mexicans and foreign immigrants to engage as entrepreneurs in commercial society in South Texas attests to the relative openness of the US economy to people from different backgrounds, especially in the American West and the borderlands, as compared to its historically exclusive society. This analysis of class as it intersects with race and ethnicity is important to a fuller understanding of historical change. The nature of the US economy has been such that it has presented opportunities, albeit not without barriers and limitations, to a wide variety of individuals willing to seize them. This promise of the American dream eventually had an impact on the opening up of US society in the late twentieth century. Inevitably, people who met each other in business became acquainted with and more accepting of each other in different spheres of life as well.

The uncertainty of success in a capitalist economy permeated life in the South Texas border region as it did elsewhere, making the pursuit of the American dream elusive. The prevalence of failure among all ethnic groups and all sizes of businesses in this time period underscores that reality. Economic cycles often determined the fate of South Texas residents. The ability to start over again after failure, not failure itself, was crucial to ongoing persistence and participation in the business class. Some individuals (and groups) were able to do this more successfully than others; gender, ethnicity, size of business, and business networks all played a role. Prominent business owners generally had an easier time coping with failure because they had larger networks of associates with capital who were willing to lend to help them start over. By contrast, discrimination created conditions (such as the segregated towns) that made many ethnic Mexican businesspeople more vulnerable to the business cycle and therefore made it more difficult for them to start afresh. Class could sometimes mitigate the effects of discrimination, especially in the older border towns. It is also important not to overlook the drive, creativity, and ability of individual business owners. The history of success, failure, and persistence reveals that considerations of class, ethnicity, and gender cannot be viewed in isolation from either the business cycle or the characteristics of the individual entrepreneur because all worked together to determine who would ultimately prosper.

This study indirectly raises questions about the nature of the business community in northeastern Mexico during this period and the extent to which it either mirrored or differed from that of South Texas. Since my research did not include specific information about the numbers, characteristics, experiences, creditors, and customers of business owners in northern Mexico unless they had corresponding businesses in South Texas, these questions provide a fruitful area for further scholarly inquiry. A related question is why some business owners chose to stay or settle in northeastern Mexico rather than South Texas in this period.

Despite the presence of long-standing and extensive economic links between South Texas and northeastern Mexico, political and legal conditions in the two places clearly differed, and it was during this period that the gap in business opportunities and living conditions between the United States and Mexico widened considerably. The United States emerged from the Civil War with a much stronger federal government and proceeded to expand political, military, and economic control over its territory in such a way as to create a stable state in a relatively short period of time. In the United States, federal and state laws protected private property and contractual rights, facilitated the growth of banks and other credit facilities, eased lending across state lines, and encouraged risk taking by providing ways to protect some property from creditors and discharge debt when it became too burdensome to bear. These laws, among others, helped to create a stable business environment in which entrepreneurs with varying degrees of resources were willing to start a wide variety of enterprises. They also fostered the development of a relatively large and growing middle class.

By contrast, in this period, the political and legal environment of Mexico was less stable and predictable, a situation attributable in part to US dominance over the Mexican economy between about 1880 and 1910. During the seemingly stable years of the Porfiriato, certain investors, many of whom were American businessmen, received subsidies and favors over others. They helped to create a highly export-dependent economy that led to extremes in income inequality and barriers to upward mobility. The Mexican Revolution, which represented a reaction to those developments, actually did little to change certain features of the Porfiriato, which remained entrenched in subsequent decades. Credit was highly concentrated and available primarily to the elite. Monopolies and oligopolies, which the Mexican state protected through a variety of laws and subsidies, controlled most industries. Political instability reigned after 1910 and until 1934, when Lázaro Cárdenas was elected president. The loss of hundreds of thousands of acres of land by private landowners during and after the Revolution underscored the tentative nature of private property rights. The Revolutionary Constitution of 1917 gave the Mexican government the right to limit ownership of private property, especially among elites, in order to protect the public interest. Even though Mexico endeavored to create a middle class of farmers in the 1930s with its irrigation projects on redistributed land, the credit available to them as well as to other kinds of business owners remained limited. Much of the Mexican economy continued to be within the control of the state, large businesses, and wealthy individuals. Small business owners, as well as other members of the middle class, represented a smaller percentage of the population than in the United States.[3]

The extent to which this different business environment of Mexico shaped the business class of northeastern Mexico remains to be determined. Perhaps proximity to the United States enhanced access to credit and markets for entrepreneurs along the border in ways lacking for entrepreneurs deeper in Mexico. Examining in more detail the eastern European Jews, Syrians, and ethnic Mexicans who did business and chose to live permanently in the towns of northeastern Mexico between 1880 and 1940 would provide greater insight into this question.

World War II and the postwar era changed Mexico, the United States, and the border region. It stimulated war-related industrialization in the American West, expanded military bases even into South Texas, hastened the trend toward large, corporate-owned farms, and accelerated urbanization. Although hundreds of people continued to own small businesses throughout the South Texas border region, increasing numbers worked for someone else. Improved relations between Mexico and the United States enhanced transnational trade. In the aftermath of the war, US businesses and financiers returned to Mexico as relations between the nations improved. In the 1960s, Mexico's Border Industrialization Program stimulated the rise of the *maquiladoras,* American-owned assembly plants set up in the Mexican border towns, where they could take advantage of cheap labor. Most dealt in automobile parts, electrical appliances and components, textiles, chemical products, and, later, computer technology, which were then sold across the border duty free. Hundreds of people moved to work in these plants, creating explosive growth in towns on the south side of the border, from Matamoros to Tijuana. *Maquiladoras* sprang up in Reynosa, Nuevo Laredo, Piedras Negras, and Ciudad Acuña.

Economic relations between the United States and Mexico in the 1990s bore an uncanny resemblance to the Porfiriato. In 1994, US financiers took advantage of the devaluation of the peso to invest substantial sums in railroads, mines, oil and gas, manufacturing, and food processing and distribution but not so much in land. The North American Free Trade Agreement of 1994 (NAFTA), which lowered tariff barriers among the United States, Canada, and Mexico, enhanced transnational trade but also exacerbated the wealth gaps that existed between the United States and Mexico. Instead of developing more of a local market, Mexico continued its dependence on export-oriented trade with the United States, especially in agricultural products, and US companies were more able to take advantage of low labor costs in Mexico. Deep inequalities between elites in Mexico and others persisted. During the 1990s and into the early 2000s, thousands of Americans settled in Mexico, attracted by low prices, and thousands more vacationed there on a regular basis. At the same time, thousands of Mexicans moved north into the United States, seeking better opportunities and higher wages; these migrants did not consist simply of undocumented, migratory workers but also included middle-class Mexicans, often highly educated, who have moved into business and the professions in the United States.[4]

All of these developments contributed to even more mixing of US and Mexican culture and society throughout the US-Mexico borderlands and created a more complex urban environment along the Río Bravo/Rio Grande. The influx of low-skilled workers seeking jobs in the *maquiladoras* and on the corporate farms actually increased poverty throughout South Texas and northeastern Mexico. Migratory farmworkers settled in *colonias* or shantytowns in unincorporated areas on the margins of towns that lacked basic services like electricity, adequate sewer systems, and potable water. Laborers seeking work in the *maquiladoras* of Reynosa, Matamoros, and Nuevo Laredo often lived in even worse conditions. Neighborhoods consisted of hundreds of small wooden and cardboard shacks lining dirt roads that turn to a thick, almost impassable mud when it rains.[5]

At the same time, the Mexican American middle class in South Texas steadily expanded, building on the achievements of earlier generations. After World War II, the Mexican American middle class became a national, not just a borderland, phenomenon. The rising economic and educational status of Mexican Americans and their increasing visibility in the political arena made it virtually impossible for Anglo-Americans to continue to segregate them as they had in the 1920s and 1930s. Educational opportunities improved with the passage of the GI Bill, and thousands of Mexican American college students began attending the University of Texas–Pan American, Texas Southmost College, Texas A&M International University, located in Laredo (formerly Texas A&I University at Laredo, founded in 1969), and, most recently, the University of Texas at Brownsville (founded in 1991). Education became increasingly important for middle-class status; although small businesses persisted in South Texas towns in the latter twentieth century, the path to the middle class for most shifted to the professions and white-collar employment. By the late twentieth century, ethnic Mexicans constituted an overwhelming majority of the residents along the South Texas border. In 2000, people of Mexican descent or ethnicity constituted 84.3 percent of the population of Cameron County, 88.3 percent of the population of Hidalgo County, 85 percent of Dimmit County, 75.5 percent of Val Verde County, and 94.3 percent of Webb County.[6] Although Anglo-Americans and a few descendants of the Spanish, Italian, German, French, Jewish, and Syrian immigrants continued to live in the area, many moved to other places. The children and grandchildren of the Jews who had settled along the border in the late nineteenth and early twentieth centuries began migrating to the larger Texas cities of Dallas, Houston, Austin, and San Antonio after World War II and increasingly moved out of retail and into the professions.

The migration from country to city accelerated in the late twentieth century. Today, the vast majority of the residents of South Texas live in urban areas. The border towns themselves are now almost indistinguishable from other US cities, filled as they are with car lots, chain restaurants, and shopping malls, the outward symbols of US consumer culture and Americans' ongoing desire to achieve a higher and higher standard of living. Although agriculture and ranching remain mainstays of the economy, corporate enterprises have taken over much of the countryside. A drive south on Highway 77 from Corpus Christi passes through miles of brush land inhabited largely by cattle, much of it still owned by the King Ranch, now a corporation. In the lower Rio Grande Valley, the acres of grapefruit and orange orchards are diminished, but fields of spinach, onion, cabbage, carrots, and cotton still extend for miles. Only a few of the old white frame houses put up by the early farmers are still standing. Sometimes you can see them down narrow roads framed with palms. John Shary's palatial home, still nestled among palm trees near grapefruit orchards, has been bought by individuals planning to turn it into a bed-and-breakfast inn.

With the rise of the drug cartels in the twenty-first century, violence has wracked the border once again, nearly one hundred years after the Mexican Revolution of 1910. People wonder what the impact will be. Monterrey, once a "model for developing countries," is now a "symbol of Mexico's drug war chaos, sucked down into a dark spiral of gangland killings, violent crime, and growing lawlessness." What will happen to business on the border? Will the drug cartels foreclose opportunities even more than the Revolution once did? Will the drug wars threaten the prosperity of residents of South Texas? The violence has already led to the migration out of Mexico of businesspeople such as Marío Ramos, who had an industrial tubing business in Monterrey. In 2011, he received a call demanding money, and then gunmen shot up his property and set fire to one of his trucks. Like those fleeing the Mexican Revolution for Texas in 1913, he left Mexico behind and fled with his family to San Antonio, seeking to start a new life.[7]

The history of entrepreneurs in the South Texas border region reveals a number of things about the nature of commercial society and business opportunity in the borderlands and in the United States as a whole. It shows that the multicultural, multinational, globalized business class of the twenty-first century is not really new but had its roots in a variety of historical borderland environments like the one along the Río Bravo/Rio Grande. It reveals that the US and Mexican economies and societies have long been inextricably intertwined and that cooperation, perhaps even more so than conflict, has historically characterized relations between and among Mexicans, US citizens, and foreign immigrants in the borderlands in their struggle to make a living and pursue profits. It reveals that events in Mexico and in the United States, business cycles, the presence or absence of favorable legal, financial, and transportation infrastructure, and a variety of local conditions could either facilitate or hinder entrepreneurial activity. Business opportunities were therefore, in part, a product of the business environment. Credit played a particularly critical role because it supplied capital to people with little or no resources of their own. The expansion of decentralized, widely available credit in the United States explains some of the reasons the country developed a sizeable middle class; it became an important feature of the US economy that borderlanders were able to take advantage of in their quest for opportunity and success.

Opportunity, however, was not only shaped by the business environment but was also a product of one's own making; people were not simply victims of their circumstances. The experiences of ethnic Mexican business owners, farmers, and ranchers, who faced the greatest number of obstacles and barriers to success, are especially instructive in this regard. Evidence that they survived and sometimes thrived in a period of harsh discrimination, coupled with the fact that a Mexican American middle class emerged in the towns of South Texas in the 1920s and 1930s, shows the importance of individual initiative and agency in shaping outcomes. The decision by many eastern European Jews, Syrians, Italians, Spaniards, and others to leave oppressive conditions in their homelands, settle down in and adapt to the borderland environment by cultivating contacts on both sides of the border, and ultimately create successful enterprises provides another illustration of the importance of individual initiative and creativity. Additionally, hundreds of Anglo-Americans who left homes, families, and long-standing roots in the South and Midwest faced trials in their efforts to forge a new life along the border and had to make choices to either persist or leave.

In another interesting parallel to the 1880–1940 period, the recent recession in the United States and its tepid economic recovery, the constriction of credit, and the looming bankruptcies of major corporations and cities like Detroit and San Bernardino all remind us that the elusive nature of success did not disappear after the Great Depression. Despite the relatively wide array of economic opportunities that the United States has offered over the course of its history to an increasingly pluralistic group of people, the unevenness of the promise of the American dream and the ambiguity of its outcome have not changed. Success has never been guaranteed, and the potential of failure, loss, or downward mobility has never been eliminated. The history of South Texas borderland entrepreneurs suggests that resilience, creativity, and persistence, along with a loose grasp of material things, are among the most important qualities to cultivate in the face of uncertainty. In her brief memoir about life on the border in the early decades of the twentieth century, Donna Hooks Fletcher perhaps best summarized this outlook. "Of course I've made my share of mistakes—who hasn't? I saw the early boom days wax and wane, and shared in the deflation of land values. My financial resources took another beating during the late 20s and early 30s which, combined with other factors, closed my department store. As my material wealth began to slip away, I sought strength from God, the one source that never fails, doing my level best and leaving the results to Him."[8]

APPENDIX 1

APPENDIX 1. Businesses reported in R. G. Dun reference books, selected South Texas towns

TOWN	1901		1910		1918		1925		1930		1938	
	Total	Hispanic	Total	Hispanic	Total	Hispanic	Total	Hispanic	Total	Hispanic	Total	Hispanic
Asherton	–	–	11	1 (9%)	13	3 (23%)	20	5 (25%)	32	12 (37%)	17	4 (23%)
Brownsville	53	26 (49%)	138	65 (47%)	161	76 (47%)	240	111 (46%)	318	122 (38%)	369	115 (31%)
Carrizo Springs	3	0	8	0	28	1 (3%)	22	1 (4%)	39	1 (2%)	59	2 (3%)
Crystal City	–	–	2	0	13	2 (15%)	23	2 (9%)	76	23 (30%)	95	15 (15%)
Del Rio	44	0	68	4 (5%)	100	20 (20%)	132	32 (24%)	170	33 (19%)	209	53 (25%)
Eagle Pass	45	6 (13%)	42	8 (19%)	105	27 (26%)	101	39 (39%)	90	40 (44%)	110	45 (40%)
Harlingen	–	–	18	3 (16%)	31	9 (29%)	101	20 (20%)	243	32 (13%)	341	25 (7%)
Laredo	128	44 (34%)	132	62 (49%)	270	135 (50%)	338	173 (51%)	381	202 (53%)	410	193 (47%)
Mercedes	–	–	39	15 (38%)	39	10 (25%)	106	30 (28%)	152	41 (26%)	145	36 (25%)
Mission	–	–	11	3 (27%)	69	27 (39%)	115	35 (30%)	128	36 (28%)	154	43 (28%)
Rio Grande City	19	15 (79%)	22	17 (77%)	59	42 (71%)	46	32 (69%)	71	56 (78%)	66	43 (65%)
Roma	11	11 (100%)	9	9 (100%)	20	20 (100%)	21	21 (100%)	26	25 (96%)	24	22 (91%)
San Diego	24	9 (37%)	31	11 (35%)	41	26 (63%)	41	25 (61%)	42	26 (62%)	63	48 (76%)
Totals	327	111 (33%)	531	198 (18%)	949	398 (41%)	1,306	526 (40%)	1,768	649 (37%)	2,061	644 (31%)

Sources: *The Mercantile Agency Reference Books, State Pocket Edition, Texas.* New York: R. G. Dun & Co., 1901, 1910, 1938; *The Mercantile Agency Reference Books.* New York: R. G. Dun & Co., 1918, 1925; *Dun & Bradstreet Reference Book, State Pocket Edition, Texas.* New York: Dun & Bradstreet, 1938.

APPENDIX 2

APPENDIX 2. Sample of large businesses reported in R. G. Dun reference books, selected South Texas towns

SIZE	1901	1910	1918	1925	1930	1938
$1m	0	1	3	5	10	21
Non-Hispanic	0	1	2	5	9	21
Hispanic	0	0	1	0	1	0
$200K–1m	2	7	11	14	26	25
Non-Hispanic	1	6	8	12	24	23
Hispanic	1	1	3	2	2	2
$75–200K	4	11	15	45	64	31
Non-Hispanic	2	9	11	33	55	26
Hispanic	2	2	4	12	9	5
$35–75K	6	23	35	47	65	64
Non-Hispanic	4	18	24	38	50	51
Hispanic	2	5	11	9	15	13
Total	12	42	64	111	165	141
Non-Hispanic	7 (58%)	34 (81%)	45 (70%)	88 (79%)	138 (84%)	121 (86%)
Hispanic	5 (41%)	8 (19%)	19 (30%)	23 (21%)	27 (16%)	20 (14%)

Note: Sample includes Asherton, Brownsville, Carrizo Springs, Crystal City, Del Rio, Eagle Pass, Harlingen, Laredo, Mercedes, Mission, Rio Grande City, Roma, San Diego, San Ygnacio (only years 1901, 1910, 1930, and 1938), and Zapata (only years 1901, 1910, 1930, and 1938).

Sources: *The Mercantile Agency Reference Books, State Pocket Edition, Texas.* New York: R. G. Dun & Co., 1901, 1910, 1930); *The Mercantile Agency Reference Books.* New York: R. G. Dun & Co., 1918, 1925; *Dun & Bradstreet Reference Book, State Pocket Edition, Texas.* New York: Dun & Bradstreet, 1938.

APPENDIX 3

APPENDIX 3. Sample of small businesses reported in R. G. Dun reference books, selected South Texas towns

SIZE	1901	1910	1918	1925	1930	1938
$20–35K	12	16	32	32	42	38
Non-Hispanic	8	13	20	18	33	25
Hispanic	4	3	12	14	9	13
$10–20K	17	22	39	56	105	76
Non-Hispanic	12	13	34	43	83	69
Hispanic	5	9	5	13	22	7
$3–10K	44	117	137	160	203	195
Non-Hispanic	26	97	83	118	143	141
Hispanic	18	20	54	42	60	54
$500–3K	65	149	127	235	328	442
Non-Hispanic	41	84	72	118	169	286
Hispanic	24	65	55	117	159	156
$500	113	153	293	351	374	592
Non-Hispanic	66	69	120	108	112	265
Hispanic	47	84	173	243	262	327
Totals	251	457	628	834	1052	1343
Non-Hispanic	153 (61%)	276 (60%)	329 (52%)	405 (48%)	540 (51%)	786 (58%)
Hispanic	98 (39%)	181 (40%)	299 (48%)	429 (51%)	512 (49%)	557 (42%)

Note: Sample includes Asherton, Brownsville, Carrizo Springs, Crystal City, Del Rio, Eagle Pass, Harlingen, Laredo, Mercedes, Mission, Rio Grande City, Roma, San Diego, San Ygnacio (only years 1901, 1910, 1930, and 1938), and Zapata (only years 1901, 1910, 1930, and 1938).

Sources: *The Mercantile Agency Reference Books, State Pocket Edition, Texas.* New York: R. G. Dun & Co., 1901, 1910, 1930; *The Mercantile Agency Reference Books.* New York: R. G. Dun & Co., 1918, 1925; *Dun & Bradstreet Reference Book, State Pocket Edition, Texas.* New York: Dun & Bradstreet, 1938.

APPENDIX 4

APPENDIX 4. Women-owned businesses reported in R. G. Dun reference books, selected South Texas towns

CITY	1901 Anglo	1901 Hispanic	1910 Anglo	1910 Hispanic	1918 Anglo	1918 Hispanic	1925 Anglo	1925 Hispanic	1930 Anglo	1930 Hispanic	1938 Anglo	1938 Hispanic
Asherton	–	–	0	0	0	0	0	0	1	0	2	0
Brownsville	7	0	3	1	4	2	5	3	7	7	17	15
Carrizo Springs	0	0	0	0	2	0	1	0	1	0	8	0
Crystal City	–	–	0	0	0	0	1	0	1	0	4	1
Del Rio	1	0	3	0	5	0	3	1	8	0	10	9
Eagle Pass	5	0	3	0	2	0	0	3	0	4	1	3
Harlingen	–	–	0	0	1	0	2	1	7	0	16	0
Laredo	6	3	3	3	3	3	5	4	4	5	12	12
Mercedes	–	–	0	0	2	1	2	1	1	3	7	3
Mission	–	–	0	0	2	0	1	0	1	0	2	2
Rio Grande City	0	1	0	1	1	1	1	0	0	2	1	2
Roma	0	0	0	0	0	0	0	1	0	1	0	1
San Diego	1	1	2	0	2	0	1	1	1	0	0	0
Totals:	20	5	14	5	24	7	22	15	32	22	80	48

Sources: *The Mercantile Agency Reference Books, State Pocket Edition, Texas.* New York: R. G. Dun & Co., 1901, 1910, 1930; *The Mercantile Agency Reference Books* (New York: R. G. Dun & Co., 1918, 1925); *Dun & Bradstreet Reference Book, State Pocket Edition, Texas.* New York: Dun & Bradstreet, 1938.

APPENDIX 5

APPENDIX 5. Credit ratings for businesses* reported in R. G. Dun reference books, selected South Texas towns

CREDIT RATING	1901	1910	1918	1925	1930	1938
High	8	23	36	64	98	92
Non-Hispanic	4 (3%)**	18 (7%)	27 (8%)	53 (10%)	91 (12%)	85 (10%)
Hispanic	4 (5%)	5 (4%)	9 (4%)	11 (3%)	7 (1%)	7 (1%)
Good	54	87	138	203	283	214
Non-Hispanic	34 (24%)	68 (25%)	103 (29%)	153 (29%)	207 (28%)	170 (20%)
Hispanic	20 (25%)	19 (15%)	35 (17%)	50 (15%)	76 (15%)	44 (10%)
Fair	73	161	220	314	462	442
Non-Hispanic	52 (37%)	119 (43%)	135 (38%)	218 (41%)	303 (40%)	316 (36%)
Hispanic	21 (26%)	42 (33%)	85 (42%)	96 (30%)	159 (32%)	126 (28%)
Limited	87	128	161	269	413	596
Non-Hispanic	51 (36%)	67 (25%)	86 (25%)	104 (20%)	151 (20%)	294 (34%)
Hispanic	36 (44%)	61 (48%)	75 (37%)	165 (51%)	262 (52%)	275 (61%)

Notes: Sample includes Asherton, Brownsville, Carrizo Springs, Crystal City, Del Rio, Eagle Pass, Harlingen, Laredo, Mercedes, Mission, Rio Grande City, Roma, San Diego, San Ygnacio (only years 1901, 1910, 1930, and 1938), and Zapata (only years 1901, 1910, 1930, and 1938).

*Only businesses with credit ratings are included; many businesses received no rating because there was inadequate information to evaluate their status.

**Percentages represent the percentage of non-Hispanic or Hispanic owners in a particular category out of the total non-Hispanic or Hispanic owners for a given year.

Sources: *The Mercantile Agency Reference Books, State Pocket Edition, Texas.* New York: R. G. Dun & Co., 1901, 1910, 1930; *The Mercantile Agency Reference Books* (New York: R. G. Dun & Co., 1918, 1925); *Dun & Bradstreet Reference Book, State Pocket Edition, Texas.* New York: Dun & Bradstreet, 1938.

NOTES

ABBREVIATIONS

BLHBS   Baker Library Historical Collections, Harvard Business School
BLUCB   Bancroft Library, University of California–Berkeley
CAH   Dolph Briscoe Center for American History, University of Texas–Austin
HLSC   Huntington Library Special Collections
JHSC   John H. Shary Papers
LRGV   Lower Rio Grande Valley Historical Collection
NARA   National Archives and Records Administration, Fort Worth, TX
NLBC   Nettie Lee Benson Collection, University of Texas–Austin
SMU   Southern Methodist University
TAMUK   South Texas Archives, Texas A&M–Kingsville
TJHS   Texas Jewish Historical Society Records, Dolph Briscoe Center for American History, University of Texas–Austin
TXSLA   Texas State Library and Archives
UTPA   Special Collections, University of Texas–Pan American
UTSA   Special Collections, University of Texas–San Antonio

Bankruptcy cases are all part of Record Group 21, National Archives and Records Administration, Fort Worth. For ease of reference, I identify them by the division of the court in which they are filed as follows:

Brownsville Case No.   Southern District of Texas, Brownsville Division
Corpus Christi Case No.   Southern District of Texas, Corpus Christi Division
Del Rio Case No.   Western District of Texas, Del Rio Division
Laredo Case No.   Southern District of Texas, Laredo Division
San Antonio Case No.   Western District of Texas, San Antonio Division

INTRODUCTION

1. Z. S. Armstrong, "Dallas Writer Finds Real Mexican Border Not along the Tortuous Rio Grande," *Dallas Morning News,* July 1, 1928, 5.

2. "50 Percent Drop in Business Here," *Laredo Times,* December 19, 1929. *In re: Vicente Cantú,* Brownsville Case No. 235 (1928); *Manuscript Census,* Hidalgo County, 1920; *In re: W. L. Bradbury,* Brownsville Case No. 55 (1919).

3. Blackford, *History of Small Business in America,* 4–5; Buder, *Capitalizing on Change,* 1–2, 50–1.

4. "A White Red Man," *Pioneer Magazine,* February 1927, 30. For his bankruptcy case, see *In re: Joseph Netzer,* Laredo Case No. 50 (1922).

5. Ruben Edelstein, "Anecdotes about Papa, Some Tales of Early Rio Grande History with Memories of My Father, a Valley Pioneer," TJHS, Austin. For his bankruptcy case, see *In re: Morris Edelstein,* Brownsville Case No. 436 (1932).

6. "Pioneer in Ranching and Oil," *Laredo Times,* December 27, 1937, 1; "Los Ojuelos Ranch Owner Succumbs, 1937," *San Antonio Express,* December 27, 1937, Vertical Files, CAH. Also see *In re: Eusebio García,* Laredo Case No. 138 (1935).

7. By "frontier," I mean a zone of contact and exchange, a place where people of different cultures, ethnicities, and economies meet and contend with each other for power and resources. David Weber, *Spanish Frontier in North America,* 12–13.

8. Ibid.; Martínez, *Border People,* 5. My use of the term "borderland" contrasts with another definition of borderlands as a space over which nation-states have not yet exerted control. Adelman and Aron draw a distinction between the nineteenth-century "borderlands" and the later "bordered lands." See Adelman and Aron, "From Borderlands to Borders."

9. By examining these other groups, I seek to add to a relatively new body of literature about the diversity of European and Middle Eastern immigrants in the American West and the US-Mexico borderlands. Matthew Frye Jacobson has explored the long and difficult process through which immigrants from southern and eastern Europe eventually became considered "white" or "Caucasian" by the dominant Anglo society in the United States, a process of civic assimilation. Jacobson, *Whiteness of a Different Color.* More recently, Katherine Benton-Cohen has looked at the process of becoming American in the borderlands, specifically Arizona, as the categories of "white" and "Mexican" developed. She shows how Serbs, Italians, Slavs, Finns, and others were not always readily accepted as "white." Benton-Cohen, *Borderline Americans.* Another recent work that explores the rich diversity of ethnic groups in the West is Andrews, *Killing for Coal.* More and more works about Jews in the West are being published, but there is more to be explored. One of the most recent is Rosenbaum, *Cosmopolitans.* Stone, *Chosen Folks,* examines the development of Jewish identity in Texas using the frontier as an interpretive framework.

10. The major borderland subregions include Southern California and Baja California, Arizona and Sonora, New Mexico–West Texas (El Paso)–Chihuahua, and South Texas/Northeastern Mexico. Martínez, *Border People,* 54–55. My study has been informed by world systems theory. Hall, *Social Change in the Southwest,* 237–48. Broadly speaking, prior to the early twentieth century, South Texas was on the remote periphery of an expanding system of world capitalism centered in western Europe and the northeastern United States. South Texas' incorporation into this capitalist world economy occurred gradually and unevenly, bringing with it social and political changes. Independent businesspeople were involved in the process of incorporation. Chase-Dunn and Hall, *Rise and Demise;* Wallerstein, *Modern World System III.* Armando Alonzo has pointed out the significance of the railroads, along with other factors, to the development of South Texas and northeastern Mexico in this period. Alonzo, "Orígenes de una sociedad economía binacional."

11. Mora-Torres, *Making of the Mexico Border,* 86–92, 126–65; Tijerina, *Tejano Empire,* 122–36; De León, *Tejano Community,* 50–112.

12. Stambaugh and Stambaugh, *Lower Rio Grande Valley;* Allhands, *Gringo Builders.*

13. Most of the literature about South Texas deals with race relations, the development

of identity, labor relations between Anglo-American farmers and Mexican migrant workers, and the dispossession of the Tejano landholding elite in the nineteenth century. The most comprehensive study of the region is still Montejano, *Anglos and Mexicans in the Making of Texas*. It primarily traces changes in race relations between Anglos and Mexicans over time. Some of the other important works dealing with South Texas include Alonzo, *Tejano Legacy;* De León, *Tejano Community;* Johnson, *Revolution in Texas;* Young, *Catarino Garza's Revolution;* Tijerina, *Tejano Empire*. Works on the Mexican side of the lower Rio Grande include Alonso, *Thread of Blood;* Mora-Torres, *Making of the Mexico Border;* Walsh, *Building the Borderlands*. For a history of nineteenth-century merchants in northeastern Mexico, see González-Quiroga, "Conflict and Cooperation," 39–52; Cerutti, Burguesía, *Capitales & industria en el norte de México*. A recent dissertation discusses the significance of a new regime of labor and racial relations that emerged in South Texas in the early twentieth century, which the federal government of the United States eventually adopted in the Bracero Program of the 1940s and which private growers across the country began to implement as well. John Weber, "Shadow of the Revolution." Another recent dissertation examines the illegal commerce along the border, essentially the underside of what this book covers. Diaz, "Contrabandista Communities." See also Valerio-Jiménez, *River of Hope*.

14. For the business history of Laredo, see Adams, *Conflict and Commerce on the Rio Grande*. The trend in business history since the 1970s has been toward studies of big business, primarily located in the northeastern and midwestern regions of the United States because of their impact on the US economy as a whole. The seminal work is Chandler, *Visible Hand*. More recently, business historians have shown an interest in small, individual business owners and have begun exploring the roles of women and African Americans as entrepreneurs. Very few of these studies have been located in the West, and none along the US/Mexico border. This is beginning to change. Wills, *Boosters, Hustlers, and Speculators* explores the central role of entrepreneurs as well as the federal government in the growth of the two cities when they were on the edge of western Anglo-American settlement in that part of the country. A notable, recent book about individual entrepreneurs in the West is Sparks, *Capital Intentions*. A recent work that combines elements of social history and business history in a study of local merchants is English, *By All Accounts*.

15. *Webster's New World Dictionary of the American Language* (1979), s.v. "entrepreneur." The word "entrepreneur" has been a contested term among historians and others. Joseph Schumpeter argues that innovation was at the heart of entrepreneurship, which in turn drove capitalism. Once bureaucracies took over, they stifled entrepreneurship. Schumpeter, *Capitalism, Socialism, and Democracy*. In contesting this thesis, Harold Livesay suggested that "entrepreneurship" is the "art of aggressive management, practiced by an innovative, growth-oriented manager." He argued that "dominant individuals hold the key to enduring success" in all kinds of businesses. Contrary to Schumpeter, who argued that entrepreneurs engaged in "creative destruction" as they built their businesses into larger and larger bureaucracies, thereby spelling the end of capitalism, Harold Livesay contended for the persistence of entrepreneurship in large enterprise and hence the persistence of capitalism. Livesay, "Entrepreneurial Domi-

nance," 4–5, and "Entrepreneurial Persistence." I have adopted a broader definition of the term "entrepreneur" more in line with recent works about women-owned businesses and African American businesses that would encompass anyone engaged in any type of self-employment or independent business enterprise, including small and medium-sized proprietors and entrepreneurially minded farmers and ranchers. See Kwolek-Folland, *Incorporating Women,* 5; Sparks, *Capital Intentions,* 6–7; and Levenstein, "African-American Entrepreneurship," 106–108.

16. Mansel Blackford includes family farmers in his definition of small businesses. He argues that they were entrepreneurial in outlook even in colonial times. Blackford, *History of Small Business in America,* 22–24.

17. The contours of the middle class in the United States are difficult to identify despite the broad use of the term. Class is something that evolves and changes and is specific to place and time. It cannot be defined purely as an economic category because it involves not only occupation and income but also lifestyle, beliefs, education, and other cultural factors. E. P. Thompson, *Making of the English Working Class,* 9–11. There is a growing body of scholarly literature about the middle class in the United States. Stuart Blumin has argued that the American middle class emerged out of a rising business class in the late 18th and 19th centuries. Some members of this business class became elite while the majority became middle class. I have found Stuart M. Blumin's analysis to be particularly helpful in my own study of an emerging business class along the border. Blumin, *Emergence of the Middle Class,* 108–37. Heather Cox Richardson has studied the developing consciousness of an American middle class that emerged after the Civil War. She argues that "a new, economically powerful middle class, one that was largely white and unwilling to include in its ranks people of color," united around ideals of self-help and individualism. Heather Cox Richardson, *West from Appomattox,* 1, 343–45. For further work on the subject, see Bledstein and Johnston, *Middling Sorts;* Johnston, *Radical Middle Class.*

18. Bledstein, "Introduction," 18. The term "small business" is as elusive as that of "entrepreneur." It is a relative term, and virtually all businesses in South Texas were small compared to the dominant corporations in the United States and elsewhere. Some scholars have used a functional approach to determining size. They look for simple management style as opposed to elaborate hierarchies and a focus on local rather than national or international markets. Blackford, *History of Small Business in America,* 1–2. Even this definition might be problematic in some cases because family farmers often produced for national markets. The R. G. Dun & Company Reference Books provide some statistics that help determine what was small in the South Texas border region. They do not include farmers and ranchers but do cover virtually all kinds of businesses in the towns. For purposes of this study, I am combining the size and functional approaches. In Appendix 1, I have tables for both large and small businesses in the region. Small ranchers have one thousand or fewer acres of land, and small farmers are those with two hundred acres or fewer. Also included in this definition is the idea of a simple management style with relatively few employees, which was true of more than 90 percent of the businesses in South Texas.

19. Einegal, "Revolutionary Promises," 253.

20. Hochschild, *Facing Up to the American Dream,* xvii. For a history of the development of the American dream, see Jillson, *Pursuing the American Dream.*

21. Hart, *Empire and Revolution,* 2.

22. Scase and Goffee, *Entrepreneurial Middle Class,* 9–27, 187–92.

23. The major work focusing exclusively on the Mexican American middle class in South Texas is Richard A. García, *Rise of the Mexican American Middle Class,* 3–4. It covers a limited time period, the 1930s, and examines only the situation in the city of San Antonio, not the counties along the Mexican border. I have built on his understanding of the development of middle-class consciousness among a group of ethnic Mexican businesspeople and professionals in the 1930s.

24. Buenger and Pratt, *But Also Good Business,* 40–49; Olegario, *Culture of Credit,* 1–12.

25. Levy, *Freaks of Fortune.*

26. Withington, "Happy Combination in Southwest Texas," *Cattleman,* March 1916, 49.

27. *México de afuera* consists of areas outside of the nation of Mexico where Mexican people have retained and established their Mexican culture in the United States. Monroy, *Rebirth,* 4, 38–40. *México de afuera* is encompassed within "Greater Mexico" as defined by Américo Paredes in *Texas-Mexican Cancionero.* Greater Mexico includes not only the Republic of Mexico but also areas inhabited by ethnic Mexicans where Mexican culture has a strong influence within the United States. This includes especially the American Southwest. See also Calderón, *Narratives of Greater Mexico.*

CHAPTER 1: BORDERLANDS IN TRANSITION

1 . Juan Nepomuceno Cortina, "Proclamation," Difficulties on the Southwestern Frontier, H. Exec. Doc. No. 52, 36th Cong., 1st Sess., March 29, 1860, pp. 70–72. For the full description of the raid from which my partial description is taken, see Jerry D. Thompson, *Cortina,* 37–46. For an official report of the raid, see "Depredations on the Frontiers of Texas," Report of United States Commissioners to Texas, H. Exec. Doc. No. 39, 42d Cong., 3d Sess., December 16, 1872. For more interpretations of Cortina, see Callahan, "Mexican Border Troubles," 165–94; Paredes, "With His Pistol in His Hand," 134, 138–40.

2. John H. Hemphill to President James Buchanan, October 8, 1859, Difficulties on the Southwestern Frontier, H. Ex. Doc. No. 52, 36th Cong., 1st Sess., March 29, 1860, p. 33.

3. Schumpeter, *Capitalism, Socialism, and Democracy,* 82–83. "Creative destruction" is the process of change inherent in capitalism that results from innovation—new goods, new methods of production, and new forms of transportation and industrial organization that displace the old.

4. Montejano, *Anglos and Mexicans in the Making of Texas,* 20–21.

5. Alonzo, *Tejano Legacy,* 15–17, 29–32, 41–44; David Weber, *Spanish Frontier in North America,* 194.

6. Alonzo, *Tejano Legacy,* 25–46.

7. Paredes, "With His Pistol in His Hand," 7–15; Alonzo, *Tejano Legacy,* 45, 66; Graf, "Economic History of the Lower Rio Grande Valley," 15–19; Hinojosa, *Borderlands Town in Transition: Laredo,* 23–24.

8. For livestock numbers, see Alonzo, *Tejano Legacy,* 75. For details about the raids and peace agreements, see David Weber, *Spanish Frontier in North America,* 44, 183, 194, 210–15; de la Teja, *San Antonio De Béxar,* 99–101.

9. DeLay, *War of a Thousand Deserts,* 15.

10. Salvucci, "Origins of the US-Mexican Trade"; David Weber, *Mexican Frontier,* 122–44; Reséndez, *Changing National Identities at the Frontier,* 93–123; Roell, *Matamoros and the Texas Revolution,* 27–37.

11. Montejano, *Anglos and Mexicans in the Making of Texas,* 15–20.

12. Graf, "Economic History of the Lower Rio Grande Valley," 29–35, 46–49; Alonzo, *Tejano Legacy,* 68–74; Buchenau, *Tools of Progress,* 3–5, 16.

13. Hart, *Empire and Revolution,* 23–24.

14. Sibley, "Charles Stillman," 229–30.

15. Graf, "Economic History of the Lower Rio Grande Valley," 2.

16. The most common form of credit at the time was mercantile credit. Mercantile credit was extended by wholesalers, most of whom resided in Europe and the eastern United States prior to the Civil War, to middlemen and retailers in order to ship goods in exchange for a future promise to pay for them. Typically, mercantile credit was "unsecured," meaning that the buyer did not pledge any collateral when he ordered goods from the wholesaler. Olegario, *Culture of Credit,* 26–29.

17. García, "Don Francisco Yturria"; Graf, "Economic History of the Lower Rio Grande Valley," 405. For the important role of merchants in capitalist development, see Nobles, "Rise of Merchants: "[Merchants] were economic and cultural innovators, the central agents of social transformation in their communities" (5).

18. Russell N. White, *State, Class, and the Nationalization,* 4–11.

19. Graf, "Economic History of the Lower Rio Grande Valley," 125–27.

20. Kelley, *River of Lost Dreams,* 44–56, 73–82; Graham, *Kings of Texas,* 18–22; Jerry D. Thompson, *Wild and Vivid Land,* 68.

21. Griswold del Castillo, *Treaty of Guadalupe Hidalgo,* 81, 187.

22. Utley, *Indian Frontier of the American West,* 45, 56.

23. Nina Veregge, "Transformations of Spanish Urban Landscapes in the American Southwest, 1821–1900," http://jsw.library.arizona.edu/3504/veregge/veregge.html (accessed November 20, 2013). For more detail about the design of towns in the borderlands, see Reps, *Forgotten Frontier.*

24. Herbert G. Davenport to J. L. Allhands, December 21, 1927, Box 34A, Folder A1963–014, J. L. Allhands Collection, TAMUK; Amberson, McAllen, and McAllen, *I Would Rather Sleep in Texas,* 105–108.

25. Graf, "Economic History of the Lower Rio Grande Valley," 256–63; Johnson and Gusky, *Bordertown,* 52–57.

26. *Manuscript Census,* Eagle Pass, Maverick County, 1860.

27. Braudaway, "'Origins.'"

28. Texas, vol. 5, pp. 45–85; Texas, vol. 9, pp. 2–10; Texas, vol. 16, pp. 1–4; Texas, vol. 18, p. 360; Texas, vol. 23, p. 40; Texas, vol. 27, pp. 178–94; Texas, vol. 31, p. 8; Texas, vol. 33, pp. 316–26, R. G. Dun & Co. Credit Report volumes, Baker Library Historical Collections, Harvard Business School.

29. Baud and Van Schendel, "Toward a Comparative History of Borderlands," 224. This period just after the drawing of the boundary line is the "infant borderland." In this stage, "[p]reexisting social and economic networks are still clearly visible, and people on both sides of the border are connected by close kinship links. National identities are still vague and undefined. Regional inhabitants can opt for a future on either side of the border, and some groups may cherish the hope that the new boundary may disappear. The border is still a potentiality rather than a social reality." Regarding the process of incorporation, see Hall, *Social Change in the Southwest,* 237–48.

30. Texas, vol. 5, p. 45, R. G. Dun & Co. Credit Report volumes, BLHBS.

31. Texas, vol. 27, pp. 178, 190, R. G. Dun & Co. Credit Report volumes, BLHBS.

32. Texas, vol. 33, p. 323, R. G. Dun & Co. Credit Report volumes, BLHBS.

33. Texas, vol. 23, p. 40, R. G. Dun & Co. Credit Report volumes, BLHBS.

34. Texas, vol. 5, pp. 53, 58, 62, 65, 69, R. G. Dun & Co. Credit Report volumes, BLHBS.

35. Texas, vol. 5, p. 70/6, R. G. Dun & Co. Credit Report volumes, BLHBS.

36. Mora-Torres, *Making of the Mexico Border,* 29–36, 66–69.

37. Texas, vol. 9, p. 10, R. G. Dun & Co. Credit Report volumes, BLHBS.

38. Texas, vol. 5, p. 50, R. G. Dun & Co. Credit Report volumes, BLHBS.

39. Texas, vol. 5, p. 50, R. G. Dun & Co. Credit Report volumes, BLHBS.

40. Texas, vol. 5, p. 55, R. G. Dun & Co. Credit Report volumes, BLHBS.

41. Texas, vol. 5, p. 55, R. G. Dun & Co. Credit Report volumes, BLHBS.

42. Graf, "Economic History of the Lower Rio Grande Valley," 210–12. For a general discussion of smuggling across borders, see the introduction to Carey and Marak, eds., *Smugglers, Brothels, and Twine.*

43. Texas, vol. 5, p. 44, R. G. Dun & Co. Credit Report volumes, BLHBS.

44. Texas, vol. 5, p. 45, R. G. Dun & Co. Credit Report volumes, BLHBS.

45. Texas, vol. 9, p. 10, R. G. Dun & Co. Credit Report volumes, BLHBS.

46. Chance, *José María de Jesús Carvajal;* Shearer, "Carvajal Disturbances." Historians have disagreed over whether the Merchants' War was a filibustering expedition by Stillman and his associates to bring the commercial cities of Tamaulipas, especially Matamoros, into the United States or whether it was primarily the local merchants' reaction to Mexican tariff policy.

47. Adams, *Conflict and Commerce on the Rio Grande,* 79–87 (smuggling in and around Laredo); Kearney and Knopp, *Boom and Bust,* 82–83, 103–107, 153 (smuggling in Matamoros/Brownsville). For a full treatment of the policy of zona libre in Mexico, which was hotly contested at times, see Herrera Pérez, *La zona libre.*

48. Thomas P. Robb, F. J. Mead, and Richard H. Savage, "Report of United States Commissioners to Texas to Hon. Hamilton Fish, Secretary of State," in *Depredations on the Frontiers of Texas,* H. Exec. Doc. 39, 42nd Cong., 3d Sess., December 16, 1872, 40.

49. Graf, "Economic History of the Lower Rio Grande Valley," 359–60, 404–405; Ericson, *Banks and Bankers in Early Texas,* 14–25, 79.

50. Texas, vol. 5, p. 53, R. G. Dun & Co.; Texas, vol. 5, pp. 58, 59, 66, R. G. Dun & Co. Credit Report volumes, BLHBS.

51. Texas, vol. 5, pp. 48–49, 54, 65, 70/71, R. G. Dun & Co. Credit Report volumes, BLHBS. The Mercantile Agency credit reports have a number of entries indicating that merchants had closed or failed.

52. Texas, vol. 5, p. 45, R. G. Dun & Co. Credit Report volumes, BLHBS.

53. Lieut. W. H. Chatfield, *The Twin Cities of the Border and the Country of the Lower Rio Grande* (1893), pp. 21–22, LRGV, UTPA.

54. Kearney and Knopp, *Boom and Bust,* 120–48.

55. Thompson, *Cortina,* 96–199.

56. Texas, vol. 5, pp. 46, R. G. Dun & Co. Credit Report volumes, BLHBS.

57. Texas, vol. 5, pp. 70/71 and 70/72, R. G. Dun & Co. Credit Report volumes, BLHBS.

58. Hart, *Revolutionary Mexico,* 105–107, 135–36.

59. Adams, *Conflict and Commerce on the Rio Grande,* 89–92, 115. Patricio's full name was Patrick Milmo O'Dowd. Milmo avoided the fate of his father-in-law, who was executed in 1867 by the forces of Porfirio Díaz for supporting the French Maximilian.

60. "Excerpts from Notes Written by Yetta Edelstein, Date Unknown, Received July 12, 1981," Box 3A169, TJHS; Chatfield, *Twin Cities of the Border,* 22. *Manuscript Census,* Brownsville, 1880 and 1900; Texas, vol. 5, p. 70/79, R. G. Dun & Co. Credit Report volumes, BLHBS.

61. Zapata, "Historical Archaeology of Roma, Texas," 86–93.

62. Hinojosa, *Borderlands Town in Transition,* 76–80.

63. Texas, vol. 33, pp. 318, 320, R. G. Dun & Co. Credit Report volumes, BLHBS.

64. Texas, vol. 33, pp. 317, 326, R. G. Dun & Co. Credit Report volumes, BLHBS.

65. Appleby, *Relentless Revolution,* 88.

66. González-Quiroga, "Conflict and Cooperation," 39–52.

67. Olegario, *Culture of Credit,* 108–109, 115.

68. Texas, vol. 27, p. 194, R. G. Dun & Co. Credit Report volumes, BLHBS.

69. Texas, vol. 5, p. 58, R. G. Dun & Co. Credit Report volumes, BLHBS.

70. Texas, vol. 5, p. 59, R.G. Dun & Co. Credit Report volumes, BLHBS.

71. Texas, vol. 5, p. 70/14, R. G. Dun & Co. Credit Report volumes, BLHBS.

72. Texas, vol. 33, pp. 322–23, R. G. Dun & Co. Credit Report volumes, BLHBS.

73. Texas, vol. 33, p. 323, R. G. Dun & Co. Credit Report volumes, BLHBS.

74. Texas, vol. 9, p. 2, R. G. Dun & Co. Credit Report volumes, BLHBS.

75. Texas, vol. 5, p. 56, R. G. Dun & Co. Credit Report volumes, BLHBS.

76. Texas, vol. 5, p. 45, 48, R. G. Dun & Co. Credit Report volumes, BLHBS.

77. Texas, vol. 5, pp. 70/71, 73, R. G. Dun & Co. Credit Report volumes, BLHBS.

78. Texas, vol. 9, p. 5, R. G. Dun & Co. Credit Report volumes, BLHBS.

79. *Manuscript Census,* Cameron County, Brownsville, 1880; *Manuscript Census,* Hidalgo County, 1880; *Manuscript Census,* Starr County, Rio Grande City, 1880; *Manu-*

script Census, Webb County, Laredo, 1880; *Manuscript Census,* Maverick County, Eagle Pass, 1880.

80. Montejano, *Anglos and Mexicans in the Making of Texas,* 70–74.

81. Graf, "Economic History of the Lower Rio Grande Valley," 55.

82. I reviewed the entire manuscript census for Starr, Webb, and Cameron counties for 1850. Although census records are notoriously unreliable, they do give us important data from which we can develop patterns. I counted 96 merchants, 12 from France, 11 from Germany, 8 from Ireland, 4 from Italy, 4 from England, 4 from Spain, 1 from Switzerland, 1 from Denmark, 1 from Scotland, 1 from Poland, 3 from Mexico, and 46 from the United States. Of those from the United States, 23 were from New England (New York, Pennsylvania, New Jersey) and Washington, DC. Another 19 came from southern states, including Kentucky, and the rest came from various areas in the Midwest and West. I counted 437 farmers, 415 of whom were identified as either Mexican or Texas Mexican. There was one black farmer, and the remaining 21 were Anglo Americans or Europeans. *Manuscript Census,* Rio Grande Valley, 1850.

83. Hämäläinen, *Comanche Empire,* 190–98, 220–32.

84. John L. Haynes to J. Hemphill and A. J. Hamilton, October 1, 1859, *Difficulties on the Southwestern Frontier,* H. Exec. Doc. No. 52, 36th Cong., 1st Sess., March 29, 1860.

85. David Weber, *Foreigners in Their Native Land,* 154–56.

86. Herbert G. Davenport to J. L. Allhands, December 21, 1927, J. L. Allhands Collection, TAMUK; Griswold del Castillo, *Treaty of Guadalupe Hidalgo,* 65.

87. Greaser, *New Guide to Spanish and Mexican Land Grants,* 135–36.

88. *Manuscript Census,* Nueces County, 1850.

89. Graham, *Kings of Texas,* 33–43, 59–66.

90. Acuña, *Occupied America,* 29–31; Graham, *Kings of Texas,* 115–23, 128–29; Rubio, *Stolen Heritage,* 136–40.

91. Report of the United States Commissioners to Texas, *Depredations on the Frontiers of Texas,* pp. 10–19; Adams, *Conflict and Commerce on the Rio Grande,* 98. For works on the Texas Rangers, see the classic seminal study, Webb, *Texas Rangers,* and a recent revisionist, comparative analysis, Graybill, *Policing the Great Plains.*

92. Out of 343 land claims presented to the commission, only 78 were denied. Fifty-one of the claims were based on *ejidos* of Matamoros, land that became part of Brownsville, and were denied because the claimants were found to be tenants, not owners. That means that only about 27 claims by Tejano rancho owners were denied. Greaser and de la Teja, "Quieting Title to Spanish and Mexican Land Grants." Other works discussing the process of validating land grants include Mawn, "Land-Grant Guarantee"; McNeely, "Mexican-American Land Issues," 35.

93. Montejano, *Anglos and Mexicans in the Making of Texas,* 36; Monday and Vick, *Petra's Legacy,* 7–23, 40, 167; Amberson et al., *I Would Rather Sleep in Texas,* 66–67, 135–61, 200–201.

94. *Manuscript Census,* Maverick County, 1860.

95. Alonzo, *Tejano Legacy,* 196–98, 203–204, 209; Paul Carlson, *Texas Woollybacks,* 49.

96. *Manuscript Census,* Cameron, Zavala, Maverick, Kinney, Uvalde, Dimmit counties, 1880; Taylor, "Historical Note on Dimmit County," 79–83; De León, *Tejano Community,* 50–52.

97. *Manuscript Census,* Encinal and Duval counties, 1860 and 1880; Alonzo, *Tejano Legacy,* 279. Duval County had 22 Hispanic merchants, out of a total of 65 in the 1870s. Texas, vol. 9, pp. 2–10, R. G. Dun & Co. Credit Report volumes, BLHBS.

98. State Tax Rolls, Starr County, 1860, TXSLA.

99. Texas, vol. 5, pp. 45, 48, R. G. Dun & Co. Credit Report volumes, BLHBS; Anders, *Boss Rule in South Texas,* 5–6.

100. State Tax Rolls, Cameron, Hidalgo, Starr, and Zapata counties, 1880, TXSLA; Alonzo, *Tejano Legacy,* 227–39.

101. Hall, *Social Change in the Southwest,* 237–48; Montejano, *Anglos and Mexicans in the Making of Texas,* 8, 18–21; Bourke, "American Congo," 592; Hubert J. Miller, Ramón Guerra interview, oral history tape recording, McAllen, TX, December 1976, LRGV, UTPA; Hubert J. Miller, Estéban García interview, oral history tape recording, Rio Grande City, TX, January 1978, LRGV, UTPA.

CHAPTER 2: FORGING A LANDSCAPE OF OPPORTUNITY (1880–1940)

1. "The First Train," *Brownsville Herald,* July 5, 1904, 1.

2. Julia Cameron Montgomery, *A Little Journey through the Lower Rio Grande Valley of Texas: The Magic Valley* (Houston: Southern Pacific Lines, 1928), p. 64, Box 1: Shary Citrus Brochures, Series 11, JHSC, UTPA.

3. Kearney and Knopp, *Border Cuates,* 125.

4. St. John, *Line in the Sand,* 63–65. For more about transnational ties in the western border region, see Truett, *Fugitive Landscapes.* For a discussion of the role of railroads in the development of the West, see Orsi, *Sunset Limited,* xiv–xv, 56–57. For a discussion of the communication network that was a part of the overall transportation and communication infrastructure, see Chandler, *Visible Hand,* 188–208.

5. Stephen F. Austin considered all of Texas a place of "crossings"; a person could get to New Mexico, Chihuahua, or any of the western Mexican states by passing through Texas. Lamar, *Texas Crossings,* 1.

6. Klein, *Genesis of Industrial America,* xi, 1–2, 83–85, 88, 105–106.

7. A. K. Owen, "Memorial of A. K. Owen, C. E. Relative to the Survey of the Austin-T Pacific Route," House Misc. Doc. 20, 45th Cong., 3d Session, February 13, 1879, in *The Survey of the Austin-Topolovampo Pacific Route,* vol. 3, Topolovampo Collection, HLSC.

8. Ibid.

9. As cited in Hart, *Empire and Revolution,* 167.

10. Hart, *Empire and Revolution,* 2, 59–67.

11. Haber, Maurer, and Razo, *Politics of Property Rights,* 47–51.

12. Hart, *Revolutionary Mexico,* 129–62; Hart, *Empire and Revolution,* 124–26, 152.

13. Regarding Mexican railroads and US involvement in railroad building, see Hart, *Empire and Revolution*, 106–30; Meyer, Sherman, and Deeds, *Course of Mexican History*, 331. For a discussion of Texas railroads, see Barr, *Reconstruction to Reform*, 11; Buenger and Pratt, *But Also Good Business*, 20; Chandler, *Visible Hand*, 88; Reed, *History of the Texas Railroads*, 48–53, 129–43. For a discussion of the Canadian and US railway network, see Currie, "British Attitudes toward Investment"; Kemble, "Transpacific Railroads, 1869–1915."

14. Hart, *Revolutionary Mexico*, 138–39.

15. "Col. Lott to Be Buried Today at Kingsville," *Brownsville Herald*, March 30, 1915, 2; "untitled," *Galveston Daily News*, November 17, 1881, 1; Bill Walraven, "Uriah Lott, Railroad Builder," *Corpus Christi Caller Times*, January 18, 1959, 10-J. For a biography of Lott, see Allhands, *Uriah Lott*.

16. "Railway Interests," *New York Times*, September 2, 1882, 2; "What the Papers throughout Texas Are Talking About," *Galveston Daily News*, February 15, 1889, 10.

17. "A Talk with Railroad Builder," *Brownsville Daily Herald*, October 18, 1902, 2.

18. J. L. Allhands, "Rio Grande Valley of Texas Notebook," Box 36B, J. L. Allhands Collection, TAMUK; "Letter from B. F. Yoakum to J. L. Allhands, 29 December 1929," Folder 5, Box 34A, J. L. Allhands Collection, TAMUK.

19. Allhands, "Rio Grande Valley of Texas Notebook."

20. Cronon, *Nature's Metropolis*, 74, 81, 324–33. For a discussion of the significance of the railroad and the telegraph to economic and cultural change in this period, see Chandler, *Visible Hand*, 81–187; Trachtenberg, *Incorporation of America*, 19, 22, 25, 38, 58–59.

21. Adams, *Conflict and Commerce on the Rio Grande*, 128–29; "The New Laredo Customs House," *Laredo Daily Times*, September 20, 1888, 1; "Gate City Gatherings," *San Antonio Daily Express*, April 13, 1889, 2.

22. "An Able Article," *Laredo Daily Times*, May 1, 1890, 1; Adams, *Conflict and Commerce on the Rio Grande*, 102–103. For an example of the ads proclaiming Laredo as the gateway to Mexico, see the *Galveston Daily Times*, August 7, 1889, 5.

23. Deverell, *Whitewashed Adobe*, 133–35; "Wonderful Growth," *New York Times*, May 29, 1890, 5.

24. "Wonderful Growth," 5.

25. "Eagle Pass Gleanings: No Boom but Steady Growth," *San Antonio Daily Express*, April 22, 1889, 1; Sanborn Maps, Eagle Pass, 1894, 1900, 1905, and 1910, and Del Rio, 1900, 1906, and 1909, CAH.

26. Chatfield, *Twin Cities of the Border*, 30–32; Mary E. McGary, "Past and Present Meet at Brownsville," *Dallas Morning News, News Magazine Supplement*, March 3, 1913, 5; Letter from C. H. Maris to J. E. Russell, October 7, 1910, *In re: J. E. Buckley*, Brownsville Case No. 5 (1911).

27. Walsh, *Building the Borderlands*, 41, 68–72.

28. Hutson, "Texas Fever in Kansas, 1866–1930," 80, 85–88; Clark, "Texas Fever in Oklahoma," 429–31.

29. Graham, *Kings of Texas,* 168; Webb, *Great Plains,* 205–55; Hart, *Empire and Revolution,* 177–81.

30. Lasater, *Falfurrias,* 76: *Handbook of Texas Online,* s.v. "Benavides, Texas," http://www.tshaonline.org/handbook/online/articles/BB/hjb4.html (accessed June 11, 2010); Handbook of Texas Online, s.v. "Hebbronville, Texas," http://www.tshaonline .org/handbook/online/articles/HH/hgh5.html (accessed June 11, 2010).

31. Skaggs, *Prime Cut,* 61–62. For a detailed study of the survey and sale of the public lands in Mexico, see Holden, *Mexico.*

32. Hart, *Revolutionary Mexico,* 138–39, 160; *History of the Cattlemen of Texas,* 65, 283–84.

33. The figures were all taken from W. H. Chatfield's list of landowners in Cameron County who had more than one thousand acres. Chatfield, *Twin Cities of the Border,* 43.

34. Walsh, *Building the Borderlands,* 26–32.

35. Pisani, *From the Family Farm to Agribusiness,* 440–41. For examples of land development in California, see "Description of Orange and Vine Lands in Los Angeles County, California for Sale by the Lake Vineyard Land & Water Association," Folder B-25, Box F-21, Ephemera, HLSC; *Facts about Lands, Productions, Climate and Water in Semi-Tropic or Southern California: What Home-Seekers, Investors, and Speculators Want to Know* (September 1887), Folder C-7, Box F21, Ephemera, HLSC; "Farms for Farmers in the Heart of California," Folder A-36, Box F-22, Ephemera, HLSC; "Ontario-Cucamonga Etiwanda Colonies: The Banner of Fruit District of Southern California," Folder A-15, Box F-22, Ephemera, HLSC. For a discussion of the different strains of agrarian reform in Mexico, see Ervin, "Formation of the Revolutionary Middle Class," 196, 200–201.

36. Walsh, *Building the Borderlands,* 23.

37. Anders, *Boss Rule in South Texas,* 143–47; Foscue, "Irrigation in the Lower Rio Grande Valley"; Stambaugh and Stambaugh, *Lower Rio Grande Valley,* 182–87. For a study of the Jagou plantation, see Neck, "History of Esperanza Ranch."

38. Chatfield, *Twin Cities of the Border,* 4.

39. B. F. Yoakum, "Farmers Can Solve High Cost of Living: Railroad Man Seeks Co-Operation of the Agriculturalist," *Texas Magazine,* May, 1911, 45–46.

40. F. A. Briggs, "Irrigation Growth in Rio Grande Valley," *Dallas Morning News,* May 28, 1911, 23; Tom Finty Jr., "Lower Rio Grande Irrigation Works," *Dallas Morning News,* December 13, 1906, 26; Hart, *Revolutionary Mexico,* 137–38; Hubert J. Miller, James Franklin Ewers interview, oral history tape recording, McAllen, TX, December 29, 1981, LRGV, UTPA; Stambaugh and Stambaugh, *Lower Rio Grande Valley,* 190, 232.

41. Sanborn Maps, Mercedes, 1917 and 1925; Mission, 1919 and 1925, CAH.

42. Allhands, *Gringo Builders,* 11–12, 38–44, 95–99; Stambaugh and Stambaugh, *Lower Rio Grande Valley,* 170–71, 180–88.

43. Hill, *Lon C. Hill, 1862–1935. In re: Rentfro Banton Creager,* Brownsville Case No. 553 (1935). More details about the developers and the areas they developed may be found in Allhands, *Gringo Builders,* 11–12, 38–44, 95–99; Stambaugh and Stambaugh, *Lower Rio Grande Valley,* 170–71, 180.

44. Allhands, "Rio Grande Valley of Texas Notebook"; US Bureau of the Census, *Thirteenth Census, Agriculture,* vol. VII, 708; William Leshner, "In the Lower Rio Grande Valley," *Texas Magazine,* October 1910, 66–68; L. H. Romig, "The Town of Mission: Metropolis of the Western Part of the Lower Rio Grande Valley," *Texas Magazine,* January 1911, 84–85.

45. Hubert J. Miller, James Franklin Ewers interview; see Bankruptcy Schedules in *In re: Sam A. Robertson,* Brownsville Case No. 54 (1919) and *In re: Lon C. Hill,* Brownsville Case No. 60 (1920). Allhands, *Gringo Builders,* 169; Stambaugh and Stambaugh, *Lower Rio Grande Valley,* 188. For a complete history of the sugar cane industry in the Valley, see Ratkin, "Rio Grande Valley Sugar Cane Industry."

46. Wellington Brink, "Mr. Bermuda Onion Moves to Town," *Farm and Ranch,* April 3, 1920, 1–2; Lea, *King Ranch,* vol. 2, 505–506; Tiller, *Texas Winter Garden,* 26; Mont Wyman, "His Honor, the Texas Onion," *Texas Magazine,* January 1911, 21–25.

47. "Asherton Famous Export Center," *Pioneer Magazine,* April 1927, 13.

48. *In re: Browne Land and Cattle Company, Santa Helena Improvement Company, James A. Browne, and A. Albert Browne,* Brownsville Case No. 53 (1919); Graham, *Kings of Texas,* 198; US Bureau of the Census, *Thirteenth Census, Agriculture,* vol. VII, 678–700; Lasater, *Falfurrias,* 72–76, 77–91.

49. US Bureau of the Census, *Fifteenth Census, Agriculture,* vol. II, part 2, 1488–1507; "Early History of Rio Grande City," Box 3L401, Starr County Scrapbook, WPA Records, CAH; "Historic Town on Verge of New Life," *San Antonio Light,* October 19, 1925; "Rio Grande City Rich in Both Past and Prospects," *San Antonio Express,* December 5, 1924, 24.

50. "150,000 Population in Near Future for San Antonio," *San Antonio Light,* May 18, 1909, 14; "Eyes on Mexican Lands," *Galveston Daily News,* June 26, 1909; "San Antonio Is Center," *Daily Express,* January 23, 1910; "Texas Locators Advertisement," *San Antonio Gazette,* April 27, 1907, 8. There are hundreds of advertisements in Texas newspapers between 1907 and 1910 for Mexican lands. Some examples include the following: International Land and Investment Company, "A Serious Word to Contemplating Investors to Mexican Lands," *San Antonio Gazette,* September 14, 1907, 10; "Hallam Colonization Co. Advertisement," *Brownsville Daily Herald,* September 7, 1907, 3; "A. J. Greiner & Co. Advertisement," *San Antonio Gazette,* April 6, 1907, 8; "Mexican Lands," *San Antonio Light and Gazette,* December 9, 1909, 14; "Mexican Lands," *San Antonio Light and Gazette,* February 24, 1910, 14; "O. C. Hillebrandt Company Advertisement," *Galveston Daily News,* May 2, 1910, 5; "Westervelt Realty Co. Advertisement," *San Antonio Gazette,* April 27, 1907, 8.

51. Hart, *Revolutionary Mexico,* 149, 404 n31; "Heavy Travel to Mexico," *Laredo Times,* March 22, 1908, 9; Sandos, "Mexican Revolution and the United States," 103–104; Walsh, *Building the Borderlands,* 72–74.

52. Mora-Torres, *Making of the Mexico Border,* 166–91.

53. Katz, *Secret War in Mexico,* 19.

54. Haber, *Industry and Underdevelopment,* citing James W. Wilkie and Paul D. Wilkins, "Quantifying the Class Structure of Mexico, 1895–1970," in James W. Wilkie

and Stephen Haber, eds., *Statistical Abstract of Latin America,* vol. 21, 577–90 (Los Angeles: University of California, Latin America Center, 1981); McGerr, *Fierce Discontent,* 15, 24, 43.

55. Haber, Maurer, and Razo, *Politics of Property,* 47–51; Hart, *Empire and Revolution,* 266–72; Sánchez, *Becoming Mexican American,* 19–22.

56. For a full analysis of the movement, see Young, *Catarino Garza's Revolution.*

57. Meyer, Sherman, and Deeds, *Course of Mexican History,* 493.

58. There have been different interpretations of the causes of the Mexican Revolution, but foreign domination of Mexican business and the sense that opportunities were being siphoned away certainly played an important part. A thorough discussion of the Mexican Revolution is beyond the scope of this book. The historiography on the subject is exhaustive. One major interpretation that focuses on Mexican sources of the conflict is Alan Knight's two-volume work. Knight, *Mexican Revolution.* John Mason Hart disagrees with his interpretation and primarily blames US investment and exploitation of Mexico's resources for the conflict in Hart, *Revolutionary Mexico.* See also Womack, "Mexican Revolution, 1910–1920," 125–26.

59. "Letter from H. P. Drought to William Mackensie, 2 November 1915," Volume: Alliance Trust Company, January 4, 1915–December 26, 1918, Box 15, H. P. Drought & Co. Collection, UTSA.

60. "Consul Williams Arrives with Party of Americans," *Laredo Times,* March 19, 1916; "Investigation of Mexican Affairs, Hearing before a Subcommittee on Foreign Relations, United States Senate, S. Res. 106, Partial Report of Committee," Box 17, Folder: National Association for the Protection of American Rights in Mexico, Letters, Quimichis Colony Records, HLSC. One of the most tragic stories was that of Rosalie Evans, who returned in the early 1920s to try to maintain her hacienda near Puebla after the death of her husband. She was shot and killed by *agraristas* on her way to Mexico City. Pettus, *Rosalie Evans Letters from Mexico.*

61. Various letters, Box 1, Folder 1, Quimichis Colony Records, HLSC; "Cancel Policies," *Laredo Times,* February 12, 1911, 3; "National Association for the Protection of American Rights in Mexico, Letters," Box 17, Quimichis Colony Records, HLSC.

62. "Anniversary of the First Attack on Nuevo Laredo," *Laredo Times,* March 19, 1916, 3; "Carranzistas Driven Back by Federals," *San Antonio Light,* March 20, 1913, 1; "Chronology from Diary of John Randall Peavey," Folder of Miscellaneous Materials, LRGV, UTPA; Transcript of Hubert J. Miller, John Randall Peavey interview, oral history tape recording, 1982, LRGV, UTPA.

63. Machado, "Mexican Revolution," 4–13; J. D. Jackson, "Livestock Conditions in Mexico," *Cattleman,* March 1916, 43; Kenneth D. Oliver, "Getting Them out of Mexico," *Cattleman,* May 1916, 25–27.

64. Harris and Sadler, *Texas Rangers and the Mexican Revolution,* 40–44, 291–93; Johnson, *Revolution in Texas,* 83–84, 128–31; transcript of John Randall Peavey interview; "Train Wrecked, Passengers Robbed and Killed," *Brownsville Herald,* October 19, 1915, 1.

65. Johnson, *Revolution in Texas,* 85–88, 113–24; Ramón Guerra interview; Pierce,

Brief History, 90–93. For an analysis of the roles of federal, state, and local troops along the border, see Don M. Coerver, "Wire Me before Shooting": Federalism in (In)action— the Texas-Mexico Border during the Revolution, 1910–1920," in Richmond and Haynes, eds., *Mexican Revolution,* 35–57.

66. "Anonymous Letter to Albert Fall, April 17, 1920," Box 17, Quichimis Colony Records, HLSC; "Laredo Embargo Raised," *Dallas Morning News,* June 11, 1911; "Nuevo Laredo Is Evacuated," *Dallas Morning News,* April 24, 1914; "Nuevo Laredo Stores Close," *Dallas Morning News,* June 20, 1916.

67. Allhands, *Gringo Builders,* 95–99, 177–79, 257–62; Anders, *Boss Rule in South Texas,* 140–47; *In re: Sam A. Robertson,* Brownsville Case No. 54 (1920); *In re: Lon C. Hill,* Brownsville Bankruptcy Case No. 60, 1920; letter from F. W. Seabury to Harlingen Land & Water Company, February 14, 1916, and letter from H. M. Skelton to Lon C. Hill, September 13, 1917, Box 3G38, Lon C. Hill Papers, CAH; Warranty Deeds with Vendor's Liens, Henrietta King to Lon C. Hill, Box 3G38, Lon C. Hill Papers, CAH; Lon C. Hill, to J. F. Rodgers, August 16, 1927, Box 3E458, Lon C. Hill Papers, CAH; Zelden, *Justice Lies in the District,* 40–44.

68. Johnson, *Revolution in Texas,* 120–24; *In re: Eutiquio Pérez,* Brownsville Case No. 31 (1915).

69. Anders, *Boss Rule in South Texas,* 215–18; transcript of John Randall Peavey interview.

70. Mora-Torres, *Making of the Mexico Border,* 126–65; John Weber, "Shadow of the Revolution," 57–61, 98–99.

71. Hernandez, *Migra!,* 21–27.

72. John M. Hart, "Introduction," in Richmond and Haynes, *Mexican Revolution,* 2.

73. Moray L. Applegate, "Letter to the Board of Compania Hacienda De Quimichis," Quimichis Colony Records, HLSC. Regarding American investment in Mexico after the revolution, see Buchenau, *Tools of Progress,* 90–98; Middleton, *Railway Supplies in Mexico.*

74. Quoted in Sempich, "Down the Rio Grande," 440.

75. Anders, *Boss Rule in South Texas,* 143–46; "Crop Experiments Mark Valley's Development," *Valley Star Monitor–Herald,* February 9, 1941; "Map of Sharyland," JHSC, UTPA; Silva-Bewley, *Legacy of John H. Shary,* 42–45.

76. "Secretary's Report," Folder 6, Box 1, San Antonio Fruit Exchange Records, HLSC.

77. "John H. Shary," *Brownsville Herald,* November 8, 1945; Wallace, "John H. Shary—Believer," 190–91.

78. "Progreso Haciendas: Citrus Fruit and Farm Lands in the Lower Rio Grande Valley of Texas," Folder 40, Box 1: Shary Citrus Brochures, Series 11, JHSC, UTPA.

79. "Land Boom from 1922 to 1930 in Valley Was More like Gold Rush," Box 3L117, *Brownsville Herald,* Cameron County Scrapbook, WPA Records, CAH. The 1920 tax schedules for Cameron and Hidalgo counties reveal that the land developers still owned thousands of acres of land, which they had likely been unable to sell during the revolution.

80. US Bureau of the Census, *Thirteenth Census, Agriculture,* vol. VII, 707–13; US Bureau of the Census, *Fifteenth Census, Irrigation of Agricultural Lands,* 3–13.

81. US Bureau of the Census, *Thirteenth Census, Agriculture,* vol. VII, 655–77; US Bureau of the Census, *Fifteenth Census, Agriculture,* vol. II, part 2, 941–1083; Watson, *Lower Rio Grande Valley and Its Builders,* 152–53; Chambers, "Lower Rio Grande Valley of Texas"; "Grocery Store Advertisement," *Ames Daily Tribune,* February 11, 1937, 7; US Bureau of the Census, *Sixteenth Census, Agriculture,* vol. I, part 26, *Texas,* 18–69.

82. US Bureau of the Census, *Fifteenth Census, Texas, Statistics by Counties,* 6–66; US Bureau of the Census, *Fifteenth Census, Irrigation of Agricultural Lands,* 13; Tiller, *Texas Winter Garden,* 26, 28, 31–35, 54.

83. "Asherton Famous Export Center," 13; "Carrizo Springs—Hub of the Winter Garden," *Pioneer Magazine,* April 1927, 14; "The Green Gold Mine," *Pioneer Magazine,* April 1927, 15; Matt Russell, "Cotulla, Onion Center," *Texas Magazine,* October 1911, 80; US Bureau of the Census, *Fifteenth Census, Agriculture,* vol. II, part 2, 941–1083.

84. Sandos, "Mexican Revolution and the United States," 135.

85. Walsh, *Building the Borderlands,* 69.

86. Ibid., 49–63, 101–108; Ervin, "Formation of the Revolutionary Middle Class," 200–201.

87. Walsh, *Building the Borderlands,* 108–11.

88. Hinton and Olien, *Oil in Texas,* 116; Tom Lillie, "Five Wells Completed in Active Week in Laredo District," *Laredo Times,* December 8, 1929, 4; Tom Lillie, "Starr County Well Most Important District Completion," *Laredo Times,* November 25, 1929, 4; *Texas Almanac,* 268–72; "Texas Charters," *Dallas Morning News,* July 25, 1935. Gold Rule Developing Company Prospectus, *In re: Bor-Tex Oil Company,* Laredo Case No. 46 (1920); *In re: Rentfro Banton Creager,* Brownsville Bankruptcy Case No. 553 (1935); *In re: Nick Doffing,* Brownsville Case Nos. 604, 621 (1936).

89. "Laredo, Texas: The Gateway to Mexico" (Laredo: Laredo Chamber of Commerce, 1926), 10, Ephemera, DeGolyer Library, SMU.

90. Nugent, *Into the West,* 132, 135, 174.

91. US Bureau of the Census, *Fifteenth Census, Reports by States, Montana to Wyoming,* 941–1083; US Bureau of the Census, *Sixteenth Census, Population,* 990–1009; Montejano, *Anglos and Mexicans in the Making of Texas,* 160–61, 167–69.

92. "Laredo and Webb County Progress Rapidly," *Laredo Times,* September 20, 1930, 1; "Laredo Fast Gaining Mexican Trade," *Laredo Times,* December 10, 1929, 1; "Shipments to Mexico Heavy," *Laredo Times,* August 2, 1914, 1; "Trade Relations between the United States and Mexico on the Increase," *Laredo Times,* July 25, 1925, 1; "Laredo, Texas: The Gateway to Mexico," 7.

CHAPTER 3: SEIZING OPPORTUNITY

1. "Invest Now," *San Antonio Light,* January 25, 1914, 31; "The Western Union Telegraph Co.," *Laredo Times,* October 18, 1914, 6.

2. González and Cotera, *Life along the Border,* 110; letter from Alonso S. Perales to Ben Garza, June 22, 1928, Box 1, Folder 3, Andrés de Luna Collection, LULAC Papers, NLBC.

3. Alexis de Tocqueville, *Democracy in America,* ed. Richard D. Heffner (New York: Signet Classic, 2001), 131.

4. Appleby, *Relentless Revolution,* 167, 177; Buder, *Capitalizing on Change,* 1–3, 45; Sullivan, Warren, and Westbrook, *Fragile Middle Class,* 260.

5. Appleby, *Relentless Revolution,* 221. For a discussion of the development of the middle class and its values in early America, see Appleby, "Social Consequences of American Revolutionary Ideals"; Wood, *Radicalism of the American Revolution,* 229–369.

6. Jillson, *Pursuing the American Dream.* For the relationship between the "standard of living" and the American middle class, see Moskowitz, *Standard of Living.* For a study of the growing importance of consumption in the United States in this period, see Cohen, *Consumer's Republic,* 18–61.

7. Wrobel, *Promised Lands,* 14, 25, 56, 58–60.

8. "Along the Way," *Farm and Ranch,* July 21, 1906, 1; Gulf Coast Lines, "The Gulf Coast Country," Folder 9, Box 1: Shary Citrus Brochures, Series 11, JHSC, UTPA; C. H. Matson, *The Gulf Coast of Texas: Winter Vegetable Garden of America* (Chicago: Rock Island–Frisco Lines, 1906), Eugene C. Barker Texas History Collection, CAH.

9. Bourke, "American Congo," 604; Lewis N. Hale, "Semi-Tropical Texas," *Texas Magazine,* January 1911, 11.

10. McGary, "Past and Present Meet at Brownsville," 1.

11. L. N. Olmsted and Southwestern Land Company Vice President and General Sales Manager, "Sharyland," Folder 1, Box 1: Shary Citrus Brochures, Series 11, JHSC, UTPA.

12. "The Golden Story of Sharyland, Where Nature Produces the Sweetest Citrus Fruits," Folder 6, Box 1: Shary Citrus Brochures, Series 11, JHSC, UTPA; "Harlingen, in the Lower Rio Grande Valley of Texas: The City That Citrus Built," Vertical Files, CAH; Montgomery, *Little Journey,* 17, 62. For discussion of the influence of the exotic and foreign on American consumption and leisure, see Greenfield, "'Game of One Hundred Intelligences'"; Hoganson, "Cosmopolitan Domesticity."

13. Montgomery, *Little Journey,* 5, 49. Also see the Nick Doffing Co., "Golden Groves: The Lower Rio Grande Valley," Box 1: Shary Citrus Brochures, Series 11, JHSC, UTPA; Missouri Pacific Railroad Company, "The Beautiful Valley of the Lower Rio Grande," Pamphlet Collection, DeGolyer Library, SMU; Missouri Pacific Lines, "South Texas and the Winter Garden District," Eugene C. Barker Texas History Collection, CAH.

14. Hale, "Semi-Tropical Texas," 11. For examples of the emphasis on irrigation, see "Citrus Tree: Facts and Potentialities of the Lower Rio Grande Valley's Great Industry," Folder 32, Box 1: Shary Citrus Brochures, Series 11, JHSC, UTPA; Chamber of Commerce, "Catarina: In the Heart of the Winter Garden District of Southwest Texas," Eugene C. Barker Texas History Collection, CAH; "Down Where the Golden Grapefruit Grows: Adams Gardens in the Heart of the Lower Rio Grande Valley," Folder 50, Box 1: Shary Citrus Brochures, Series 11, JHSC, UTPA; Missouri Pacific Lines, "South Texas and the Winter Garden District." For a discussion of the American myth of turning the desert into a garden, see Smith, *Virgin Land.*

15. Matson, *Gulf Coast of Texas,* 4.

16. W. H. Withington, "The Happy Combination in Southwest Texas," 50–51.

17. "Golden Story of Sharyland." For more examples of the use of the semitropical metaphor in literature about South Texas, see Charles F. C. Ladd, "Adam's Gardens: In the Heart of the Lower Rio Grande Valley," Folder 29, Box 1: Shary Citrus Brochures, Series 11, JHSC, UTPA; "Prospectus, Progreso Development Company," Folder 50, Box 1: Shary Citrus Brochures, Series 11, JHSC, UTPA. For an example of a Southern California brochure using the "semitropical" metaphor, see *Facts about Lands, Productions, Climate, and Water in Semi-Tropic or Southern California: What Home-Seekers, Investors, and Speculators Want to Know* (September 1887), Folder C-7, Box F-21, Ephemera, HLSC.

18. Theodore M. Plummer, "The Land of Opportunity," *Gulf Coast Magazine* (July 1907): 77–8. For more comparisons to California, see "Gulf Coast Country Developers," *Gulf Coast Magazine* (July 1908); Victor H. Schoffelmayer, "The Magic Valley—Its Marvelous Future," *Texas Geographic Magazine,* Spring 1939, 16–31. See also C. J. Jones, *Homes in South-Western Texas 50,000 Acres Equal to the Best Valley Lands in California Sold in Tracts to Suit at from $2 to $3 per acre on time to suit purchasers* (San Francisco: P. E. Daugherty & Co., 1881), 6–7, HLSC. California and Texas promoters used similar themes. There are many examples of Southern California promotional literature between 1880 and 1940 in two boxes located in the Ephemeral files in Special Collections at the Huntington Library, Boxes F-21 and F-22.

19. Jordan, "Perceptual Regions in Texas," 293–307, 293, 296–97, 300. A perceptual region is one that exists in the minds of ordinary people who live there but is very much influenced by promotional literature about the region. Fox, "Architecture in Brownsville." For studies of the creation of the Spanish fantasy heritage in New Mexico and California, see Montgomery, *Spanish Redemption;* Starr, *Inventing the Dream.*

20. Schoffelmayer, "Magic Valley—Its Marvelous Future," 31.

21. "Laredo, Texas: Gateway to Mexico," 2.

22. "Eagle Pass, Maverick County, a Coming Border City," *Texas Magazine,* April 1911, 74–75; Fred I. Meyers, "Prosperous Del Rio," *Texas Magazine,* July 1910, 83–84; T. C. Richardson, "Woolly, but Not So Terribly Wild," *Farm and Ranch,* September 20, 1924, 1.

23. "Progreso Haciendas"; Montgomery, *Little Journey,* 5. The classic work on "separate spheres" is Cott, *Bonds of Womanhood.* For a study of that ideology in the West, see Jeffrey, *Frontier Women.* For a discussion of how images of modern amenities signaled the incorporation of borderland places, see Mora, *Border Dilemmas,* 171–73.

24. "Golden Story of Sharyland"; Plummer, "Land of Opportunity," 76.

25. "Mercedes, Queen City of the Valley: the lower Rio Grande Valley of Texas; a winter garden for the world, where summer spends the year" (Mercedes, TX: American Rio Grande Land and Irrigation Co., 1925), Pamphlet Collection, Degolyer Library, SMU; Leshner, "In the Lower Rio Grande Valley," 67.

26. "El Jardin: The Garden Spot of the Lower Rio Grande Valley," Folder 4, Box

1: Shary Citrus Brochures, Series 11, JHSC, UTPA; "Errand Boy to Bank President," *Pioneer Magazine,* February 1927, 29; "He Knows His Onions," *Pioneer Magazine,* April 1927, 12.

27. "Beautiful Valley of the Lower Rio Grande"; "Golden Story of Sharyland"; Moskowitz, *Standard of Living,* 9–11.

28. Julia Cameron Montgomery, *The Citrus Tree: Facts and Potentialities of the Lower Rio Grande Valley's Great Industry, Supplement to Monty's* (Brownsville, 1924), 28–29, Folder 32, Box 1: Shary Citrus Brochures, JHSC, UTPA; "Golden Story of Sharyland"; "Progreso Haciendas." For reference to voluntary associations, including churches, as markers of middle-class status, see Blumin, *Emergence of the Middle Class,* 192–229. For a discussion of the role of ideology and religion among the middle class, see Applegate, "Henry Ward Beecher and the 'Great Middle Class'"; Reiser, "Secularization Reconsidered."

29. Excursions, Boxes 1 and 2, JHSC, UTPA; "Sam Perl," Folder 7, Box 3a169, TJHS.

30. F. O. Alin to J. M. Donaldson, Postmaster, Kansas City, Missouri, April 6, 1921, Transcript of Testimony of Rush D. Simmons, March 25, 1924, p. 348, Folder 54: US Senate Hearings, alleged land fraud in Cameron and Hidalgo counties, Texas, Box 3, Series 6: Legal Actions and Lawsuits, 1917–1940, JHSC, UTPA.

31. Simmons Exhibit 1, Transcript of Testimony of Rush D. Simmons, March 24, 1924, pp. 72–73, Folder 51: US Senate Hearings, alleged land fraud in Cameron and Hidalgo counties, Texas, Box 3, Series 6: Legal Actions and Lawsuits, 1917–1940, JHSC, UTPA. Kearney and Knopp, *Border Cuates,* 196.

32. "Heavy Travel to Mexico," *Laredo Times,* March 22, 1908, 9.

33. Rodolfo A. de la Garza, "Who Are You," *LULAC News* 2, no. 1 (September 1932), 1, LULAC papers, NLBC.

34. Jordan, "Century and a Half of Ethnic Change," 398–99.

35. Foley, *From Peones to Politicos,* 3. For the trend of migration out of the midwestern and northern Great Plains states into the Sunbelt states, see Cassetti, "Manufacturing Productivity and Snowbelt-Sunbelt Shifts"; Perry and Watkins, *Rise of the Sunbelt Cities.*

36. Martha Anderson, Dr. Earl Reed interview, oral history tape recording, McAllen, Texas, August 16, 1982, LRGV, UTPA; Martha Anderson, George Strohmeyer interview, oral history tape recording, Hidalgo County, Texas, May 17, 1983, LRGV, UTPA; James Franklin Ewers interview; Robert E. Norton, Charles W. Griffith interview, oral history tape recording, San Juan, Texas, April 29, 1982, LRGV, UTPA; Robert E. Norton, Elma Krumdieck Koch Dutschman interview, oral history tape recording, Pharr, Texas, April 11, 1982, LRGV, UTPA; Robert E. Norton, Maurice B. Cramer interview, oral history tape recording, Hidalgo County, Texas, March 8, 1983, LRGV, UTPA; Edna Salinas, Mildred Fagg interview, oral history tape recording, Hidalgo County, Texas, April 7, 1987, LRGV, UTPA.

37. White, *"It's Your Misfortune and None of My Own,"* 186–87. Census records and local publications such as Watson, *Lower Rio Grande Valley and Its Builders,* reveal that

most of the newcomers were families from the Midwest, something that most secondary sources acknowledge.

38. Jordan, "Century and a Half of Ethnic Change," 385–422.

39. "Caroline Chatfield Says Today," *Laredo Times,* October 18, 1935, 10.

40. Gonzalez, *Culture of Empire,* 123–25; Montejano, *Anglos and Mexicans in the Making of Texas,* 159–60, 220–34; Nugent, *Into the West,* 203, 206.

41. Field Notes, Folder 12:19, Carton 12, Paul Schuster Taylor Papers, BLUCB; Foley, *From Peones to Politicos,* 47.

42. Robert E. Norton, Andrew Champion interview, oral history tape recording, Donna, Texas, August 22, 1982, LRGV, UTPA; Anders, *Boss Rule in South Texas,* 169–70, 276–81; Richardson, *West from Appomattox,* 128, 230, 306; Montejano, *Anglos and Mexicans in the Making of Texas,* 143–51; "Guerra Dynasty of Starr County in Last Stand," *McAllen Monitor,* July 27, 1934.

43. Blackford, *History of Small Business in America,* 4.

44. Danbom, *Born in the Country,* 135–49; St. John, "Divided Ranges," 117.

45. Jeffrey M. Pilcher, "Fajitas and the Failure of Refrigerated Meatpacking in Mexico: Consumer Culture and Porfirian Capitalism," *Americas* 60, no. 3 (January 2004): 412–13. For an example of a rancher who sold fresh meat locally, see *In re: Ignacio Lozano,* Case No. 9 (Laredo, 1902).

46. For some records of cattle crossings in the late nineteenth century, see the *Laredo Times,* June 28, 1897, and June 30, 1897; Machado, "Mexican Revolution"; J. D. Jackson, "Livestock Conditions in Mexico," *Cattleman,* March 1916, 43; Kenneth D. Oliver, "Getting Them Out of Mexico," *Cattleman,* May 1916, 25–27.

47. Anders, *Boss Rule in South Texas,* 45; Lasater, *Falfurrias,* 45, 76–90, 235, 253; "Letter from H. P. Drought to W. D. Mcdougall, 13 October 1922," Box 16, H. P. Drought Collection, UTSA; "Letter from H. P. Drought to W. D. Mcdougall, 28 November 1922," Box 16, H. P. Drought Collection, UTSA. For more information about Lasater, see the Edward Cunningham Lasater Papers, 1860–1930, CAH.

48. William H. Dusenberry, "The Mexican Agricultural Society, 1879–1914," *Americas* 12, no. 4 (April 1956): 385–98; Lasater, *Lasater Philosophy of Cattle Raising,* 58; Graham, *Kings of Texas,* 209–11.

49. Lasater, *Lasater Philosophy of Cattle Raising,* 1.

50. "Calves Advance at Fort Worth," *San Antonio Express,* October 21, 1925, 19; "Cow Men Hear Warning by Expert," *San Antonio Light,* March 22, 1935; "Round-Up Notes: A Reliable Report of Range Conditions and Representative Sales of the Past Months," *Cattleman,* July 1923, 45; S. G. Rubinow, "Agricultural Progress," *Cattleman,* March 1916, 83–89; "We Sold $180,000,000 of Meat in 11 Months," *San Antonio Light,* June 24, 1906, 24; "Why Beef Prices Increase," *San Antonio Light,* February 3, 1913, 4; "World Depression Plainly Shown by US Export Report," *San Antonio Light,* November 30, 1930, 23.

51. A. C. Williams, "Cattle Raisers' Association of Texas: Something of Its History," *Cattleman,* March 1915, 13–16; Schlebecker, *Cattle Raising on the Plains,* 33.

52. *History of the Cattlemen of Texas,* vii–ix, 30.

53. Carlson, *Texas Woollybacks,* 33, 51, 112–13, 189–206; Hornby, *Going Around,* 34; Meyers, "Prosperous Del Rio," 83.

54. Foley, *From Peones to Politicos,* 4–5; Foley, *White Scourge,* 10–11; Tiller, *Texas Winter Garden,* 35.

55. Miller, James Franklin Ewers interview; Shary Excursions, Box 1, JHSC, UTPA.

56. Letter from the Office of the Secretary, Rio Grande Valley Development League, undated, *In re: S. M. Williams,* Brownsville Case No. 25 (1919); *In re: W. L. Bradbury,* Brownsville Case No. 55 (1919); *In re: Alby Richard Juby,* Brownsville Case No. 559 (1935); *In re: George Hackney,* Case No. 249 (1928); Norton, Elma Krumdieck Koch Dutschman interview.

57. Creditor Meeting Transcript, pp. 4–6, *In re: Jacob Blair Vincent,* San Antonio Case No. 1709 (1933); *In re: James Frances Braden,* Del Rio Case No. 111 (1935).

58. Montejano, *Anglos and Mexicans in the Making of Texas,* 173; Paul S. Taylor, "Field Notes, December 10, 1928," Folder 12:13, Carton 12, Paul Schuster Taylor Papers, BLUCB.

59. US Bureau of the Census, *Fourteenth Census, Agriculture,* vol. VI, part 2, 664–86; US Bureau of the Census, *Fifteenth Census, Agriculture,* vol. II, part 2, 1370; Silva-Bewley, *Legacy of John H. Shary,* 87.

60. Robert E. Norton, Howard Millen interview, oral history tape recording, San Juan, TX, April 15, 1992, LRGV, UTPA; *In re: Ira Ragsdale,* Brownsville Case No. 61 (Mission, 1920); *In re: William C. Duncan,* Brownsville Case No. 109 (Donna, 1922). For other examples of tenant farmers, see *In re: Leo Schimerowski,* Brownsville Case No. 112 (Alamo, 1922); *In re: Leo Gaynor,* Brownsville Case No. 113 (San Juan, 1922); *In re: W. E. Gaynor,* Brownsville Case No. 113 (San Juan, 1922). Saunders, "Bentsen Brothers, Empire Builders," 258–60.

61. Lasater, *Falfurrias,* 72–91.

62. *In re: Alice and Martha Furman,* Brownsville Case No. 526 (Donna, 1934); *In re: Mrs. Ethel Ralston McManus,* Brownsville Case No. 620 (Edinburg, 1936); *In re: Mrs. Annie Penry,* Brownsville Case No. 781 (Weslaco, 1941).

63. Yoakum, "Farmers Can Solve High Cost of Living," 45–46.

64. M. W. Holland, "Team Work in the Rio Grande Valley: Farmer Tours and Community Organizations Promote Co-Operative Spirit," *Farm and Ranch,* March 5, 1921, 1.

65. Ibid.; see TexaSweet Advertisements in the *Hutchinson News,* January 16, 1930; *Muscatine Journal and News-Tribune,* February 6, 1931; *Hamilton Evening Journal,* November 24, 1932; *Lethbridge Herald,* January 15, 1933.

66. Miller, James Franklin Ewers interview. The relevant laws include the Irrigation District Act, ch. 122, 1905 Tex. Gen. Laws 235; Irrigation Act of 1913, ch. 171, 1913 Tex. Gen. Laws 358; and Irrigation Act of 1917, ch. 88, 1917 Tex. Gen. Laws 211.

67. Buder, *Capitalizing on Change,* 54, 90; Montejano, *Anglos and Mexicans in the Making of Texas,* 159–61. For a detailed study of the formation of labor relations in South Texas and how the work arrangement spread to the rest of the nation, see John Weber, "Shadow of the Revolution."

68. See Schedule B-2 in the following cases: *In re: W. L. Bradbury,* Brownsville Case No. 55 (1919); *In re: George Wiley,* Brownsville Case No. 90 (1921); *In re: Odessa and Ida Bickelhaupt,* Brownsville Case No. 91 (1922); *In re: J. T. Simpson,* Brownsville Case No. 126 (1922); *In re: James Baldwin,* Brownsville Case No. 329 (1930); *In re: Frank Barfield,* Brownsville Case No. 593 (1936); *In re: Frank Eli Clark,* Brownsville Case 595 (1936); *In re: George Molby,* Brownsville Case No. 598 (1936). These are samples; there are hundreds of similar cases.

69. US Bureau of the Census, *Fifteenth Census, Agriculture,* vol. II, part 2, 1028, 1038, 1051–56.

70. For examples of the clubs, see entries in the *Standard Blue Book of the United States of America,* vol. 14, and the *Standard Blue Book of the United States of America, 1929–30,* vol. 15. For a discussion of the importance of clubs and associations in American life and among the middle class, see Blumin, *Emergence of the Middle Class,* 192–229.

71. See listings in the *Texas State Gazetteer,* 1890, DeGolyer Library, SMU.

72. *The Mercantile Agency Reference Book, Texas Pocket Edition, 1901.* New York: R. G. Dun & Co., 1901, 75–76; *Dun & Bradstreet Reference Book, Texas Pocket Edition, 1938.* New York: Dun & Bradstreet, 1938, 99–102, 174–75; *The Mercantile Agency Reference Book, Texas Pocket Edition, 1910.* New York: R. G. Dun & Co., 1910, 56–57, 101; *The Mercantile Agency Reference Book, 1925,* vol. 227. New York: R. G. Dun & Co., 1925, 2744.

73. *In re: Palm Valley Canning Company,* Brownsville Case No. 680 (1938).

74. For example, out of 92 border businesses in 1918 with more than $20,000 in assets, 70 could be identified in terms of ethnicity and/or birthplace of owners. (The rest were mainly branches of corporations from outside the area.) Of those, only 22 were Anglo-Americans born in the United States. The rest consisted of Jews, Syrians, ethnic Mexicans and Hispanics, and a variety of European immigrants. By 1938, there were 180 businesses with a net worth in excess of $20,000. Among the 104 where ownership could be identified, approximately 41 were Anglo-Americans from the United States. These statistics come from my database and are based on figures taken from *The Mercantile Agency Reference Book, 1918* and the *Dun & Bradstreet Reference Book, Texas Pocket Edition, 1938.*

75. For examples of the kinds of assets and debts held by artisans, see bankruptcy schedules in *In re: Edward and Mildred Hays d / b / a Hays & Sons,* Brownsville Case No. 511 (1934) (plumber); *In re: R. B. Suttle,* Brownsville Case No. 262 (1929) (carpenter).

76. Barton, "At the Edge of the Storm," 222–23; McCrossen, "Drawing Boundaries between Markets, Nations, and Peoples, 1650–1940," 12–20.

77. *In re: A. Schmidt & Co.,* Laredo Case No. 8 (1900); *In re: Henry Dewey Tobias,* Brownsville Case No. 174 (1925); *In re: Roy Lowry,* Del Rio Case No. 74 (1930). For similar examples, see *In re: Louis Lindheim,* San Antonio Case No. 258 (1903) (Del Rio); *In re: Joseph Vale,* Brownsville Case No. 1 (1909).

78. *1926 Standard Blue Book of the United States of America,* 15, 21, 79.

79. Diaz, "Contrabandista Communities," 59, 63, 102–106, 202; Northrup and Turney, *Encyclopedia of Tariffs and Trade in US History*, vol. 1, 114–15, 146–47, 183, 248–50, 294–95, 403, 434–35.

80. For examples of Anglos selling primarily or exclusively to other Anglos, see Schedule B-2, Personal Property, Lists of Accounts Receivable in the following cases: *In re: J. E. Buckley*, Brownsville Case No. 5 (1911) (Mercedes); *In re: Paul Barnett*, Brownsville Case No. 8 (1913) (San Benito); *In re: Alfred P. Hall*, Brownsville Case No. 38 (1917) (McAllen); *In re: J. M. Todd*, Brownsville Case No. 94 (1922) (Donna); *In re: John Rutledge*, Brownsville Case No. 231 (1928) (Brownsville); *In re: L. B. Winans*, Brownville Case No. 304 (1929) (San Benito); *In re: John T. Cardwell*, Brownsville Case No. 332 (1930) (McAllen); *In re: W. H. Putegnat Company, Inc.*, Brownville Case No. 401 (1931) (Brownsville); *In re: Robert Burdette Ernest*, Brownsville Case No. 633 (1937) (Harlingen).

81. Montejano, *Anglos and Mexicans in the Making of Texas*, 240–41; Tiller, *Texas Winter Garden*, 36. Even in other towns, Anglos did sell to ethnic Mexicans, so there was not a clear dividing line between which merchants served which communities. *In re: Henry W. Earnest, Harry G. Earnest, and Josephine Earnest*, Laredo Case No. 16 (1905) (Millet, La Salle County); *In re: Oscar B. Kessler*, Del Rio Case No. 9 (1911) (Knippa, Uvalde County).

82. Bankruptcy Schedules, *In re: James A. Hockaday*, Brownsville Case No. 130 (1923); Transcript of Creditors' Meeting, *In re: Lee Reader*, Brownsville Case No. 148 (1924); Transcript of Creditors' Meeting, p. 1, *In re: Monty Fuller Colvin*, Brownsville Case No. 428 (1932); Bankruptcy Schedules, *In re: Robert Alder Jeffreys*, Brownsville Case No. 715 (1939); *Dun & Bradstreet Reference Book, State Pocket Edition; Mercantile Agency Reference Book, 1918*.

83. Stanley C. Green, *Border Biographies*, vol. 1, 127–28.

84. "Adding to the Cost," *Laredo Times*, January 28, 1917, 8; "Buying at Home," *Laredo Times*, July 15, 1925; "The Home Trade," *Laredo Times*, February 2, 1913; "The Postal Rates," *Laredo Times*, May 14, 1925.

85. Chatfield, "Twin Cities of the Border," 22, 25. Texas, vol. 5, pp. 60–61, 70/13, 85, R. G. Dun & Co. Credit Report volumes, BLHBS.

86. Transcript of Creditors' Meeting, *In re: A. H. Allen*, Brownsville Case No. 158 (1924), 2.

87. *In re: Lee Dillon*, San Antonio Case No. 1282 (1928); *In re: Joseph Netzer*, Laredo Case No. 50 (1922); *In re: Mrs. Louis Pasco*, Laredo Case No. 11 (1902).

88. Transcript of Creditors' Meeting, *In re: Crystal City Dress Shop*, Del Rio Case No. 129 (1940).

89. "Local Items," *Brownsville Daily Herald*, March 2, 1909, 3.

90. "City News," *Brownsville Herald*, September 23, 1915, 3; "Little Locals," *Laredo Times*, December 9, 1917, 8; "Spring Frocks Are Modeled at Style Show," *Brownsville Herald*, March 11, 1934, 9. *In re: Ruth Runkle*, Brownsville Case No. 303 (1929); *In re: Mary and Katherine Miller*, Brownsville Case No. 313 (1930); *In re: Dorothy L. Haas*, Brownsville Case No. 259 (1928). For examples of Eva Preuss's advertisements, see the

Brownsville Herald, January 3, 4, 10, 11, 17, 18, 22, 23, 24, 1920. Usually, they appear on the third, fourth, or fifth page.

91. *In re: Sudie Knoblauch,* San Antonio Case No. 1873 (1935).

92. Bowles, ed., *Donna Hooks Fletcher,* 35–40, 44–45, 48–51.

CHAPTER 4: SEARCHING FOR THE AMERICAN DREAM

1. "Immigration Soup Bunch," *Laredo Times,* October 22, 1907, 1.

2. US Bureau of the Census, *Fourteenth Census, Population,* vol. III, 1022–24.

3. Higham, *Strangers in the Land,* 65.

4. "John T. Rossetti Murdered by Two Unknown Assassins," *Laredo Times,* March 18, 1917, 9.

5. "Would-Be Immigrants," *Laredo Weekly Times,* April 4, 1922, 10.

6. Paul S. Taylor, "Field Notes," Folder 12:17, Carton 12, Paul Schuster Taylor Papers, BLUCB.

7. Jacobson, *Whiteness of a Different Color,* 8, 88–95.

8. See Bankruptcy Schedules in the following cases: *In re: George Federolf,* Brownsville Case No. 41 (1917); *In re: J. W. Petrie,* Brownsville Case No. 118 (1922); *In re: John Walsdorf,* Brownsville Case No. 706 (1939); *In re: Julius and Kate Johnson,* Brownsville Case No. 720 (1939). Transcript of Creditor Meeting, *In re: Peter and Clara Dicken,* Brownsville Case No. 658 (1937); *Manuscript Census,* Hidalgo County, 1920. For other farmers in the area from Germany, Norway, and Switzerland, see *In re: George Federolf,* Brownsville Case No. 41 (1917); *In re: Frank Leverman,* Brownsville Case No. 123 (1922); *In re: Anton Mertens,* Brownsville Case No. 169 (1925); *In re: Fred and Minnie Stauffer,* Brownsville Case No. 692 (1938); *In re: Julius Alfred and Kate Johnson,* Brownsville Case No. 720 (1939).

9. Bankruptcy Schedules and Creditor Meeting Transcript, *In re: Joseph Netzer,* Laredo Case No. 50 (1922); "White Red Man," 30. For information about Buenz, see Green, *Border Biographies,* vol. 2, 13; *Mercantile Agency Reference Book, 1918.*

10. "Celestino Barreda," Vertical Files, CAH; *The Mercantile Agency Reference Book, State Pocket Edition, Texas, 1930.* New York: R. G. Dun & Co., 1930, 106; *Standard Blue Book of the United States of America, 1929–30,* 80; *In re: Celestino P. Barreda,* Brownsville Case No. 535 (1935).

11. Carlos Cuellar, "The House of Armengol"; Green, *Border Biographies,* vol. 1, 3–5. *In re: Antonio Valls Armengol,* Laredo Case No. 136 (1934).

12. "Mrs. Champion Passes Away at the Age of 93 Years," *Brownsville Herald,* March 18, 1922, 1.

13. Green, *Border Biographies,* vol. II, 132; *Manuscript Census,* Webb County, 1930.

14. Kraut, *Huddled Masses,* 15–51, 112–13; "By the Thousand, Arriving Subjects of King Humbert: Italians Rush for America," *New York Times,* May 10, 1891; "The Greek Texans," University of Texas Institute of Texan Cultures, http://www.texancultures .com (accessed April 30, 2010); "The Immigration Movement," *Galveston Daily News,* March 24, 1905, 6; "Val Verde County, Where Nature Has Been Prodigal," *Del Rio–Re-*

cord News, April 20, 1905, 4–6; *In re: James Margas,* Laredo Case No. 76 (1927); *In re: Santiago Pappas,* Laredo Case No. 140 (1935); *Manuscript Census,* Maverick County, Eagle Pass, 1920; "Spiro Allis Dies," *Brownsville Herald,* January 4, 1933, 7; "Impressive Ceremony Marks Betrothal of Miss Anita Marinos," *Laredo Times,* July 4, 1937, 2. The analysis contained in my database of the R. G. Dun & Co. statistics shows that most individuals with Greek and Italian surnames had small businesses.

15. *The Mercantile Agency Reference Book, State Pocket Edition, Texas, 1930,* 106. "Black Hand in San Antonio," *Dallas Morning News,* December 10, 1908, 3; "Eleven Arrested in San Antonio Conspiracy Case," *Dallas Morning News,* May 16, 1930, 2; *In re: Manuel Vela,* Laredo Case No. 91 (1929); *In re: Oscar García,* Brownsville Case No. 273 (1929).

16. "Eagle Pass Transaction Involves $130,000 Stock," *Galveston Daily News,* April 17, 1921, 15; "Italians to Revive Annual Custom of Celebrating Columbus Day in San Antonio," *San Antonio Express,* June 21, 1936, 10-C; Sanborn Map, Eagle Pass, 1916, 2, CAH.

17. "Bruni as Pioneer Wool Merchant," *Pioneer Magazine,* February 1927, 17; "A. M. Bruni Made Laredo History," *Laredo Times,* special edition, November 23, 1937, 2.

18. *In re: Antonio Barreda,* Brownsville Case No. 565 (1935); Field Notes, Folder 12:13, Paul Schuster Taylor Papers, BLUCB; Benton-Cohen, *Borderline Americans.*

19. Stone, *Chosen Folks,* 4.

20. Gordon, *Great Arizona Orphan Abduction,* 198; Rischin, "Jewish Experience in America," 32–40; Rosenbaum, *Cosmopolitans,* 37; Caroline Luce, "Reexamining Los Angeles' 'Lower East Side': Jewish Bakers Union Local 453 and Yiddish Food Culture in 1920s Boyle Heights," in Karen S. Wilson, ed., *Jews in the Los Angeles Mosaic* (Los Angeles: University of California Press, 2013), 27–30.

21. One of the best examples of this is found in the Jewish community of Los Angeles. Karen S. Wilson, "Becoming Angelinos," in Wilson, ed., *Jews in the Los Angeles,* 11–12.

22. "A Brief History of the Levines of Harlingen," Box 3J163, TJHS; "Sam Rosen Memoir," Folder: People by Occupation, Merchants, Box 3A168, TJSH; Stone, *Chosen Folks,* 138.

23. Morrison I. Swift, "Immigration Ideas," *Boston Herald,* February 7, 1924.

24. Marcus, *To Count a People,* 211; "Jews Coming West," *Laredo Times,* October 30, 1910, 9; "Jews in Texas History," *Jewish Herald Voice, Sesquicentennial Passover,* April 24, 1986; Stone, *Chosen Folks,* 81–93. For examples of movement between San Antonio and the border, see *Transcript of Creditors' Meeting, In re: William Epstein,* Laredo Bankruptcy Case No. 156 (1937), 24–25, 41; *Transcript of Creditors' Meeting, In re: Sam Greenfield,* Brownsville Bankruptcy Case No. 73 (1921), 1.

25. See, for example, short, untitled sections about Jewish businesses closing on the holy days in the *Laredo Times,* October 7, 1883, 4; *Laredo Times,* October 9, 1905, 3; *Laredo Times,* September 9, 1909; "Laredo, Texas," *Encyclopedia of Southern Jewish Communities,* http://isjl.org/history/archive/tx/laredo.html (accessed June 30, 2013). For population figures, see Marcus, *To Count a People,* 211–15.

26. "Sam Perl," Folder 7, Box 3A169, TJHS, Center for American History, University of Texas at Austin; Harriett Denise Joseph and Sondra Shands, "Sam Perl: Mr. Friendship and Mr. Temple Beth-El of Brownsville, Texas," *Locus: A Historical Journal of Regional Perspectives on National Topics* 5 (Spring 1993): 145–62.

27. "A Brief History of the Levines of Harlingen," Levine Folder (Harlingen), Box 3J163, TJHS.

28. Levinson, "American Jews in the West"; Olegario, *Culture of Credit,* 121, 128–29; Stone, *Chosen Folks,* 78; Toll, "Jewish Merchant and Civic Order," 83. For scholarship about Jews and farming, see Taylor Spence, "Jeffersonian Jews: The Jewish Agrarian Diaspora and the Assimilative Power of Western Land, 1882–1930," *Western Historical Quarterly* 41, no. 3 (Autumn 2010): 327–51, and Ellen Eisenberg, "From Cooperative Farming to Urban Leadership," in *Jewish Life in the American West: Perspectives on Migration, Settlement, and Community,* ed. Ava Fran Kahn (Los Angeles: Autry Museum of Western Heritage in association with the University of Washington Press, Seattle, 2002), 113–32.

29. Olegario, *Culture of Credit,* 127.

30. Transcript of Creditors' Meeting, *In re: Sam Greenfield,* Brownsville Case No. 73 (1921).

31. Transcript of Creditors' Meeting, *In re: Esidor Pupkin,* Brownsville Case No. 23 (1915); *In re: Ben, Milton, Joe, and Alex Pupkin, Pupkin Brothers,* Brownsville Case No. 295 (1929).

32. Leach, *Land of Desire,* 91–92.

33. A. A. Champion, "Letter to Ruben Edelstein," Box 3A169, TJHS, CAH; "Early Settler at Rio Grande City Dead," *San Antonio Express,* March 10, 1936; "May 25, 1988, Info about Ben Freudenstein," Folder 7, Box 3A169, TJHS; "Morris A. Hirsch Succumbs after Lingering Illness," *Laredo Times,* February 25, 1925, 6; "Pierre Block & Company, Inc., Opens Customs Brokerage House," *Laredo Daily Times,* June 23, 1928, 1; "Rio Grande Merchant Who Waited Forty Years for Railroad, Dies 16 Years after Wish Fulfilled," *San Antonio Express,* March 15, 1936, 10; "Casa Raul Founder Dies at 93," *Laredo Morning Times,* July 16, 2001, 3A; "Laredo, Texas," *Encyclopedia of Southern Jewish Communities.*

34. Morris Riskind, "Letter to Ruthe Weingarten, August 21, 1988," Folder 7, Box 3A170, TJHS; Morris Riskind, "Letter to Ruthe Weingarten, September 30, 1988," Folder 7, Box 3A170, TJHS; *The Mercantile Agency Reference Book, State Pocket Edition, Texas, 1930,* 106.

35. *The Mercantile Agency Reference Book, 1925,* 2761; *Dun & Bradstreet Reference Book, State Pocket Edition, Texas, 1938,* 252; William J. Munter, "History of the Jews of Texas' Middle Corridor," Folder 7, Box 3A170, TJHS.

36. "Fallecio Ayer un Conocido Comerciante," *Tiempo Laredo,* August 17, 1934; Green, "History of Laredo's Jewish Community," 26–29.

37. "History of the Sol Freed Family in Texas," Folder 6, Box 3A164, TJHS; "Jews Coming West"; *In re: S. C. and M. B. Freed,* Laredo Case No. 49 (1922).

38. "Brownsville Historical Association Newsletter," Folder 7, Box 3A169, TJHS; Green, "History of Laredo's Jewish Community," 21, 27, 31, 34; Munter, "History of the Jews of Texas' Middle Corridor"; *Brownsville Historical Association Newsletter,* November–December, date unknown, Box 3a169, Folder 7, TJHS.

39. Ruben Edelstein, "Anecdotes about Papa, Some Tales of Early Rio Grande History with Memories of My Father, a Valley Pioneer," Box 4Ad103, TJHS; Ruthe Weingarten, "Interview with Ruben Edelstein, Field Visit, Brownsville," Folder 6, Box 3A169, TJHS, CAH. "Store Stories/Edelstein's Better Furniture," *Southwest Furniture News,* April–May, 1970, in Folder 5: People by Occupation, Mayors to Merchants, Box 3A168, TJHS. Schedule B, *In re: Morris Edelstein,* Brownsville Case No. 436 (Brownsville, 1932).

40. "May 25, 1988, Info about Ben Freudenstein"; Champion, "Letter to Ruben Edelstein"; "For 48 Years the Name of L. Daiches Has Stood Out in Jewelry World Here," *Laredo Times,* special edition, November 23, 1937; Green, "History of Laredo's Jewish Community," 19; "Morris A. Hirsch Succumbs after Lingering Illness"; "Slides Exhibit: Jewish Life in Brownsville—a Salute to the State of Texas on Its Sesquicentennial," Folder 6, Box 3A169, TJHS.

41. Ruthe Weingarten, "Interview of Eva Silberman," Folder 6, Box 3A169, TJHS; Ruthe Weingarten, "Description of Survey Questionnaire, Survey Report Summary," Box 3J163, TJHS.

42. "History of the Sol Freed Family in Texas"; Hubert J. Miller, Dr. Octavío García interview, oral history tape recording, McAllen, Texas, October 18, 1975, LRGV, UTPA; "Pierre Block & Company, Inc., Opens Customs Brokerage House," *Laredo Daily Times,* June 23, 1928, 1.

43. Green, "History of Laredo's Jewish Community," 38; "Jews in Texas History," *Jewish Herald Voice, Sesquicentennial Passover.*

44. F. A. Chapa letter dated June 5, 1917, Folder: Selig Deutschman, Box 3A190, TJHS.

45. Miller, Dr. Octavío Garcia interview; "Oscar Sommer: An Extraordinary Man," Folder 7, Box 3A169, TJHS; Stone, *Chosen Folks,* 196.

46. Jewish merchants sold to both Anglos and ethnic Mexicans or almost exclusively to ethnic Mexicans. *In re: Laurence Solomon,* Del Rio Case No. 54 (1924); *In re: Sam Greenfield,* Brownsville Case No. 73 (1921) (Mission); *In re: Henry Plenn,* Brownsville Case No. 283 (1929) (Brownsville); *In re: Joe Barasch,* Brownsville Case No. 355 (1931) (Harlingen); *In re: Max Yacker,* Brownsville Case No. 426 (1932) (Mercedes); *In re: Joseph Grossman,* Brownsville Case No. 475 (1933) (McAllen). Edelstein, "Anecdotes about Papa," 45, 48; Green, "History of Laredo's Jewish Community," 23.

47. Stone, *Chosen Folks,* 2–5.

48. Haber, *Industry and Underdevelopment,* 171.

49. Tibawi, *Modern History of Syria,* 175–76; Gutiérrez, *Walls and Mirrors,* 51–5, 69–73; "New Gateway for Foreign Nationals," *Laredo Daily Times,* February 9, 1906, 1; Sekaly, "Syrian-Lebanese Immigration," 28–41, 55–57.

50. "Federal Court Fines One More Reyista," *Brownsville Herald,* December 7,

1912, 1; "Interpreter Here," *Brownsville Herald,* December 8, 1914, 8; "Mexico Puts Up the Bars," *Brownsville Herald,* August 24, 1907, 2.

51. "Deported to Mexico," *Laredo Times,* September 17, 1904, 3; "Did Clever Detective Work?" *Laredo Times,* October 19, 1913; "How Syrians Got In," *Dallas Morning News,* February 3, 1907; "Immigrants Held at Laredo," *Dallas Morning News,* March 9, 1912; "Local Items," *Brownsville Herald,* January 6, 1907, 6; "Many Immigrants Detained," *Laredo Times,* October 3, 1912; "Many Syrians Barred," *Dallas Morning News,* January 7, 1907; "New Gateway for Foreign Nationals," *Laredo Daily Times,* 1; "Plot to Escape Frustrated," *Laredo Times,* January 2, 1914; "Sore-Eyed Syrians," *Dallas Morning News,* June 24, 1907; "Syrians at Eagle Pass Ordered Deported," *Dallas Morning News,* January 7, 1903; "Syrians Returned to Mexico," *Laredo Times,* February 2, 1914; "Guarding the Nation's Doors," *San Antonio Light,* May 20, 1917, 11.

52. "Declares Syrians Loyal to America," *Dallas Morning News,* July 5, 1918; Haney-López, *White by Law,* 1–2; "Holds Syrians Are White," *Dallas Morning News,* September 13, 1914. Abraham Kazen and family, *Manuscript Census,* Laredo, Webb County, 1920; Emil Ayoub and family, *Manuscript Census,* San Benito, Cameron County, 1920; Joe and George Sahadi, *Manuscript Census,* San Patricio County, 1920.

53. "Syrians Contribute $119," *San Antonio Light,* May 10, 1917, 5; "Syrian Maronites to Build Church," *San Antonio Express,* August 13, 1932, 3. "Last Rites Set for Reverend Nageem," *San Antonio Light,* July 2, 1939, 11.

54. "Obituary: Matilde Karam Showery," *McAllen Monitor,* February 4, 1996; *Syrian and Lebanese Texans;* "Work of Syrian Peddlers," *Dallas Morning News,* October 2, 1911, 1. *In re: George Sahadi,* Brownsville Case No. 157 (1924); *The Mercantile Agency Reference Book, State Pocket Edition, Texas, 1930,* 526.

55. "Last Rites Set for Reverend Nageem"; "Syrian Maronites to Build Church"; "Syrians Contribute $119." *In re: H. M. Haik,* Brownsville Case No. 70 (1921); *In re: Antone Joseph,* Brownsville Case No. 98 (1922); *In re: Alex Hamauei,* Brownsville Case No. 138 (1923); *In re: James Ayoub,* Brownsville Case No. 228 (1928); *In re: Mike Joseph,* Brownsville Case No. 400 (1931); *In re: Joseph Shahady,* Laredo Case No. 58 (1924); *In re: Emil Ayoub,* Brownsville Case No. 460 (1932).

56. "Philip Kazen Has Made Fast Rise in His Chosen Profession," *Laredo Times,* special edition, November 23, 1937, 6; *Syrian and Lebanese Texans,* 5; Watson, *Lower Rio Grande Valley and Its Builders,* 336.

57. The term "Iowa on the border" comes from Bowman, "Blood Oranges." For a discussion of "greater Mexico," see Gutiérrez, "Migration, Emergent Ethnicity, and the 'Third Space'"; Paredes, *"With His Pistol in His Hand,"* 7–15. Regarding European entrepreneurs in Mexico, see Buchenau, *Tools of Progress,* 11–37.

CHAPTER 5: NAVIGATING CHANGE

1. Transcript of Creditors' Meeting, *In re: Alonso Ancira,* Laredo Case No. 53 (1923).

2. Martínez, *Border People,* 34–41, 59–60.

3. Lillian Weems Baldridge, "Old Ranches of Valley like Feudal Times; Had Own Churches, Stores, Plazas and Homes," *Brownsville Herald,* December 6, 1942, 3-G.

4. Terry G. Jordan, "The 1887 Census of Texas' Hispanic Population," *Aztlan* 12 (1982): 271–78.

5. Arreola, *Tejano South Texas,* 46–47; Jordan, "1887 Census of Texas' Hispanic Population," 273.

6. Bourke, "American Congo"; Tijerina, *Tejano Empire,* 21–44; *Manuscript Census,* Hidalgo County, 1880.

7. González and Cotera, *Life along the Border,* 109–10.

8. State Tax Rolls, Hidalgo County, 1920, TXSLA; *Manuscript Census,* Hidalgo County, 1880; García, "Don Francisco Yturria," 10–21; Harding and McCoy, "Francisco Yturria and Heirs," 91; Watson, *Lower Rio Grande Valley and Its Builders,* 291.

9. Tijerina, *Tejano Empire,* 129–30; David Weber, *Foreigners in Their Native Land,* 154–56.

10. Young, "Red Men, Princess Pocahontas, and George Washington," 51.

11. Baldridge, "Old Ranches of Valley like Feudal Times."

12. Maude McKnight Dopp, "Zapata County Historical Sketch," June 28, 1938, Zapata County Scrapbook, Box 2Q112, WPA Records, TJHS, CAH.

13. US Bureau of the Census, *Thirteenth Census, Population,* 844, 850; US Bureau of the Census, *Sixteenth Census, Population,* 804, 806; "Contestant Closes in Election Hearing," *Galveston Daily News,* February 18, 1919, 1; *Manuscript Census,* Starr County, 1920. For more about Starr County, see "Rio Grande City Rich in Both Past and Prospects," *San Antonio Express,* December 5, 1924, 2A.

14. "Early History of Rio Grande City," Starr County Scrapbook, Box 3L401, WPA Records, CAH.

15. Texas State Tax Rolls, Cameron, Hidalgo, Starr, and Webb Counties, 1930, TXSLA; *Manuscript Census,* Starr County, Zapata County, 1920.

16. Alonzo, *Tejano Legacy,* 169–75.

17. State Tax Rolls, Starr County, 1880 and 1910, TXSLA.

18. State Tax Rolls, Starr County, 1940, TXSLA.

19. Foley, *From Peones to Politicos,* 50–51.

20. Continuing to own land north and south of the river until at least the 1930s were the families of Esteban García, Octavío García, Cayetano Barrera, the de la Viña family, the Benavides family of Laredo, and Manuel Guerra's family of Starr County and Mier, Mexico. Anders, *Boss Rule in South Texas,* 44; Elena Farías Barrera, "Cayetano Barrera of La Reforma Ranch," in *Roots by the River,* ed. Valley By-Liners, 82–83; Green, *Guillermo Benavides Family,* 4, 26–35; Miller, Dr. Octavío García interview; Miller, Esteban García interview.

21. Anders, *Boss Rule in South Texas,* 44; State Tax Rolls, Starr County, 1910, 1930, and 1940, TXSLA.

22. Miller, Esteban García interview; Kipp Shackleford, "A Master of the Breed," *Cattleman,* September 1985, 47–56.

23. Green, *Guillermo Benavides Family,* 10, 31–33.

24. González and Cotera, *Life along the Border,* 69–70; Green, *Guillermo Benavides Family,* 4, 26–35. Transcript of Creditors' Meeting, *In re: Volpe Brothers,* Laredo Case

No. 125 (1932). For examples of their roles in the lives of businesspeople in the city, see *In re: Rafael Martínez,* Laredo Case No. 78 (1928); *In re: Manuel Cruz,* Laredo Case No. 115 (1931); *In re: Pablo Chapa,* Laredo Case No. 141 (1935).

25. Green, *Border Biographies,* vol. 1, 51–52; "Los Ojuelos Ranch Owner Succumbs."

26. "Mexican Property," 25 Tex. Bar J. 661 (1962); William M. Ryan, "Aliens—Right of an Alien to Own Land in Texas," 7 Tex. L. Rev. 607, 610–614 (1928–1929). Act Relating to the Rights, Powers, and Disabilities of Aliens, ch. 134, § 1, 1921 Tex. Gen. Laws.

27. Miller, Dr. Octavío García interview; *Standard Blue Book of the United States of America, 1929–30,* 82.

28. Viña, *Emigrantes de Asturias,* 48–51, 60–68; Washington, "Judge Juan Manuel De La Viña," 82–83.

29. Isbel, "Man from Lightning Ranch," 107–109. *In re: Melchor Mora,* Brownsville Case No. 586 (1935); *In re: Irene and Plutarco de la Viña,* Brownsville Case No. 586 (1935); *In re: P. de la Viña,* Brownsville Case No. 733 (1939).

30. Miller, Esteban García interview; Miller, Ramón Guerra interview; *In re: Feliciana Cisneros de Rotge,* Brownsville Case Nos. 571 and 583 (1935). *In re: T. T. Margo,* Brownsville Case No. 15 (1914). For examples of small landowners, see *In re: Julian Palacios,* Laredo Case No. 1 (1900); *In re: Margarito López,* Laredo Case No. 2 (1900) (Duval County); *In re: Jesús López,* Laredo Case No. 3 (1900) (Duval County); *In re: Francisco López,* Laredo Case No. 4 (1900) (Duval County); *In re: Pedro López,* Laredo Case No. 5 (1900); *In re: Martin and Petra Valadez,* Laredo Case No. 6 (1900) (Duval County); *In re: T. T. Margo,* Brownsville Case No. 15 (1914) (Starr County); *In re: Calixta Salinas de Muniz joined pro forma by her husband, Leopoldo Muniz, Sr.,* Brownsville Case No. 591 (1936) (Starr County); *In re: Pedro Salinas,* Brownsville Case No. 592 (1936) (Starr County); *In re: Fidel Salinas,* Brownsville Case No. 596 (1936); *In re: Jose Solis,* Brownsville Case No. 673 (1937) (Cameron County); *In re: Jose Maria Guerra,* Brownsville Case No. 761 (1940) (Starr County). The 1910 and 1920 census records for Duval County indicate that the Duval County landowners stayed on their land for at least a couple of decades after 1900. Julian Palacios, Margarito López, Jesús López, Francisco López, and Pedro López were all from Mexico. Martin and Petra Valadez were born in Texas. *Manuscript Census,* Duval County, 1910 and 1920.

31. US Bureau of the Census, *Thirteenth Census, Agriculture,* vol. VII, 678–700; Kenneth McCallan, "Railroads Promise Rio Grande City Prosperity," *The San Antonio Light,* October 19, 1924, pt. 2, p. 5; *Mercantile Agency Reference Book, State Pocket Edition, Texas, 1932,* 645.

32. *In re: Juan Acevedo,* Laredo Case No. 135 (1934); *Manuscript Census,* Webb County, 1930; *In re: Francisco Farías,* Laredo Case No. 157 (1938).

33. US Bureau of the Census, *Fourteenth Census, Agriculture,* vol. VI, part 2, 683, 685; US Bureau of the Census, *Fifteenth Census, Agriculture,* 1399, 1401. For evidence of Mexicans leasing land and working as tenant farmers, see *In re: Antonio Barreda,* Brownsville Case No. 565 (1935) and *Gaston, Pierre, and Robert Block,* Brownsville Case No. 628 (1936).

34. State Tax Rolls, Zapata County, 1930, TXSLA; *US Census of Agriculture, Texas, First Series,* 75–78. Rates dropped to 16 percent in Zapata County and to 23 percent in Starr County.

35. Transcript of Creditors' Meeting, pp. 5–6, *In re: Donato Saldivar,* Brownsville Case No. 77 (1921); *In re: D. Benavides & Sons,* Brownsville Case No. 22 (1915) (Cameron County); Transcript of Creditors' Meeting, *In re: Eutiquio Pérez,* Brownsville Case No. 31 (1915) (Cameron County); *In re: C. C. Yznaga and O. A. Yznaga,* Brownsville Case No. 69 (Cameron County) (1921). For more examples of landowners and ranchers operating small businesses, see *In re: Feliciana Cisneros de Rotge,* Brownsville Case No. 571 (1935) (Cameron, Kleberg, Jim Wells counties); *In re: Calixta Salinas de Muniz joined pro forma by her husband, Leopoldo Muniz, Sr.,* Brownsville Case No. 591 (1936) (Starr County); *In re: Pedro Salinas,* Case No 592 (1936) (Starr County); *In re: Fidel Salinas,* Case No. 596 (1936) (Starr County).

36. Arreola, *Tejano South Texas,* 45–55; García, *Rise of the Mexican-American Middle Class,* 3–4; Gutiérrez, *Walls and Mirrors,* 44. Every Mexican businessperson whose origins I could trace was from Tamaulipas, Nuevo León, Coahuila, or San Luis Potosí. See also Alonzo, "Orígenes de una sociedad economía binacional," 74. For migration statistics in the Winter Garden region, see Taylor, *Mexican Labor in the United States,* 26–36. See Appendix 1 for numbers of Hispanic business owners.

37. Bankruptcy records reveal that Hispanic businesspeople sold to ethnic Mexicans in the local area as well as in various parts of Mexico. For a sampling of these, see *In re: A. H. Dodier and Jose Dodier d/b/a A. H. Dodier & Bros.,* Laredo Case No. 54 (1923); *In re: D. Benavides & Sons,* Brownsville Case No. 22 (1915); *In re: Augustine D. Domínguez,* Laredo Case No. 51 (1923); *In re: Arturo, Martin, and Ludovico Volpe,* Laredo Case No. 125 (1932). *In re: Jesús R. Flores,* Laredo Case No. 70 (1925); *In re: Enrique González d/b/a González Furniture and Mattress Company,* Brownsville Case No. 398 (1931); *In re: Volpe Brothers, Arturo, Ludovico, and Martin Volpe,* Laredo Case No. 125 (1932); *In re: Jorge Luna, Luna Coffee Co.,* Brownsville Case No. 443 (1932). See also "Account Books, 1931–42," Papers of Manuel Guerra, UTPA. For examples of advertisements of cross-border businesses, see *El Cronista del Valle,* 1924–1930.

38. Transcript of Creditors' Meeting, *In re: Hijinio Salinas,* Brownsville Case No. 36 (1916); *In re: Sierra & Castillo,* Brownsville Case No. 21 (1914); Editorial Field Copy, Stanley H. Holm, P. W., Piedras Negras, Coahuila, Folder 1, County Material, Maverick County, Box 4J190, WPA Records, CAH; R. Taylor Cole, "The Mexican in Maverick County," Oliver Weeks Collection, LULAC General Collection, NLBC.

39. Young, "Red Men, Princess Pocahontas, and George Washington," 48–85.

40. Paul S. Taylor, "James Sullivan Interview, Field Notes," Folder 12:13, Carton 12, Paul Schuster Taylor Papers, BLUCB.

41. *Standard Blue Book of the United States of America, 1929–30,* 14. The Social Register is a section within the *Standard Blue Book.*

42. Buchenau, *Tools of Progress,* 96–97. *In re: Justo R. Guerra,* Brownsville Case No. 182 (1926); *In re: Ernest Fernandez,* Brownsville Case No. 269 (1929); *In re: José Martínez,* Brownsville Case No. 461 (1932); *In re: Zenón Peña,* Laredo Case No. 83 (1928).

43. *Standard Blue Book of the United States of America, 1925,* 122; *Standard Blue Book of the United States of America, 1929–30,* 88–89, 94.

44. *In re: Aurelia de Treviño,* Corpus Christi Case No. 88 (1922) (immigrated from Mexico), *Manuscript Census,* Duval County, 1920; *Manuscript Census,* San Antonio, Bexar County, 1930; *In re: Mrs. Guillarmina G. Marques,* Brownsville Case No. 390 (1931); *In re: Feliciana Cisneros de Rotge,* Brownsville Case Nos. 571 and 583 (1935); *In re: Mrs. Eliza Martínez de Richer,* Laredo Case No. 164 (1940) (immigrated from Mexico in 1914), *Manuscript Census,* Webb County, 1930; *In re: Luz González de Baldearina,* Brownsville Case No. 62 (1920); *In re: Felicidad Gutiérrez de Lockwood,* Laredo Case No. 165 (1941).

45. Arreola, *Tejano South Texas,* 83–87; Sanborn Maps, Del Rio 1924, 7, CAH.

46. For some examples of inventories revealing types of goods carried, see *In re: Nicéforo Buitrón,* Laredo Case No. 11 (1902); *In re: Marcial Treviño,* Del Rio Case No. 1 (1906); *In re: Guadalupe Medrano,* Del Rio Case No. 15 (1913); *In re: Santos Ruiz Vasques,* Del Rio Case No. 88 (1932); *In re: Gregorio Sosa,* Brownsville Case No. 63 (1920). Customer lists reveal that Mexican merchants sold primarily to ethnic Mexicans, and in several of the cases, they identified their customers as primarily farm laborers. *In re: Julian Villarreal,* Brownsville Case No. 43 (1917) (Harlingen); *In re: Higinio Cantú,* Brownsville Case No. 50 (1918) (Raymondville); *In re: Guadalupe González Benavides,* Brownsville Case No. 146 (1924) (Mission); *In re: Juan Bautista Galaviz,* Del Rio Case No. 80 (1931) (Del Rio); *In re: Santos Ruiz Vasques,* Del Rio Case No. 88 (1932) (Uvalde); *In re: Melquiades García,* Laredo Case No. 103 (1931). Stephen Haber discusses the consumer market of Mexico and contrasts it with the more expansive ones in Europe and the United States in *Industry and Underdevelopment,* 29–31.

47. "Catarina: In the Heart of the Winter Garden District of Southwest Texas"; "Gulf Coast Country"; Wallace Thompson, "Trading with Mexico: Markets, Credits, Laws," Folder: National Association for the Protection of American Rights in Mexico, Letters, Box 17, Quichimis Colony Records, HLSC.

48. Paul S. Taylor, "Field Notes," Folder 12:23, Carton 12, Paul Schuster Taylor Papers, BLUCB.

49. Letter from Paul H. Frier, Acting Camp Manager, to W. A. Canon, Assistant Regional Director, Farm Resettlement Administration, May 3, 1941, Farm Resettlement Administration Records, Record Group 96, NARA.

50. Domosh, "Selling Civilization."

51. Paredes, *George Washington Gómez,* 155–56.

52. González, *Culture of Empire,* 75–83; Montejano, *Anglos and Mexicans in the Making of Texas,* 162–63, 223–26.

53. García, *Mexican Americans,* 27; Taylor, "Field Notes, December 10, 1928."

54. Miller, Esteban García interview; Miller, Ramón Guerra interview.

55. Miller, Dr. Octavío García interview.

56. Rubén R. Lozano, "LULAC Subsidiaries," October 1932, 1.

57. Walsh, *Building the Borderlands,* 98–104, 123–34; "Home Seekers Enter Mexico to Buy Lands," *Eagle Pass Daily Guide,* January 9, 1931, 1.

58. García, *Rise of the Mexican-American Middle Class,* 4–15, 253–54; Tomás A. Garza, "Food for Thought," *LULAC News,* October 1931, 4, LULAC Archives, NLBLC; "Latin-US Group Form Service Body," *Brownsville Herald,* September 22, 1929; Alonso Perales, "The Unification of the Mexican American," Box 1, Folder 13, Oliver Weeks Collection, *La Prensa,* September 6, 1929, LULAC Archives, NLBC. For a complete study of the League of United Latin American Citizens and its role as a civil rights organization, see Orozco, *No Mexicans, Women, or Dogs Allowed.*

59. "Are Texas-Mexicans 'Americans'?" *LULAC News,* April 1932, 7–8, LULAC Archives, NLBLC; J. T. Canales, "The Romans of Today," *LULAC News,* February 1932, 5, LULAC Archives, NLBLC; Tomás A. Garza, "LULAC a Future Power," *LULAC News,* February 1932, LULAC Archives, NLBLC.

60. Monroy, *Rebirth,* 259; Mora-Torres, *Making of the Mexico Border,* 200–204.

61. Andrés de Luna, "Letter to Public Forum Chronicle, Corpus Christi, Texas," and "Letter from Alonso S. Perales to Ben Garza, June 22, 1928," Folder 3, Box 1, Andrés de Luna Collection, LULAC General Collection, NLBC; Ezequiel D. Salinas, "The Need for LULAC," *LULAC News,* October 1937, LULAC Archives, NLBC; Stock, *Main Street in Crisis,* 41–62.

62. "Ben Garza Spent Life in Hard Work and Activity for Civic Betterment," *LULAC News,* March 1937, LULAC Archives, NLBC; "Ramón L. Longoria," *LULAC News,* July 1937, 5–6.

63. N. Aguilar, "Salesmanship," *LULAC News,* October 1931, 11–12, LULAC Archives, NLBC; Evaristo G. Ruiz, "True Salesmanship," *LULAC News,* December 1932, 11, LULAC Archives, NLBC.

64. Anonymous, "An Ideal LULAC Family," Box 1, Folder 12, Alicia Dickerson Montemayor Papers, LULAC General Collection, NLBC.

65. Orozco, *No Mexicans, Women, or Dogs Allowed,* 221–30.

CHAPTER 6: ACCESSING CREDIT

1. Transcript of Creditors' Meeting, pp. 2–3, Schedule A-3, *In re: Garza and Muñoz, Antonio Garza and Donato Cortez Muñoz,* Del Rio Case No. 82 (1931); *Manuscript Census,* Del Rio, 1930.

2. Balleisen, *Navigating Failure,* 26–28; Cassis and Collier, *Capitals of Capital,* 73; Haber, Maurer, and Razo, *Politics of Property Rights,* 79–80; Schumpeter, *Theory of Economic Development,* 95–115. For information on Mexico's credit industry, see Maurer, *Power and the Money.*

3. Chandler, *Visible Hand,* 209–39; Cronon, *Nature's Metropolis,* 325–26; Moeckel, *Development of the Wholesaler,* 13–20, 65–73, 81–90, 142–52; Olegario, *Culture of Credit,* 21–9.

4. Transcript of Hearing on Fraud Claim of Central Shoe Company against Sierra and Castillo, *In re: Sierra and Castillo,* Brownsville Case No. 21(1914); Chandler, *Visible Hand,* 219–20; Moeckel, *Development of the Wholesaler,* 142–43.

5. R. G. Dun & Co., "Mercantile Agency's Reporter's Manuel," R. G. Dun & Co. Collection, BLHBC; Norris, *R. G. Dun & Co., 1841–1900,* 34, 40–41, 47, 57–59, 92.

6. Chandler, *Visible Hand,* 215–24, 282–83; Hansen, "Commercial Associations," 86–91.

7. George F. Hoar, R-Massachusetts, 49th Cong., 1st Sess., 17 *Congressional Record* 4853–54 (1886). A brief account of Senator Hoar's role in negotiating and passing the Bankruptcy Act of 1898 may be found in Hoar, *Autobiography of Seventy Years,* vol. 2, 300–303. For a study of creditor's roles in the passage of the bankruptcy act, see Hansen, "Commercial Associations," 86–87, 91; Hansen, "Origins of Bankruptcy Law."

8. Friedman, *American Law in the Twentieth Century,* 386–87; Merkel, "Origins of an Expanded Federal Court Jurisdiction"; Zelden, *Justice Lies in the District,* 34.

9. An Act to establish a uniform system of bankruptcy throughout the United States, ch. 541, 30 Stat. 544 (1898); Annual Report of the Attorney General, 56th Cong., 2nd Sess., House Doc. 9, Exec. Docs. 4121 (1900), 388; Annual Report of the Attorney General, 58th Cong., 3rd Sess., House Doc. 9, Exec. Docs. 4811 (1904), 155–56; Annual Report of the Attorney General, 59th Cong., 1st Sess., Exec. Docs. 4970, Exhibit 4 (1905), 94.

10. See Bankruptcy Schedules, *In re: Henry Stein,* San Antonio Case No. 87 (1899); *In re: Louis Lindheim,* San Antonio Case No. 258 (1903); *In re: Mrs. Louis Pasco,* Laredo Case No. 11 (1902); *In re: Henry W. Earnest, Harry G. Earnest, and Josephine Earnest,* Laredo Case No. 16 (1904); *In re: Guadalupe Cuevas,* Laredo Case No. 25 (1907); *In re: José Martínez d/b/a Martínez Drug Store,* Brownsville Case No. 461 (1932).

11. Schedule A-3, *In re: The Franklin Bros. Co., Inc.,* Laredo Case No. 122 (1932). Harris, *Merchant Princes,* 201, 207; Ornish, *Pioneer Jewish Texans,* 73–76; Lehman Sanger, "A History of the Firm of Sanger Brothers," Folder 6: People by Occupation, Merchants, Box 3A168, TJHS. For more information about Jewish cross-country supply networks, see Olegario, *Culture of Credit,* 120–27.

12. Cuéllar, "House of Armengol"; Green, *Border Biographies, vol. 1,* 3–5. For examples of lending by these suppliers, see Schedule A-3 in the following cases: *In re: Guadalupe Cantú,* Brownsville Case No. 411 (1931); *In re: Porfirio Villanueva,* Brownsville Case No. 199 (1927); *In re: Justo R. Guerra,* Brownsville Case No. 182 (1926); *In re: Eustalio Peña,* Brownsville Case No. 191, (1926); *In re: Antonio Alonso,* Brownsville Case No. 161 (1924); *In re: H. C. Stephens,* Brownsville Case No. 34 (1915); *In re: David Chapa,* Brownsville Case No. 24 (1915); *In re: Joseph Veltmann,* San Antonio Case No. 148 (1900); *In re: James Bird Cavender,* San Antonio Case No. 173 (1901); *In re: George Warren Ames,* San Antonio Case No. 290 (1904).

13. Norris, *R. G. Dun & Co., 1841–1900,* 34, 40–41, 47, 57–59, 92–93, 157. Letter from R. G. Dun & Co. to J. E. Buckley, October 3, 1910, *In re: J. E. Buckley,* Brownsville Case No. 5 (1911). Mercantile agencies asked Edward Sisk for a statement of his assets and liabilities in 1904. Transcript of Creditors' Meeting, *In re: Edward D. Sisk,* Laredo Case No. 18 (1904). Unfortunately, it does not appear that R. G. Dun's records of the creditworthiness of borrowers in Mexico have survived. Librarians at the Baker Library, which houses the R. G. Dun Collection, have no records or reference books for Mexico.

14. Olegario, *Culture of Credit,* 115.

15. *In re: Eustaquio Vallejo and Ma. de los Angeles Castellanos Vallejo,* Brownsville Case No. 265 (1932); *In re: DC Decker d/b/a Decker's Grocery & Market,* Brownsville

Case No. 449 (1932). During the period from 1898 to 1941, 138 bankruptcy cases filed by Tejano and Mexican merchants reveal that they borrowed from a wide variety of suppliers across the United States. More illustrative examples include *In re: Bruno Rios*, Corpus Christi Case No. 23 (1914); *In re: F. G. Vela*, Corpus Christi Case No. 67 (1918); *In re: A. Ancira*, Laredo Case No. 53 (1923); *In re: Celestino and Hilario Gomez d/b/a S. Gomez & Sons*, Brownsville Case No. 302 (1929).

16. Transcript of Creditors' Meeting, pp. 33–35, *In re: Guadalupe Cuevas*, Laredo Case No. 25 (1907); *In re: Oscar Sommer*, Brownsville Case 455 (1932).

17. Transcript of Creditors' Meeting, pp. 6–14, 21–22, *In re: G. W. Cook*, Brownsville Case No. 74 (1921).

18. Schedule A-3, *In re: Oscar Sommer*, Brownsville Case No. 455 (1932); Schedule A-3, *In re: Romulo Martínez*, Laredo Case No. 109 (1931). For other individuals who borrowed money from merchants in Mexico, see *In re: Flavio Vargas*, Laredo Case No. 48 (1921); *In re: Marcos M. Treviño*, Laredo No. 63 (1925); *In re: Donato Saldivar*, Brownsville Case No. 77 (1921); *In re: Vicente Cantú*, Brownsville Case No. 235 (1928); *In re: Luis E. García*, Brownsville Case No. 342 (1930).

19. Statistics are based on my database, which in turn is a compilation of statistics from *Dun & Bradstreet Reference Book, State Pocket Edition, Texas, 1938* and *Mercantile Agency Reference Book, Texas Pocket Edition, 190. In re: Mrs. Louis Pasco*, Laredo Case No. 11 (1902); *The Mercantile Agency Reference Book, State Pocket Edition, Texas, 1901*, 358; *In re: Mrs. D. P. Stoner*, Laredo Case No. 68 (1925); *In re: Mrs. Guillarmina Marques*, Brownsville Case No. 390 (1932); *The Mercantile Agency Reference Book, 1925*, 2744, 2791; *The Mercantile Agency Reference Book, State Pocket Edition, Texas, 1930*, 108; *The Mercantile Agency Reference Book, State Pocket Edition, Texas, 1932*, 87.

20. *The Mercantile Agency Reference Book, State Pocket Edition, Texas, 1901*, 75; *The Mercantile Agency Reference Book, 1918*, Texas, 12; *The Mercantile Agency Reference Book, 1925*, 2745; *The Mercantile Agency Reference Book, State Pocket Edition, Texas, 1930*, 526.

21. Leach, *Land of Desire*, 10–12.

22. Buenger, *But Also Good Business*, 16–17; Ericson, "Origins of the Texas Bill of Rights," 458–60; Freyer, *Producers and Capitalists*, 85–91.

23. Carlson, *Monetary and Banking History of Texas*, 51–52; *The Mercantile Agency Reference Book, State Pocket Edition, Texas, 1901*, 42; Monday and Vick, *Petra's Legacy*, 167; *In re: Louis Lindheim*, San Antonio Case No. 258 (1903).

24. *Manuscript Census*, Duval County, 1900; *In re: Margarito Lopez, Jesús Lopez, Francisco Lopez, and Pedro Lopez*, Laredo Case Nos. 2, 3, 4, 5 (1900); *In re: Martin and Petra Valadez*, Laredo Case No. 6 (1900).

25. Gressley, *Bankers and Cattlemen*, 183, 187–88, 208; Kerr, *Scottish Capital on the American Credit Frontier*, 1–2, 134, 183.

26. Gressley, *Bankers and Cattlemen*, 192–97; Kerr, *Scottish Capital on the American Credit Frontier*, 1–2, 132, 183.

27. Gressley, *Bankers and Cattlemen*, 195, 201–202; "Letter from H. P. Drought to William Mackensie, 19 April 1918," Alliance Trust Company, January 4, 1915–December 26, 1918, Box 15, H. P. Drought Collection, Institute of Texan Cultures, UTSA.

28. Lea, *King Ranch,* 498.

29. H. P. Drought: Northern Counties Investment Trust, Ltd., Loan Registers, Box 61, Loans 60 and 67; Loan Registers, Box 63, Loan 180, H. P. Drought Collection, UTPA. For numbers of Tejano borrowers, see Alonzo, *Tejano Legacy,* 237–38.

30. Letter from H. P. Drought to William Mackensie, January 13, 1915, "Alliance Trust Company, January 4, 1915–December 26, 1918," Box 15, H. P. Drought Collection, UTSA.

31. Loan Nos. 1300, 1336, 1371, Loan Registers, Box 75, H. P. Drought Collection, UTSA.

32. Buenger, *But Also Good Business,* 19, 39–44; Ericson, *Banks and Bankers in Early Texas,* 6–13; Adams, *Conflict and Commerce on the Rio Grande,* 115–16; Carlson, *Monetary and Banking History of Texas,* 21–22, 42, 50–54; "National Bank at Browns-ville," *Galveston Daily News,* May 3, 1891; *In re: William Andrew Bonnet,* Del Rio Case No. 2 (1908), and *In re: William Wallace Collier,* Del Rio Case No. 5 (1909), NARA.

33. See Schedule A-2, Creditors Holding Security, in the following cases: *In re: Rentfro Banton Creager,* Brownsville Case No. 553 (1935); *In re: Al Parker Securities, Inc.,* Brownsville Case No. 584 (1935); *In re: Celestino Barreda,* Brownsville Case No. 585 (1935).

34. Buenger, *But Also Good Business,* 40–49; Gressley, *Bankers and Cattlemen,* 143–45; *The Mercantile Agency Reference Book, 1918,* 81.

35. Buenger, *But Also Good Business,* 19, 39–41; Grant and Crum, *Development of State Chartered Banking in Texas,* 39. For a discussion of how national banks found ways around the restrictions and engaged in forms of indirect mortgage lending, see Keehn and Smiley, "Mortgage Lending by National Banks." For examples of the kinds of loans made to ranchers by national banks, see Schedule A(2), *In re: Samuel Alonzo Yates,* Laredo Case No. 41 (1917); Schedule A(2), *In re: James Wright McAda,* Laredo Case No. 59 (1924); Schedule A(2), *In re: Jessie Coward,* Corpus Christi Case No. 120 (1925); Schedule A(2), *In re: Jes Baker,* Del Rio Case No. 62 (1926); Schedule A(2), *In re: Ira Calloway and Winnie Louise Green,* Del Rio Case No. 108 (1935).

36. Buenger, *But Also Good Business,* 41, 49; Carlson, *Monetary and Banking History of Texas,* 50–51; Grant and Crum, *Development of State Chartered Banking in Texas,* 40–44. Texas allowed state-chartered banks in towns of fewer than 2,500 residents to begin with $10,000 in capital. In towns of 2,500 to 10,000, state banks had to have at least $25,000 to open. For cities with more than 20,000 inhabitants, a bank could not open until it had at least $100,000.

37. "Statistical Reports of the Banks of the Lower Rio Grande Valley," *Brownsville Herald,* September 5, 1913, 1; *The Mercantile Agency Reference Book, 1918,* Texas, 82; *The Mercantile Agency Reference Book, 1925,* 2834–42; *The Mercantile Agency Reference Book, State Pocket Edition, Texas, 1910,* 69–77.

38. "Advertisement, Brownsville Bank & Trust," *Brownsville Daily Herald,* October 13, 1913. For a discussion of the importance of local banks to a community, see Blackford, *History of Small Business in America,* 68.

39. "Alliance Trust Company, January 4, 1915–December 26, 1918." H. P. Drought

to W. D. McDougal, July 31, 1919, "Alliance Trust Company, December 27, 1918–June 2, 1921," Box 15, H. P. Drought & Co. Collection, UTSA; Benedict, *Farm Policies of the United States, 1790–1950,* 147–48; Carlson, *Monetary and Banking History of Texas,* 70.

40. *San Antonio Daily Express,* May 31, 1899, 6; *San Antonio Daily Express,* February 18, 1900, 18; Schedule A(2), *In re: Benjamin Avent Borroum,* San Antonio Case No. 308 (Del Rio, 1904); Schedule A(3), *In re: Albert Mitchell,* San Antonio Case No. 358 (Uvalde, 1905); Schedule A(2), *In re: John William Gallagher,* Laredo Case No. 17 (San Diego, 1904). Schedule A(2), *In re: Bub Davenport,* Del Rio Case No. 49 (1923); San Antonio Cattle Loan Company, Schedule A(2), *In re: John S. Strait,* San Antonio Case No. 1874.

41. See Schedule A-2, Creditors Holding Securities in *In re: Eleanor Petty Jennings,* Del Rio Case No. 46 (1923) and in *In re: Bub and Fred Davenport,* Del Rio Case Nos. 48 and 49 (1923), NARA. For another similar debt profile, see *In re: Robert Johnson Raney,* Del Rio Case No. 58 (1925), NARA.

42. *In re: Eusebio García,* Laredo Case No. 138 (1935); Green, *Border Biographies,* vol. 2, 39; *In re: F. G. Treviño, Albert G. Treviño, and Benito G. Treviño,* Laredo Case No. 158 (1938).

43. *In re: T. T. Margo,* Brownsville Case No. 15 (1914); *In re: José Maria Guerra,* Brownsville Case No. 761 (1940); *In re: Juan Acevedo,* Laredo Case No. 135 (1934); *In re: Francisco Farías,* Laredo Case No. 157 (1938).

44. *In re: José R. Salinas,* Brownsville Case No. 745 (1940); US Bureau of the Census, *Thirteenth Census, Agriculture,* vol. VII, 678–70; US Bureau of the Census, *Fourteenth Census, Agriculture,* vol. VI, part 2, 740–46; US Bureau of the Census, *Fifteenth Census, Agriculture,* vol. II, part 2, 1574–85.

45. Miller, James Franklin Ewers interview; US Bureau of the Census, *Fourteenth Census, Agriculture,* vol. VI, 740–46. For evidence of farmers borrowing from the land companies, see Excursion Box 1, JHSC, UTPA and Schedule A-2, Creditors Holding Securities, *In re: George Molby,* Brownsville Case No. 150 (1924); *In re: George Hackney,* Brownsville Case No. 249 (1928); *In re: Charles Woolf,* Brownsville Case No. 288 (1929). *In re: Ira Ragsdale,* Case No. 61 (Brownsville, 1920). For other examples of Anglo farmers borrowing from state banks, see Schedule A-2, Creditors Holding Securities and Schedule A-3, Creditors whose claims are unsecured, in the following cases: *In re: W. L. Bradbury,* Brownsville Case No. 55 (1920); *In re: Ira Ragsdale,* Brownsville Case No. 61 (1920); *In re: Steve Pfeiffer,* Brownsville Case No. 110 (1922); *In re: Frank P. Carl,* Brownsville Case No. 111 (1922); *In re: Leo Gaynor,* Brownsville Case No. 113 (1922); In re: J. W. Petrie, Brownsville Case No. 118 (1922). These only provide samples; there are many more farm cases involving loans from state banks.

46. *In re: H. O. Berset,* Brownsville Case No. 271 (1929); *In re: Steve Pfeiffer,* Brownsville Case No. 346 (1930). For the expansion of installment debt in the United States generally, see Calder, *Financing the American Dream,* 158–208.

47. For examples of loans by state and national banks to ethnic Mexicans, see the bankruptcy schedules in the following cases: *In re: C. C. Oznaga and O. A. Yznaga,* Brownsville Case No. 69 (1921) (Cameron County Bank of La Feria); *In re: Hijinio*

Salinas d / b / a Salinas Mercantile Co., Brownsville Case No. 36 (1916) (First National Bank of Brownsville); *In re: Cristóbal Rodríguez,* Brownsville Case No. 77 (1920) (First State Bank & Trust Co. of McAllen); *In re: Donato Saldivar,* Brownsville Case No. 86 (1921) (First National Bank of Brownsville); *In re: D. Benavides & Sons,* Brownsville Case No. 22 (1915) (Brownsville Bank & Trust Co.); *In re: Julian Villarreal,* Brownsville Case No. 43 (1917) (First National Bank of Brownsville, Merchants National Bank, Planters State Bank of Harlingen, State Bank & Trust of Brownsville); *In re: Alejandro Saenz,* Brownsville Case No. 75 (1921) (First State Bank & Trust Co.); *In re: Tomas Guerra,* Brownsville Case No. 209 (1927) (Capitol Sate Bank of Edinburg); *In re: Ernest Fernandez,* Brownsville Case No. 269 (1929) (First National Bank, State National Bank, Merchants National Bank, all of Brownsville); *In re: Manuel García Gomez,* Brownsville Case No. 739 (1940) (First National Bank of Brownsville).

48. Haber, "Industrial Concentration and Capital Markets." For a discussion of the connections between the Mexican government and banking during the Porfirian era, see Maurer and Gomberg, "When the State Is Untrustworthy."

49. Maurer, *Power and the Money,* 1–8, 18–19, 91, 100.

50. Reports of banking failures in Mexico appeared in a number of local newspapers. Associated Press, "Mexican Secretary Decries Reports of Financial Crisis: Bank Failures Declared Not to Foretell Panic," *San Antonio Light,* November 17, 1922, 14; "Politics Are Affected by Bank Failures: Financial Crisis in Mexico Accentuates Political Crisis," *San Antonio Light,* December 20, 1922, 20.

51. Individuals living in South Texas who borrowed money from Mexican institutions and financiers included the following: *In re: Flavio Vargas,* Laredo Case No. 48 (1921), *In re: Marcos M. Treviño,* Laredo Case No. 63 (1925); *In re: Romulo Martínez,* Laredo Case No. 109 (1931); *In re: Vicente Cantú,* Brownsville Case No. 235 (1928); *In re: Luis E. García,* Brownsville No. 342 (1930).

52. Grant, *Money of the Mind,* 107; William J. McAdoo, "Federal Reserve System, the 'Shock Absorber,' Proves to Be Nation's Credit Foundation after Years of Operation," *Dallas Morning News,* October 24, 1915; Grant and Crum, *Development of State Chartered Banking in Texas,* 114, 129–39; Miller, James Franklin Ewers interview.

53. *In re: Rafael Martínez,* Brownsville Case No. 78 (1928); "Man Assigns Assets after Bank Closes," *Dallas Morning News,* February 29, 1928, 2; "Ex-Bankers to Be Tried May 9," *Dallas Morning News,* April 11, 1928, 2; "Laredo Banker Faces Second Trial Monday," *Dallas Morning News,* December 2, 1929, 2.

54. "Suit to Collect Sum Lost in Bank Closing Is Filed," *Dallas Morning News,* August 10, 1932, 2; Schedules, *In re: Al Parker Securities Co.,* Brownsville Case No. 584 (1935).

55. "Suit to Collect Sum Lost in Bank Closing Is Filed"; Schedules, *In re: Al Parker Securities Co.,* Brownsville Case No. 584 (1935). Evidence of the bank failures was gathered from proofs of claim filed by the Texas banking commissioner or receiver for the various banks in the following cases: *In re: James Howze,* Brownsville Case No. 482 (1933); *In re: J. T. Taylor,* Brownsville Case No. 489 (1933); *In re: Moses and Patterson,* Brownsville Case No. 491 (1933); *In re: Roy Bertram Roberts,* Brownsville Case No. 492 (1933); *In re: Harper & Fitzgerald,* Brownsville Case No. 496 (1933); *In re: T. J. Mauck,*

Brownsville Case No. 524 (1934); *In re: Rentfro Banton Creager,* Brownsville Case No. 553 (1935); James Franklin Ewers interview; Ramon Guerra interview.

56. *Dun & Bradstreet Reference Book, State Pocket Edition, Texas, 1938,* 908–44.

57. "Over 300 Ask for Loans on 1935 Farming," *Eagle Pass Daily Guide,* April 20, 1935, 2. *In re: Francisco Farías,* Laredo Case No. 157 (1938); *In re: Francisco, Benito, and Alberto Treviño,* Laredo Case No. 158 (1938); Transcript of Testimonies, December 22, 1938, Testimony of Karl Duddleston, Secretary Treasurer of the Lyford & McAllen National Farm Loan Association, *In re: La Feria Water Control and Improvement District, Cameron County No. 3,* Brownsville Case No. 684 (1938).

58. Gressley, *Bankers and Cattlemen,* 142.

59. Tex. Const., art. XVI, § 15, interpret. commentary (Vernon 1993). The constitutional provision in force between 1898 and 1941 read as follows: "All property, both real and personal, of the wife, owned or claimed by her before marriage, and that acquired afterward by gift, devise or descent, shall be her separate property; and laws shall be passed more clearly defining the rights of the wife, in relation as well to her separate property as that held in common with her husband. Laws shall also be passed providing for the registration of the wife's separate property." The relevant statute in force at the time was Tex. Rev. Civ. Stat. art. 2851 (1879).

60. See the Transcript of Creditors' Meeting in the following cases: *In re: Oscar B. Kessler,* Del Rio Case No. 9 (1911); *In re: David Chapa,* Brownsville Case No. 24 (1915); *In re: Gregorio Sosa,* Brownsville Case No. 63 (1920); *In re: Mauricio Zertuche,* Del Rio Case No. 40 (1921), 11.

61. Goodman, "Emergence of the Homestead Exemption," 489. For examples of this, see *In re: Robert L. Skinner,* Brownsville Case No. 9 (1913); *In re: A. H. Allen,* Brownsville Case No. 158 (1924).

62. For example, see *In re: Will Collingwood,* Brownsville Case No. 766 (1940) (Mary C. Keslear was the primary creditor); *In re: Lex Hugh Clark,* Del Rio Case No. 33 (1918) (Cynthia Yates leased space to him in a building for his store); *In re: Zack Hancock Eppler,* San Antonio Case No. 850 (1921) (borrowed $2,400 from Mrs. R. S. Grantland to buy a truck); *In re: Lloyd Blair,* San Antonio Case No. 854 (1921) (borrowed money from Mrs. J. M. Benskin); *In re: Clinton Lafayette Smith,* San Antonio Case No. 1123 (1925) (also borrowed money from Mrs. J. M. Benskin); *In re: William T. Barnhouse,* Corpus Christi Case No. 29 (1915) (owed money to Mrs. R. O'Donnell); *In re: R. G. Leal,* Brownsville Case No. 134 (1923) (Josefina Longoria).

63. Green, *Guillermo Benavides Family,* 4, 26–35; Green, *Border Biographies,* vol. 2, 29–30. Examples of individuals who borrowed from Rosa and Teresa include *In re: Manuel Cruz,* Laredo Case No. 115 (1931); *In re: Volpe Brothers,* Laredo Case No. 125 (1932); *In re: Albert Urbahn,* Laredo Case No. 128 (1933); *In re: Juan Acevedo,* Laredo Case No. 135 (1934); *In re: Antonio Valls Armengol,* Laredo Case No. 136 (1934); *In re: Pablo Chapa,* Laredo Case No. 141 (1935).

64. Transcript of Creditors' Meeting, December 14, 1914, *In re: Miguel García Brownsville,* Case No. 14 (1914); Transcript of Creditors' Meeting, July 18, 1904, *In re: Edward Sisk,* Laredo Case No. 18 (1904).

65. J. T. Canales, "Usury," *LULAC News* 1, no. 12 (July 1932), 5, LULAC Archives, NLBC; Transcription of *El Paladin,* May 10, 1929, pp. 4–7, Box 1, Folder 10, Oliver Douglas Weeks Collection, LULAC General Collection, NLBC. For insight into attitudes about debt and credit in Texas in general, see "The Credit System," *Dallas Morning News,* February 19, 1890; "The Penalties of Extravagance and Debt," *Dallas Morning News,* February 6, 1911, 6; "The Curse of the Credit System," *Dallas Morning News,* January 4, 1901; "Housewife Opposed to Credit System," *Dallas Morning News,* January 13, 1914, 4.

66. "Credit and Helpfulness of the Mortgage System," *Dallas Morning News,* December 19, 1892; "Credit System a Necessity," *Dallas Morning News,* April 25, 1890; Alfonso Johnson, "Credit System Is of Great Benefit if Rightly Used," *Dallas Morning News,* June 22, 1924.

67. Calder, "From 'Consumptive' Credit to 'Consumer'"; Harry J. Steinbreder, "Why Installment Buying of Machinery Is Sound Business Practice," *Executive's Magazine,* February 1931, 17–18, 26, 28. Regarding the expansion of consumer credit, see Calder, *Financing the American Dream;* Hyman, *Debtor Nation.*

CHAPTER 7: FACING FAILURE

1. Statement of Facts, *In re: Joseph Netzer,* Laredo Case No. 50 (1923).

2. Sandage, *Born Losers,* 11. Small, independent businesses have always had a relatively high failure rate. Balleisen, *Navigating Failure,* 1–6; Sullivan, Warren, and Westbrook, *As We Forgive Our Debtors,* 108–21.

3. Olegario, *Culture of Credit,* 29.

4. *In re: George W. Cook,* Brownsville Case No. 74 (1921).

5. Transcript of Creditors' Meeting, *In re: Sam Greenfield,* Brownsville Case No. 73 (1921). He was not the only merchant who filed that year from the area. There were several others who probably experienced the same problems. *In re: B. A. Cropper,* Brownsville Case No. 67 (1921); *In re: E. L. Weatherford,* Brownsville Case No. 68 (1921); *In re: M. H. Haik,* Brownsville Case No. 70 (1921); *In re: Mrs. Donna Fletcher,* Brownsville Case No. 71 (1921); *In re: Forrest E. Hester,* Brownsville Case No. 72 (1921); *In re: George W. Cook,* Brownsville Case No. 74 (1921); *In re: Forrest Thorman,* Brownsville Case No. 78 (1921); *In re: Cam Hill and C. J. January,* Brownsville Case No. 79 (1921); *In re: J. H. Woodstock,* Brownsville Case No. 80 (1921). A total of twenty-three merchants from the lower Rio Grande Valley filed for bankruptcy in 1921.

6. *In re: Sierra and Castillo,* Brownsville Case No. 21 (1914).

7. Ibid.; *In re: Luz González de Balderina,* Brownsville Case No. 62 (1920). For more examples of small ethnic Mexican customer accounts, see Schedule B(3) in the following cases: *In re: D. Benavides & Sons,* Brownsville Case No. 22 (1915); *In re: Porfirio Villanueva,* Brownsville Case No. 199 (1927); *In re: Marcial Treviño,* Del Rio Case No. 1 (1906); *In re: Manuel Cortes Muñoz and Consuelo Paredes de Muñoz,* Del Rio Case No. 123 (1938); *In re: Zaragoza Domínguez,* Laredo Case No. 89 (1929); *In re: Donaciano Castillo,* Brownsville Case No. 137 (1923); *In re: Celestino and Hilario Gomez,* Brownsville Case No. 302 (1929).

8. *In re: Eutiquio Pérez,* Brownsville Case No. 31 (1915).

9. González, "America Invades the Border Towns"; Transcript of Creditors' Meeting, Schedule A-3, *In re: Garza and Muñoz, Antonio Garza and Donato Cortez Muñoz,* Del Rio Case No. 82 (1931).

10. *In re: Mrs. Louis Pasco,* Laredo Case No. 11 (1902); *In re: Pedro Zavaleta,* Brownsville Case No. 141 (1923); *In re: Isadore Goodman,* Laredo Case No. 110 (1931). "$26,000 Loss Sustained in Laredo Warehouse Fire," *Dallas Morning News,* May 22, 1919; "Fire Record," *Dallas Morning News,* March 25, 1905; "Fire Record: Big Fire at Laredo," *Dallas Morning News,* December 26, 1902; "Texas Fire Losses Are High," *Laredo Times,* October 1, 1931, 2.

11. *In re: Guadalupe Medrano,* Del Rio Case Nos. 14 and 15 (1913); *In re: Manuel Cortes Muñoz and Consuelo Paredes Muñoz,* Del Rio Case No. 123 (1938); *In re: Rafael Rangel,* Laredo Case No. 10 (1902): December 17, 1936; letter from Mrs. Strawbridge to R. L. Rowland, *In re: W. P. and Lucile Strawbridge,* Brownsville Case No. 597 (1936); *In re: August Linnard,* Brownsville Case No. 539 (1934); *In re: Max Tavss,* Brownsville Case No. 610 (1936); Transcript of Creditors' Meeting, pp. 21–22, *In re: G. W. Cook,* Brownsville Case No. 74 (1921).

12. *In re: Narciso Alanis,* Laredo Case No. 47 (1920); *In re: Flavio Vargas,* Laredo Case No. 48 (1921).

13. Lea, *King Ranch,* 593; "Only Big Rains Can Save Texas Cattle," *Dallas Morning News,* September 19, 1917; Schlebecker, *Cattle Raising on the Plains,* 61–62.

14. Transcript of Creditors' Meeting, July 20, 1917, pp. 14–15, 31–32, *In re: S. M. Hargrove,* Brownsville Case No. 46 (1917); Transcript of Creditors' Meeting, July 20, 1917, pp. 14–15, 31–32, *In re: S. M. Hargrove,* Brownsville Case No. 46 (1917); letter from Dario Sanchez to John C. Scott, August 6, 1917, *In re: Samuel Alonzo Yates,* Laredo Case No. 41 (1917); Transcript of Creditors' Meeting, *In re: Lee Dillon,* San Antonio Case No. 1282 (1928).

15. *In re: Salvador A. Armstrong,* San Antonio Case No. 992 (1923); Machado, "Mexican Revolution"; "Proclamation for Quarantine Signed," *Dallas Morning News,* February 2, 1922; Clark, "Texas Fever in Oklahoma."

16. "Cotton Boll Weevil," *San Antonio Daily Light,* January 19, 1898, 1; Delcurto, Halstead, and Halstead, "Citrus Industry in the Lower Rio Grande Valley"; "Farm Cooperative Work and the Citrus Fruit Industry," *Brownsville Herald,* December 1, 1914, 11; "Ridding Valley of the Boll Weevil," *Brownsville Herald,* June 13, 1919, 6; "Statewide War on Boll Weevil Is Inaugurated," *Brownsville Herald,* September 18, 1922, 1; "Texas Vegetable Shipments Show Big Increase," *Laredo Times,* January 19, 1931.

17. Transcript of Creditors' Meeting, June 29, 1923, p. 4, *In re: Bub and Fred Davenport,* Case Nos. 48 and 49 (1923).

18. Danbom, *Born in the Country,* 186–87; Transcript of Creditors' Meeting, June 29, 1923, p. 4, *In re: Bub and Fred Davenport,* Case Nos. 48 and 49 (1923); Lasater, *Falfurrias,* 205, 243, 253–55; H. P. Drought to W. D. Macdougal, November 28, 1922, Alliance Trust Company Correspondence 1922, MS 69, Box 16, H. P. Drought Collection, UTPA.

19. *Dun & Bradstreet Reference Book, State Pocket Edition, Texas, 1938,* 400; *The*

Mercantile Agency Reference Book, 1925, 2791; *The Mercantile Agency Reference Book, Texas Edition, 1930,* 106–107.

20. Mann, *Republic of Debtors,* 255–63.

21. Blackford, *History of Small Business in America,* 70; Chandler, *Visible Hand; In re: Guadalupe Medrano,* Del Rio Case Nos. 14 and 15 (1913); Transcript of Creditors' Meeting, p. 4, *In re: Don Lázaro Champion,* Brownsville Case No. 40 (1917); *In re: G. W. Cook,* Brownsville Case No. 74 (1921); *In re: Eloy Peña,* San Antonio Case No. 2011 (1938).

22. Transcript of Creditors' Meeting, *In re: Arthur Joel Chaney,* Brownsville Case No. 783 (1941); Transcript of Creditors' Meeting, pp. 2–3, 15, *In re: Richard Masters,* Del Rio Case No. 67 (1927). For more examples of bankruptcy filings of former merchants who failed at farming, see *In re: Valerius Dietrich,* Brownsville Case No. 642 (1937); *Manuscript Census,* Albany, Pennsylvania, 1920. *In re: Ed Maule,* Brownsville Case No. 163 (1924); *Manuscript Census,* Hidalgo County, 1920.

23. *In re: David Chapa,* Brownsville Case No. 364 (1931).

24. M. Coppard, "Report of Investigation in the Matter of Raymond Palmer Saylor," *In re: Raymond Saylor,* Del Rio Case No. 38 (1921); Transcript of Creditors' Meeting, pp. 5–6, *In re: Guadalupe Cuevas,* Laredo Case No. 25(1907); Transcript of Creditors Meeting, December 2, 1920, p. 16, *In re: Gregorio Sosa,* Brownsville Case No. 63 (1920).

25. Transcript of Creditors' Meeting, p. 24, *In re: Mauricio Zertuche,* Del Rio Case No. 40 (1921).

26. Transcript of Creditors' Meeting, p. 7, *In re: A. Schmidt & Co.,* Laredo Case No. 8 (1900).

27. Letter to Postmaster General William H. Hays signed by more than six hundred farmers, August 16, 1921, Simmons Exhibit 1, Transcript of Testimony of Rush D. Simmons, p. 68, Folder 51: US Senate Hearings, alleged land fraud in Cameron and Hidalgo counties, Texas, Box 3, Series 6: Legal Actions and Lawsuits, 1917–1940, JHSC, UTPA.

28. Simmons Exhibit 1, Transcript of Testimony of Rush D. Simmons, March 24, 1924, pp. 72–88, Folder 51: US Senate Hearings, alleged land fraud in Cameron and Hidalgo counties, Texas, Box 3, Series 6: Legal Actions and Lawsuits, 1917–1940, JHSC, UTPA; F. O. Alin, Fullerton, North Dakota to J. M. Donaldson, Post Office, Kansas City, MO, April 6, 1921, Transcript of Testimony of Rush D. Simmons, March 25, 1924, p. 348, Folder 54: US Senate Hearings, alleged land fraud in Cameron and Hidalgo counties, Texas, Box 3, Series 6: Legal Actions and Lawsuits, 1917–1940, JHSC, UTPA.

29. Testimony of Rush D. Simmons, March 25, 1924, pp. 247–8, Folder 53: US Senate Hearings, alleged land fraud in Cameron and Hidalgo counties, Texas, Box 3, Series 6: Legal Actions and Lawsuits, 1917–1940, JHSC, UTPA.

30. Transcript of Testimony of Rush D. Simmons, March 25, 1924, p. 244, Folder 53: US Senate Hearings, alleged land fraud in Cameron and Hidalgo counties, Texas, Box 3, Series 6: Legal Actions and Lawsuits, 1917–1940, JHSC, UTPA.

31. Transcript of Testimony of Rush D. Simmons, March 24, 1924, p. 138, Folder 52: US Senate Hearings, alleged land fraud in Cameron and Hidalgo counties, Texas, Box 3, Series 6: Legal Actions and Lawsuits, 1917–1940, JHSC, UTPA; Transcript of

Testimony of Rush D. Simmons, March 25, 1924, p. 250, Folder 53: US Senate Hearings, alleged land fraud in Cameron and Hidalgo counties, Texas, Box 3, Series 6: Legal Actions and Lawsuits, 1917–1940, JHSC, UTPA.

32. Miller, James Franklin Ewers interview. Ewers was the attorney who handled many of these cases.

33. John Weber, "Shadow of the Revolution," 96–97.

34. Zelden, *Justice Lies in the District,* 135. For information about how the Depression affected agriculture, see Danbom, *Born in the Country,* 185–99. For the origins and impact of the Great Depression on a national level, see Galbraith, *Great Crash, 1929;* Kennedy, *Freedom from Fear;* McElvaine, *Great Depression.*

35. Testimony of J. T. Wise, chief deputy tax assessor of Webb County, Transcript of Creditors' Meeting, *In re: Franklin Brothers, Inc.,* Laredo Case No. 99 (1931).

36. "Calles to Reach Border in a Few Days," *Laredo Times,* December 11, 1929; "Relations of Two Laredos at Normal," *Laredo Times,* December 27, 1929, 1; "Valls Refuses to Grant Immunity," *Laredo Times,* December 13, 1929.

37. "Business Men Have Backs to Wall," *Laredo Times,* December 30, 1929, 1; "Meeting Called Monday in Effort to Solve Business Situation," *Laredo Times,* December 29, 1929, 1.

38. "50 Percent Drop in Business Here," *Laredo Times,* December 19, 1929, 1; "Attorney Says Mexico Can't Dictate," *Laredo Times,* December 18, 1929, 1; "No Action on Consulate Taken," *Laredo Times,* December 18, 1929, 1; "Merchants of Monterrey Complain," *Laredo Times,* December 19, 1; "Santibanez Appeals to Governor Moody," *Laredo Times,* December 20, 1929, 1; "Valls Answers Estrada Statement," *Laredo Times,* December 24, 1929, 1; "Meeting Hall Overflows as Laredoans Gather to Solve Business Crisis," *Laredo Times,* December 31, 1929, 1; "Laredo Port Opens Friday," *Eagle Pass Daily Guide,* January 15, 1930, 1.

39. Testimony of Mose Franklin, Transcript of March 7, 1931 hearing, *In re: Franklin Brothers, Inc.,* Laredo Case No. 99 (1931); State Tax Rolls, Webb County, Summary of Property and Values thereof, 1930, 1936, and 1940, TXSLA; Tom Lillie, "Five Wells Completed in Active Week in Laredo District," *Laredo Times,* December 8, 1929, 4.

40. Transcript of March 7, 1931 hearing, *In re: Franklin Brothers, Inc.,* Laredo Case Nos. 122 and 123 (1932); *In re: Shapu & Frelich,* Laredo Case No. 134 (1934); *In re: Manuel Cruz,* Laredo Case No. 114 (1931) and *In re: Francisco Vizcaya Ibañez,* Laredo Case No. 118 (1932); Transcript of Evidence, *In re: Carlos Otal,* Laredo Case No. 121 (1932). Ibañez was a one-half owner of the wholesale house J. Armengol.

41. *In re: Laredo Robert E. Lee Hotel, Inc.,* Laredo Case No. 112 (1932); *In re: John O. Buenz Lumber Company,* Laredo Case No. 116 (1932); Green, *Border Biographies,* vol. 2, 13–14; *In re: James K. Kepley,* Laredo Case No. 86 (1929); *In re: Kepley Production Company,* Laredo Case No. 130 (1936); *In re: James K. Kepley,* Laredo Case No. 137 (1935). Kepley was called one of the "finest, fastest oil men in this great oil state." "Kepley, an Oil Man and Aviator," *Laredo Times,* special edition, November 23, 1937; *In re: Texas Gas Utilities,* Del Rio Case Nos. 100 and 114 (1934 and 1936).

42. "Fall Shearing Season Opens," *Eagle Pass Daily Guide,* August 26, 1931; Miller, Esteban García interview; Miller, Ramon Guerra interview; "Ranch Owners Secured

Valuation of $7 Acre," *Eagle Pass Daily Guide,* June 24, 1931; "Texas Sheepmen See Better Times Ahead," *Eagle Pass Daily Guide,* January 7, 1931; *In re: Albert Urbahn,* Laredo Case No. 128 (1933); *In re: Eusebio Garcia,* Laredo Case No. 138 (1935). Examples of other ranching bankruptcies in the 1930s include *In re: Mack Henry Gobble,* Del Rio Case No. 77 (1930); *In re: Roy Jack Davenport,* Del Rio Case No. 89 (1932); *In re: Frank Otis Landrum,* Del Rio Case No. 103 (1934); *In re: Jones and Montgomery,* Del Rio Case No. 104 (1934); *In re: William Albert Humphreys,* Del Rio Case No. 107 (1935); *In re: Ira and Winnie Green,* Del Rio Case No. 108 (1935); *In re: James Murrah,* Del Rio Case No. 116 (1936).

43. "Laredo Will Ship Citrus in Carlots," *Dallas Morning News,* September 4, 1929; "Webb County Citrus Association Elects," *Dallas Morning News,* July 5, 1928; *In re: Antonio Valls Armengol,* Laredo Case No. 136 (1934); *In re: James G. Sullivan,* San Antonio Case No. 1553 (1931).

44. Dobie, *Cow People,* 143.

45. "García, Eusebio," Vertical Files, CAH; Green, *Border Biographies,* vol. 2, 39; "Los Ojuelos Ranch Owner Succumbs"; *In re: Eusebio García,* Laredo Case No. 138 (1935); Texas State Tax Rolls, Webb County, 1940, TXSLA.

46. There were 486 cases filed in Brownsville between 1930 and 1941, 70 in Laredo, and 60 in Del Rio. For descriptions of the conditions in the area, see Bankruptcy Petition, *In re: Robb Hotel Company,* Brownsville Case No. 543 (1934); Bankruptcy Petition, *In re: Cameron County Water Improvement District No. 1,* Brownsville Case No. 520 (1934); Transcript of Creditors' Meeting, *In re: Emmett Houston Kasey,* Brownsville Case No. 515 (1934).

47. "Land Boom from 1922 to 1930 in Valley Was More like Gold Rush," *Brownsville Herald,* Cameron County Scrapbook, Folder 4, Box 3L117, WPA Records, CAH; State Tax Rolls, Cameron County, 1930, 1933, 1935, and 1940, Hidalgo County, 1930, 1933, 1935, and 1940, and Starr County, 1930, 1935, and 1940, TXSLA.

48. For information about price declines for fruit, see Petition, *In re: Cameron County Water Improvement District No. 1,* Brownsville Case No. 520 (1934); "Fruit Market Dull in Texas," *Eagle Pass Daily Guide,* September 18, 1931. For lists of delinquent taxpayers, see the *Hidalgo County Independent,* January 15, 1932. For more information about uncollected taxes, see Transcript of Appellate Record, filed May 31, 1938, p. 9, *In re: Edinburg Consolidated Independent School District,* Brownsville Case No. 671 (1937); Transcript of Testimonies, December 22, 1938, Testimony of Matthew Moore, President and General Manager of La Feria Water Control and Improvement District No. 3, pp. 39–46, *In re: La Feria Water Control and Improvement District, Cameron County No. 3,* Brownsville Case No. 684 (1938). *In re: Valley Gin Company,* Brownsville Case Nos. 551 and 728 (1935 and 1939).

49. For a general discussion of the effect of bank failures on mortgages, see Danbom, *Born in the Country,* 201–202. For information about foreclosures and bankruptcies, see Transcript of Creditors' Meeting, p. 38, Herbert Van Vliet, Brownsville Case No. 660 (1937); Transcript of Creditors' Meeting, p. 7, *In re: James Fisher McClintock,* Brownsville Case No. 635 (1937); Transcript of Testimonies, December 22,

1938, Testimony of Karl Duddleston, Secretary-Treasurer of the Lyford and McAllen Farm Loan Association, p. 92, *In re: La Feria Water Control and Improvement District, Cameron County No. 3,* Brownsville Case No. 684 (1938). For descriptions of the difficulties of ordinary people and reversion to a system of barter and exchange, see Miller, James Franklin Ewers interview; Miller, Ramon Guerra interview; Trisha Williams, Mrs. Crockett interview, oral history tape recording, Hidalgo County, Texas, 1985, LRGV, UTPA.

50. Hearing Transcript, December 22, 1938, Testimony of Ralph Agar, pp. 148–149, *In re: La Feria Water Control and Improvement District, Cameron County No. 3,* Brownsville Case No. 684 (1938); *In re: Al Parker Securities,* Brownsville Case No. 584 (1935) and *In re: Al Francis Parker,* Brownsville Case No. 668 (1937); *In re: Rentfro Banton Creager,* Brownsville Case No. 553 (1935); *In re: Nick Doffing Company,* Brownsville Case Nos. 604 and 621 (1936).

51. "Time Is Here When Creditors and Debtors Must Unite," *Hidalgo County Independent,* January 27, 1933, 1.

52. Bankruptcy Petition, *In re: Robb Hotel Company,* Brownsville Case No. 543 (1934); Bankruptcy Petition, *In re: Cameron County Water Improvement District No. 1,* Brownsville Case No. 520 (1934); Transcript of Creditors' Meeting, *In re: Emmett Houston Kasey,* Brownsville Case No. 515 (1934); Bankruptcy Petition, p. 6, *In re: Rio Grande Valley Gas Company,* Brownsville Case No. 574 (1935); *In re: Valley Gin Company,* Brownsville Case No. 551 (1935).

53. Transcript of Trial, October 15, 1936, p. 22, *In re: Nick Doffing Co.,* Brownsville Case No. 621 (1936).

54. "Hurricane Due to Hit Coast Today," *Edinburg Daily Review,* September 4, 1933; "Reporter Recalls 1933 Labor Day Hurricane," *Edinburg Daily Review,* August 18, 1983; Rocio Patricia Rodríguez, Henrietta Kassabaum interview, oral history tape recording, Hidalgo County, Texas, June 24, 1987, LRGV; UTPA.

55. "Haven't Lost Faith, Says Non-Resident Owner Visiting Here," *Edinburg Daily Review,* September 7, 1933; Norton, Elma Krumdieck Koch Dutschman interview; Norton, Howard Millen interview; Transcript of Creditors' Meeting, *In re: Peter and Clara Dicken,* Brownsville Case No. 658 (1937).

56. 1933 Letter from Emmett Houston Kasey to McKesson Drug Company, *In re: Emmett Houston Kasey,* Brownsville Case No. 515 (1934).

57. Ralph Agar, Tax Assessor, Testimony, December 22, 1933, pp. 102, 118–19, *In re: La Feria Water Control and Improvement District, Cameron County No. 3,* Brownsville Case No. 684 (1938).

58. Transcript of Hearing, April 1939, pp. 38–39, *In re: Herbert Van Vliet,* Brownsville Case No. 660 (1937); Transcript of Hearing on Motion to Dismiss, p. 7, *In re: James Fisher McClintock,* Brownsville Case No. 635 (1937).

59. "Hard-Hit Farmers Still Clinging to Autos and Radios," *Eagle Pass Daily Guide,* September 9, 1931, 1.

60. *In re: Cameron County Water Improvement Districts 1, 2, 5, and 6,* Brownsville Case Nos. 520, 521, 686, 698, 699, 754, 756; *In re: Hidalgo County Road Districts 1, 2, 3,*

292 Notes to Pages 207–209

4, 5, 6, 7, and 8, Brownsville Bankruptcy Cases 530, 531, 532, 533, 534, 535, 536, 537; *In re: Willacy County Water Control and Improvement District No. 1,* Brownsville Case Nos. 557 and 762; *In re: Hidalgo County Drainage District No. 1,* Brownsville Case Nos. 527 and 707; *In re: Hidalgo County Water Control and Improvement District Nos. 1, 2, and 5,* Brownsville Case Nos. 661, 674, and 757; *In re: La Feria Water Control and Improvement District, Cameron County No. 3,* Brownsville Case Nos. 594 and 694; *In re: Donna Irrigation District,* Brownsville Case No. 702.

61. Transcript of Hearing, p. 21, *In re: City of Pharr,* Brownsville Case No. 700 (1938), *In re: City of San Benito,* Brownsville Case No. 726 (1939); *In re: City of Brownsville,* Brownsville Case No. 755 (1940).

62. *In re: City of Donna,* Brownsville Case No. 697 (1938); *In re: City of Pharr,* Brownsville Case No. 700 (1938); *In re: City of San Benito,* Brownsville Case No. 726 (1939); *In re: City of Brownsville,* Brownsville Case No. 755 (1940); *In re: City of Lyford,* Brownsville Case No. 750 (1940); *In re: City of Edinburg,* Brownsville Case No. 764 (1940); *In re: City of San Juan,* Brownsville Case No. 791 (1941); *In re: City of Mercedes,* Brownsville Case No. 793 (1941); *In re: Edinburg Consolidated School District,* Brownsville Case No. 671 (1937); *In re: Mercedes Independent School District,* Brownsville Case No. 712 (1939); *In re: Mission Independent School District,* Brownsville Case No. 749 (1940); *In re: Tabasco Consolidated Independent School District,* Brownsville Case No. 753 (1940); *In re: Brownsville Independent School District,* Brownsville Case No. 780 (1941).

63. This conclusion is drawn from a sampling of oral histories conducted by students and faculty at the University of Texas–Pan American. Yolanda Juarez, Aurora Villanueva interview, oral history tape recording, LRGV, UTPA; Yolanda Juarez, Francisco Orneles, oral history tape recording, LRGV, UTPA; Yolanda Juarez, Robert Ramírez, oral history tape recording, LRGV, UTPA; Hubert J. Miller, James Franklin Ewers interview; Hubert J. Miller, Ramon Guerra interview; Williams, Mrs. Crockett interview.

64. Juarez, Robert Ramírez interview; Juarez, Francisco Orneles interview.

65. John Weber, "Homing Pigeons, Cheap Labor."

66. "Mexican Families Returning to Mexico," *Eagle Pass Daily Guide,* February 7, 1930, 1; "Mexicans Leave US in Search of Employment," *Eagle Pass Daily Guide,* November 27, 1931, 1; Dodd Vernon, "Through the Valley," *Edinburg Daily Review,* March 21, 1933; Miller, Esteban García interview. In the Southern District of Texas federal court, the one that governed the lower Rio Grande Valley, there were 275 deportation cases in 1929, and the numbers rose to 2,081 in 1930 and 1,831 in 1931. Zelden, *Justice Lies in the District,* 98–99.

67. "Del Rio Wages War on Hoboes," *Eagle Pass Daily Guide,* September 1, 1931, 1; "Valley Overloaded, People Hunting Work," *Eagle Pass Daily Guide,* February 4, 1930, 1.

68. Danbom, *Born in the Country,* 233–35; Montejano, *Anglos and Mexicans in the Making of Texas,* 271; letter from Nick Doffing to Seabury, Taylor, and Wagner, September 4, 1936, *In re: The Nick Doffing Company,* Brownsville Case No. 621 (1936).

69. Bowman, "Blood Oranges," 215; Tiller, *Texas Winter Garden,* 34–35; US Bureau of the Census, *Fourteenth Census, Agriculture; US Census of Agriculture 1945,* 18–69.

70. "History of the Sol Freed Family in Texas"; Weingarten, "Description of Survey

Questionnaire, Survey Report Summary"; US Bureau of the Census, 1935 *Census of Business,* vol. 1, 22–23; US Bureau of the Census, *Fifteenth Census,* vol. I, *Retail Distribution,* part III, 1061; US Bureau of the Census, 1935 *Census of Business,* vol. II, *Retail Distribution,* 73.

71. J. T. Canales, "Get Acquainted," *LULAC News* 2, no. 3 (November 1932), 4, LULAC Archives, NLBC.

72. "Pulse of Texas Business Gets Stronger Each Day," *Eagle Pass Daily Guide,* December 30, 1931, 1; " 'Market Sound,' Saith the Bankers," *Laredo Times,* November 6, 1929; "1931 to Be Great Year," *Eagle Pass Daily Guide,* December 31, 1930, 1.

73. "Looking Ahead," *Eagle Pass Daily Guide,* January 2, 1932, 1; Vernon, "Through the Valley," *Edinburg Daily Review;* Whisenhunt, *Depression in Texas,* 7–9.

74. "A Come Back at Sixty: The Story of a Ruined Man Who Made a Success at Sixty as Told Anonymously to Herbert Croly," *Saturday Evening Post,* December 17, 1932, 8–9, 64–66.

CHAPTER 8: STARTING OVER

1. "Heavy Trade for Holiday," *Laredo Times,* November 6, 1929.

2. For a study of the development of the life insurance industry, see Sharon Ann Murphy, *Investing in Life.*

3. US Const., art. I, § 8. Friedman, *History of American Law,* 269 71, 549 51; Mann, *Republic of Debtors;* Warren, *Bankruptcy in United States History,* 52–58, 95–115; Sullivan Warren, and Westbrook, *As We Forgive Our Debtors,* 8–9. For a study of the 1841 Act, see Balleisen, *Navigating Failure.* For a study of the 1867 Act, see Elizabeth Lee Thompson, *Reconstruction of Southern Debtors.*

4. Coleman, *Debtors and Creditors in America,* 8–15, 25, 37.

5. Ashford, "Jacksonian Liberalism and Spanish Law"; Balleisen, *Navigating Failure,* 170; Nackman, "Anglo-American Migrants to the West." Local Texas judges seldom ruled in favor of American creditors who tried to pursue collection efforts against Texas colonists. See also Cantrell, *Stephen F. Austin,* 43–54, 61–69.

6. Tex. Const. art. XVI, § 50, interp. commentary (Vernon 1993). Cornyn, "Roots of the Texas Constitution," 1193–94; Goodman, "Emergence of the Homestead Exemption," 476–81; McKnight, "Protection of the Family Home." Texas is the only state that has ever adopted a business homestead exemption. See Tex. Const., art. XVI, § 15, interpret. commentary (Vernon 1993).

7. Tex. Rev. Civ. Stat. Ann. art. 3832 (Vernon 1966).

8. Jackson, *Logic and Limits of Bankruptcy Law,* 225–78; Will, "Economic Transformation, Legal Innovation, and Social Change," 119. Cf. Sullivan, Warren, and Westbrook, *Fragile Middle Class,* 26, 259–61. For information about Mexican insolvency and Mexican insolvency laws, see Bodayla, "Bankers vs. Diplomats."

9. *Stellwagen v. Clum,* 245 US 605, 607 (1918); Friedman, *American Law in the Twentieth Century,* 389; Zelden, *Justice Lies in the District,* 46–53.

10. An Act to establish a uniform system of bankruptcy throughout the United States, ch. 541, 30 Stat. 544 (1898); Gilbert, *Collier on Bankruptcy.*

11. Representative Hatton W. Sumners, D-Texas, 72nd Congress, 2nd Sess., 76 *Congressional Record* 2902 (1932). The laws may be found at Act of March 3, 1933, ch. 204, §§ 75, 76, 77, 47 Stat. 1474 (1933); Municipal Bankruptcy Act of May 24, 1934, ch. 345, 48 Stat. 798. Section 77 essentially incorporated state equity receivership provisions. For a brief history of the development of equity receivership laws, the precursors to bankruptcy corporate reorganization, see Skeel, *Debt's Dominion,* 48–70.

12. The Chandler Act of 1938 adopted the New Deal vision in Chapter X, created for large corporate reorganizations. It required an independent trustee in all reorganization cases involving more than $250,000 in debt. This trustee proposed a reorganization plan, removing control from the hands of the lawyers, bankers, and existing management, thereby reducing the control of banks like J.P. Morgan over corporate America. The Chandler Act left in place the railroad reorganization provisions and the provisions for small corporate reorganizations, embodied in Chapter XI. Unlike Chapter X, Chapter XI provisions allowed existing management to remain in control. Skeel, *Debt's Dominion,* 74–75, 101–27; Friedman, *American Law in the Twentieth Century,* 386–87.

13. Statement of Facts of Testimony Taken at Hearing Had on the 23rd day of February, A.D., 1927, *In re: Mrs. Elizabeth Lyford King,* Case No. 189 (1926); Coleman, *Debtors and Creditors in America,* 272; Mann, *Republic of Debtors,* 3; Sandage, *Born Losers,* 36, 237–47.

14. Transcript of Creditors' Meeting, *In re: Henry Lee and Madge Brandon,* Brownsville Case No. 613 (613); Transcript, Hearing on Involuntary Petition, January 17, 1936, p. 6, *In re: George W. Sutherland,* Corpus Christi Case No. 366 (1936). For examples of cases where creditor action precipitated a filing, see *In re: Henry Stein,* San Antonio Case No. 87 (1899) (sheriff's sale); *In re: Oscar B. Kessler,* Del Rio Case No. 9 (1911) (filed after a judgment entered); *In re: George Molby,* Brownsville Case No. 150 (1924) (pending lawsuits filed against him); *In re: Parker and Louise Ayers,* Brownsville Case No. 566 (1935) (filed to try to stop a foreclosure proceeding).

15. Order, *In re: Margarito Osuña,* Laredo Case No. 77 (1927); Transcript of Hearing, *In re: Carlos Otal,* Laredo Case No. 121 (1932); *In re: Joseph Rosenblum,* Laredo Bankruptcy Cases 92, 93, and 94 (1929); letter from John A. Pope to John C. Scott, January 10, 1921, *In re: Narciso Alanis,* Laredo Case No. 47 (1920); Green, *Border Biographies,* vol. 2, 109–10.

16. *In re: Tomás Cantú,* San Antonio Case No. 57 (1899).

17. *In re: Volpe Brothers,* Laredo Case No. 125 (1932).

18. An Act to establish a uniform system of bankruptcy throughout the United States, ch. 541, 30 Stat. 544, §§ 2 and 4 (1898). Examples of cases involving Spanish-language translators include *In re: Enrique Zuñiga,* Brownsville Case No. 751 (1940); *In re: Fidel Salinas,* Brownsville Case No. 596 (1936); *In re: Placido Herrera and Marcelo Cantú d/b/a Placido Herrera & Co.,* Brownsville Case No. 42 (1917). A search for all bankrupt debtors in the manuscript census records uncovered 143 individuals with Spanish surnames who appear to have been ethnic Mexicans and 5 individuals born in Spain. The census reveals information about birthplace and ethnicity. Of the 143 ethnic Mexicans in the census, 92 were born in Mexico, 50 were born in Texas, and 1 was

born in New Mexico. *Manuscript Census,* Cameron, Hidalgo, Starr, Willacy, Jim Hogg, Webb, Val Verde, and Duval counties, 1880, 1900, 1910, 1920, and 1930.

19. The statistics are based on an analysis of the following: (1) all bankruptcy cases filed in the Brownsville federal court between 1898 and December 7, 1941; (2) all bankruptcy cases filed in the Laredo federal court between 1898 and December 7, 1941, except for 15 cases located in Jim Wells and Nueces counties; (3) all bankruptcy cases filed in the Del Rio court between 1898 and December 7, 1941; (4) 53 bankruptcy cases filed in the San Antonio federal court between 1898 and December 7, 1941, from the relevant Southwest Texas counties in this study; (5) 26 bankruptcy cases filed in the Corpus Christi federal district court between 1898 and December 7, 1941, from the relevant South Texas counties in this study. Bankruptcy Case Files, 1898–1942: United States District Court for the Southern District of Texas, Brownsville Division, Laredo Division, and Corpus Christi Division, RG 21 NARA; Bankruptcy Case Files, 1898–1942: United States District Court for the Western District of Texas, San Antonio Division and Del Rio Division, RG 21 NARA. Among those found in the census, about 826, only 15 were unable to read and write.

20. *In re: Lon C. Hill,* Brownsville Case No. 60 (1920); *In re: Rentfro Banton Creager,* Brownsville Case No. 553 (1935); *In re: Al Frances Parker,* Brownsville Case No. 668 (1937); *In re: Benjamin Borroum,* Del Rio Case No. 308 (1904); *In re: Mrs. Donna H. Fletcher,* Brownsville Case No. 71 (1921); *In re: Samuel Finley Ewing,* Brownsville Case No. 656 (1937); *In re: Morris Edelstein,* Brownsville Case No. 436 (1932); *In re: Franklin Brothers,* Laredo Case Nos. 122 and 123 (1931); *In re: Shapu & Frelich,* Laredo Case No. 134 (1934); *In re: Antonio Barreda,* Brownsville Case No. 565 (1935); *In re: Celestino Pardo Barreda,* Brownsville Case No. 585 (1935); *In re: Ernesto Urustastegui,* Brownsville Case No. 339 (1930); *In re: J. B. Symonds,* Brownsville Case Nos. 18 and 376 (1914 and 1931).

21. An Act to establish a uniform system of bankruptcy throughout the United States, ch. 541, 30 Stat. 544 (1898); Tex. Rev. Civ. Stat. art. 3832 (Vernon's 1966); Harris, *Merchant Princes,* 218–19; Skeel, *Debt's Dominion,* 6–7.

22. *In re: M. M. Peña,* Brownsville Case No. 561 (1935); *In re: Leon Russell d/b/a Russell Pharmacy,* Brownsville Case No. 340 (1930).

23. *In re: Antonio Barreda,* Brownsville Case No. 565 (1935); *Dallas Morning News,* February 5, 1943, section 1, p. 14.

24. *In re: James B. Underwood,* Brownsville Case No. 58 (1920); *Manuscript Census,* Brewster County, 1930; *In re: Aaron Braunstein,* Brownsville Case No. 65 (1921); *Manuscript Census,* Bexar County, 1930; Transcript of Creditors' Meeting, *In re: Morris T. Kaplan,* Brownsville Case No. 206 (1927). Out of 164 entrepreneurs with businesses in the towns who could be traced, 136 returned to proprietorship, and 28 pursued employment for someone else.

25. "Store Stories/Edelstein's Better Furniture," *Southwest Furniture News,* April–May, 1970, Folder 5, People by Occupation, Mayors to Merchants, Box 3A168, TJHS, CAH. *In re: Bruno Rios,* Corpus Christi Case No. 23 (1914); *In re: Tomás Guerra,* Brownsville Case No. 209 (1927); *In re: Guadalupe Cantú,* Brownsville Case No. 411

(1931); *Dun & Bradstreet Reference Book, State Pocket Edition, Texas, 1938,* 100. Aaron Nelsen, "Edelstein's Sold after 102 Years," *Brownsville Herald,* January 29, 2008, http://www.brownsvilleherald.com/business/article_20db4bad-83ee-5aeb-851c -160d66d73202.html (accessed December 17, 2013).

26. Transcript of Creditors' Meeting, *In re: Robert Burdette,* Brownsville Case No. 633 (1937); *In re: John P. McGuire,* Brownsville Case No. 281 (1929).

27. *In re: Margarito Lopez, Jesus Lopez, Francisco Lopez, and Pedro Lopez,* Laredo Case Nos. 2, 3, 4, 5 (1900); *In re: Walter Wade McClain,* Brownsville Case No. 11 (1922); *In re: W. C. Schultz,* Brownsville Case No. 166 (1925).

28. *In re: William Knippa,* Del Rio Case No. 79 (1931).

29. *In re: John W. Sullivan,* Laredo Case No. 15 (1903); *In re: William Doyle,* Del Rio Case No. 12 (1912); *In re: Frank Stafford Weaver,* Del Rio Case No. 30 (1917); In re: Albert Urbahn, Laredo Case No. 128 (1935); *In re: Louis Lindheim,* San Antonio Case No. 258 (1905).

30. *In re: Charles Blair,* San Antonio Case No. 854 (1921); *Manuscript Census, Real County,* 1930; *In re: Osee Clifton Pope,* Case No. 1201 (1926); *Manuscript Census, Edwards County,* 1930; *In re: Benjamin Avent Borroum,* Case No. 308 (1904); "Borroum Family, Pioneer Cattlemen and Trail Drivers: B. A. Borroum Narrates Experiences and Events of the Trail in Early Drives," *Pioneer Magazine,* June 1925, 15; Florence Fenley, "Mrs. Lillie Lee Armstrong," *Uvalde Leader-News,* October 31, 1954, "Armstrong, Sal," Vertical File, CAH. For an example of ranchers who lost their land but continued as a cattle trader, see *In re: Frank Stafford Weaver,* Del Rio Case 30 (1917); *Manuscript Census,* El Paso, 1920. For those who continued small stock farms, see *In re: Rovert Edwin Nutt,* Del Rio Case No. 53 (1923); *In re: Alvin Forest Hope,* Del Rio Case No. 56 (1925); *In re: Jes Baker,* Del Rio Case No. 62 (1926); *Manuscript Census,* Edwards County and Uvalde County, 1930.

31. McElvaine, *Great Depression,* 147–49. Bankruptcy Act of March 3, 1933, 72d Cong., ch. 204, 47 Stat. 1467, § 75. Blackorby, "William Lemke." The act essentially allowed farmers to scale down their mortgages to the value of their property, retain the property for a period of five years regardless of the due date of the debt by paying a reasonable rental value to the secured creditor, and, at the end of five years, purchase the property from the secured creditor by paying its appraised value, which was usually less than the amount owed. Act of June 28, 1934, 73rd Cong., ch. 869, 48 Stat. 1289. Louisville Joint Stock Land Bank v. Radford, 295 US 555 (1935). The revised statute reducing the five-year period to three years, giving the secured creditor the right to force a public sale of its collateral and bid in the amount of the debt and also allowing the farmer to redeem the property within ninety days by paying the auction price plus interest. Act of August 28, 1935, ch. 792, 49 Stat. 942, 943–45. King, ed., *Collier on Bankruptcy* § 1200.01[b].

32. Examples of cases filed to stop a foreclosure include *In re: Cantrell Eben Bryan,* Brownsville Case No. 544 (1935); *In re: Plutarco and Irene de la Viña,* Brownsville Case No. 590 (1936); *In re: Oliver and Ruby Newcomer,* Brownsville Case No. 690 (1938); *In re: Eusebio Garcia,* Laredo Case No. 138 (1935). Examples of cases where the farmer negotiated a deal with the main creditor and dismissed the case include *In re: Frank Eli*

Clark, Brownsville Case No. 599 (1936); *In re: David O. States,* Brownsville Case No. 600 (1936); *In re: Francisco, Alberto, and Benito Treviño,* Laredo Case No. 158 (1938).

33. *In re: Oliver and Grace Newcomer,* Brownsville Case No. 690 (1938).

34. *Dun & Bradstreet Reference Book, State Pocket Edition, Texas, 1938,* 527–28.

35. Transcript of Creditors' Meeting, p. 7, *In re: A. Schmidt & Co.,* Laredo Case No. 8 (1900).

36. Interrogatories to Edward Pfeffer, *In re: William Pfeffer,* Laredo Case No. 13 (1902).

37. See Schedule A-3 in the following cases: *In re: James Ayoub,* Brownsville Case No. 228 (1928); *In re: James and William Ayoub,* Brownsville Case No. 315 (1930); *In re: Savage Brothers,* Brownsville Case No. 96 (1922); *In re: Savage Wholesale Grocery Co., Inc.,* Brownsville Case No. 345 (1930).

38. "Lon C. Hill Founded City of Harlingen," *Brownsville Herald,* May 10, 1936, 9.

39. Bankruptcy Schedules, *In re: Lon C. Hill,* Brownsville Case No. 60 (1920); "Harlingen Founder to Be Paid Tribute," *Houston Press,* July 29, 1932, Cameron County Scrapbook, Box 3L117, WPA Records, CAH; "Lon Hill Is 76 Now," *Dallas Morning News,* August 1, 1932.

40. "White Red Man," 30.

41. Transcript of Creditors' Meeting, *In re: Botts and Chambers,* Case No. 37 (1916); "Sympathy for Others Gives Sam Botts Real Hold on Valley Folk," *Brownsville Herald,* Cameron County Scrapbook, Box 3L117, WPA Records, CAH.

42. Florence Fenley, "Sal Armstrong, Cattleman," *Cattleman,* October 1939, 45, 48; C. L. Douglas, "Sal Armstrong, Son of the Brush Country, Hits Town," *Fort Worth Press,* March 7, 1940, Vertical Files, CAH; Florence Fenley, "Mrs. Lillie Lee Armstrong," "Armstrong, Sal," Vertical Files, CAH; *In re: Salvador Armstrong,* Case No. 992 (1923).

43. *In re: L. E. Snavely,* Brownsville Case No. 30 (1915) and *In re: Levi Snavely,* Brownsville Case No. 663 (1937); Watson, *Lower Rio Grande Valley and Its Builders,* 283. Snavely's 1915 case was an involuntary one filed by his creditors.

44. "He Knows His Onions," 12; *In re: James Garfield Sullivan,* San Antonio Case Nos. 573 and 1553 (1913 and 1931).

45. Will, "Economic Transformation, Legal Innovation, and Social Change," 119.

46. Sullivan, Warren, and Westbrook, *Fragile Middle Class,* 26, 258–61; Jackson, *Logic and Limits of Bankruptcy Law,* 228–52. For a discussion of how European ideas influenced the New Deal, see Rodgers, *Atlantic Crossings,* 409–84. Although Europe significantly expanded its social welfare programs over the course of the twentieth century, it has never had very liberal bankruptcy laws. Until recently, the United States, on the other hand, passed increasingly liberal bankruptcy laws providing an ever-expanding range of options for debtors, while keeping social welfare programs to a minimum.

CONCLUSION

1. Hart, *Empire and Revolution,* 503–504.

2. For a classic study on the subject of socioeconomic mobility in the Northeast, see Thernstrom, *Other Bostonians.*

3. Haber, *Industry and Underdevelopment,* 64–65, 124; Mayagoitia, *Layman's Guide to Mexican Law,* 15.

4. Hart, *Empire and Revolution,* 459–81; Evans, "Nothing New about NAFTA," 73–85, 81–82.

5. Hart, *Empire and Revolution,* 403, 446–51; Evans, "Nothing New about NAFTA," 73.

6. US Bureau of the Census, *Profile of General Demographic Characteristics: 2000,* 32, 65, 109, 234, and 241. For a study of social class in South Texas today, specifically the lower Rio Grande Valley, see Richardson, *Batos, Bolillos, Pochos, and Pelados.*

7. "Special Report: If Monterrey Falls, Mexico Falls," Reuters, June 1, 2011, http://www.reuters.com/article/2011/06/01/us-mexico-drugs-monterrey-idUSTRE7502 VG20110601 (accessed December 17, 2013).

8. Bowles, *Donna Hooks Fletcher,* 51.

BIBLIOGRAPHY

MANUSCRIPT COLLECTIONS AND ARCHIVES

Baker Business Historical Collections, Baker Library, Harvard Business School

Center for American History, University of Texas at Austin

    Creager, Rentfro B. Papers.

    Hill, Lon C. Papers.

    Lasater, Edward Cunningham. Papers, 1860–1930.

    Mercantile Agency Reference Books, The. State Pocket Editions. Texas. New York: R. G. Dun & Co., 1901, 1910, 1930, 1932.

    Sanborn Maps.

    Vertical Files.

    Works Progress Administration Files.

DeGolyer Library, Southern Methodist University

    Dun & Bradstreet Reference Book, The. State Pocket Edition. Texas. New York: Dun & Broadstreet, 1938.

    Ephemera.

    Texas State Gazetteer and Business Directory. 1892.

Drought, H. P., and Company Records. Special Collections. University of Texas–San Antonio

Dun, R. G., & Co. Credit Report Volumes. Baker Library, Harvard Business School.

Huntington Library Special Collections

    Ephemera.

    Quichimis Colony Records.

    San Antonio Fruit Exchange Collection.

    Topolobampo Collection.

League of United Latin American Citizens (LULAC) Archives, Nettie Lee Benson Latin American Collection, University of Texas at Austin

    de Luna, Andrés. Papers.

    LULAC News.

    Montemayor, Alicia Dickerson. Papers.

    Weeks, Oliver Douglas. Papers.

National Archives and Records Administration, Fort Worth, Texas

    Bankruptcy Docket Books and Case Files, United States District Court for the Southern District of Texas, Brownsville, Corpus Christi, and Laredo Divisions, in Records of the District Courts of the United States, Record Group 21, National Archives and Records Administration—Southwest Region (Fort Worth).

    Bankruptcy Docket Books and Case Files, United States District Court for the Western District of Texas, San Antonio and Del Rio Divisions, in Records of the District Courts of the United States, Record Group 21, National Archives and Records Administration—Southwest Region (Fort Worth).

Shary, John H. Collection. University of Texas–Pan American, Library Archives.

Taylor, Paul Schuster. Papers. Bancroft Library, University of California at Berkeley.

Texas State Tax Rolls, Texas State Library and Archives Commission, Austin, Texas.

University of Texas–Pan American, Special Collections, Oral History, Rio Grande Valley
    Historical Collection.

GOVERNMENT DOCUMENTS

Federal Manuscript Census Schedules. Tenth, Twelfth, Thirteenth, Fourteenth, and
    Fifteenth Censuses of the United States, 1880, 1900, 1910, 1920, and 1930.

US Bureau of the Census. *Census of Business, Retail Distribution 1935,* vols. I and II.
    Washington, DC: United States Government Printing Office, 1937.

US Bureau of the Census. *Profile of General Demographic Characteristics: 2000.* Wash-
    ington, DC: United States Government Printing Office, 2001.

US Bureau of the Census. *Thirteenth Census of the United States, Population,* vol. III.
    Washington, DC: United States Government Printing Office, 1913.

US Bureau of the Census. *Thirteenth Census of the United States, Agriculture,* vol. VII.
    Washington, DC: United States Government Printing Office, 1913.

US Bureau of the Census. *Fourteenth Census of the United States, Agriculture,* vol. VI.
    Washington, DC: United States Government Printing Office, 1922.

US Bureau of the Census. *Fourteenth Census of the United States, Population,* vol. III.
    Washington, DC: United States Government Printing Office, 1923.

US Bureau of the Census. *Fifteenth Census of the United States Taken in the Year 1930:
    Texas, Statistics by Counties.* Washington, DC: Government Printing Office, 1931.

US Bureau of the Census. *Fifteenth Census of the United States, Population,* vol. III, part
    2. Washington, DC: United States Government Printing Office, 1932.

US Bureau of the Census. *Fifteenth Census of the United States, Agriculture,* vol. II, part
    2. Washington, DC: United States Government Printing Office, 1932.

US Bureau of the Census. *Fifteenth Census of the United States: 1930, Irrigation of
    Agricultural Lands, Texas.* Washington, DC: United States Government Printing
    Office, 1932.

US Bureau of the Census. *Fifteenth Census of the United States Taken in the Year 1930:
    Reports by States, Montana to Wyoming,* vol. III. Washington, DC: Government
    Printing Office, 1932.

US Bureau of the Census. *Fifteenth Census of the United States, Retail Distribution,* vol.
    I, part 3. Washington, DC: United States Government Printing Office, 1934.

US Bureau of the Census. *Sixteenth Census of the United States, Population,* vol. II, part
    6. Washington, DC: United States Government Printing Office, 1943.

US Bureau of the Census. *Sixteenth Census of the United States, Agriculture,* vol. I, part
    26, *Texas.* Washington, DC: United States Government Printing Office, 1946.

US Bureau of the Census. *Sixteenth Census of the United States, Agriculture, Texas,*
    First Series. Washington, DC: United States Government Printing Office, 1946.

US Bureau of the Census. *US Census of Agriculture 1945.* Washington, DC: United
    States Government Printing Office, 1946.

NEWSPAPERS AND PERIODICALS

Brownsville Daily Herald
Cattleman
Corpus Christi Caller Times
Dallas Morning News
Del Rio–Record News
Eagle Pass Daily Guide
Edinburg Daily Review
El Cronista del Valle
Farm and Ranch Magazine
Galveston Daily News
Hidalgo County Independent
Laredo Daily Times
Laredo Times
Laredo Weekly Times
McAllen Monitor
New York Times
Pioneer Magazine
San Antonio Express
San Antonio Gazette
San Antonio Light
San Antonio Light and Gazette
Saturday Evening Post
Texas Magazine
Tiempo Laredo
Valley Star Monitor–Herald

BOOKS AND ARTICLES

Acuña, Rodolfo. *Occupied America: A History of Chicanos,* 4th ed. New York: Longman, 2000.

Adams, John A. *Conflict and Commerce on the Rio Grande: Laredo, 1755–1955.* College Station: Texas A&M University Press, 2008.

Adelman, Jeremy, and Stephen Aron. "From Borderlands to Borders: Empires, Nation-States, and the Peoples in between in North American History." *American Historical Review* 104, no. 3 (1999): 814–41.

Allhands, J. L. *Gringo Builders.* Joplin, MO, Texas: Private Printing, 1931.

———. *Uriah Lott.* San Antonio: Naylor, 1949.

Alonso, Ana María. *Thread of Blood: Colonialism, Revolution, and Gender on Mexico's Northern Frontier.* Hegemony and Experience. Tucson: University of Arizona Press, 1995.

Alonzo, Armando Cantú. *Tejano Legacy: Rancheros and Settlers in South Texas.* Albuquerque: University of New Mexico Press, 1998.

———. "*Orígenes* de una sociedad economía binacional: El noreste de México y el sur de Texas, 1848–1940." In *Territorio y ciudades en el noreste de México al inicio del siglo XXI,* ed. Roberto García Ortega, Socorro Arzaluz Solano, and Jesús Manuel Fitch Osuna, 59–88. Tijuana: El Colegio de la Frontera Norte, 2009.

Amberson, M. Margaret McAllen, James A. McAllen, and Margaret H. McAllen. *I Would Rather Sleep in Texas: A History of the Lower Rio Grande Valley and the People of the Santa Anita Land Grant.* Austin: Texas State Historical Association, 2003.

Anders, Evan. *Boss Rule in South Texas: The Progressive Era.* Austin: University of Texas Press, 1982.

Andrews, Thomas G. *Killing for Coal: America's Deadliest Labor War.* Cambridge, MA: Harvard University Press, 2008.

Appleby, Joyce. "The Social Consequences of American Revolutionary Ideals in the Early Republic." In *The Middling Sorts: Explorations in the History of the American Middle Class,* ed. Burton J. Bledstein and Robert D. Johnston, 31–49. New York: Routledge, 2001.

———. *The Relentless Revolution: A History of Capitalism.* New York: Norton, 2010.

Applegate, Debby. "Henry Ward Beecher and the 'Great Middle Class': Mass-Marketed Intimacy and Middle-Class Identity." In *The Middling Sorts: Explorations in the History of the American Middle Class,* ed. Burton J. Bledstein and Robert D. Johnston, 107–24. New York: Routledge, 2001.

Arreola, Daniel D. *Tejano South Texas: A Mexican American Cultural Province.* Austin: University of Texas Press, 2002.

Ashford, Gerald. "Jacksonian Liberalism and Spanish Law in Early Texas." *Southwestern Historical Quarterly* 57 (July 1953): 1–37.

Balleisen, Edward J. *Navigating Failure: Bankruptcy and Commercial Society in Antebellum America.* Chapel Hill: University of North Carolina Press, 2001.

Barr, Alwyn. *Reconstruction to Reform: Texas Politics, 1876–1906.* Dallas: Southern Methodist University Press, 2001.

Barton, Josef. "At the Edge of the Storm: Northern Mexico's Rural Peoples in a New Regime of Consumption, 1880–1940." In *Land of Necessity: Consumer Culture in the United States–Mexico Borderlands,* ed. Alexis McCrossen, 217–47. Durham: Duke University Press, 2009.

Baud, Michiel, and Willem Van Schendel. "Toward a Comparative History of Borderlands." *Journal of World History* 8, no. 2 (1997): 211–42.

Benedict, Murray R. *Farm Policies of the United States, 1790–1950: A Study of Their Origins and Development.* New York: Twentieth Century Fund, 1953.

Benton-Cohen, Katherine. *Borderline Americans: Racial Division and Labor War in the Arizona Borderlands.* Cambridge, MA: Harvard University Press, 2009.

Blackford, Mansel G. *A History of Small Business in America,* 2nd ed. Chapel Hill: University of North Carolina Press, 2003.

Blackorby, Edward C. "William Lemke: Agrarian Radical and Union Party Presidential Candidate." *Mississippi Valley Historical Review* 49 (June 1962): 67–84.

Bledstein, Burton J. "Introduction: Storytellers to the Middle Class." In *The Middling Sorts: Explorations in the History of the American Middle Class,* ed. Burton J. Bledstein and Robert D. Johnston, 1–25. New York: Routledge, 2001.

———, and Robert D. Johnston. *The Middling Sorts: Explorations in the History of the American Middle Class.* New York: Routledge, 2001.

Blumin, Stuart M. *The Emergence of the Middle Class: Social Experience in the American City, 1760–1900.* New York: Cambridge University Press, 1989.

Bodayla, Stephen D. "Bankers vs. Diplomats: The Debate over Mexican Insolvency." *Journal of Interamerican Studies and World Affairs* 24, no. 4 (1982): 461–82.

Bourke, John G. "An American Congo." *Scribner's* (1894).

Bowles, David, ed. *Donna Hooks Fletcher: Life and Writings.* Donna, TX: VAO Publishing, 2012.

Bowman, Timothy "Blood Oranges: Citriculture, Colonialism, and the Making of Anglo-American Identity in the Lower Rio Grande Valley Borderlands during the Twentieth Century." PhD diss., Southern Methodist University, 2011.

Braudaway, Douglas. "The 'Origins' of Del Rio, Texas: Documenting Myths and Mything Documentation." *Journal of South Texas* 23, no. 1 (2010): 47–64.

Buchenau, Jürgen. *Tools of Progress: A German Merchant Family in Mexico City, 1865–Present.* Albuquerque: University of New Mexico Press, 2004.

Buder, Stanley. *Capitalizing on Change: A Social History of American Business.* Chapel Hill: University of North Carolina Press, 2009.

Buenger, Walter L., and Joseph A. Pratt. *But Also Good Business: Texas Commerce Banks and the Financing of Houston and Texas, 1886–1986.* College Station: Texas A&M University Press, 1986.

Calder, Lendol G. "From 'Consumptive' Credit to 'Consumer' Credit: E. R. A. Seligman and the Moral Justification of Consumer Debt." *Essays in Economic and Business History* 14 (1996): 185–206.

———. *Financing the American Dream: A Cultural History of Consumer Credit.* Princeton, NJ: Princeton University Press, 1999.

Calderón, Héctor. *Narratives of Greater Mexico.* Austin: University of Texas Press, 2004.

Callahan, Manuel. "Mexican Border Troubles: Social War, Settler Colonialism, and the Production of Frontier Discourse, 1848–1880." PhD diss., University of Texas, 2003.

Cantrell, Gregg. *Stephen F. Austin: Empresario of Texas.* New Haven, CT: Yale University Press, 1999.

Carey, Elaine Carey, and Andrae Marak, eds. *Smugglers, Brothels, and Twine: Historical Perspectives on Contraband and Vice in North America's Borderlands.* Tucson: University of Arizona Press, 2012.

Carlson, Avery Luvere. *A Monetary and Banking History of Texas from the Mexican Regime to the Present Day, 1821–1929.* Fort Worth: Fort Worth National Bank, 1930.

Carlson, Paul Howard. *Texas Woollybacks: The Range Sheep and Goat Industry.* College Station: Texas A&M University Press, 1982.

Cassetti, Emilio. "Manufacturing Productivity and Snowbelt-Sunbelt Shifts." *Economic Geography* 60 (1984): 313–24.

Cassis, Youssef, and Jacqueline Collier. *Capitals of Capital: A History of International Financial Centres, 1780–2005.* Cambridge: Cambridge University Press, 2006.

Cerutti, Mario. *Burguesía, capitales & industria en el norte de México: Monterrey y su ámbito regional (1850–1910).* Monterrey: Facultad de Filosofía y Letras, Universidad Autónoma de Nuevo León, 1989.

Chambers, William T. "Lower Rio Grande Valley of Texas." *Economic Geography* 6, no. 4 (October 1930): 364–73.

Chance, Joseph E. *José María de Jesús Carvajal: The Life and Times of a Mexican Revolutionary.* San Antonio: Trinity University Press, 2006.

Chandler, Alfred. *The Visible Hand: The Managerial Revolution in American Business.* Cambridge, MA: Belknap/Harvard, 1977.

Chase-Dunn, Christopher, and Thomas D. Hall. *Rise and Demise: Comparing World Systems.* Boulder: Westview, 1997.

Clark, J. Stanley. "Texas Fever in Oklahoma." *Oklahoma Chronicles* 29, no. 1 (1951): 429–43.

Cohen, Lizabeth. *A Consumer's Republic: The Politics of Mass Consumption in Postwar America.* New York: Knopf, 2003.

Coleman, Peter J. *Debtors and Creditors in America: Insolvency, Imprisonment for Debt, and Bankruptcy, 1607–1900.* Madison: State Historical Society of Wisconsin, 1974.

Cornyn, John. "The Roots of the Texas Constitution: Settlement to Statehood." *Texas Tech Law Review* 26 (1995): 1089–1194.

Cott, Nancy F. *The Bonds of Womanhood: "Woman's Sphere" in New England, 1780–1835,* 2nd ed. New Haven, CT: Yale University Press, 1997.

Cronon, William. *Nature's Metropolis: Chicago and the Great West.* New York: Norton, 1991.

Cuéllar, Carlos E. "The House of Armengol: Doing Business on the Rio Grande Border, 1881–1939." Master's thesis, Texas A&M International University, 1990.

Currie, A. W. "British Attitudes toward Investment in North American Railroads." *Business History Review* 34, no. 2 (1960): 194–216.

Danbom, David B. *Born in the Country: A History of Rural America.* Baltimore: Johns Hopkins University Press, 1995.

De León, Arnoldo. *The Tejano Community, 1836–1900.* Dallas: Southern Methodist University Press, 1982.

DeLay, Brian. *War of a Thousand Deserts: Indian Raids and the US-Mexican War.* New Haven, CT: Yale University Press, 2008.

Delcurto, J. M., E. W. Halstead, and H. F. Halstead. "The Citrus Industry in the Lower Rio Grande Valley of Texas." *Texas Department of Agriculture Bulletin* 75 (1923).

Deverell, William Francis. *Whitewashed Adobe: The Rise of Los Angeles and the Remaking of Its Mexican Past.* Berkeley: University of California Press, 2004.

Diaz, George. "Contrabandista Communities: States and Smugglers in the Lower Rio Grande Borderlands, 1848–1945." PhD diss., Southern Methodist University, 2010.

Dobie, J. Frank. *Cow People.* Boston: Little, Brown, 1964.

Domosh, Mona. "Selling Civilization: Toward a Cultural Analysis of America's Economic

Empire in the Late Nineteenth and Early Twentieth Centuries." *Transactions of the Institutes of British Geographers* 29, no. 4 (2004): 453–67.

Einegal, Susanne. "Revolutionary Promises Encounter Urban Realities for Mexico City's Middle Class, 1915–1928." In *The Making of the Middle Class: Toward a Transnational History,* ed. A. Ricardo López and Barbara Weinstein, 253–66. Durham: Duke University Press, 2012.

Encyclopedia of Southern Jewish Communities. http://isjl.org/history/archive/tx/laredo.html (accessed July 1, 2013).

English, Linda. *By All Accounts: General Stores and Community Life in Texas and Indian Territory.* Norman: University of Oklahoma Press, 2013.

Ericson, Joe E. "Origins of the Texas Bill of Rights." *Southwestern Historical Quarterly* 62, no. 4 (April 1959): 457–66.

———. *Banks and Bankers in Early Texas, 1835–1875.* New Orleans: Polyanthos, 1976.

Ervin, Michael A. "The Formation of the Revolutionary Middle Class during the Mexican Revolution." In *The Making of the Middle Class: Toward a Transnational History,* ed. Ricardo López and Barbara Weinstein, 196–222. Durham: Duke University Press, 2012.

Evans, Sterling. "Nothing New about NAFTA: The Trade in Commodities and the Economic Seamlessness of the US-Mexican Border." *Journal of the West* 47, no. 3 (Summer 2008): 73–86.

Foley, Douglas E. *From Peones to Politicos: Class and Ethnicity in a South Texas Town, 1900–1987,* 1st rev. ed. Austin: University of Texas Press, 1988.

Foley, Neil. *The White Scourge: Mexicans, Blacks, and Poor Whites in Texas Cotton Culture.* American Crossroads. Berkeley: University of California Press, 1997.

Foscue, Edwin J. "Irrigation in the Lower Rio Grande Valley of Texas." *Geographical Review* 23, no. 3 (July 1933): 457–63.

Fox, Stephen. "Architecture in Brownsville: The Twentieth Century." In *Studies in Matamoros and Cameron County History,* ed. Anthony Knopp, Milo Kearney, and Antonio Zavaleta, 283–346. Brownsville: University of Texas at Brownsville and Texas Southmost College, 1997.

Freyer, Tony A. *Producers and Capitalists: Constitutional Conflict in Antebellum America.* Charlottesville: University Press of Virginia, 1994.

Friedman, Lawrence M. *A History of American Law,* 2d ed. New York: Simon and Schuster, 1985.

———. *American Law in the Twentieth Century.* New Haven, CT: Yale University Press, 2004.

Galbraith, John Kenneth. *The Great Crash, 1929,* 2d ed. Boston: Houghton Mifflin, 1961.

García, Lilia M. "Don Francisco Yturria: Beginnings of a South Texas Entrepreneur." *Journal of South Texas* 21, no. 1 (Spring 2008): 10–21.

García, Mario T. *Mexican Americans: Leadership, Ideology, and Identity, 1930–1960.* Yale Western Americana Series. New Haven, CT: Yale University Press, 1989.

García, Richard A. *Rise of the Mexican-American Middle Class: San Antonio, 1929–1941.* College Station: Texas A&M University Press, 1991.

Gilbert, Frank B. *Collier on Bankruptcy: A Treatise on the Law and Practice of Bank-ruptcy under the National Bankruptcy Act of 1898.* New York: Matthew, Bender, 1927.

Gonzalez, Gilbert G. *Culture of Empire: American Writers, Mexico, and Mexican Immi-grants, 1880–1930.* Austin: University of Texas Press, 2004.

González, Jovita. "America Invades the Border Towns." *Southwest Review* 15, no. 4 (1930): 469–77.

———, and María Eugenia Cotera, eds. *Life along the Border: A Landmark Tejana The-sis.* Elma Dill Russell Spencer Series in the West and Southwest. College Station: Texas A&M University Press, 2006.

González-Quiroga, Miguel Ángel. "Conflict and Cooperation in the Making of Texas-Mexico Border Society, 1840–1880." In *Bridging National Borders in North Amer-ica: Transnational and Comparative Histories,* ed. Benjamin Heber Johnson and Andrew R. Graybill, 33–58. Durham: Duke University Press, 2010.

Goodman, Paul. "The Emergence of the Homestead Exemption in the United States: Accomodation and Resistance to the Market Revolution, 1840–1880." *Journal of American History* 80, no. 2 (1993): 476–98.

Gordon, Linda. *The Great Arizona Orphan Abduction.* Cambridge, MA: Harvard Univer-sity Press, 1999.

Graf, Leroy P. "The Economic History of the Lower Rio Grande Valley, 1820–1875." PhD diss., Harvard University, 1942.

Graham, Don. *Kings of Texas: The 150-Year Saga of an American Ranching Empire.* Hoboken, NJ: Wiley & Sons, 2003.

Grant, Joseph M., and Lawrence L. Crum. *The Development of State Chartered Bank-ing in Texas: From Predecessor Systems until 1970.* Austin: Bureau of Business Research, University of Texas, 1978.

Graybill, Andrew. *Policing the Great Plains: Rangers, Mounties, and the North American Frontier, 1875–1910.* Lincoln: University of Nebraska Press, 2007.

Greaser, Galen D. *New Guide to Spanish and Mexican Land Grants in South Texas.* Austin: Texas General Land Office, 2009.

———, and Jesús F. de la Teja. "Quieting Title to Spanish and Mexican Land Grants in the Trans-Nueces: The Bourland and Miller Commission." *Southwestern Historical Quarterly* 95, no. 4 (1992): 444–64.

Green, Stanley C. *The Guillermo Benavides Family: A History.* Laredo: Border Studies Center, 1993.

———. "A History of Laredo's Jewish Community." *Journal of South Texas* 11, no. 1 (1996): 19–38.

———. *Border Biographies.* Vol. 1. Laredo, TX: Border Studies Center, 2000.

———. *Border Biographies.* Vol. 2. Laredo, TX: Border Studies Center, 2000.

Greenfield, Mary C. "'The Game of One Hundred Intelligences': Mahjong, Materials, and the Marketing of the Asian Exotic in the 1920s." *Pacific Historical Review* 79, no. 3 (2010): 329–59.

Gressley, Gene M. *Bankers and Cattlemen.* New York: Knopf, 1966.

Griswold del Castillo, Richard. *The Treaty of Guadalupe Hidalgo: A Legacy of Conflict.* Norman: University of Oklahoma Press, 1990.

Gutiérrez, David G. *Walls and Mirrors: Mexican Americans, Mexican Immigrants, and the Politics of Ethnicity.* Berkeley: University of California Press, 1995.

———. "Migration, Emergent Ethnicity, and the 'Third Space': The Shifting Politics of Nationalism in Greater Mexico." *Journal of American History* 86, no. 2 (1999): 481–517.

Haber, Stephen H. *Industry and Underdevelopment: The Industrialization of Mexico, 1890–1940.* Stanford, CA: Stanford University Press, 1989.

———. "Industrial Concentration and Capital Markets: A Comparative Study of Brazil, Mexico, and the United States." *Journal of Economic History* 51, no. 3 (September 1991): 559–90.

———, Noel Maurer, and Armando Razo. *The Politics of Property Rights: Political Instability, Credible Commitments, and Economic Growth in Mexico, 1876–1929.* Political Economy of Institutions and Decisions. Cambridge: Cambridge University Press, 2003.

Hall, Thomas D. *Social Change in the Southwest, 1350–1880.* Lawrence: University Press of Kansas, 1989.

Hämäläinen, Pekka. *The Comanche Empire.* New Haven, CT: Yale University Press, 2008.

Haney-López, Ian. *White by Law: The Legal Construction of Race.* New York: New York University Press, 1996.

Hansen, Bradley A. "Commercial Associations and the Creation of a National Economy: The Demand for Federal Bankruptcy Law." *Business History Review* 72 (1988): 86–113.

———. "The Origins of Bankruptcy Law in the United States, 1789–1898." PhD diss., Washington University, 1996.

Harding, Nola Martin, and Dorothy Abbott McCoy. "Francisco Yturria and Heirs." In *Roots by the River: A Story of a Texas Tropical Borderland,* ed.Valley By-Liners, 91–94. Canyon, TX: Staked Plains Press, 1978.

Harris, Charles H., and Louis R. Sadler. *The Texas Rangers and the Mexican Revolution: The Bloodiest Decade, 1910–1920.* Albuquerque: University of New Mexico Press, 2004.

Harris, Leon A. *Merchant Princes: An Intimate History of Jewish Families Who Built Great Department Stores.* New York: Harper & Row, 1979.

Hart, John M. *Revolutionary Mexico: The Coming and Process of the Mexican Revolution,* 10th anniversary ed. Berkeley: University of California Press, 1997.

———. *Empire and Revolution: The Americans in Mexico since the Civil War.* Berkeley: University of California Press, 2002.

Hernandez, Kelly Lytle. *Migra!: A History of the U.S. Border Patrol.* American Crossroads. Berkeley: University of California Press, 2010.

Herrera Pérez, Octavio. *La zona libre: Excepción fiscal y conformación histórica de la frontera norte de México.* Mexico City: Secretaría de Relaciones Exteriores, Mexico, Dirección General del Acervo Histórico Diplomático, 2004.

Higham, John. *Strangers in the Land: Patterns of American Nativism, 1860–1925.* New Brunswick, NJ: Rutgers University Press, 2002.

Hill, Kate Adele. *Lon C. Hill, 1862–1935: Lower Rio Grande Valley Pioneer.* San Antonio: Naylor, 1973.

Hinojosa, Gilberto Miguel. *A Borderlands Town in Transition: Laredo, 1755–1870.* College Station: Texas A&M University Press, 1983.

Hinton, Diana Davids, and Roger M. Olien. *Oil in Texas: The Gusher Age, 1895–1945,* 1st ed. Clifton and Shirley Caldwell Texas Heritage Series. Austin: University of Texas Press, 2002.

History of the Cattlemen of Texas: A Brief Resume of the Live Stock Industry of the Southwest and a Biographical Sketch of Many of the Important Characters Whose Lives Are Interwoven Therein. Degolyer Library Cowboy and Ranch Life Series. Austin: Texas State Historical Association, 1991. Reprint of 1914 ed.

Hoar, George F. *Autobiography of Seventy Years.* Vol. 2. New York: Scribner's Sons, 1903.

Hochschild, Jennifer L. *Facing Up to the American Dream: Race, Class, and the Soul of the Nation.* Princeton Studies in American Politics. Princeton, NJ: Princeton University Press, 1995.

Hoganson, Kristin. "Cosmopolitan Domesticity: Importing the American Dream, 1865–1920." *American Historical Review* 107, no. 1 (2002): 53–83.

Holden, Robert H. *Mexico and the Survey of Public Lands: The Management of Modernization, 1876–1911.* DeKalb: Northern Illinois University Press, 1994.

Hornby, Harry P. *Going Around: Almost 60 Years of Life in Southwest Texas.* Uvalde: Hornby, 1945.

Hutson, Cecil Kirk. "Texas Fever in Kansas, 1866–1930." *Agricultural History* 68, no. 1 (Winter 1994): 80–88.

Hyman, Louis. *Debtor Nation: The History of America in Red Ink.* Princeton, NJ: Princeton University Press, 2011.

Isbel, Frances Wyatt. "Man from Lightning Ranch: Melchor Mora, Peace Officer." In *Rio Grande Round-Up: Story of a Tropical Texas Borderland,* ed. Valley By-Liners, 107–112. Mission: Border Kingdom, 1980.

Jackson, Thomas H. *The Logic and Limits of Bankruptcy Law.* Cambridge, MA: Harvard University Press, 1986.

Jacobson, Matthew Frye. *Whiteness of a Different Color: European Immigrants and the Alchemy of Race.* Cambridge, MA: Harvard University Press, 1998.

Jeffrey, Julie Roy. *Frontier Women: The Trans-Mississippi West, 1840–1880.* New York: Hill and Wang, 1979.

Jillson, Cal. *Pursuing the American Dream: Opportunity and Exclusion over Four Centuries.* Lawrence: University Press of Kansas, 2004.

Johnson, Benjamin H. *Revolution in Texas: How a Forgotton Rebellion and Its Bloody Suppression Turned Mexicans into Americans.* New Haven, CT: Yale University Press, 2003.

———, and Jeffrey Gusky. *Bordertown: The Odyssey of an American Place.* New Haven, CT: Yale University Press, 2008.

Johnston, Robert D. *The Radical Middle Class: Populist Democracy and the Question of Capitalism in Progressive Era Portland, Oregon.* Princeton, NJ: Princeton University Press, 2003.

Jordan, Terry G. "Perceptual Regions in Texas." *Geographical Review* 68, no. 3 (June, 1978): 293–307.

———. "Research Note: The 1887 Census of Texas' Hispanic Population." *Aztlan* 12, no. 2 (1982): 271–78.

———. "A Century and a Half of Ethnic Change in Texas, 1836–1986." *Southwestern Historical Quarterly* 89, no. 1 (1986): 385–422.

Katz, Friedrich. *The Secret War in Mexico: Europe, the United States, and the Mexican Revolution.* Chicago: University of Chicago Press, 1981.

Kearney, Milo, and Anthony K. Knopp. *Boom and Bust: The Historical Cycles of Matamoros and Brownsville.* Austin: Eakin, 1991.

———. *Border Cuates: A History of the US-Mexican Twin Cities.* Austin: Eakin, 1995.

Keehn, Richard H., and Gene Smiley. "Mortgage Lending by National Banks." *Business History Review* 51, no. 4 (1977): 474–91.

Kelley, Pat. *River of Lost Dreams: Navigation on the Rio Grande.* Lincoln: University of Nebraska Press, 1986.

Kemble, John Haskell. "The Transpacific Railroads, 1869–1915." *Pacific Historical Review* 18, no. 3 (August 1949): 331–43.

Kennedy, David. *Freedom from Fear: The American People in the Great Depression.* Oxford: Oxford University Press, 1999.

Kerr, William Gerald. *Scottish Capital on the American Credit Frontier.* Austin: Texas State Historical Association, 1976.

King, Lawrence P., ed. *Collier on Bankruptcy,* 15th ed., vol. 8. New York: Bender, 1974.

Klein, Maury. *The Genesis of Industrial America, 1870–1920.* New York: Cambridge University Press, 2007.

Knight, Alan. *The Mexican Revolution.* 2 vols. Cambridge Latin American Studies. Cambridge: Cambridge University Press, 1986.

Kraut, Alan M. *The Huddled Masses: The Immigrant in American Society, 1880–1921,* 2nd ed. Wheeling, IL: Harlan Davidson, 2001.

Kwolek-Folland, Angel. *Incorporating Women: A History of Women and Business in the United States.* New York: Twayne, 1998.

Lamar, Howard Robert. *Texas Crossings: The Lone Star State and the American Far West, 1836–1986.* Austin: University of Texas Press, 1991.

Lasater, Dale. *Falfurrias: Ed C. Lasater and the Development of South Texas.* College Station: Texas A&M University Press, 1985.

Lasater, Laurence M. *The Lasater Philosophy of Cattle Raising.* El Paso: Texas Western Press, University of Texas at El Paso, 1972.

Lea, Tom. *The King Ranch.* 2 vols. Boston: Little, Brown, 1957.

Leach, William. *Land of Desire: Merchants, Power, and the Rise of a New American Culture.* New York: Vintage, 1994.

Levenstein, Margaret. "African-American Entrepreneurship: The View from the 1910 Census." *Business and Economic History* 24 (1995):106–22.

Levinson, Robert E. "American Jews in the West." *Western Historical Quarterly* 5, no. 3 (1974): 285–94.

Levy, Jonathan. *Freaks of Fortune: The Emerging World of Capitalism and Risk in America.* Cambridge, MA: Harvard University Press, 2012.

Livesay, Harold. "Entrepreneurial Persistence through the Bureaucratic Age." *Business History Review* 51 (1977): 415–43.

———. "Entrepreneurial Dominance in Business Large and Small, Past and Present." *Business History Review* 63 (1989): 1–19.

Machado, Manuel A., Jr. "The Mexican Revolution and the Destruction of the Mexican Cattle Industry." *Southwestern Historical Quarterly* 79, no. 1 (1975): 1–20.

Mann, Bruce H. *Republic of Debtors: Bankruptcy in the Age of American Independence.* Cambridge, MA: Harvard University Press, 2002.

Marcus, Jacob Rader. *To Count a People: American Jewish Population Data, 1585–1984.* Lanham, MD: University Press of America, 1990.

Martínez, Oscar J. *Border People: Life and Society in the US-Mexico Borderlands.* Tucson: University of Arizona Press, 1994.

Maurer, Noel. *The Power and the Money: The Mexican Financial System, 1876–1932.* Stanford, CA: Stanford University Press, 2002.

———, and Andrei Gomberg. "When the State Is Untrustworthy: Public Finance and Private Banking in Porfirian Mexico." *Journal of Economic History* 64, no. 4 (December 2004): 1087–1107.

Mawn, Geoffrey P. "A Land-Grant Guarantee: The Treaty of Guadalupe Hidalgo or the Protocol of Querétero." *Journal of the West* 14 (Fall 1975): 49–63.

Mayagoitia, Alberto. *A Layman's Guide to Mexican Law.* Albuquerque: University of New Mexico Press, 1976.

McCrossen, Alexis. "Drawing Boundaries between Markets, Nations, and Peoples, 1650–1940." In *Land of Necessity: Consumer Culture in the United States–Mexico Borderlands,* ed. Alexis McCrossen, 3–47. Durham: Duke University Press, 2009.

McElvaine, Robert S. *The Great Depression: America, 1929–1941.* New York: Times Books, 1984.

McGerr, Michael E. *A Fierce Discontent: The Rise and Fall of the Progressive Movement in America, 1870–1920.* New York: Free Press, 2003.

McKnight, Joseph W. "The Protection of the Family Home from Seizure by Creditors: The Sources and Evolution of a Legal Principle." *Southwestern Historical Quarterly* 86 (April 1983): 369–99.

McNeely, John. "Mexican-American Land Issues in the United States." In "The Role of the Mexican American in the History of the Southwest." Unpublished conference papers. Edinburg: Pan American College, 1969, http://eric.ed.gov/?id=ED046592 (accessed December 17, 2013).

Merkel, Philip L. "The Origins of an Expanded Federal Court Jurisdiction: Railroad Development and the Ascendancy of the Federal Judiciary." *Business History Review* 58 (1984): 336–58.

Meyer, Michael C., William L. Sherman, and Susan M. Deeds. *The Course of Mexican History,* 8th ed. New York: Oxford University Press, 2007.

Middleton, Philip Harvey. *Railway Supplies in Mexico.* New York: Railway Business Association, 1919.

Moeckel, Bill Reid. *The Development of the Wholesaler in the United States, 1860–1900.* New York: Garland, 1986.

Monday, Jane Clements, and Frances Brannen Vick. *Petra's Legacy: The South Texas Ranching Empire of Petra Vela and Mifflin Kenedy.* College Station: Texas A&M University Press, 2007.

Monroy, Douglas. *Rebirth: Mexican Los Angeles from the Great Migration to the Great Depression.* Berkeley: University of California Press, 1999.

Montejano, David. *Anglos and Mexicans in the Making of Texas, 1836–1986.* Austin: University of Texas Press, 1987.

Montgomery, Charles H. *The Spanish Redemption: Heritage, Power, and Loss on New Mexico's Upper Rio Grande.* Berkeley: University of California Press, 2002.

Mora, Anthony P. *Border Dilemmas: Racial and National Uncertainties in New Mexico, 1848–1912.* Durham: Duke University Press, 2011.

Mora-Torres, Juan. *The Making of the Mexico Border: The State, Capitalism, and Society in Nuevo León, 1848–1910.* Austin: University of Texas Press, 2001.

Moskowitz, Marina. *Standard of Living: The Measure of the Middle Class in Modern America.* Baltimore: Johns Hopkins University Press, 2004.

Murphy, Sharon Ann. *Investing in Life: Insurance in Antebellum America.* Baltimore: Johns Hopkins University Press, 2010.

Nackman, Mark E. "Anglo-American Migrants to the West: Men of Broken Fortunes? The Case of Texas, 1821–1846." *Western Historical Quarterly* 5 (October 1974): 441–55.

Neck, Raymond W. "History of Esperanza Ranch: A Significant Agricultural and Scientific Site, Brownsville, Texas." In *More Studies in Brownsville History,* ed. Milo Kearney, 267–74. Brownsville: Pan American University at Brownsville, 1989.

Nobles, Gregory. "The Rise of Merchants in Rural Market Towns: A Case Study of Eighteenth-Century Northampton, Massachusetts." *Journal of Social History* 24, no. 1 (1990): 5–23.

Norris, James D. *R. G. Dun & Co., 1841–1900: The Development of Credit Reporting in the Nineteenth Century.* Westport, CT: Greenwood, 1978.

Northrup, Cynthia Clark, and Elaine C. Prange Turney. *Encyclopedia of Tariffs and Trade in US History.* 3 vols. Westport, CT: Greenwood, 2003.

Nugent, Walter T. K. *Into the West: The Story of Its People.* New York: Knopf, 1999.

Olegario, Rowena. *A Culture of Credit: Embedding Trust and Transparency in American Business.* Cambridge, MA: Harvard University Press, 2006.

Ornish, Natalie. *Pioneer Jewish Texans: Their Impact on Texas and American History for Four Hundred Years, 1590–1990.* Dallas: Texas Heritage Press, 1989.

Orozco, Cynthia. *No Mexicans, Women, or Dogs Allowed: The Rise of the Mexican American Civil Rights Movement.* Austin: University of Texas Press, 2009.

Orsi, Richard J. *Sunset Limited: The Southern Pacific Railroad and the Development of the American West, 1850–1930.* Berkeley: University of California Press, 2005.

Paredes, Américo. *"With His Pistol in His Hand," a Border Ballad and Its Hero.* Austin: University of Texas Press, 1958.

———. *A Texas-Mexican Cancionero.* Austin: University of Texas Press, 1976.

———. *George Washington Gómez: A Mexicotexan Novel.* Houston: Arte Publico, 1990.

Perry, David C., and Alfred J. Watkins. *The Rise of the Sunbelt Cities.* Beverly Hills, CA: Sage, 1977.

Pettus, Daisy Caden. *The Rosalie Evans Letters from Mexico.* Indianapolis: Bobbs-Merrill, 1926.

Pierce, Frank C. *A Brief History of the Lower Rio Grande Valley.* Menasha, WI: Banta, 1917.

Pisani, Donald J. *From the Family Farm to Agribusiness: The Irrigation Crusade in California and the West, 1850–1931.* Berkeley: University of California Press, 1984.

Ratkin, Gary Alan. "An Economic History of the Rio Grande Valley Sugar Cane Industry, 1870–1922." Master's thesis, Rice University, 1963.

Reed, S. G. *A History of the Texas Railroads and of Transportation Conditions under Spain and Mexico and the Republic and the State,* 2d ed. Houston: St. Clair, 1941.

Reiser, Andrew Chamberlin. "Secularization Reconsidered: Chataqua and the De-Christianization of Middle-Class Authority, 1880–1920." In *The Middling Sorts,* ed. Burton J. Bledstein and Robert D. Johnston, 136–49. New York: Routledge, 2001.

Reps, John William. *The Forgotten Frontier: Urban Planning in the American West before 1890.* Columbia: University of Missouri Press, 1981.

Reséndez, Andrés. *Changing National Identities at the Frontier: Texas and New Mexico, 1800–1850.* Cambridge: Cambridge University Press, 2005.

Richardson, Chad. *Batos, Bolillos, Pochos, and Pelados: Class and Culture on the South Texas Border.* Austin: University of Texas Press, 1990.

Richardson, Heather Cox. *West from Appomattox: The Reconstruction of America after the Civil War.* New Haven, CT: Yale University Press, 2007.

Richmond, Douglas W., and Sam W. Haynes, eds. *The Mexican Revolution: Conflict and Consolidation, 1910–1940.* College Station: Texas A&M University Press, 2013.

Rischin, Moses. "The Jewish Experience in America: A View from the West." In *Jews of the American West,* ed. Moses Rischin and John Livingston, 26–47. Detroit: Wayne State University Press, 1991.

Rodgers, Daniel T. *Atlantic Crossings: Social Politics in a Progressive Age.* Cambridge, MA: Belknap, 1998.

Roell, Craig H. *Matamoros and the Texas Revolution.* Denton: Texas State Historical Association, 2013.

Rosenbaum, Fred. *Cosmopolitans: A Social and Cultural History of the Jews of the San Francisco Bay Area.* S. Mark Taper Foundation Imprint in Jewish Studies. Berkeley: University of California Press, 2009.

Rubio, Abel G. *Stolen Heritage: A Mexican-American's Rediscovery of His Family's Lost Land Grant.* Austin: Eakin, 1993.

Salvucci, Richard J. "The Origins of the US-Mexican Trade, 1825–1884: 'Hoc opus, hic labor est.'" *Hispanic American Historical Review* 71, no 4 (1991): 698–735.

Sánchez, George J. *Becoming Mexican American: Ethnicity, Culture, and Identity in Chicano Los Angeles, 1900–1945.* Oxford: Oxford University Press, 1993.

Sandage, Scott A. *Born Losers: A History of Failure in America.* Cambridge, MA: Harvard University Press, 2005.

Sandos, James Anthony. "The Mexican Revolution and the United States, 1915–1917: The Impact of Conflict in the Tamaulipas-Texas Frontier upon the Emergence of Revolutionary Government in Mexico." PhD diss., University of California at Berkeley, 1978.

Saunders, Freddie Milam. "The Bentsen Brothers, Empire Builders." In *Roots by the River: A Story of a Texas Tropical Borderland,* ed. Valley By-Liners, 258–62. Canyon, TX: Staked Plains Press, 1978.

Scase, Richard, and Robert Goffee. *The Entrepreneurial Middle Class.* London: Croom Helm, 1982.

Schlebecker, John T. *Cattle Raising on the Plains, 1900–1961.* Lincoln: University of Nebraska Press, 1963.

Schoffelmayer, Victor H. "The Magic Valley—Its Marvelous Future." *Texas Geographic Magazine* (1939): 16–31.

Schumpeter, Joseph A. *Capitalism, Socialism, and Democracy.* Harper Perennial Modern Thought Edition ed. New York: HarperCollins, 2007.

———. *The Theory of Economic Development: An Inquiry into Profits, Capital, Credit, Interest, and the Business Cycle,* 15th ed. New Brunswick: Transaction, 2010.

Sekaly, Jo Carolyn Gibbs. "The Syrian-Lebanese Immigration into Southeast Texas and Their Progeny." Master's thesis, Lamar University, 1987.

Sempich, Frederich. "Down the Rio Grande: Tracing This Strange, Turbulent Stream on Its Long Course from Colorado to the Gulf of Mexico." *National Geographic Magazine,* October 1939, 415–54.

Shearer, Ernest C. "The Carvajal Disturbances." *Southwestern Historical Quarterly* 55, no. 2 (1951): 201–30.

Sibley, Marilyn McAdams. "Charles Stillman: A Case Study in Entrepreneurship on the Río Bravo, 1861–1865." *Southwestern Historical Quarterly* 77, no. 2 (1973): 227–40.

Silva-Bewley, S. Zulema. *The Legacy of John H. Shary: Promotion and Land Development in Hidalgo County, South Texas, 1912–1930.* Edinburg: University of Texas–Pan American Press, 2001.

Skaggs, Jimmy M. *Prime Cut: Livestock Raising and Meatpacking in the United States, 1607–1983.* College Station: Texas A&M University Press, 1986.

Skeel, David A. Jr. *Debt's Dominion: A History of Bankruptcy Law in America.* Princeton, NJ: Princeton University Press, 2001.

Smith, Henry Nash. *Virgin Land: The American West as Symbol and Myth.* Cambridge, MA: Harvard University Press, 1950.

Sparks, Edith. *Capital Intentions: Female Proprietors in San Francisco, 1850–1920.*
    Luther H Hodges Jr. And Luther H. Hodges Sr. Series on Business, Society, and the
    State. Chapel Hill: University of North Carolina Press, 2006.

St. John, Rachel. "Divided Ranges: Trans-Border Ranches and the Creation of National
    Space along the Western Mexico–US Border." In *Bridging National Borders in
    North America: Transnational and Comparative Histories,* ed. Benjamin H. John-
    son and Andrew R. Graybill, 116–40. Durham: Duke University Press, 2010.

——. *Line in the Sand: A History of the Western US-Mexico Border.* Princeton, NJ:
    Princeton University Press, 2011.

Stambaugh, J. Lee, and Lillian Stambaugh. *The Lower Rio Grande Valley.* San Antonio:
    Naylor, 1954.

Standard Blue Book of the United States of America, The. Vol. 14. South Texas ed. San
    Antonio: Standard Blue Book, 1926.

Standard Blue Book of the United States of America, 1929–30, The. Vol. 15. South Texas
    ed. San Antonio: Standard Blue Book, 1930.

Starr, Kevin. *Inventing the Dream: California through the Progressive Era.* Americans
    and the California Dream. New York: Oxford University Press, 1985.

Stock, Catherine McNicol. *Main Street in Crisis: The Great Depression and the Old Middle
    Class on the Northern Plains.* Chapel Hill: University of North Carolina Press, 1992.

Stone, Bryan Edward. *The Chosen Folks: Jews on the Frontiers of Texas.* Jewish History,
    Life, and Culture. Austin: University of Texas Press, 2010.

Sullivan, Teresa A., Elizabeth Warren, and Jay Lawrence Westbrook. *As We Forgive Our
    Debtors: Bankruptcy and Consumer Credit in America.* New York: Oxford Univer-
    sity Press, 1989.

——. *The Fragile Middle Class: Americans in Debt.* New Haven, CT: Yale University
    Press, 2000.

Syrian and Lebanese Texans, The. The Texians and the Texans. San Antonio: University
    of Texas at San Antonio, Institute of Texan Cultures, 1974.

Taylor, Paul S. "Historical Note on Dimmit County, Texas." *Southwestern Historical
    Quarterly* 34, no. 2 (1930): 79–90.

——. *Mexican Labor in the United States Migration Statistics,* vol. IV. Berkeley: Uni-
    versity of California Press, 1933.

Teja, Jesús F. de la. *San Antonio de Béxar: A Community on New Spain's Northern Fron-
    tier,* 1st ed. Albuquerque: University of New Mexico Press, 1995.

Texas Almanac: State and Industrial Guide, Texas Centennial Edition, 1936. Reprint,
    Dallas: William P. Clements Center for Southwest Studies, Southern Methodist
    University, 2006.

Thernstrom, Stephan. *The Other Bostonians: Poverty and Progress in the American
    Metropolis, 1880–1970.* Boston: Harvard University Press, 1964.

Thompson, E. P. *The Making of the English Working Class.* Paperback ed. New York:
    Vintage, 1963.

Thompson, Elizabeth Lee. *The Reconstruction of Southern Debtors: Bankruptcy after the
    Civil War.* Athens: University of Georgia Press, 2004.

Thompson, Jerry D. *A Wild and Vivid Land: An Illustrated History of the South Texas Border.* Austin: Texas State Historical Association, 1997.

———. *Cortina: Defending the Mexican Name in Texas,* 1st ed. Fronteras Series. College Station: Texas A&M University Press, 2007.

Tibawi, A. L. *A Modern History of Syria, including Lebanon and Palestine.* London: Macmillan, St. Martin's, 1969.

Tijerina, Andrés. *Tejano Empire: Life on the South Texas Ranchos,* 1st ed. Clayton Wheat Williams Texas Life Series. College Station: Texas A&M University Press, 1998.

Tiller, James Weeks. *The Texas Winter Garden: Commercial Cool-Season Vegetable Production.* Research monograph no. 33. Austin: Bureau of Business Research, University of Texas at Austin, 1971.

Toll, William. "The Jewish Merchant and Civic Order in the Urban West." In *Jewish Life in the American West: Perspectives on Migration, Settlement, and Community,* ed. Ava F. Kahn, 13–31. Los Angeles: Autry Museum of Western Heritage in association with University of Washington Press, Seattle, 2002.

Trachtenberg, Alan. *The Incorporation of America: Culture and Society in the Gilded Age.* New York: Hill and Wang, 1982.

Truett, Samuel. *Fugitive Landscapes: The Forgotten History of the US-Mexico Borderlands.* New Haven, CT: Yale University Press, 2006.

Utley, Robert M. *The Indian Frontier of the American West, 1846–1890.* Albuquerque: University of New Mexico Press, 1984.

Valerio-Jiménez, Omar S. *River of Hope: Forging Identity and Nation in the Rio Grande Borderlands.* Durham: Duke University Press, 2013.

Valley By-Liners. *Roots by the River: A Story of a Tropical Texas Borderland.* Canyon, TX: Staked Plains Press, 1978.

Viña, José Jesus Ponce y de la. *Emigrantes de Asturias, the Story of the De La Viña Family of Edinburg.* Edinburg: M.A.P. Publishers, 1996.

Wallace, Lucy H. "John H. Shary—Believer." In *Roots by the River: A Story of a Texas Tropical Borderland,* ed. Valley By-Liners, 188–93. Canyon, TX: Staked Plains Press, 1978.

Wallerstein, Immanuel. *The Modern World System III: The Second Era of Great Expansion of the Capitalist World System, 1730–1840s.* San Diego: Academic Press, 1989.

Walsh, Casey. *Building the Borderlands: A Transnational History of Irrigated Cotton along the Mexico-Texas Border.* College Station: Texas A&M University Press, 2008.

Warren, Charles. *Bankruptcy in United States History.* Cambridge, MA: Harvard University Press, 1935.

Washington, Ann Reed. "Judge Juan Manuel De La Viña." In *Roots by the River: A Story of a Texas Tropical Borderland,* ed. Valley By-Liners, 82–84. Canyon, TX: Staked Plains Press, 1978.

Watson, Mrs. James. *The Lower Rio Grande Valley and Its Builders.* Mission, TX: Lower Rio Grande Valley and Its Builders, Inc., 1931.

Webb, Walter Prescott. *The Texas Rangers: A Century of Frontier Defense,* 2d ed. Austin: University of Texas Press, 1965.

———. *The Great Plains.* Reprint, Lincoln: University of Nebraska Press, 1981.

Weber, David J. *Foreigners in Their Native Land: Historical Roots of the Mexican Americans.* Albuquerque: University of New Mexico Press, 1973.

———. *The Mexican Frontier, 1821–1846: The American Southwest under Mexico.* Albuquerque: University of New Mexico Press, 1982.

———. *The Spanish Frontier in North America.* New Haven, CT: Yale University Press, 1992.

Weber, John William, III. "The Shadow of the Revolution: South Texas, the Mexican Revolution, and the Evolution of Modern American Labor Relations." PhD diss., College of William and Mary, 2008.

———. "Homing Pigeons, Cheap Labor, and Nativists: Immigration Reform and the Deportation of Mexicans from South Texas in the 1920s." *Western Historical Quarterly* 44, no. 2 (Summer 2013): 167–86.

Whisenhunt, Donald. *The Depression in Texas: The Hoover Years,* 2d ed. Boston: American Press, 1995.

White, Richard. *"It's Your Misfortune and None of My Own": A History of the American West.* Norman: University of Oklahoma Press, 1991.

White, Russell N. *State, Class, and the Nationalization of the Mexican Banks.* New York: Crane Russak, 1992.

Wiebe, Robert. *The Search for Order, 1877–1920.* New York: Hill and Wang, 1980.

Will, Susan. "Economic Transformation, Legal Innovation, and Social Change: A Case Study of Bankruptcy Lawyers." PhD diss., University of California at Irvine, 1999.

Wills, Jocelyn. *Boosters, Hustlers, and Speculators: Entrepreneurial Culture and the Rise of Minneapolis and St. Paul, 1849–1883.* St. Paul: Minnesota Historical Society Press, 2005.

Wilson, Karen S. "Becoming Angelinos." In *Jews in the Los Angeles Mosaic,* ed. Karen S. Wilson, 11–24. Los Angeles: University of California Press, 2013.

Womack, John, Jr. "The Mexican Revolution, 1910–1920." In *Mexico since Independence,* ed. Leslie Bethell, 125–200. Cambridge: Cambridge University Press, 1991.

Wood, Gordon S. *The Radicalism of the American Revolution.* New York: Vintage, 1993.

Wrobel, David M. *Promised Lands: Promotion, Memory, and the Creation of the American West.* Lawrence: University Press of Kansas, 2002.

Young, Elliott. "Red Men, Princess Pocahontas, and George Washington: Harmonizing Race Relations in Laredo at the Turn of the Century." *Western Historical Quarterly* 29, no. 1 (1998): 48–85.

———. *Catarino Garza's Revolution on the Texas Mexico Border.* Durham: Duke University Press, 2004.

Zapata, José E. "A Historical Archaeology of Roma, Texas." Master's thesis, University of Texas–San Antonio, 2002.

Zelden, Charles L. *Justice Lies in the District: The U.S. District Court, Southern District of Texas, 1902–1960.* College Station: Texas A&M University Press, 1993.

INDEX